The Mind of James Madison

This book provides a compelling and incisive portrait of James Madison the scholar and political philosopher. Through extensive historical research and analysis of Madison's heretofore underappreciated 1791 "Notes on Government," this book casts Madison's scholarly contributions in a new light, yielding a richer, more comprehensive understanding of his political thought than ever before. Tracing Madison's intellectual investigations of republics and philosophers – both ancient and modern – this book invites readers to understand the pioneering ideas of the greatest American scholar of politics and republicanism – and, in the process, to discover anew the vast possibilities and potential of that great experiment in self-government known as the American republic.

COLLEEN A. SHEEHAN is Professor of Politics and Director of the Matthew J. Ryan Center for the Study of Free Institutions and the Public Good at Villanova University, where she teaches courses in American political thought and politics and literature. She has served in the Pennsylvania House of Representatives and is currently a member of the Pennsylvania State Board of Education. She is the author of *James Madison and the Spirit of Republican Self-Government* (Cambridge, 2009); the coeditor of *Friends of the Constitution: Writings of the Other Federalists 1787–1788* (1998); and the author of numerous articles on the American founding and on eighteenth-century political and moral thought, which have appeared in such journals as the *William and Mary Quarterly*, *American Political Science Review*, *Review of Politics*, and *Persuasions: The Jane Austen Journal*.

"This is the most important book published on James Madison in my lifetime. It makes available to the general public for the first time in its original form a little book, known as 'Notes on Government,' that Madison began drafting, as a sequel to *The Federalist*, while he was a Congressman in the early 1790s. Moreover, it makes this unfinished treatise available in a critical edition with detailed notes citing the passages from earlier works that Madison references; and, as a supplement, it provides an elaborate, readable introduction, tracing the evolution of Madison's thinking and analyzing this neglected work. Scholars will find this book indispensable. Students of the American founding and of American government more generally will be forced to rethink."

– Paul A. Rahe,
Charles O. Lee and Louise K. Lee Chair in the Western Heritage,
Hillsdale College

"Colleen Sheehan places James Madison's 'Notes on Government' in the history of political thought and thus further reveals Madison as a political philosopher and not just a partisan tactician. In addition to this important discovery, she has included Madison's 'Notes' in a book that is now indispensable for seminars in American political thought and the early republic."

– Jeremy D. Bailey,
Ross M. Lence Distinguished Teaching Chair
and Associate Professor,
Political Science and Honors,
University of Houston

The Mind of James Madison

The Legacy of Classical Republicanism

COLLEEN A. SHEEHAN
Villanova University

CAMBRIDGE
UNIVERSITY PRESS

University Printing House, Cambridge CB2 8BS, United Kingdom

One Liberty Plaza, 20th Floor, New York, NY 10006, USA

477 Williamstown Road, Port Melbourne, VIC 3207, Australia

4843/24, 2nd Floor, Ansari Road, Daryaganj, Delhi - 110002, India

79 Anson Road, #06-04/06, Singapore 079906

Cambridge University Press is part of the University of Cambridge.

It furthers the University's mission by disseminating knowledge in the pursuit of education, learning and research at the highest international levels of excellence.

www.cambridge.org
Information on this title: www.cambridge.org/9781108404983

First published 2015
First paperback edition 2017

A catalogue record for this publication is available from the British Library

Library of Congress Cataloging in Publication data
Sheehan, Colleen A.
The Mind of James Madison: The Legacy of Classical Republicanism /
Colleen A. Sheehan, Villanova University.
pages cm
Includes bibliographical references and index.
ISBN 978-1-107-02947-7 (Hardback)
1. Madison, James, 1751-1836–Political and social views. 2. United States–Politics and government–Philosophy. 3. United States–Politics and government–1783-1809. 4. Republicanism–United States–History–18th century. 5. Representative government and representation–United States–History–18th century. 6. Political science–United States–History–18th century. I. Title.
E342.S54 2015
973.5′1092–dc23 2014024203

ISBN 978-1-107-02947-7 Hardback
ISBN 978-1-108-40498-3 Paperback

For my mother and the memory of my father

"Mr. Maddison is a character who has long been in public life; and what is very remarkable every Person seems to acknowledge his greatness. He blends together the profound politician, with the Scholar."

William Pierce of Georgia,
delegate to the Constitutional Convention

Contents

Preface

Winston Churchill once said that a man has to choose whether to nail his life to the cross of thought or the cross of action. But Churchill managed to do both and to do them well, although it is surely the case that we remember him more for his statesmanship. Like Churchill, James Madison was both a statesman and a scholar, as William Pierce of Georgia noted in his character sketch of "Mr. Maddison" at the Constitutional Convention. Americans are more aware of Madison as the fourth President of the United States than they are of his scholarly writings. I think, though, that it was in the realm of ideas rather than practical political jockeying that Madison most excelled and found his vocation. He was a good but, honestly, not great politician. While he had a natural aptitude for legislative committee work, he was a poor orator. He was, however, an exceptional scholar of politics and political philosophy and, in particular, a brilliant pioneer in the study of republican government in the modern world. The following pages are meant to acquaint readers and citizens with Madison's discoveries and groundbreaking ideas as he engaged in a study of ancient and modern republicanism. Readers are also invited to experience with Madison the excitement he felt when he believed he had discovered the republic "for which philosophy has been searching, and humanity been sighing, from the most remote ages."[1]

Shortly after the formation of the new Constitution and the publication of *The Federalist* essays, and immediately following the close of the first session of Congress in March 1791, Madison burrowed in among his papers and books in his rented room at Mrs. House's Boarding House on 5th and Market in Philadelphia. His plan was to investigate further the problems and prospects

[1] "Spirit of Governments," *PJM*, 14:234.

of republican government. To accomplish this "little task,"[2] he engaged in extensive research into diverse texts of history and political philosophy, and he penned an outline portending a comprehensive treatise on politics.

Many years ago, when I first discovered his outline and the accompanying notes, I was both intrigued and perplexed. The "Notes on the Foundations of Government," as William B. Allen first referred to them (or what I refer to as the "Notes on Government"), clearly indicated a vast and rich inquiry into the foundations of government. At the same time, they seemed like a mosaic with some of the pieces missing or in shards. Enough of the mosaic was there to know I was looking at something of potentially very great value; enough was missing that I knew I had my work cut out for me for some time to come. Like Madison, I would have to burrow in among my books and papers to complete my task.

Following Madison's mind through the "Notes on Government" has required as much patience as it has research. After extensive investigation and study, I began fitting the pieces of Madison's intricate mosaic into place, and in time, the perplexing gave way to a pattern of understanding. Madison's project in the "Notes" sought to answer the following challenging questions: Can republican government – government by the people – be rescued from the internal diseases and external dangers that so often meant its demise throughout history? Could a remedy be found for these ailments that had eluded the classical philosophers? How did the protections for liberty that Montesquieu advanced shield individuals from the arbitrary and capricious actions of men in power? Did Montesquieu's robust and pivotal defense of liberty in *The Spirit of Laws* constitute the final remedy or did the celebrated French philosopher neglect, overlook, or sacrifice too much? Would it be possible – is it desirable – to reclaim the classical dedication to the cultivation of civic character that Montesquieu abandoned without jeopardizing the security of individuals against arbitrary power?

Given the nature of Madison's "Notes on Government," this book is necessarily a work of literary archaeology. Textual sites are mapped out for exploration; as Madison excavates one, he prepares the ground for the next. His intellectual journey brings us to stops along the way that are rich and varied. At the end of his travels, Madison arrived at a place that was, from his prospect, a political landscape of philosophical elegance.

•••

In seeking to explore, understand, and explain the mind of Madison, I have tried to remain as true as possible to Madison's own work as well as to how he would have read and understood the thinkers and texts he studied. Accordingly, I have consulted Madison's handwritten manuscript of the "Notes on Government" and associated materials; the transcriptions of these

[2] Madison to Jefferson, March 13, 1791, *PJM*, 13:405.

documents are included in Part II of this work. I have included in Part II writings by Madison that he cited in the "Notes on Government," except *The Federalist* and his *Notes of Debates in the Federal Convention of 1787*, which are much too lengthy to include and are readily available in print or online. I have annotated Madison's works for the ease of the readers. Where Madison refers to a specific text, I provide the pertinent passage. Jean Jacques Barthélemy, whom Madison cited heavily, often referenced other works, and I have also included his notes. For the sake of clarity, I have continued to number my own footnotes and have lettered and indented Barthélemy's footnotes. For the *National Gazette* essays, which are not in the collection of Madison's papers held by the Library of Congress, I have transcribed these articles from their originally published newspaper format. In some of these newspaper essays, Madison included references. These are indicated with an explanation at the start of the note.

I have also attempted to discern whether Madison would have read a given text in translation or in the original. With regard to Barthélemy's *Voyage du Jeune Anacharsis en Grèce* (*Travels of Anacharsis the Younger in Greece*), he read these volumes in the original French. (Thomas Jefferson sent these volumes to him in 1789, shortly after they were published.) I have used the only English translation published of Barthélemy's work and checked it against the original French, correcting the translation whenever necessary. If more than one English translation is available for texts Madison read (or probably read) in the original – for example, in the case of Montesquieu's *The Spirit of Laws* and Aristotle's *Politics* – I have used the most literal translation available today.

Acknowledgments

I am indebted to the Earhart Foundation and in particular to Ingrid A. Gregg and David Kennedy for their generous support of my research for this volume.

As this project has been in the offing for some years, a host of fine graduate students have contributed to this work. I am grateful to them for their dedication, willingness to wrestle with complex ideas, and patience with some very messy handwriting in a few of the original eighteenth-century documents. To Laura Butterfield, Andy Bausch, Kasey Neil, Charles Meyers, Sam West, Clyde Ray, and Graham Gormley, I extend my sincere thanks. You have done yeoman's work, which (as you know) Madison would have considered a virtue.

I am grateful to David Mattern of the University of Virginia's Papers of James Madison Project for his knowledge and kind assistance with corrections to the "Additional Notes on Government," as printed in Part II of this volume. Indeed, I owe a special note of gratitude to the editors of *The Papers of James Madison*. Their painstaking labor and exceptional editing of Madison's writings for decade upon decade has greatly enabled and enhanced contemporary scholarship on Madison. In my own case, it was in the volumes they produced that I first read Madison's correspondence and writings at length and encountered his ideas in detail. As a graduate student, I remember anticipating the publication of each new volume, saving my meager wages for months to be able to make each purchase. My debt to these editors is profound, and it is one I cannot readily repay.

Brian Satterfield and Mark Shiffman, colleagues of mine at Villanova, have kindly helped with certain French, Latin, and Greek translations of texts cited by Madison in the "Notes on Government" and Party Press Essays. It is always a nice excuse to impose on them for their accrued wisdom and acumen – just to have the chance to spend a bit more time in company and conversation with them.

I would not have been able to pursue research on the subject matter of this book if it were not for the expertise of Bente Polites, Special Collections

Librarian of Falvey Memorial Library at Villanova University. Early on in this venture, Bente was able to obtain some rare French texts for me to study, without which I would have had to abandon this project. She also directed the library's purchase of Barthélemy's *Travels of Anacharsis the Younger in Greece* (1806) and supported the digitization of this work by Michael Foight, Special Collections and Digital Library Coordinator at Falvey Library.

Renowned scholars and good friends Ralph Lerner and Paul A. Rahe have generously read earlier drafts of this manuscript and have offered extensive comments and suggestions. Their knowledge of ancient and modern political philosophy and the depth of their thoughtfulness are unsurpassed. They have prompted me to rethink and refine some of my ideas in this text, and I believe the volume is stronger and will be of more lasting value as a result.

I owe an especially great debt of gratitude to my mentor and dear friend Bill Allen, who has been an inspiration to me in my study of Madison and the American founding over the course of many years. His profound understanding of the American republic is matched only by his consummate dedication to its principles.

In the last phase of the work on this volume, I had the assistance of two incomparable graduate students: Brenda Hafera and Alexios Alexander. We met together almost every day for a number of weeks at the Ryan Center at Villanova. During that time, we transcribed, we edited, we disputed grammar, we debated ideas, and we engaged in more than our share of raillery. Despite all the long hours and hard work, we knew we were fortunate to be spending our time together thinking about the most fundamental questions of free government.

I also want to thank, most deeply and sincerely, Lewis Bateman of Cambridge University Press. Over the course of our last project and this current one, Lew has put up with me like a family member who tolerates the foibles and unpunctuality of another.

My husband and best friend, Jack Doody, has always been exceptionally supportive of my scholarly research and work and of my penchant for virtually "living" in the eighteenth century. Indeed, he has not been averse to sharing a wintry Sunday afternoon with me gossiping about our good friends: Mr. Madison and Mr. Jefferson (or Mr. Darcy and Elizabeth Bennet, for that matter). I cannot thank him enough for his willingness to share with me what I love so much.

This book builds on the original preliminary work I did on the "Notes on Government" ("The Politics of Public Opinion: James Madison's 'Notes on Government,'" *William and Mary Quarterly* 49, no. 3 [1992]: 609–27). It is an extension of the work I began in *James Madison and the Spirit of Republican Self-Government* (Cambridge University Press, 2009), particularly Chapter 7. The discussion of David Hume's views herein draws freely on "Public Opinion and the Formation of Civic Character in Madison's Republican Theory," *Review of Politics* 67, no. 1 (2005): 37–48.

Abbreviations for sources

The Federalist	Hamilton, Alexander, James Madison, and John Jay. *The Federalist Papers*. Edited by Clinton Rossiter. New York: Mentor Books, 1999.
LOC	Madison, James. *The James Madison Papers, 1723–1836*. Library of Congress. http://memory.loc.gov/ammem/collections/madison_papers/.
MJM	Sheehan, Colleen A. *The Mind of James Madison: The Legacy of Classical Republicanism*. Cambridge: Cambridge University Press, 2014.
Politics	Aristotle. *Politics*. Translated by Carnes Lord. Chicago: University of Chicago Press, 1984.
PJM	Madison, James. *The Papers of James Madison*. Edited by William T. Hutchinson, William M. E. Rachal, Robert A. Rutland et al. 35 vols. to date. Chicago and Charlottesville: University of Chicago Press and University Press of Virginia, 1962–.
PTJ	Jefferson, Thomas. *The Papers of Thomas Jefferson*. Edited by Julian P. Boyd and J. Jefferson Looney et al. 48 vols. to date. Princeton: Princeton University Press, 1950–.
SOL	Montesquieu, Charles de Secondat, Baron de. *The Spirit of the Laws*. Translated by Thomas Nugent. New York: Hafner Press, 1949.
Voyage	Barthélemy, Jean Jacques. *Voyage du Jeune Anacharsis en Grèce dans le Milieu du Quatrième Siècle Avant l'Ère Vulgaire*. 8 vols. Paris, 1788. Barthélemy, Jean-Jacques. *Travels of Anacharsis the Younger in Greece*. Translated by William Beaumont. 7 vols. and an eighth in quarto. London: J. Johnson et al., 1806. The English translation is used herein and has been digitized by Michael Foight, Special Collections and Digital Library Coordinator, Falvey Memorial Library of Villanova University.

WJA Adams, John. *The Works of John Adams*. Edited by Charles Francis Adams. 10 vols. Boston, 1850-1856; Reprint, Freeport, NY: Books for Libraries Press, 1969.

WJM Madison, James. *The Writings of James Madison*. Edited by Gaillard Hunt. 9 vols. New York: G. P. Putnam's Sons, 1900-1910.

Influence of the size of a nation on Government . . . page. 1
——— of external danger on Government. . ——— 10
——— of the Stage of Society on Government ——— 16
——— of Public opinion on Government . . ——— 22
——— of Education on Government ——— 30
——— of Religion on Government ——— 35
——— of Domestic slavery on Government 40
——— of Dependent dominions on Government . . 46
Checks devised in democracies marking self-distrust — 49
True reasons for keeping the great departments of power separate 55

Federal Governments 65
Government of United States 75

Best distribution of people in Republic . . . 82

The articles in this volume were written after the commencement of the new government, as is proved, among other circumstances by frequent references to "Travels of Anacharsis," first published in 1789.

Handwritten page from James Madison's "Notes on Government." In addition to functioning as an outline and table of contents for his "Notes on Government," this handwritten page displays the contour of Madison's comprehensive project in political philosophy.
Source: Courtesy of James Madison Papers, Manuscript Division, Library of Congress, mjm 28_1771_1794

R. Smith's Brewery, 20 South 5th Street, Philadelphia, PA, 1859. Prior to becoming a brewery in the mid-19th century, this building on the corner of Philadelphia's 5th and Market Streets was under the care of Mary House. It was in her stately Boarding House that James Madison resided while researching and developing his "Notes on Government" in 1791. This is also where he stayed during the Constitutional Convention in the summer of 1787, and in general when he resided in Philadelphia from 1780 to 1793.
Source: Courtesy of Free Library of Philadelphia, Print and Picture Department

PART I

1

An itinerant scholar in Mr. Jefferson's library

Had they been in their native Virginia, they would have considered the spring-like March day a prelude to an overture of cherry blossoms just around the season's corner. But the comforts of home were for them many days' journey away and, for the elder of the two, essentially had been so since summer 1784. Still, the mild and pleasant Philadelphia day could tempt even a displaced southerner, especially if it might be whiled away with one's closest friend. Thus, with anticipation, Secretary of State Thomas Jefferson sat at his writing desk on the morning of March 13, 1791. Jotting a note to his fellow Piedmonter residing in the city, Jefferson invited James Madison to join him and a small party for an afternoon outing, followed by dinner at his table. Jefferson knew that his friend had been spending long sedentary hours in scholarly research since the close of the First Congress a week prior, and he was anxious to bolster his health and share in his company. Perhaps, he wrote Madison, you will also come stay at my lodgings. "When I get my library open, you will often find a convenience in being close at hand to it."[1]

As was his wont, Jefferson was undertaking extensive renovations to his domicile. Even in his rented residence on High Street (now Market Street) in the temporary capital city, he was architecturally altering and rearranging things to accommodate his style of social entertaining and studious retreat, including adding an upstairs library to the back of his residence to house his extensive book collection. Although the new room was still under construction in mid-March 1791, he had already unpacked his books. Madison had likely requested the loan of some volumes for his current project or perhaps was already borrowing books from Jefferson's collection, and Jefferson was eager to provide him easier access to them. Madison accepted his friend's invitation for a

[1] *PTJ*, XIX:551.

ride in the countryside but politely declined the offer to relocate from his room at Mrs. House's Boarding House, pleading:

> I am just settled in my harness for compleating the little task I have allotted myself. My papers and books are all assorted, around me. A change of position would necessarily give some interruption – & some trouble on my side whatever it might do on yours.[2]

Most scholars accept the claim that the "little task" Madison was engaged in at this juncture was the correction of his "Notes of Debates" of the Federal Convention.[3] If this were the case, however, Madison would hardly have protested the move as troublesome. For this task, he needed only his Convention notes and William Jackson's journal of proceedings, and it would not have been a great bother to move these two moderately sized sets of papers. Madison claimed the move would be incommodious because he had his "papers and books" all spread about him. The emendation of the Convention notes required neither access to Jefferson's library nor the use of any *books* at all. Surely, Madison would not have made such a spurious excuse to his dear friend and confidante.

As Jefferson undoubtedly understood, Madison's "little task" was hardly a trifling project. However impressive Madison's contribution to *The Federalist* may have been – which Jefferson thought "the best commentary on the principles of government which ever was written"[4] – the fruits of those labors did not satisfy Madison himself. Just three years later, Madison was intensely engaged in a "more thorough investigation" of the important subject he had undertaken as Publius. In spring 1791, Madison produced a set of writings that rivaled his previous study of republican government in scope and substance. Indeed, these "Notes on Government"[5] constitute the most ambitious philosophical project of Madison's scholarly career.

THE COMPOSITION OF THE "NOTES ON GOVERNMENT"

The "Notes on Government" are designated as the "Notes for the *National Gazette* Essays" by the editors of *The Papers of James Madison*. The editors have set the approximate composition of these writings between late 1791 and early 1792 and have identified their purpose as draft material for some of the occasional pieces Madison published in Freneau's newspaper in

[2] *PJM*, 13:405.

[3] *PTJ*, XIX:547n; Cf. *PJM*, 10:8 and 13:406n1. See also Charles R. Keller and George W. Pierson, "A New Madison Manuscript Relating to the Federal Convention of 1787," *American Historical Review* 36, no. 1 (October 1930): 17–30. It should also be noted that there is no evidence to support the supposition that Madison even had his Convention debates notes with him in Philadelphia at this time. His book memorandum of August 1790, for example, does not list this material as destined for the capital city; see *PJM*, 13:286–89.

[4] Jefferson to Madison, November 18, 1788, *PJM*, 11:353.

[5] *MJM*, 123; *PJM*, 14:157–69.

1791–1792.[6] An examination of the general design and purpose of the "Notes," however, demonstrates that the designation "Notes for the *National Gazette* Essays" (or Party Press Essays) is too narrow and inadvertently misleading. While the editors of *The Papers of James Madison* are correct to claim that some of the *National Gazette* articles rely on material found in the "Notes" and that certain segments of some of the essays are virtually identical to portions of the "Notes," a comparison of the content of the "Notes" to that of the nineteen Party Press Essays reveals that nearly two-thirds of the Party Press Essays are not based on the "Notes." In turn, more than half the headings in the "Notes" are dedicated to subjects that the Party Press Essays do not address.[7] Moreover, in the Party Press Essays, Madison did not follow the outline of the "Notes" or attempt to treat the various influences on government systematically, as he did in the "Notes on Government."

The approximate dateline assigned to the composition of the "Notes" by the editors of *The Papers of James Madison* is between December 19, 1791, and March 3, 1792. It is more likely, however, that Madison composed the "Notes" in late winter 1790/early spring 1791, beginning about the time the congressional session ended in early March, when he mentioned to Jefferson that he had just settled in to work on a "little" scholarly task.

It is doubtful, for example, that Madison was engaged in work on the "Notes" later than December 12, 1791. On this date, his first *National Gazette*

[6] *MJM*, 123–65; *PJM*, 14:157–69. The manuscript is in the LOC, Washington, DC. Although the editors of *The Papers of James Madison* classify this material as "Notes for the *National Gazette* Essays," they claim only that this notebook material "is the basis for five essays" and that it "served only as an early draft for the essays" (see *PJM*, 14:110–11n).

[7] Similarities between the sets of writings include subjects discussed in the first heading/chapter of the "Notes on Government" ("Influence of the size of a nation on Government"), which are also taken up in three of his Party Press Essays: "Public Opinion," "Government," and "Parties" (*MJM*, 245; 246; 249; *PJM*, 14:170; 178–79; 197–98). The Party Press Essay "Government" includes material found in the second chapter of the "Notes," titled "Influence of External Danger on Government"; the *National Gazette* essays "Public Opinion" and "British Government" include material found in Chapter 4 of the "Notes": "Influence of Public Opinion on Government"; the essay "Dependent Territories" is based on "Influence of Dependent Dominions on Government" from the "Notes" (see Sheehan, "Madison's Party Press Essays," *Interpretation: A Journal of Political Philosophy* 17, no. 3 [Spring 1990]: 376–77), and *MJM*, 237; *PJM*, 17:559–60; the Party Press Essay "Government of the United States" (*MJM*, 254; *PJM*, 14:217–19) is based on Chapter 12 of the "Notes" ("Government of United States"); and the essay "Republican Distribution of Citizens" (*MJM*, 258; *PJM*, 14:244–46) is similar to the last chapter of the "Notes," titled "Best distribution of people in Republic." Twelve of the nineteen Party Press Essays are not based on material found in the "Notes," and seven of the thirteen chapters of the "Notes" are not explicitly related to the *National Gazette* essays. However, some of the themes set forth and developed in the Party Press Essays – for example, the idea that the will of the society is dependent on the reason of the society (see "Spirit of Governments" and "Universal Peace") – are clearly presaged by the Party Press Essay "Public Opinion," which is based on the fourth chapter of the "Notes," titled "Influence of Public Opinion on Government."

article based on the "Notes" was published;[8] had he started the project after the publication of one or more of the Party Press Essays based on the "Notes," he would almost certainly have cited his published work in the "Notes" rather than waste time rewriting arguments and passages he had already committed to paper – and which were in a more polished form.[9] Prior to December 1791, then, when might he have had the time and the requisite materials at his disposal to compose the "Notes"?

It is unlikely that Madison researched and wrote the "Notes" in the period between the end of April and mid-October 1791. The material he used and cited in the "Notes" was located in Philadelphia, and save for a brief period between August 23 and September 2, he was away from the capital city during this time. During the short interim when he was in Philadelphia, his friends were eager to share in his company, and there is no reason to believe he did not gratify their wishes. Indeed, Jefferson's letter to Madison in the waning summer days of 1791 is a charming depiction of the warm and close friendship they shared, showing how much he and Madison's other friends delighted in his company and missed him when deprived of it for any length of time. On August 18, Jefferson impatiently wrote to Madison: "Try to arrive here on Tuesday time enough (say by 4 o clock) to come & dine with E. Randolph, Ross &c. half a dozen in all en petite comite." Jefferson also noted George Washington's eagerness to have him with them: "All your acquaintances are perpetually asking if you are arrived. It has been the first question from the President every time I have seen him for this fortnight. If you had arrived before dinner to-day, I had a strong charge to carry you there. Come on then & make us all happy."[10] Surely, Madison hurried along his way, but if the adage that absence makes the heart grow fonder is true, then there were fonder hearts greeting Mr. Madison on his return to Philadelphia, for he was not able to reach the city until about five days later.

The tempo of Madison's late spring 1791 was robust, characterized by upstate New York travels and lake country air. It was a time in which he seems

[8] On December 12, 1791, "Dependent Territories" appeared in the *National Gazette*, an article which was clearly based on "Influence of dependent dominions on Government" in the "Notes on Government."

[9] When, for example, he wished to include in the "Notes" arguments from his Convention notes and certain *Federalist* essays, he simply cited the texts. The one reference to the *National Gazette* essays in the "Notes" is to the entire set of published essays and appears at the very end of the "Notes on Government," indicating that it was likely added at a later date. In addition, in the very first essay of the series – "Population and Emigration" – written on November 19 and published on November 21, 1791, Madison's reference to Pliny the Younger was gleaned from his reading of the sixth volume of Barthélemy's *Voyage of Anacharsis*, as the editors of *The Papers of James Madison* duly note (*MJM*, 230; *PJM*, 14:118 and 14:122n1). Accordingly, Madison was studying Barthélemy's work, upon which he heavily relied in the "Notes," at least as early as November 1791.

[10] Jefferson to Madison, August 18, 1791, *PJM*, 14:71.

to have attempted to improve his generally poor health and particularly to mend from an illness he had suffered in April. After touring through northern New York with Jefferson in May and June, he planned a trip to the Boston area. Despite his good intentions and active pace, his health relapsed during July, forcing him to cancel his intended excursion east. Added to this were other sundry setbacks, which would have compromised his plans anyway. And as (bad) luck would have it, his horse was simultaneously suffering from ill health, which seems to have caused Madison almost as much anxious concern as his own malady. The recurrence of Madison's poor health earned from Edmund Randolph the fretful advice of a fellow Virginian and longtime friend. Hearing from Jefferson that Madison had recovered from his recent bilious attack, Randolph conveyed to Madison his satisfaction of knowing that he was better, but he simultaneously counseled him to abstain from study when he returned to Philadelphia in the autumn.[11] Undoubtedly, Randolph believed that Madison's summer relapse was a lingering effect of the debilitating spring attack caused by excessive scholarly strain, and he hoped to parry yet another repeat performance in the coming fall when Madison was again to be at home with his books.

Fortunately, Madison's friends' anxieties were not prophetic. His health throughout the fall and ensuing winter was apparently quite good. (Fortunately, his horse also recovered.) Arriving in Philadelphia from Montpelier via Mount Vernon on October 22, 1791, he immediately thrust himself into public business. As one would expect, the beginning of the congressional session was a very busy period, which Madison himself noted. His lack of leisure time lasted at least through the end of the month and most likely for some time beyond.[12] Besides devoting his attention to pressing public business that fall, he dashed off a number of articles for the newly established Philadelphia newspaper. During the past summer, Philip Freneau had finally agreed to establish and edit this newspaper, and on October 31, he began publication of the *National Gazette*.

In addition to the lack of time for scholarly activity at Madison's disposal during the final months of 1791, it seems reasonable to surmise the following: upon his return to Philadelphia in the autumn of that year, with a mound of public work facing him and Freneau's expectation that he contribute to the new semi-weekly publication, Madison felt the rush of the season and simply used or polished some things he had already written. In fact, we know he did precisely this with respect to the fourth and fifth Party Press Essays on

[11] See Edmund Randolph to Madison, July 21, 1791, *PJM*, 14:51.

[12] See Madison's letter to his father, James Madison Sr., October 30, 1791, *PJM*, 14:90. In this letter, Madison wrote: "Being obliged to attend immediately on my arrival [October 22] to Public business I have not been able to give the attention to yours & that of others which I wished."

"Money," which were published in mid-December 1791 but were actually written in 1779–1780.[13]

In all likelihood, then, Madison penned the "Notes on Government" prior to the start of his spring travels at the end of April 1791. In March and April, following Congress' adjournment on March 2, Madison had leisure time to pursue scholarly endeavors and also had access to the materials he employed in the "Notes." Many of the sources Madison cited in the "Notes" were included in his August 1790 list of books to be sent to the new capital city at Philadelphia for his relocation there that fall.[14] A few of the sources he referred to in the "Notes," however, were borrowed from the book collection Jefferson had transported to Philadelphia, which Jefferson was not able to unpack until at least December 1790 or more probably January 1791.[15] Accordingly, Madison's "Notes" were likely not written after the end of April 1791 and could not have been written prior to December 1790. Indeed, he probably began gathering data for the "Notes on Government" in February 1791, anticipating the project he intended to work on after the close of public business the following month. One of the citations under the heading of "Federal Governments" refers to Ebenezer Hazard's unpublished manuscript of the *Records of the United Colonies of New England*, a source Madison apparently only had access to in mid-February by way of Jefferson.[16]

Given the time needed to compose the notebook and the access to materials used therein, it seems very likely that Madison was working on the "Notes on Government" in early 1791. Accordingly, the claim that these notes were composed as preliminary drafts for some of the *National Gazette* essays cannot be accurate; the *National Gazette* was not yet in existence. In fact, during this

[13] *MJM*, 238–244; *PJM*, 1:302–10.

[14] Madison's 1790 book list is reprinted in *PJM*, 13:286–89.

[15] See *PJM*, 14:168–69nn14–15, 29. Cf. E. Millicent Sowerby, *Catalogue of the Library of Thomas Jefferson*, 5 vols. (Washington, DC: Library of Congress, 1952); *PTJ*, XVIII:350, 579, 600.

[16] Ebenezer Hazard's manuscript concerned the first Anglo-American compact of federal union. The material cited by Madison in the "Notes" was contained in the second volume of Hazard's *Historical Collections*, which would not be published until 1794. Prior to this, there existed only one copy of this material, which was in Jefferson's possession in winter 1791. In compliance with Hazard's request, Jefferson inspected this portion of his manuscript and then returned it to him on February 18, 1791 (see *PTJ*, XIX:287–89n; cf. Sowerby, III:238–39). According to Hazard, he was presently in the process of obtaining an agreement for publication and was anxious to have the one copy of the *Records of the United Colonies of New England* back in his hands (see Fred Shelley, "Ebenezer Hazard: America's First Historical Editor," *William and Mary Quarterly* 12 [1955]: 61–63). Hazard secured a publication contract in late February 1791 and fulfilled it over the next three years. It is doubtful that Hazard would have loaned out any of the manuscript during this period of preparation for printing. Thus, if Madison actually examined Hazard's *Records* of the four New England colonies – and one would presume he at least perused the material he cited in "Notes" – then he probably did so in February 1791, when the *Records* were temporarily in Jefferson's possession.

period, there was not yet any certainty that Freneau would even take up the task of founding and editing a newspaper in Philadelphia.[17]

THE DESIGN AND PURPOSE OF THE "NOTES ON GOVERNMENT"

Madison recorded his "Notes on Government" in a bound notebook, with pages numbered from one to ninety-nine. These pages are prefaced by a table of contents, printed on the verso of the first page.[18] The table of contents consists of thirteen divisions or chapters, with pagination listed as follows:

X Influence of the size of a nation on Government. . . . . page. 1
——of external danger on Government. 10
——of the Stage of Society on Government. 16
—X– of Public opinion on Government. 22
——of Education on Government. 30
——of Religion on Government 35
—X– of Domestic slavery on Government. 40
—X– of Dependent dominions on Government 46
X Checks devised in democracies marking self-distrust. 49
True reasons for keeping the great departments of power separate. . . . 55
X Federal Governments. 65
X Government of United States. 75
X Best distribution of people in Republic. 82

Although many of the pages of the notebook are left blank, ten of the thirteen chapters contain at least preliminary, if not fairly extensive, information. The portion of the notebook filled by Madison equals approximately seventeen typed, double-spaced pages. The design of the "Notes on Government" reveals an outline and envisioned project much broader and more philosophically systematic than preliminary drafts for newspaper opinion pieces would require. The outline commences with the question of political stability, framed in terms of the influences that contribute to the preservation or destruction of governments. It culminates in a description of a new kind of federal republic that is superior to all past governments in its potential to achieve the safety, liberty, and happiness of its citizens.

[17] See Jefferson to Philip Freneau, February 28, 1791, *PTJ*, XIX:351; Madison to Jefferson, May 1, 1791, *PJM*, 14:15, 18n2; Jefferson to Madison, May 9, 1791, *PJM*, 14:18; Madison to Jefferson, July 10, 1791, *PJM*, 14:43; Jefferson to Madison, July 21, 1791, *PJM*, 14:49–50; Madison to Jefferson, July 24, 1791, *PJM*, 14:52; Philip Freneau to Madison, July 25, 1791, *PJM*, 14:57; and editorial note, *PJM*, 14:56–57.

[18] *PJM*, 14:168n. See the facsimile of the original first page of Madison's "Notes," in Madison's hand, printed on *MJM*, xvi at the beginning of this volume.

The first eight headings, or chapters, form the first section of the "Notes" and concern the various influences on government. This section is subdivided into two parts: Chapters 1 through 3 deal with the spatial, temporal, and external circumstances of political society and their influence on government. First and foremost, Madison considered the size of the territory; he then investigated the issues of external danger and the stage of society, emphasizing how these factors interact with territorial size to stabilize or destabilize the political order. Chapters 4 through 8 constitute the second subsection, which focuses on the influences on government that result from the views, beliefs, mores, and manners of the people. The subject of the fourth chapter is the influence of public opinion on government, which is the central concern of the entire first section. The other chapters of this section pertain to the influences on government by way of their influence on public opinion – whether by affecting the mode of forming public opinion or by directly shaping the citizens' views and mores.

The second section of the "Notes" encompasses Chapters 9 through 12; it focuses on the prudential devices and structural components that may be employed to impede or promote the force of opinion in popular government, including checks on decision-making power, separation of powers, and federalism. The concluding chapter constitutes the final section of the notebook; it describes the plan for the way of life of a free and virtuous republic, which Madison proffered as an archetype to republican statesmen for successive political improvements. The "Notes on Government" move from a concern for the stability of the political order to a concern for the liberty and ultimately the happiness of the citizens, reflecting a deliberate progression from the lowest but most immediate political objective to the highest human aspiration.

The design of the "Notes" reveals Madison's intent to treat the subject of government methodically and comprehensively. Although the number of pages Madison filled in his notebook is not extensive, the substantial amount of reference material, the breadth of historical study, and the depth of philosophical analysis unmistakably indicate an envisioned undertaking much beyond the production and publication of a few occasional pieces. While Madison's essays for the Party Press are certainly more theoretically complex than the average newspaper opinion piece, they do not reflect the latitude and complexity of analysis evident in the pages of his "Notes on Government" and are rather more akin to the politicized approach of *The Federalist*. Although the analysis is thoughtful and often penetrating in these two newspaper collections, neither set of essays is, strictly speaking, a work of political philosophy. The contrast in the style of speech of *The Federalist* and the Party Press Essays on the one hand and that of the "Notes on Government" on the other serves to illustrate this distinction. The former is written in the rhetorical style conjoined to politics, appealing to the reason, interests, and prejudices of a particular people in particular circumstances. The newspaper articles are essentially op-ed pieces (although some of the most substantive and brilliant ones that ever appeared in an American newspaper, to be sure). As such, they are appropriately identified as political tracts. Alternatively, in the "Notes," Madison is not confined by the various rhetorical constraints associated with the political speech of the stump, assembly, or newspaper; here, he speaks not as a politician but as a philosophical scholar, unfettered by the particularistic concerns of a specific people, time, or place. For example, in the "Notes," he treats the subject of slavery in the southern states of America candidly and harshly, without rhetorical euphemism or political caution. As far as I know, he never published this piece or any revised version of it. Other (unpublished) text and topics in the "Notes," such as Minos' reception of divine laws at the Cave of Jupiter or checks on popular orators employed in ancient Greece, seem rather far removed from the concerns of everyday eighteenth-century American life. In the final chapter of the "Notes," Madison envisions the contours of the best political order and the way of life of its inhabitants, offering a window to his conception of the character and spirit of the men and women he considers fitting citizens of a genuine republic.

The "Notes on Government" are laden with citations to the most renowned philosophical and historical texts, indicating extensive research on these works and their themes, hardly any of which are used in the published *National Gazette* pieces. For example, in the "Notes," Madison studied Xenophon, Plato, Aristotle, Thucydides, Strabo, Dionysius of Halicarnassus, Livy, Plutarch, Montesquieu, Gibbon, Robertson, Pownall, Moyle, Franklin, and contributors to the *Encyclopédie Méthodique*. He also cited the work of Publius as well as his own *National Gazette* essays of 1791–1792; the latter reference he likely appended to the end of his "Notes" at a future date.[19] However, it is the epical work of Jean Jacques Barthélemy, titled *Voyage du Jeune Anacharsis en Grèce dans le Milieu du Quatrième Siècle Avant l'Ère Vulgaire* (Paris, 1788), that garners the greatest number of citations and copied passages. Barthélemy's eight-volume fictional narrative on ancient Greek civilization and culture took him more than thirty years to write. Upon its release in 1789, Jefferson purchased the volumes and sent them to Madison.[20] When the temporary capital of the United States moved from New York to Philadelphia in the latter part of 1790

[19] *MJM*, 165; see *PJM*, 14:168 and 169n31.

[20] Jean Jacques Barthélemy's *Voyage du Jeune Anacharsis en Grèce dans le Milieu du Quatrième Siècle Avant l'Ère Vulgaire*, which was completed by the author in 1788 and published in 1789, was immediately purchased in multiple copies by Jefferson. On January 12, 1789, he sent a set to Madison, which, after almost a four months' journey across the Atlantic, Madison acknowledged receipt of on May 9, 1789. In a letter to Joseph Willard, March 24, 1789 (*PTJ*, XIV:697), Jefferson wrote: "The most remarkable publications we have had in France, for a year or two past, are the following. 'Les voyages d'Anacharsis par l'Abbé Barthelemi,' seven volumes, octavo. This is a very elegant digest of whatever is known of the Greeks; useless, indeed, to him who has read the original authors, but very proper for one who reads modern languages only."

and Madison made up a list of the books he would transport to the new seat of government, the complete set of Barthélemy's *Voyage* was on this select list.

Following the adjournment of the First Congress in early March 1791, Madison embarked on a study (or probably continued his study) of the Abbé Barthélemy's opus. Given the close attention he devoted to this immense work, including many of the references to original Greek texts contained therein, Madison's scholarly endeavors must have occupied him for no small period of time that late winter and early spring. Interestingly, this intense period of study followed immediately on the heels of a politically charged session of Congress during which he had served as the de facto leader of the House of Representatives and most recently had led the opposition to the establishment of a national bank. Over the past several months, Madison also had to endure a year-long serial publication of John Adams' "obnoxious principles" in John Fenno's pro-Federalist newspaper: the *Gazette of the United States*.[21] As in his earlier volumes, Adams continued his "voluminous and ponderous" defense of balanced government based on the different orders in society and criticized those (especially French politician and writer Turgot) who advocated "collecting all authority into one center, the nation."[22]

While Madison was not at this stage bent on full-scale opposition to the Federalist administration or intent on establishing the Republican Party, he was nonetheless uneasy about the influence of (what he perceived as) Adams' antirepublican views on public opinion. He was also concerned about the inroads Alexander Hamilton was making to establish a British-type fiscal system on American soil. These concerns are manifested in portions of the "Notes on Government," although no names or specific policies of the Federalist administration are explicitly mentioned. From Madison's perspective, the tone and policies that were emerging from high administrative offices and that were popular in the urban areas of the nation would, if not counteracted, threaten a fair trial of the American experiment in self-government.

The trend that Madison saw emerging from the administration over the course of the next year, leading particularly to Hamilton's "Report on Manufacturers," led to his decision to oppose the Federalist agenda and establish the Republican Party in 1792. It is not clear, however, that the earlier proposals emanating from members of the administration triggered his decision to undertake a fuller study of republican government in 1791. He may, in fact, have had the "Notes on Government" project in mind prior to his move to Philadelphia in 1790 when he drew up his list of books to transport to the new temporary capital. This would have been after Adams had made his antirepublican intentions abundantly clear (at least to Madison's way of thinking) and subsequent to the debate on funding the debt but prior to Hamilton's unveiling of his

[21] See letter of Madison to Jefferson, June 27, 1791, *PJM*, 12:182.

[22] See Madison's article of October 20, 1792, in *Dunlap's American Daily Advertiser*, *PJM*, 14:388n.

project to establish a national bank and the beginnings of party alignments. There is, for example, an emphasis on political economy and on the significance of public opinion in an advanced communicative society in the texts Madison selected to ship to his Philadelphia residence, which is also present in the "Notes."

We do not know whether Madison intended to present to the public the fuller picture of republicanism he outlined in the "Notes" or – if he did mean to do so – when and in what form. It may not have been a decision Madison himself had yet made in spring 1791. What is evident, however, is that despite the political concerns that are implicit in this material, the "Notes on Government" primarily reveal the efforts and temperament of a scholar. Indeed, given the comprehensive scope and philosophic analysis that characterize the "Notes," it is possible that Madison planned at some point to produce a scholarly treatise on politics.[23] Certainly, the space reserved for further research entries in the paginated notebook indicates that he originally intended to take the project further. First, though, he wanted to work out his theory of republicanism more systematically and completely in his own mind and commit some thoughts to paper. His plan was to examine the fundamental and enduring questions of politics within the broad context of the works composed by "the great oracles of political wisdom."[24] His goal was to investigate the causes that tend toward the preservation or destruction of regimes, particularly in a republican polity, and ultimately to set forth a description of the well-ordered republic. Like Barthélemy's *Voyage du Jeune Anacharsis en Grèce*, Madison's intellectual journey in the "Notes on Government" is a retrieval of the ancient quest to vindicate republican government. In the texts of the Classics, especially Aristotle's *Politics*, Madison discovered an analysis of the problems that had plagued republicanism from its inception and had caused the failure of popular government into his own day. In his voyage to the classical world, Madison found reason to hope for the future success of the age-old experiment in self-government.

Despite the philosophic importance of the "Notes on Government" and their indispensability to understanding Madison's overarching political theory, this material has been virtually unstudied by scholars of Madison and the American founding.[25] This is perhaps understandable given that the accepted designation

[23] See William B. Allen, "Justice and the General Good: *Federalist* 51," in *Saving the Revolution: The Federalist Papers and the American Founding*, ed. Charles R. Kesler (New York: Free Press, 1987), 133–36.

[24] "Notes on the Influence of Extent of Territory on Government," *PJM*, 14:132.

[25] In addition to my preliminary work on the "Notes on Government" (see particularly "The Politics of Public Opinion: James Madison's 'Notes on Government,'" *William and Mary Quarterly* 49, no. 4 [1992], and *James Madison and the Spirit of Republican Self-Government* [Cambridge: Cambridge University Press, 2009], 156–75), William B. Allen has provided a succinct general description of Madison's "Notes on Government" in "Justice and the General Good: *Federalist* 51," 133–36; Drew McCoy, *The Last of the Fathers: James Madison and the*

of this notebook as "Notes for the *National Gazette* Essays" relegates its contents to preliminary draft essays and denies it a distinct status. While some of the *National Gazette* articles are derived from parts of the "Notes on Government," viewing the latter as merely notes for the former results in the failure to appreciate the full scholarly thrust of the "Notes."[26] Although the

Republican Legacy (Cambridge: Cambridge University Press, 1989), 235, has briefly examined Madison's account of slavery in the "Notes on Government"; Lance Banning has offered some summary remarks on the material in *The Sacred Fire of Liberty: James Madison & the Founding of the Federal Republic* (Ithaca: Cornell University Press, 1985), 349 and 521–22nn60, 65. See also Denver Brunsman, "James Madison and the National Gazette Essays: The Birth of a Party Politician," in *A Companion to James Madison and James Monroe*, ed. Stuart Leibiger (Malden, MA: Wiley-Blackwell, 2012), 147–51; Paul A. Rahe, *Republics Ancient & Modern: Inventions of Prudence: Constituting the American Regime* (Chapel Hill: University of North Carolina Press, 1994), 179, 330n150; and Carl J. Richard, *The Founders and the Classics: Greece, Rome, and the American Enlightenment* (Cambridge, MA: Harvard University Press, 1994), 273n52.

26 Madison added a line at the end of the "Notes on Government" referring to the published *National Gazette* essays, thereby including them in this notebook. While most of these essays were included in a collection of Madison's writings edited by Jack Rakove (*James Madison: Writings* [New York: Library of America, 1999]), the entire collection of Party Press Essays had yet to be published together in the same volume. As such, I have included the Party Party Press Essays of 1791–1792 in their entirety in this volume. (See Chapter 7.) Adrienne Koch, one of the twentieth century's first-rate scholars on the thought of Jefferson and Madison, once remarked that Madison's *National Gazette* essays are "papers I have long considered worthy of separate publication and wide distribution for readers today" ("James Madison and the Workshop of Liberty," *The Review of Politics* 16, no. 2 [1954]: 179). Pertinent and substantial scholarship that has discussed Madison's essays for the *National Gazette* includes: John Zvesper, "The Madisonian Systems," *The Western Political Quarterly* 37, no. 2 (1984): 236–56; Douglas W. Jaenicke, "Madison v. Madison: The Party Press Essays v. The Federalist Papers," in *Reflections on the Constitution: The American Constitution After Two Hundred Years*, eds. Richard Maidment and John Zvesper (New York: Manchester University Press, 1989), 116–47; Richard K. Mathews, *If Men Were Angels: James Madison & the Heartless Empire of Reason* (Lawrence: University Press of Kansas, 1995), 158–64; Banning, *Sacred Fire of Liberty*, 348–61; Gary Rosen, *American Compact: James Madison and the Problem of the Founding* (Lawrence: University Press of Kansas, 1999), 152–55; Saul Cornell, *The Other Founders: Anti-Federalism & the Dissenting Tradition in America, 1788–1828* (Chapel Hill: University of North Carolina Press, 1999), 166–68, 247–53; James H. Read, *Power Versus Liberty: Madison, Hamilton, Wilson, and Jefferson* (Charlottesville: University Press of Virginia, 2000), 32, 45; Larry D. Kramer, *The People Themselves: Popular Constitutionalism and Judicial Review* (Oxford: Oxford University Press, 2004), 112–14; Larry D. Kramer, "The Interest of the Man: James Madison, Popular Constitutionalism, and the Theory of Deliberative Democracy," *Valparaiso University Law Review* 41, no. 2 (2007): 697–754; Alan Gibson, "Veneration and Vigilance: James Madison and Public Opinion," *Review of Politics* 67, no. 1 (2005): 5–35, 69–76; Todd Estes, "Shaping the Politics of Public Opinion: Federalists and the Jay Treaty," *Journal of the Early Republic* 20, no. 3 (2000): 393–423; Estes, *The Jay Treaty Debate, Public Opinion, and the Evolution of Early American Culture* (Amherst: University of Massachusetts Press, 2006), 7–8, and *passim*; Greg Weiner, *Madison's Metronome: The Constitution, Majority Rule, and the Tempo of American Politics* (Lawrence: University Press of Kansas, 2012), 18, 28–29, 42, 52, 57; Teena Gabrielson, "James Madison's Psychology of Public Opinion," *Political Research Quarterly* 62 (2009): 431–44; Robert W. T. Martin, *Government by Dissent: Protest, Resistance, & Radical Democratic Thought in the Early American Republic* (New York: New York University Press,

notebook is a collection of research material, references, and unpolished entries rather than a refined and completed manuscript, this does not detract from its robust substantive importance. It does, however, add to the interpretive challenge, which is made particularly demanding by the inclusion of hundreds of citations and subcitations to other authors and sources in the "Notes." The following pages attempt to meet this challenge.

THE ARGUMENT OF THE "NOTES ON GOVERNMENT": AN OVERVIEW

In the "Notes on Government," Madison indicated that he was building on the arguments he had made in the 1780s, particularly in his preparations for and/or speeches at the Constitutional Convention, writings in *The Federalist*, and his lengthy letter to Jefferson of October 24, 1787, setting forth his ideas on the theory of federal republican government. His intent in the "Notes" was to present a "more thorough" examination of the phenomena that destroy or preserve governments, particularly popular governments. To this end, he invoked the "great oracles of political wisdom," in whose analysis, he believed, some of the most "powerful influences" on the operation of government had been "overlooked or little heeded."[27] Specifically, Madison focused on the incomplete analysis with regard to the extent and structure of government, the presence or absence of foreign danger, and the stage of society and its degree of economic and religious diversification. Of these, the issue of territorial size garnered the largest part of his attention. As in "Vices of the Political System," speeches at the Constitutional Convention, *The Federalist*, and his discursive letter to Jefferson following the Convention, in the opening chapters of the "Notes on Government," Madison examined the maladies associated with small polities; he included a discussion of both their internal weaknesses (resulting mainly from faction and instability) and their external weaknesses (with respect to security against invasion from more powerful states).

In the "Notes on Government," however, Madison moved beyond the analysis of territorial size he had presented in *The Federalist*, taking up the subject of states that are too large (or "overgrown") to provide for domestic liberty or stability.[28] Moreover, he pointed to problems associated with moderately sized

2013), 133–39, 142–43; and Brunsman, "James Madison and the National Gazette Essays," 143–58.

[27] "Notes on the Influence of Extent of Territory on Government," *PJM*, 14:132. Although these notes are not part of the 1791 notebook, the draft essay is clearly based on the first three chapters of the "Notes on Government."

[28] Madison points to the problem of overgrown states in *The Federalist* in his discussion of the need for a "practicable sphere" of territory; see especially *Federalist* 14.

states, especially England, so lauded by Montesquieu and some of his followers. Madison's analysis in the "Notes on Government" demonstrates that an equilibrium in the powers of government and in the interests and passions of the society is not sufficient to the task of regime preservation. He did not believe that the "received opinion" of his age or the approach that was generally employed provided the kind of political analysis that was necessary to achieve the ends he sought. Accordingly, he sought guidance elsewhere. He found much to assist him in his inquiry – but certainly not all that was needed – in the treatment of political society afforded by the classical historians and political philosophers. In the "Notes on Government," Madison consciously set out to revive the scope and depth of analysis employed by the Classics; he also sought to consider the treatment of institutions and constitutional structure that modern thinkers had set forth. He added to this historical-philosophical inquiry his own assessment of the various circumstantial influences on government, including the influence of external danger, stage of society, and, especially, territorial size on the operation of public opinion in government.

Over and above the notion of establishing an equilibrium in government and in society, Madison emphasized the power and authority of public opinion in determining the stability, liberty, and character of a political order. Influences on government, such as education, religion, slavery, and colonial dependence, are actually influences on public opinion, which in turn is a particularly powerful influence on government. In essence, public opinion acts as the intermediary power between the various character-forming customs and institutions of the society and governmental decisions. In all governments, public opinion is a force to be reckoned with; in popular governments, public opinion constitutes the sovereign power and is the authority behind public judgments.

In the small classical republican polity, public opinion was simply the sum of public morality, which generally consisted of the unrefined views of the majority.[29] Accordingly, there was little that was effectually done to thwart the power of a factious majority, although there were attempts to restrain popular demagogues in the assembly through various checks, such as age requirements, character examinations, banishment, and even death. The predominant modern solution to the age-old problem of the internal instability of republican government, attributed above all to Montesquieu, consisted of the functional distribution of the powers of government into three branches, which serves to check and limit governmental power, and the rival parties

[29] See Jacques Peuchet, "Discours Préliminaire," in *Encyclopédie Méthodique: Jurisprudence*, vol. 9, *Police et Municipalités* (Paris, 1789), iv–v. See also my discussion of Peuchet's theory of public opinion and public morality in Sheehan, *James Madison and the Spirit of Republican Self-Government*, 71–75.

and interests, which produce a kind of equilibrium in society. With respect to the problem of external force, Montesquieu presented his conception of the confederate republic, which combined the internal advantages of the small republic with the external power of monarchy. But as Montesquieu was fully aware, this solution was of limited value to states in modern times. The more powerful modern states of Europe were not small republics on the scale of the ancient Greek polities; they were, rather, monarchies or republics of a much larger extent, albeit not vast empires such as Rome or Persia. But just as Montesquieu ultimately situated his theory of the functional separation of powers in a relatively large modern state on the basis of a society composed of diverse economic interests and rival parties, he applied this same view of commercial diversification to develop his theory of an equilibrium among nations and the attainment of international security and peace. Although certain scientific discoveries and events had already ushered in a new age of the larger commercial nation, Montesquieu pointed the way to capitalizing on the potential of these historical developments. A plethora of scholars flocked to follow his lead, including the eighteenth-century Scottish school of philosophic historians.

Like Montesquieu, Madison also identified the fundamental problems of the classical small republic as internal insecurity caused by majority faction and external safety resulting from its obvious weakness vis-à-vis larger states, particularly powerful empires bent on conquest. However, Madison believed that neither the great oracles of ancient nor those of modern political wisdom had sufficiently remedied the internal and external dangers associated with republican government, for neither had adequately treated the ever threatening, potentially undermining force of the power of public opinion in government. Whereas the classical solution was to educate public opinion via singular institutions, the modern approach generally substituted institutional arrangements and economic self-interest, enabling them to abandon a reliance on what they perceived as the futile project in civic education and character formation. If the former was grounded in a notion of liberty that extolled the participation of the citizen but left him insecure in his person or property, the latter did not depend on an active, virtuous citizenry, but instead emphasized a narrower definition of liberty as individual security. In carefully investigating the various influences on government and, particularly, the powerful effect of public opinion on the operations of government in an extensive, federal republic, Madison believed he had discovered a way in which the safety and the liberty of citizens, including their participation in the active sovereignty of the regime, could be achieved. He believed that, at last, the constitution of government for which philosophers had been searching and humanity sighing since time immemorial could be realized. Finally, free and popular government could be rescued from the contempt it had so long incited and be recommended to the esteem and adoption of America, and, indeed, of all mankind.

Madison's response to the challenges presented by both ancient and modern political philosophy entailed a detailed and complex consideration of a variety of factors that conspire to shape public decisions; these include the size of the territory, its situation vis-à-vis foreign dangers, the stage of society, the moral views and cultural institutions of the nation, representation, separation of powers, checks and balances, federalism, the influence of the literati on public opinion, and the influence of public opinion on the carriers of public morality and ultimately on government. According to Madison's understanding, the pivotal procedural element that connects these various factors and produces an interaction among them with potentially significant salutary results is the dynamic of communication. The net result of a properly constructed republic is its effect on the difficulty or facility of communication in the society, which on the one hand produces impediments to factions and on the other promotes political deliberation at the level of the government and throughout the political community. As we shall see, Madison's republican vision required a very extensive territorial union – much larger than the moderately-sized sovereign European nations and much tighter than the league of these nations that was envisioned by many other political thinkers of his time. Indeed, Madison's republican vision brought in its wake a truly new conception of federalism. But as Madison himself well understood, the consequence of this new and very extensive territorial configuration could well be the individual's perception of himself as politically insignificant, thereby silencing his voice, which is tantamount to the very condition the tyrant seeks to perpetuate with his power. Anticipating this, Madison's design of the federal republic simultaneously provided for an environment and political process that serves to thwart the formation of majority faction but which is also capable of sustaining communicative activity and promoting the formation, refinement, and enlargement of public opinion. In his view, public opinion in a free society is grounded in the genuine and active will of the society – that is, of the majority; it is cultivated and transformed via the institutional and educational processes of the society, which in turn operate to enhance the understanding and interests of the citizens of the society.

What is strikingly evident in the pages of the "Notes" is the ambitious nature of the task Madison set for himself in his scholarly endeavors. Despite his aspirations, however, he apparently did not complete the projected work he began in the "Notes on Government." Nonetheless, the "Notes" do give us a detailed outline of the author's conceptual design and argument for the complete work. In these "Notes," Madison demonstrated the comprehensive nature of his inquiry and the depth of treatment he believed necessary to produce a study of politics that advanced beyond the "great oracles of political wisdom," thus leaving to posterity an illuminating sketch of the mind and vision of one of the chief architects of the U.S. Constitution and of his enduring and remarkable intellectual voyage.

EXCURSUS

Travels with Anacharsis

When Madison was preparing his papers for posterity, he jotted an explicatory comment at the bottom of the first page of the "Notes on Government": "These articles were written after the commencement of the new government, as is proved, among other circumstances, by frequent references to 'Travels of Anacharsis,' first published in 1789." And to be sure, Madison's "Notes on Government" are heavily laden with citations to Jean Jacques Barthélemy's *Voyage du Jeune Anacharsis en Grèce dans le Milieu du Quatrième Siècle Avant l'Ère Vulgaire*. These citations show the extent to which Madison's interests in classical Greek thought replicated a substantial portion of Barthélemy's concerns. In essence, in spring 1791, Madison set off with Anacharsis on an extraordinary voyage to the world of the Classics.

Barthélemy began work on the *Voyage of Anacharsis* in 1757 and completed it thirty-one years later. In it, he explored the art, music, literature, geography, religion, customs, laws, politics, and philosophy of Greece during its golden age. Upon its publication in 1788 (and release in 1789), the work became an instant international success, ultimately going through more than forty editions, including translations into English, German, Dutch, Italian, Spanish, Danish, Russian, modern Greek, and Armenian. It was the topic of conversation in French salons and in letters traversing the Atlantic. In Paris, gala parties were organized around the "Anacharsis" theme, replete with attendees gaily attired in classical garb and the menu a panoply of Greek cuisine. In honor of Anacharsis, a supper at Mme. Vigée-Lebrun's featured the wine of Cyprus and cake made from Corinthian honey and raisins. The hostess even invited her guests to sample a Lacedaemonian broth, which must have been something of an insult to the French palate.[30] However, Barthélemy's work was not merely a fashionable Parisian trend. Although presented in the form of a fictional travel narrative, the volumes are teeming with footnotes of supporting authority by ancient authors. They may even appear, as the translator of the first American edition put it, as "a parade of erudition." With more than 2,000 citations to Greek philosophers, historians, and poets of the classical era, Barthélemy's work is a comprehensive reference source for classical Hellenic culture and thought. It was intended to provide a wealth of information that could be useful to the "man of real learning, by enabling him to refer immediately to the original author."[31] Madison was one of the scholars who carefully read and made use of Barthélemy's texts as a reference guide to primary Greek sources.

[30] C. A. Saint-Beuve, *Portraits of the Eighteenth Century: Historic and Literary*, trans. Katharine P. Wormeley (New York: G. P. Putnam's Sons, 1905), 433.

[31] *Voyage*, 1:iii.

The *Voyage of Anacharsis* tells the story of a Scythian who arrived in Greece some years prior to the birth of Alexander the Great. Born of a native father and Greek mother, Anacharsis was conversant in both languages. Making his residence in the city of Athens, Anacharsis made several journeys into the neighboring provinces – all the while observing the manners, customs, and governments within his view. When at leisure, he devoted himself to inquiries relative to the improvement of his mind through conversations with the great men of the era, including Xenophon, Plato, Aristotle, Euclid, and Demosthenes. One can imagine the young Scythian's excitement at the start of his journey and his visit to Epaminondas, perhaps the greatest man Greece ever produced.[32] At the close of his twenty-six-year sojourn, however, Anacharsis' mood had changed, and readers experience with him a sadness at the death of Greek liberty and the foreboding picture of things to come. With the enslavement of Greece by Philip of Macedon, Anacharsis returned to his native land and made a written account of his journey. Barthélemy chose this particular era to study for two reasons: It connects the age of Pericles with that of Philip's son Alexander – the acme of Greek learning and culture – and during this period, Anacharsis witnessed "the revolution which changed the face of Greece."[33]

Between the time of Anacharsis' arrival at Thebes and the final defeat of Athenian forces at the battle of Chaeronea, freedom and civilization coincided in Greece to produce the "golden age." Military conquests and the growth of commerce resulted in a flourishing of the arts, especially in Athens, but this was accompanied by the rise of a ruinous luxury and licentiousness of mores and manners. Through the eyes of Anacharsis, we witness the simultaneous rise of civilization and loss of freedom. With the increase in prosperity and power, Greece "fell into a state of dissension which gave a surprising degree of activity to every mind. She beheld wars and victories, riches and luxury, artists and monuments, multiply at once within her bosom."[34] Toward the end of the Peloponnesian War, when Greece was threatened with the loss of empire on land and sea, "a peaceful class of citizens was labouring to secure to it for ever the empire of the mind."[35] Poetry, history, architecture, painting, sculpture, philosophy, and, especially, political and moral philosophy progressed and flourished as never before in human history.

In a public tribute to Jean Jacques Barthélemy in 1789, marking his induction into the Académie Française, the Chevalier Stanislaus Jean de Boufflers declared that the abbé had again brought to life the wonders of twenty centuries past and had opened the eyes of his countrymen to the vision of Greece at the height of its ancient splendor. When reading Barthélemy, the Chevalier continued, one feels that the maxims of the ancient Greeks are his principles, that their knowledge is in his spirit, and that their virtues are in his heart. According to Louis Jules Barbon Mancini-Mazarini, duc de Nivernais, in the sculpture by Houdon, Barthélemy's visage has an ancient character, and it could not

[32] *Voyage*, 2:81. [33] *Voyage*, 1:xiv. [34] *Voyage*, 1:343. [35] *Voyage*, 1:336.

be better placed than between the busts of Plato and Aristotle.[36] Stanislaus Jean de Boufflers believed that Barthélemy's *Voyage* must be understood as much more than merely an erudite composition. In its pages, he said, one comes to understand that freedom is a principle of life and despotism a precept of death.[37] A number of later readers of *Voyage* agreed with Boufflers' assessment, for between the lines of the text, Barthélemy appealed to the republican sensibilities of his countrymen, showing them the model of political freedom and civilization worthy of their emulation.[38]

While this interpretation of Barthélemy's text has garnered the support of some scholars, it has also been met with a substantial amount of scholarly criticism. Indeed, every interpretation of Barthélemy's *Voyage* seems to have its vocal and austere detractors. Some commentators have interpreted the work to be a clever undermining of the classical viewpoint. R. A. McNeal argues that Barthélemy linked himself to the modern philosophical outlook of Montesquieu. "He has nothing of Montesquieu in his view of Greece," declares C. A. Saint-Beuve.[39] Maurice Badolle sees behind the classical visage of the *Voyage* a criticism and rejection of the Greek idea of civilization and a tribute to Rousseau's noble savage.[40] Marie Frances Silver also interprets the work to be a clever undermining of the classical viewpoint; however, she claims that Barthélemy's model was not Rousseauian romanticism but Cartesian rationalism.[41] The *Voyage* is situated

[36] Louis Jules Barbon Mancini-Mazarini, duc de Nivernais, *Essai sur la Vie de J. J. Barthélemy* (Paris, 1795), www.archive.org/stream/oeuvresno6niveuoft/oeuvresno6niveuoft_djvu.txt.

[37] "Réponse de M. le Chevalier de Boufflers au Discours de M. l'Abbé Barthélemy, Discours Prononcé dans la Séance Publique," Le 25 Août 1789, Paris Le Louvre, www.academie-francaise.fr/reponse-au-discours-de-reception-de-jean-jacques-barthelemy.

[38] See, for example, Marie-Francis Silver, "La Grèce dans le Roman Français de l'Époque Révolutionnaire: *Le Voyage du Jeune Anacharsis en Grèce au IVe Siècle Avant l'Ère Vulgaire*" in *L'Homme et la Nature*, IX, eds. Hans-Günther Schwarz, David McNeil, and Roland Bonnel (1990), 145–55, 151–52.

[39] R. A. McNeal, "Nicholas Biddle, Anacharsis, and the Grand Tour," *Pennsylvania Magazine of History and Biography* 120, no. 3 (1996): 217–47, 243; Saint-Beuve, *Portraits of the Eighteenth Century*, 428.

[40] Maurice Badolle, *L'Abbé Jean-Jacques Barthélemy et L'Hellénisme en France dans la Seconde Moitié du XVIIIe Siècle* (Paris: Les Presses Universitaires de France, 1926), 287.

[41] Silver, "La Grèce dans le Roman Français de l'Époque Révolutionnaire," 150. Silver also interprets Barthélemy as a heretic Jesuit abbé who thought that all religions are engines of persecution (Silver, 150); in contrast, Saint-Beuve claims that Barthélemy disagreed vehemently with those around him who assaulted religion and desired its demise (*Portraits of the Eighteenth Century*, 423–24). Badolle, Silver, and McNeal praise Barthélemy for his ingenious and cleverly circumspect manner of writing. Saint-Beuve asserts that he was a "descriptive Isocrates, and nothing more" (429). Indeed, Barthélemy "has read, but not seen" (431). Certainly, Badolle is correct in discovering a complexity and nuance in Barthélemy's work despite the author's claim that *Voyage* is merely a compilation of thoughts as they occurred to the author (*L'Abbé Jean-Jacques Barthélemy et L'Hellénisme en France dans la Seconde Moitié du XVIIIe Siècle*, 258–67). Indeed, Barthélemy followed his beloved classical authors in the circumspect method of writing that he employed throughout the work. The professions to truthfulness by Plato's Socrates are legendary, as are the ironies and contradictions he employed – the latter often following the former within a few pages in the Platonic dialogues. In *Voyage*, readers may also see

somewhere between that of the Encyclopedists and Condorcet's work on human progress, she argues.[42] In contrast, Saint-Beuve contends that Barthélemy was at odds with the Encyclopedists and rejected the idea of perfectibility.[43]

I would argue that Barthélemy read the modern authors closely but did not consider himself a disciple of any of them. Rather, he saw his project as a distinct and genuine contribution to both Hellenic studies and eighteenth-century scholarship on the politics of human freedom. Like others of his age, including his friend the abbé Mably as well as Necker, Trosne, Peuchet, Turgot, and Condorcet, Barthélemy was particularly interested in the rising power of public opinion in contemporary France and the West. Like them, he explored how public opinion might be grounded in reason and moderation to produce stability and unity in a nation. However, he disagreed with those (for example, Condorcet and the physiocrats) who relied on the modern scientific approach, attempted to systematize rationality, and made *évidence* the basis for law and the guide for public morality and opinion. Instead, Barthélemy sought to rehabilitate what he believed to be the more sensible and richer approach taken by the Classics.

Barthélemy was a member of the Académie des Inscriptions et Belles-Lettres, a humanities society devoted to the study of the monuments, documents, languages, and cultures of past civilizations.[44] According to Louis Bertrand, members of the Académie des Inscriptions resisted the "eclipse of the classics" and the new spirit of scholarship influenced by Descartes' suggestion that it was no longer necessary to know Latin, Greek, or History.[45] They fought against the seventeenth-century rationalist idea and its modernizing tendency, which threatened to destroy the humanities by making them subservient to mathematics and physics. In the war between the ancients and the moderns, Barthélemy stood together with his

professions of truth and candor followed by irony and contradiction. For example, at Sparta, the native Damonax announces that all he will say will be perfectly truthful, relying on the scholarship of the great Athenian historian Thucydides and his reputation for impartiality. Damonax then proceeded to tell Anacharsis and his Athenian friend Philocles the story of the beginning of the Peloponnesian War, summarizing the speeches of the Corinthians and the King of Sparta before the Lacedemonian Assembly, as recounted by Thucydides. These two speeches offer contradictory descriptions of the same situation. Damonax also neglected the speech by the Spartan Ephor, not to mention that of the Athenian visitors. (See *Voyage*, 4:248–51; cf. Badolle, 265–76, including Barthélemy's treatment of Simonides, the teacher of Hiero.) See also Saint-Beuve's discussion of Barthélemy's strategic placement in revealing his own ideas in the volumes (434).

[42] Silver, "La Grèce dans le Roman Français de l'Époque Révolutionnaire," 149–51; see also Baddole, *L'Abbé Jean-Jacques Barthélemy et L'Hellénisme en France*, 296, and McNeal, "Nicholas Biddle, Anacharsis, and the Grand Tour," 235.

[43] Saint-Beuve, *Portraits of the Eighteenth Century*, 422, 435–36.

[44] Barthélemy entered the Académie des Inscriptions in 1747. In 1789, after the publication of *Voyage de Anacharsis*, he was invited to become a member of the Académie Française.

[45] Louis Bertrand, *La Fin du Classicisme et le Retour à l'Antique* (New York: Burt Franklin, 1897), 43–44.

friends of the Académie des Inscriptions, fighting passionately to preserve the study of antiquity in an age marked by the ascent and triumph of a soulless modern science and "to make the moderns restless in their victory."[46] In the view of many of Barthélemy's contemporaries, his *Voyage of Anacharsis* not only captured the Greek mind and spirit but represented the peak of eighteenth-century French scholarship on the side of the Classics.[47]

Barthélemy's love of freedom and profound wish for a better way of life for France parallels Anacharsis' aspirations for his fatherland. Although earlier in his travels Anacharsis determined he would never leave Greece – and, indeed, he was made an Athenian citizen – after a twenty-six-year sojourn, he returned to Scythia to devote himself to the care and enlightenment of his native countrymen. According to Diogenes Laërtius (the original, nonfictional), Anacharsis' homecoming was due to his desire to "abrogate the existing institutions of his country, being exceedingly earnest, in his fondness for Grecian customs."[48] The return of Barthélemy's Anacharsis to Scythia parallels not only that of the historical Anacharsis, but also Socrates' return to the cave in Plato's *Republic*. His return is not the Rousseauian retreat to savage nature but the classical descent from the world of ideas to the world of politics and the enduring challenge to make freedom and civilization coincide in the realm of human affairs. Anacharsis' return is the return of the citizen.

46 Bertrand, *La Fin du Classicisme*, 67.

47 See, for example, Bertrand, *La Fin du Classicisme*, 58. According to J. G. A. Pocock (*Barbarism and Religion* [Cambridge: Cambridge University Press, 2001], 2:14–26), one approach to the study of history during this period was employed by the "*érudits*," who for the most part were antiquarians associated with the scholarly endeavors of the Académie des Inscriptions. Taking a different approach to the *érudits* were the philosophical historians interested in the changes of civil society, who approached history in terms of the progress of opinion, manners, *moeurs*, and general spirit of societies. This group included such authors as William Robertson, Edward Gibbon, and David Hume. However, some scholars, including Montesquieu, combined these two approaches. While Barthélemy was clearly influenced by the antiquarianism of the *érudits*, he also sought to advance the enlightenment of men's minds and the improvement of their mores and manners through the "*commerce des idées*" (speech by Jean Jacques Barthélemy on his induction to the *Académie Française*, August 25, 1789, www.academie-francaise.fr/discours-de-reception-de-jean-jacques-barthelemy). Like other works concerned with philosophical history, Barthélemy's work was guided by an overarching question: "Would the age of Enlightenment continue, or would Europe descend into decadence and follow the ancients into decline and fall?" (I. M. C. Carhart, "The Enlightenments of J. G. A. Pocock," *Cromohs* 6 [2001], www.cromohs.unifi.it/6_2001/pocock.html); cf. Michael C. Carhart and John Robertson, "The Enlightenments of J. G. A. Pocock," *Storia della Storiografia – History of Historiography* 39 (2001): 123–51.

48 Diogenes Laërtius, *The Lives and Opinions of Eminent Philosophers*, trans. C. D. Yonge (London: George Bell & Sons, 1895), 47. The nonfictional Anacharsis was a Scythian who traveled to Greece in early sixth century BC to study Greek institutions and customs. He was the first foreigner to be made an Athenian citizen and, according to some ancient writers, was one of the Seven Sages of Greece. In Herodotus' account, when Anacharsis returned to Scythia, he was killed by his brother because he had adopted the ideas and manners of the Greeks, including certain religious views and practices anathema to the Scythians.

Barthélemy's Anacharsis spent the major portion of his political education in Greece under the tutelage of Aristotle. Barthélemy commented on the year-long, concentrated period of study that he himself devoted to a rereading and study of Aristotle's work. Anacharsis' bittersweet narrative of the golden age of Greece reflects the author's own intellectual journey, which led him to discover the limitations and the paradox of political life. Despite the difficulties that Aristotle's well-constructed polity overcomes and the hope for freedom and civilization that it engenders, Aristotle recognized that there is, finally, no solution to the political problem. According to Aristotle, there are three possible ways to conceive of human association – namely, the tribe, the empire, and the polis. The tribal association may be characterized by a certain kind of freedom, but it does not generate high artistic development or civilization. Conversely, an empire may be civilized, but it cannot be free. Aristotle taught that the polis is superior to both the tribe and empire because it is capable of freedom and civilization concurrently. However, the polis also has a central defect: Given its small size, it cannot match the military strength of the large empire. Ironically, this is a lesson we learn most dramatically from the exploits of Aristotle's most famous student, Alexander the Great. The victories of the Greek cities in the first three battles against the Persian Empire represented an amazing military feat. Ultimately, however, Alexander's triumphs marked the end to the threat of foreign domination but also led to the destruction of the liberties of the Greek citizens.[49]

If Anacharsis felt resignation in the face of Aristotle's political prognosis and the historical events that fulfilled it, Madison worked through the ideas of Aristotle and emerged with a new vision and fresh hope for republicanism. Scientific and technological progress had brought about certain improvements that enabled Madison to conceive of the establishment of a type of republican government that could boast both inner stability in the face of domestic factions and external strength in the face of foreign enemies. As Madison and Barthélemy both understood, the advances in technology in modern times made the internally destabilizing institution of slavery no longer necessary to the economic well-being of society, however much some individuals might find it beneficial to their own prosperity. Moreover, Madison believed advances in the means of communication made possible the coincidence between republican liberty and the power of empire. With this in the forefront of his mind, he delved into Aristotle's penetrating analysis of the forces that preserve and destroy regimes, and he focused on the unique strengths of the polity that emanate from the support of public opinion and its decisive influence on the preservation and vitality of the constitutional order. In spring 1791, with Barthélemy's books spread around him in his cramped quarters at Fifth and Market, Madison became a fellow traveler with Anacharsis on his *voyage imaginaire* to the world of the Classics.

[49] Leo Strauss, "Lectures on Aristotle's Politics" (Lecture XI:13–14, University of Chicago, Chicago, IL, autumn 1967). I am grateful to Joseph Cropsey for granting me permission to cite Professor Strauss' lectures.

2

Circumstantial influences on government

The first section of the "Notes on Government" consists of three chapters concerning circumstantial influences on government: territorial size, foreign danger, and the stage of society. These geographic, demographic, external, and temporal factors have an impact on the type of government that can feasibly be founded or will likely come about as a result of their powerful influence. Although the importance of these factors had been explored previously by political philosophers and historians, Madison thought that no one had yet given adequate consideration to the interaction between each of these variables and the formation of public opinion or to the extraordinary political benefits that might be accrued if one did. He thus embarked on a research project to correct the errors and advance the analysis of former thinkers and to present a markedly new way of thinking about republicanism and the politics of public opinion. To understand Madison's analysis as fully as possible, we must follow the path of his examination and retrace his study of the authors and perspectives to which he was responding. The results of this investigation, he believed, demonstrated the need for a new political calculus and offered a fresh prospect for the viability of republican government.

TERRITORIAL SIZE

Madison opened the "Notes on Government" with the issue of territorial size, immediately showing the latitude of his inquiry by citing not the Antifederalists' small republic argument but Plato's analysis (or, rather, Montesquieu's reference to Plato's argument, which strictly limits the number of citizens in a republic to 5,040).[1] Madison's reference to the Classics and their defining

[1] *Voyage*, 1:iii. The editors of *The Papers of James Madison* have noted that Montesquieu's reference to Plato's discussion of limiting the number of citizens to 5,040 is to the *Republic*; the reference is actually to Plato's *Laws*, V:737e. The Thomas Nugent translation of *The Spirit of*

characteristics of the polis, as well as to Montesquieu's consideration and treatment of this in the opening paragraph of the "Notes on Government," is indicative of the political philosophers and the questions that were foremost in Madison's mind as he prepared to launch his own examination of the things that destroy and the things that preserve government, particularly republican governments.[2]

The reference to Montesquieu's citation of Plato is followed by a quotation from Barthélemy regarding the number of men who bear arms in a well-regulated republic. Citing the *Critias*, Barthélemy argued that experience has taught that the number of arms-bearing citizens is neither more nor less than 20,000.[3] Madison's juxtaposition of Plato's differing accounts of the optimum number of citizens in a republic points to the problem of the small republic and its limited population. In the unfinished dialogue the *Critias*, which may have been intended to form a trilogy with the *Timaeus* and a third work that was never written (perhaps to be titled the *Hermocrates*), Plato planned to depict the best city "engaged in a patriotic conflict."[4] In this mythical story, the small, virtuous republic of Athens, with its 20,000 citizens bearing arms, is pitted against the vast empire of Atlantis, whose ten kings (five sets of twins descended from Poseidon) are absolute rulers in their respective cities and united together in a defensive union. Although originally law abiding, moderate, and virtuous, over time, the people of Atlantis grew to love their wealth and prosperity too much and became corrupted. According to one interpretation of the dialogue, the *Critias* was intended to represent the conflict between the city of Athens and the Persian Empire. Did Plato intend to show that the ideal city of Athens was invincible, even against a vast powerful empire, as Benjamin Jowett argues?[5] Or was the myth of Atlantis an allegory for the very real threat a foreign empire posed to Athens, which ultimately led to the demise of Greek civilization? Montesquieu leaves no doubt as to his view on the matter. His reference to the *Critias* in *The Spirit of Laws* is followed by a discussion of the conflict between the Persian Empire and the Athenian republic and then between the

Laws, cited by the editors of the *PJM*, mistakenly cites the *Republic*, Book V (Montesquieu, Charles de Secondat, Baron de, *The Spirit of the Laws*, trans. Thomas Nugent [New York: Hafner Press, 1949], 23:17, 11nm). This translation is hereafter cited *SOL*. The Cohler translation (Montesquieu, Charles de Secondat, Baron de, *The Spirit of the Laws*, trans. and eds. Anne M. Cohler, Basia Carolyn Miller, and Harold Samuel Stone [New York: Cambridge University Press, 1989], 23:17, 438nn25–26) cites both the *Republic* V:460a and *Laws* V:737e.

[2] Donald Lutz has demonstrated that the American founders referred more to Montesquieu than to any other political philosopher or thinker. See Lutz's study "The Relative Influence of European Writers on Late Eighteenth-Century American Political Thought," *American Political Science Review* 78 (1984): 189–97.

[3] *SOL*, 3:3, 21. Montesquieu also cites Plato's *Critias* at *SOL* 3:3, 21, regarding the 20,000 arms-bearing citizens in Athens. (See the *Critias*, 112d.)

[4] Benjamin Jowett, introduction to *The Dialogues of Plato*, by Plato (Dulles, VA: Thoemmes Press, 1997), III:519; *Timaeus*, III:19, 20, 393–441.

[5] Jowett, *The Dialogues of Plato*, III:525.

Macedonian Empire and Athens: "It was ever after as easy to triumph over the forces of Athens as it had been difficult to subdue her virtue," Montesquieu declared.[6]

The issue of territorial size reminds us of Publius' discussions of the subject in *The Federalist*, and in fact, Madison proceeded immediately in the "Notes" to cite "Federalists No. X et alia" as well as his Convention notes[7] and his letter "on a federal negative on State laws" to Jefferson of October 24, 1787.[8] His plan in the "Notes" was to expand his prior discussion of the internal and external problems associated with states that are too small and those that are too large or "overgrown," the latter of which included the Persian and Macedonian empires. As we shall see, Madison's "Notes" constitute a project aimed at resolving the age-old problem of the small, virtuous, but militarily weak republic versus the large, powerful, but corrupt empire that Plato depicted in the *Critias*.

In the "Notes," Madison offered a number of historical cases that exemplify the dangers inherent in republics that are too small, including Switzerland, Megara, and the ancient Italian republics. He especially made use of Barthélemy's references to Aristotle on the instability of small polities discussed in Book V, Chapter 5, of the *Politics*. "Almost all our governments," Barthélemy wrote,

> under whatever form they may be established, contain within themselves many seeds of destruction. As the greater part of the Grecian republics are confined within the narrow limits of a city, or a district, the divisions of individuals, which become the divisions of the state, the misfortunes of a war which seems to leave no resource, the inveterate and perpetually-renewed jealousy of the different classes of citizens, or a rapid succession of unforeseen events, may in a moment shake to the foundations or overturn the constitution. We have seen the democracy abolished in the city of Thebes by the loss of a battle [Aristotle, *Politics*, V:3], and in those of Heraclea, Cumae, and Megara, by the return of some principal citizens, whom the people had proscribed to enrich the public treasury with their spoils [Aristotle, *Politics*, V:5].[9]

Madison employed these ancient examples to demonstrate that when the people can too easily unite, government is unable to impede factious combinations of

[6] Montesquieu, *SOL*, 3:3, 22.

[7] The editors of *The Papers of James Madison* presume by "Convention notes" that Madison is referring to the "Notes of Debates" he recorded at the Constitutional Convention in 1787. (See "Notes on Government," *PJM*, 14:168n3.) It is possible, however, that Madison was also referring to the notes he made *for* and not simply *at* the convention. This would include his "Vices of the Political System of the United States," as well as his "Notes on Ancient and Modern Confederacies," an important set of notes that sets out not only the practical political problems faced by the nation under the Articles of Confederation but also the theoretical framework and political aims that guided Madison throughout the founding period. This reference might also include his "Memorandums for the Convention of Virginia in 1788 on the federal Constitution," which was written in preparation for the Virginia Ratifying Convention.

[8] *MJM*, 214–27; *PJM*, 10:206–20.

[9] *Voyage*, 5:247–48.

the majority against the minority. There are various conflicting claims in civilized societies that may lead to oppression by a majority, including the poor against the rich, debtors against creditors, city against city, and superior states against their colonies. The particular economic, geographic, and political circumstances that give rise to these distinctions vary from time to time and place to place. In the modern era, there are at least two factors that warrant special consideration: the "case of Black slaves" and "religious persecutions every where."[10]

Small states cannot achieve the requisite stability to preserve the constitution and form of government. But neither, Madison argued, can states that are too large. While overgrown empires "impede a combination of the people for the purpose of oppression," they tend toward tyranny and ultimately impotency, proving inadequate against external danger. In addition to the Persian and Macedonian empires, Madison listed the Assyrian, Roman, Charlemagne's, and France under Charles V as examples of overgrown territories.[11] Neither monarchies nor aristocracies are suited to a large extent of territory because the people cannot readily combine to prevent oppression by the ruler(s). In monarchies, "a very great extent of Country" prevents a good prince from possessing the requisite information to govern well. Conversely, the extensive size of the territory enables a bad prince to tyrannize over the people because he cannot be controlled by fear of popular combinations against him. Thus, in order to temper an aristocracy or monarchy, the state should be small enough to allow for popular combinations against oppression.

Madison's discussion of the comparative dangers and strengths of monarchies and republics in the "Notes on Government" was a continuation of the analysis he had begun to develop at the conclusion of his pre-Convention analysis of this subject in "Vices of the Political System of the United States." In "Vices," he argued that a "limited Monarchy tempers the evils of an absolute one,"[12] and in the "Notes," we learn that no monarchical government – not even a limited one – can succeed in a nation of "a very great extent." Whereas a monarchy or an aristocracy is tempered by limiting its size to allow for a coalition of the people against oppression, a republic is moderated by extending the territory, thereby hindering a factious coalition of the people. In small republics, the sovereign power is not sufficiently impartial toward the parts of the society that compose it; in contrast, an extensive republic tempers the problems associated with the ruling authority of a small one.[13] When

[10] "Notes on Government," *MJM*, 129; *PJM*, 14:160.

[11] With regard to France and Rome, Madison here cites William Robertson's *The History of the Reign of Emperor Charles V* and Edward Gibbon's *Decline and Fall of the Roman Empire*, respectively. The passage referring to the Roman Empire appears to be copied almost verbatim from Madison's 1787 "Memorandums for the Convention of Virginia in 1788 on the federal Constitution," *MJM*, 206; *PJM*, 10:281.

[12] "Vices of the Political System of the United States," *MJM*, 204; *PJM*, 9:357.

[13] "Vices of the Political System of the United States," *MJM*, 204; *PJM*, 9:357.

the principle of representation is combined with the size of territory, the government of a republic – unlike that of monarchy – can see everything. Moreover, in contrast to a small republic, a large republic significantly reduces the likelihood of "easy combinations" of the people on the basis of "misinformed or corrupt passions."[14]

Although Madison did not explicitly cite arguments by his fellow countrymen regarding a small republic versus a large republic, his examination was intended, in part, to correct the faulty understanding of some Americans on this subject, particularly their misconceptions regarding Montesquieu's analysis of territorial size.[15] It was also meant to correct errors made by the French author himself. In this chapter, Madison took issue with the "received opinion" that republics must operate in a small society and that monarchies are fit for a large territory.[16] The "received opinion" to which he alluded was the conventional wisdom of his day that constituted a misreading of the celebrated Montesquieu. This conventional perspective was evident in the arguments set forth by such Antifederalists as Brutus, Cato, and George Mason, as well as by such Federalists as Roger Sherman, who, on the supposed basis of the French philosopher's authority, argued that a republic cannot be extended over a large territory.[17] As Hamilton had discussed in the ninth *Federalist*, however, many of the American states were significantly larger than the territorial area Montesquieu assigned to small republics.

The subtlety and complexity of Montesquieu's method of presentation in *The Spirit of Laws* goes a long way toward accounting for the confusion that surrounded his political theory – then as well as today. Montesquieu did indeed argue that a "large empire supposes a despotic authority in the person who governs."[18]

[14] "Notes on Government," *MJM*, 129; *PJM*, 14:159; see also the Party Press Essay "Government," *MJM*, 246; *PJM*, 14:178–79.

[15] My primary aim in this study is to set forth Montesquieu's views as Madison understood them. Secondarily, I have attempted to note major or important differences of interpretation on critical points. Because Montesquieu's theory is so nuanced and complex, due at least in part to the complicated design of *The Spirit of Laws*, there is much scholarly disagreement that I cannot include in this study. For a much more extensive treatment of Montesquieu's thought and the secondary scholarly literature that has been written on it, see Paul A. Rahe, *Montesquieu and the Logic of Liberty: War, Religion, Commerce, Climate, Terrain, Technology, Uneasiness of Mind, the Spirit of Political Vigilance, and the Foundations of the Modern Republic* (New Haven: Yale University Press, 2009).

[16] See also the Party Press Essay "Government," *MJM*, 246; *PJM*, 14:178–79; this article was based on Chapters 1 and 2 of the "Notes on Government."

[17] See Sherman's speech of June 6, 1787, on the floor of the Federal Convention, in Adrienne Koch, *Notes of Debates in the Federal Convention of 1787 Reported by James Madison* (New York: W. W. Norton & Company, 1987), 75.

[18] Montesquieu, *SOL*, 8:19, 122. Montesquieu makes this same argument in *Reflections on Universal Monarchy in Europe* (VIII): "A large empire necessarily requires that the ruler should have despotic authority." Although *Reflections on Universal Monarchy in Europe* was prepared for publication in 1734, only one copy was printed before it was suppressed (see Rahe,

As the example of Rome proves,[19] a republic is not fit for a large territory; concern for the common good cannot be sufficiently "felt" or "known" in a large republic.[20] In essence, a large republic cannot sustain the degree of civic virtue that is necessary for its preservation nor is it able to overcome the "informational or epistemic problems" created by the extent of territory.[21] Consequently, Montesquieu claimed, a republic must be limited to a small territory; otherwise, it cannot subsist.[22] However, this does not answer the further difficulties Montesquieu identified – namely, that a republic small enough to sustain virtue and guard against internal military usurpation cannot prevent an excess of liberty or defend itself against external danger.[23]

In the eighteenth century, small republics based on civic virtue were, for the most part, relics of the past, replaced by the larger modern monarchical states backed by substantial military power (as exemplified particularly by France, Spain, and England). Moreover, despite the hereditary kingship and nobility who held places of political privilege in the British government, Montesquieu believed that England was more accurately categorized as a republic rather than a monarchy or, more specifically, a republic hidden under the form of a monarchy.[24] Given its size, however, the English nation was too large to accommodate the traditional republican principle of virtue; hence, Montesquieu intimates that a different principle – or principles – must form the basis of this new kind of republic. However, he did not tell us the principle(s) that forms the basis of this new republic but instead described at length the distribution of constitutional powers, the diverse passions and interests of the people, and the peaceful, commercial character of the English nation. Avoiding both absolute monarchy and extreme liberty, this nation – or at least his abstract model of this nation – represented for Montesquieu the archetype of the modern republic.[25]

In Book 11, Chapter 5, of *The Spirit of Laws*, Montesquieu tells us that the British republic is the only nation in the world whose direct end is political liberty. In the next chapter, he claimed that by establishing the functional

Montesquieu and the Logic of Liberty, 20.) Accordingly, Madison could not have read it. I cite *Reflections* to elucidate further the ideas Montesquieu presents in *The Spirit of Laws*.

19 See Montesquieu, *Considerations on the Causes of the Greatness of the Romans and Their Decline (1734)*, trans. David Lowenthal (New York: Free Press, 1965), 93–94, 189.

20 Montesquieu, *SOL*, 8:16, 120.

21 See Jacob T. Levy, "Beyond Publius: Montesquieu, Liberal Republicanism and the Small-Republic Thesis," *History of Political Thought* 27, no. 1 (2006): 51.

22 Montesquieu, *SOL*, 8:16, 120.

23 Montesquieu, *SOL*, 9:6, 129–30.

24 Montesquieu, *SOL*, 5:19, 68. Montesquieu is undoubtedly referring here to England.

25 According to Judith Shklar, Montesquieu reclaimed the republican past by "imaginatively" recreating or replacing it with "a new expansive republicanism to fit the modern political world" ("Montesquieu and the New Republicanism," in *Machiavelli and Republicanism*, eds. Gisela Bock, Quentin Skinner, and Maurizio Viroli [Cambridge: Cambridge University Press, 1990], 266–67).

separation of powers and checks and balances, England was able to achieve constitutional equilibrium and to preserve liberty. In Book 19, Chapter 27, Montesquieu expanded on his earlier analysis of the British constitution, demonstrating how the effects of commerce on the character of the English people had contributed substantially to the stability, liberty, and peaceful international dominance of the nation. In this nation, Montesquieu wrote, there are "two visible [and distinct] powers – the legislative and executive," and most people would feel affection for one and hatred, envy, or jealousy toward the other depending on what might or might not be gained at any given time.[26] Thus, even though "all the passions are free" in this nation, the constitutional distribution of powers would render the hatred between the two rival parties "powerless." In addition, the legislative power is itself divided into two parts, each of which checks the other as well as checks the executive and vice versa, thereby resulting in constitutional equilibrium.[27] This is a great advantage over ancient direct democracies, Montesquieu argued, in which the sway of skilled orators caused agitations that "always produced their effect."[28] The modern republic, by contrast, is substantially freer from "destructive prejudices," which inclines it toward commerce, thereby weakening prejudices or at least softening their effects. Moreover, a commercial nation is a kind of political incubator in which "the number of sects is increased" and "a prodigious number of small, particular interests" would form.[29]

The doctrine of separation of powers and checks and balances and the idea of establishing an equilibrium in society via a multiplication of interests and sects were, of course, two prominent themes discussed by Publius in *The Federalist* (most notably in *Federalist* 47–51 and *Federalist* 10, respectively). In the "Notes on Government" Madison revisited these important topics:

> The best provision for a stable and free Govt. is not a balance in the powers of the Govt. tho' that is not to be neglected, but an equilibrium in the interests & passions of the Society itself, which can not be attained in a small Society. Much has been said on the first. *The last deserves a thorough investigation.*[30]

Accordingly, in the "Notes," Madison's intention was to go beyond what he considered the incomplete analysis of the theory of the separation and balance of powers on the one hand and an equilibrium in the interests and passions of the society on the other. He thus indicated that all prior examinations of the subjects, including not only Montesquieu's but also his own in *The Federalist*, were deficient.

As we shall see, in Chapter 4 of the "Notes," Madison explicitly took issue with those who attributed the "boasted equilibrium" of the British government to its distribution of powers. In this first chapter, he implied that the theory of

[26] Montesquieu, *SOL*, 19:27, 307. [27] Montesquieu, *SOL*, 11:6, 157–60.
[28] Montesquieu, *SOL*, 19:27, 309. [29] Montesquieu, *SOL*, 19:27, 311–12.
[30] "Notes on Government," *MJM*, 127; *PJM*, 14:158–59; emphasis added.

separation of powers and balanced government, especially that exemplified in the English constitution and so praised by Montesquieu and others, including Vice President John Adams and Secretary of the Treasury Alexander Hamilton, had been overemphasized and overrated in terms of its role in achieving stability and liberty. Possibly with Montesquieu but almost certainly with Adams in mind, he continued to develop this argument in the "Notes": While "natural divisions" in society "should be made mutual checks on each other," it "does not follow that artificial distinctions, such as kings & nobles, should be created, and then formed into checks and balances with each other & with the people."[31] This type of defective reasoning in politics is tantamount to saying in ethics that "new vices ought to be promoted that they may control each other, because this use may be made of existing vices – avarice and vanity – cowardice & malice –&c."[32] Such an approach to political disagreement, he believed, was inconsistent with the tenets of republicanism. Instead, he argued, insofar as parties are unavoidable, they should be made to check one another – but only to the extent that they cannot be prevented or their views accommodated.

Throughout the volumes of *A Defence of the Constitutions of the United States*, Adams lavished praise on the British model of balanced government. According to Adams, the British constitution superimposed the functional separation of powers onto the different social orders of society, thereby establishing an equilibrium of the orders within the government. The excellence of the English model, he argued in the preface to the first volume of the *Defence*, was based on its blending of the classical mixed government model with European feudal institutions. Although Adams would spend hundreds of pages demonstrating the merit of this model, he admitted that a superb account of the advantages of feudal institutions had already been provided by others:

> The English have, in reality, blended together the feudal institutions with those of the Greeks and Romans; and out of all have made that noble composition, which avoids the inconveniences, and retains the advantages, of both. . . . Robertson, Hume, and Gibbon

[31] "Notes on Government," *MJM*, 129; *PJM*, 14:160. In the "Notes," Madison indicated that his discussion of natural versus artificial parties was intended to follow his discussion of equilibrium in government and society. Cf. the *National Gazette* essay "Parties," *MJM*, 249; *PJM*, 14:197–98, and the *National Gazette* essay "Who Are the Best Keepers of the People's Liberties?" *MJM*, 269–70; *PJM*, 14:426–27. See also Correa Moylan Walsh, *The Political Science of John Adams: A Study in the Theory of Mixed Government and the Bicameral System* (New York: G. P. Putnam's Sons, 1915), 258n1. Walsh argues that Madison's "little skit on *Parties* . . . is an obvious hit at Adams."

[32] See "Parties," *MJM*, 249; *PJM*, 14:197. See also Madison's November 9, 1792 "Address of the House of Representatives to the President," in which he argued that "it is not more essential to the preservation of true liberty that a Govt. shd. be always ready to listen to the representations of its Constituents, & to accomodate [*sic*] its measures to the sentiments & wishes of every part of them as far as will consist with the good of the whole than it is that the just authority of laws actually & constitutionally in force, should be steadfastly maintained" (*PJM*, 14:403).

have given such admirable accounts of the feudal institutions, and their consequences, that it would have been more discreet to have referred to them, perhaps, without saying any thing more upon the subject.[33]

But discreet, Adams was not. His prolix examination of this subject in the *Defence* was an unabashed attempt to defend and promote the philosophical historians' feudalistic model of politics or what James Harrington had called "the Gothic balance."

Keenly aware of Adams' project in the *Defence*, Madison vehemently rejected what he perceived as the antirepublican feudal model Adams so lauded, which he claimed limits "the share of the people to a third of the government ... and establishes two grand hereditary orders, with feelings, habits, interests, and prerogatives all inveterately hostile to the rights and interests of the people." Indeed, the "model established on the feudal idea ... excluded the people almost altogether."[34] To the extent that the vaunted equilibrium of the British government was constituted by a rivalry between corporate powers, Madison believed that it was not a republican model to be imitated. Indeed, as he implied clearly in the "Notes" and had previously made explicit in *Federalist* 39, the British government is not properly designated a republic at all.[35]

Despite Adams' attribution of his theory of balanced government to Robertson, Hume, and Gibbon, his own protracted exposition of the theory in the *Defence* shows that he missed or ignored the central point of their teaching. For Hume, as for Montesquieu, for example, political equilibrium was not to be primarily achieved by the clash of the rival passions that actuate the different social, hierarchical orders of men (although these passions were certainly factored into their analysis) but by the rivalry of parties and interests, particularly economic interests, in modern commercial societies. Although Adams recognized the desire for economic gain as a motivating factor for many men, he never made the conceptual leap at the root of Montesquieu's and the philosophic historian's analysis of communication and commercial politics. Madison was a more careful and a more critical reader of these historians than Adams.

TERRITORIAL SIZE AND EXTERNAL DANGER

In the eighteenth century, it was a commonly held view that Montesquieu believed a republic must operate in a small extent of territory, as one might well conclude from a reading of the first eight books of *The Spirit of Laws*. Montesquieu's discussion of this subject in Book 8, Chapter 16, however, was not his final word on the subject. In Book 9 of *The Spirit of Laws*, he made a

[33] Adams, *Defence*, vol. 1, *WJA*, 4:298.

[34] *PJM*, 11:307; "Who Are the Best Keepers of the People's Liberties?" *MJM*, 269–70; *PJM*, 14:426–27.

[35] *Federalist* 39:208–09; see also "Spirit of Governments," *MJM*, 256–57; *PJM*, 14:233–34.

fresh beginning. In the discussion concerning the relationship of laws to defensive force – and particularly with regard to the seeming dilemma that a large republic is destroyed by internal dissensions, while a small republic is destroyed by a foreign force – Montesquieu introduced the idea of the confederated republic. The federal republic, he wrote, is "a kind of assemblage of societies, that constitute a new one," and that combines "the internal advantages of a republican, together with the external force of a monarchical, government."[36] Examples of confederated states included the ancient Greek confederacies and the modern European federations of Holland, Germany, and the Swiss leagues. Of this type of association, Montesquieu named the ancient example of Lycia as the "model of an excellent confederate republic."[37] His judgment regarding the superiority of the Lycian model was due to two factors: It was composed of only republican towns (unlike the German confederacy, for example, which was constituted by republican and monarchical entities) and, given that the associated towns were not of the same size and population, voting in the general council was based on proportionate representation.

Following the brief discussion of the federal republic composed of many small states, Montesquieu proceeded to examine despotic states, monarchical states, and states in general, paying particular attention to the issue of size of territory and its bearing on the state's ability to defend itself against foreign dangers. Despotic governments tend to be large and, ultimately, self-destructive empires. In order for the despot to maintain his power, he must constantly pursue a policy of military conquest and expansion. But the more he expands his empire, the more vulnerable his government becomes vis-à-vis the enlarged borders abutted by enemy territory (and hence the need for further conquest and expansive dominion).[38] In contrast to despotic states, monarchies must be of a "moderate extent" to be at their full force; for example, "France and Spain are exactly of a proper extent" to secure themselves against foreign invasions and, presumably, to avoid the throes of despotism.[39] The examples Montesquieu provided of the moderately large unitary states are distinctively modern rather than ancient monarchies. This supplied the context for his warning against the "project of universal monarchy" attempted by Louis XIV of France and Charles V of Spain. If such a moderately large modern state tried to expand beyond a certain point, it would lose "its soul and decay... as Rome had."[40]

In contrast to France and Spain, Montesquieu presented the portrait of another moderately large modern European state – England – whose aim was not universal monarchy but liberty. (When Hume discussed "large states," he mentioned England and France as examples, thus actually signifying moderately

[36] Montesquieu, *SOL*, 9:1, 126. [37] Montesquieu, *SOL*, 9:3, 128.

[38] See Katya Long, "The 'Anti-Hobbes'? Montesquieu's Contribution to International Relations Theory," *In-Spire Journal of Law, Politics and Societies* 3, no. 2 (2008): 94–95.

[39] Montesquieu, *SOL*, 9:6, 130.

[40] Shklar, "Montesquieu and the New Republicanism," 266–67.

sized nations rather than large empires.[41]) For Montesquieu, the English constitution, at its best, served as a balance of powers model that constituted the optimal interior constitutional structure of a free government. This model also served as the archetype for an international balance of power. He believed that with regard to the international arena, an equilibrium in the European international system of sovereign nations would go a long way toward achieving security for each nation against external danger, which would in turn advance the internal, constitutional liberty of each nation. He made this point explicit in both *Reflections on Universal Monarchy in Europe* (Part VIII) and in *The Spirit of Laws* (Book 16, Chapter 6), whose passages on this subject are virtually identical. The "natural divisions" in Europe that "form several moderately-sized states" offer the prospect of maintaining authority "not incompatible with the rule of law." Moreover, the rule of law "is so conducive to the maintenance and authority" of the states that in its absence, they would become "decadent and inferior" to other states.[42] "It is this which has formed a genius for liberty that renders every part extremely difficult to be subdued and subjected to a foreign power, otherwise than by the laws and the advantage of commerce."[43]

[41] David Hume, "Idea of a Perfect Commonwealth," in *Essays: Moral, Political, and Literary*, ed. Eugene F. Miller (Indianapolis: Liberty Classics, 1985), 527. Hume wrote: "We shall conclude this subject, with observing the falsehood of the common opinion, that no large state, such as FRANCE or GREAT BRITAIN, could ever be modeled into a commonwealth, but that such a form of government can only take place in a city or small territory." This is the same essay in which Hume argued, just a page later in his conclusion, that "in a large government, which is modeled with masterly skill, there is compass and room enough to refine the democracy," leading one to infer that by "large government," he meant a government in a territory the size of England or France. If this is true, and if Madison understood Hume to mean by a "large government" a moderate-sized state and not an empire, then the discovery of the benefits of a very extensive territory – that is, an empire – would seem to belong solely to Madison.

[42] Montesquieu, Charles de Secondat, Baron de, *Reflections on Universal Monarchy in Europe*, trans. David Carrithers and Mark Waddicor (unpublished translation), Print, VIII. I am indebted to David Carrithers and Mark Waddicor for allowing me to use their unpublished translation of this important work by Montesquieu.

[43] Montesquieu, *SOL*, 17:6, 269. Ana J. Samuel, in her very thoughtful essay on "The Design of Montesquieu's *The Spirit of the Laws*: A Triumph of Freedom Over Determinism" (*American Political Science Review*, 103, no. 2 [2009]: 305–21), points out that whereas Montesquieu's initial tripartite classification of governmental types, such as tyranny, monarchy, and republic, depends on territorial size in order to remain consistent with their principles, Montesquieu's new republic, or the free regime, does not depend on the size of territory in order to be effective. "Nowhere," Samuel argues, "does Montesquieu indicate that the free regime would have to be of a particular size. His suggestion is that the political and civil laws of this regime preserve their effectiveness over whatever size territory. This is likely due to the fact that all citizens and classes are represented in and divide the powers of this government, and because, as Montesquieu reveals in Part 4, the commercial activity of this regime makes it particularly friendly with other states, lessening the need to intimidate by its size or be prepared to fight or conquer other formidable territories" (310). Samuel is certainly correct to point out that Montesquieu is silent on the issue of the territorial size of the modern commercial republic. However, it should also be

Accordingly, in his writings, Montesquieu presented at least two models of composite political association: (1) the confederate republic, composed of a number of small republics united to form an "assemblage of societies, that constitute a new one"[44] and (2) "a nation composed of many nations."[45] The former was exemplified by the old Swiss confederacy of small republican cantons; the latter was composed of a number of moderately sized states that constituted a balance of power among European nations.[46] Montesquieu juxtaposed these archetypes of political association with the paradigm of universal monarchy. After the French subjugated the barbarian nations and the Holy Roman Empire was established by Charlemagne, he argued, the establishment of universal monarchy in Europe seemed fated. But rather than unite under a single ruler, Europe divided into a number of "sovereign states." The reason for this, he claimed, was due to the opinions and habits of the Goths and Germans. If any ruler had even talked of "arbitrary power or supreme authority or power without limits, he would have been mocked by his whole army." Such are the origins of the kingdoms of Germany, Italy, France, and Aquitaine.[47] Later, when the Gothic governments declined and feudal authorities were replaced by independent, powerful monarchs with standing armies (made economically possible by the enormous increase in commerce and credit), universal monarchy again threatened Europe. But even Emperor Charles V, who acquired Burgundy, Castile, and Aragon, could not achieve European hegemony. "France everywhere separated Charles V's states, and ... [served as] the rallying point of all the rulers who wanted to defend their declining political freedom."[48]

The Europe Montesquieu knew was composed of a number of sovereign and independent states that served to limit the power of the ambitious monarchs, thereby preventing any single ruler from acquiring empire and establishing universal monarchy. At the same time, these nations were connected by mutual commercial and economic interests that rubbed up against each other, softening and polishing mores and manners. If the balance of power among the states (and the ambition of their sovereigns) made the acquisition of empire unlikely, the spirit of commerce made it less desirable, for riches could be gained by enterprise and trade as easily or more easily than by the sword. For both these reasons – but particularly with an eye to the peaceful, unifying influence of

noted that he speaks of this new republic within the context of a geopolitical environment in which there are other nations, optimally a political, economic milieu of commercial republics.

44 Montesquieu, *SOL*, 9:1, 126.

45 Montesquieu, *Reflections on Universal Monarchy in Europe*, XVIII.

46 See the incisive analysis of this subject by Long, "The 'Anti-Hobbes'? Montesquieu's Contribution to International Relations Theory," 88–101, especially 94, 97–100; Daniel H. Deudney, *Bounding Power: Republican Security Theory From the Polis to the Global Village* (Princeton: Princeton University Press, 2010), 139–42.

47 Montesquieu, *Reflections on Universal Monarchy in Europe*, X.

48 Montesquieu, *Reflections on Universal Monarchy in Europe*, XV.

mutual economic advantage – Montesquieu described modern Europe as "a nation composed of many nations."[49]

Building on Montesquieu's analysis of the emergence of the commercial republic in the modern world, a school of "philosophical historians" pursued a novel scholarly approach that sought to set forth as methodically as possible the causes of the changes in and progress of civilized society.[50] In contrast to those who read Montesquieu as teaching that a republic can only operate in a small territory, such historians as William Robertson, Edward Gibbon, and David Hume (the first two of whom Madison explicitly cites in Chapters 1 through 3 of the "Notes"; he tacitly references Hume in Chapter 4) understood Montesquieu to teach that certain historical changes had made the classical small republic generally unfeasible in the modern world. They also recognized in Montesquieu's analysis of England the description of a limited constitutional monarchy that constituted a new type of republic. This new republic is much larger than its classical variant; it owes its stability to the distribution of governmental powers and the rivalry of diverse passions and economic interests. Accordingly, in the new republic, the conflict-driven model of politics replaced the old republican traits of virtue and self-abnegation.

Robertson, Hume, and Gibbon believed that although human nature remained constant, specific developments in the history of the West had altered political and societal circumstances to such a degree that an entirely new political analysis was necessary. Two changes in particular stood out: the establishment and spread of Christianity in the West and the advent of modern science and technology. The former gave rise to the idea of a universal religion that transcends political boundaries and allegiances; the latter resulted in such new inventions as gunpowder, the compass, and the printing press. With the decline of feudal institutions, improvements in military technology, the rise of standing armies, and the centralization and consolidation of power in the hands of the monarchy, came the rebirth of wars of conquest and the possibility of a new European empire headed by a Christian king.[51] Charles V and Louis XIV were two such monarchs. Each aspired to destroy the balance of power among sovereign states established by the 1714 Treaty of Utrecht and to replace it with an empire modeled after Rome. Indeed, empire was the objective of every major

[49] Montesquieu, *Reflections on Universal Monarchy in Europe*, XVIII.

[50] As J. G. A. Pocock points out in *Barbarism and Religion* (vol. 1: *The Enlightenments of Edward Gibbon* and vol. 2: *Narratives of Civil Society* [Cambridge: Cambridge University Press, 1999, 2001]), the Scottish Enlightenment historians did not simply reject the traditional narrative approach but rather combined it with philosophical history and erudition. Cf. Ralph Lerner, "Musings in the Ruins," *Law and History Review* 19, no. 2 (2001): 435–44.

[51] See J. G. A. Pocock, "Edward Gibbon in History: Aspects of the Text in *The History of the Decline and Fall of the Roman Empire*" (The Tanner Lectures on Human Values, Yale University, New Haven, CT March 1–3, 1989, http://tannerlectures.utah.edu/_documents/a-to-z/p/pocock90.pdf).

European state at the time.[52] Montesquieu sounded the alarm of the threat of universal monarchy; Robertson, Hume, and Gibbon chimed in.

According to J. G. A. Pocock, Montesquieu and Gibbon considered Rome as the illustration of the "republican contradiction."[53] Because the republic of Rome "was virtuous it defeated its enemies; because it defeated its enemies it acquired empire." And because it acquired empire, it lost its liberty.[54] What Gibbon called the "immoderate greatness" of the Roman Empire eventually led to absolute monarchy, the loss of Roman liberty, and the ultimate downfall of the regime.[55] The essential problem that Rome symbolized was not expansion per se but rather imperialism based on military conquest and universal monarchy.[56] If the civic martial spirit had led classical republics on expeditions of expansion that eventually resulted in their demise, the large modern state headed by a monarch in command of a large standing army posed the danger of a unified military empire and the loss of civic virtue. To counteract the threat of universal monarchy and preserve the liberties of Europe, the philosophic historians adopted and expanded on Montesquieu's application of the domestic model of balanced government and commercial society to the international arena.[57] Accordingly, they promoted a confederation that would balance the

[52] Judith N. Shklar, *Montesquieu* (Oxford: Oxford University Press, 1987), 50. See also Michael Lind, "Toward a Global Society of States," *The Wilson Quarterly* (2002), www.newamerica.net/publications/articles/2002/toward_a_global_society_of_states.

[53] J. G. A. Pocock, *Virtue, Commerce, and History* (Cambridge: Cambridge University Press, 1985), 146.

[54] Prior to Montesquieu and Gibbon, Machiavelli argued that the Romans lost their liberty as a result of conquest, overexpansion, and decadence. See Rahe, *Montesquieu and the Logic of Liberty*, 36–37.

[55] See Ralph Lerner's commentary on Gibbon in *Playing the Fool: Subversive Laughter in Troubled Times* (Chicago: University of Chicago Press, 2009), especially Chapter 6. Speaking of "the philosophic historian's hard, unblinking assessment of Roman greatness," Lerner argues that "assimilation into the empire and all its attractions came at the cost of the suppression of a vital provincial public life and the acceptance of tyrannical rule" (118).

[56] João Marques de Almeida, "What Republicans Tell Us About International Society" (paper presented at BISA Annual Conference, Bradford University, Yorkshire, United Kingdom, December 2–18, 2000), 20.

[57] For example, see Hume, "Of the Balance of Power," *Essays*, 332–41. Cf. John Robertson, "Universal Monarchy and the Liberties of Europe: David Hume's Critique of an English Whig Doctrine," in *Political Discourses in Early Modern Britain*, ed. Nicholas Phillipson and Quentin Skinner (Cambridge: Cambridge University Press, 1993), 49–73. See also Almeida's insightful examination of the philosophic historians' views on international politics and social relations in "What Republicans Tell Us About International Society." According to Almeida, Hume believed that "any stable political system has to rest on an equilibrium and division of power. The international *respublica* ... must incorporate the principle of maintaining a balance between its parts, as it happens in the domestic constitution of republics ... and civilised monarchies" (30–31). See also Bruce Buchan's fine essay "Enlightened Histories: Civilization, War and the Scottish Enlightenment," *The European Legacy* 2, no. 2 (2005): 177–92. Buchan argues that Robertson's *The History of the Reign of Emperor Charles V* and Hume's *History* culminated "in the creation of independent, militarily powerful states, based on civilized and refined civil

power of a number of moderately large sovereign commercial states in order to achieve a peaceful concert of European powers. Not Rome, but the feudal system of interconnected states provided them the model they sought to build on; the Goths had demonstrated how a form of empire is possible without the loss of freedom to military despotism.[58]

Robertson, Hume, and Gibbon believed that a methodical treatment of the system of European feudal relations and the history of the emergence of a balance of power among the European states, formalized by the Treaty of Utrecht, was of critical importance to understanding the movement from feudal to commercial society. It was also of decisive political importance to curbing the threat of universal monarchy. They believed that Europe under the Utrecht system served as a powerful portrait of the civilizing and peaceful effects of the new way of life in an advanced stage of civilization. However, it lasted only until the last quarter of the eighteenth century, when it was undermined by colonial imperialism and wars involving territorial acquisition outside the continent.[59] A post-Utrecht vision of Europe thus became the pressing task for the philosophic historians, who adhered to the view of the historical progress of European thought and manners but who were also concerned about the decline and decay that accompanied the advancements in civilization. In this vein, they promoted Montesquieu's "doux commerce" thesis, believing that key developments in history had ushered in a new stage of civilized society in which mutual interests can receive accommodation, thereby providing a solution to the political and religious conflicts that had afflicted Europe.[60] It was to this vision of political and civil society that they devoted their scholarly talents and ambitions.

Madison recognized that the theory of modern national pacifism in the thought of Montesquieu and the philosophical historians was based on the effects of commerce to unite the interests of nations and soften manners, thereby tending toward international security and peace. Madison also believed that this theory did not completely leave behind the European balance of national power model but rather was superimposed on it. This was necessarily the case because the international model was rooted in a confederation of

societies. As each was aware, the formalized structure of interaction between sovereign states also provided a model of domestic social interaction, replacing action determined by private conviction with rule-governed, regulated and disciplined conduct. Montesquieu described this as a secular model of political interaction, one in which considerations of interest rather than conscience were paramount" (181). Cf. Stephen J. Rosow, "Commerce, Power and Justice: Montesquieu on International Politics," *The Review of Politics* 46, no. 3 (1984): 346–66; Albert O. Hirschman, *The Passions and the Interests: Political Arguments for Capitalism Before Its Triumph* (Princeton, NJ: Princeton University Press, 1997).

58 Pocock, "Edward Gibbon in History," 31.

59 Carhart and Robertson, "The Enlightenments of J. G. A. Pocock," 123–51, 144.

60 See Albert O. Hirschman's provocative treatment of this aspect of Enlightenment thought in *The Passions and the Interests*, 56–63.

states, which, like Lycia and the feudal states, ultimately retained their sovereignty. As a result, a sense of external political danger and the rational exercise of national interest and ambition to maintain security necessarily formed part of the equation. This meant the existence of standing armies in the European nations, making the peace of their world depend on a cold war.[61] "Fear & hatred of other nations [is] the greatest cement," Madison wrote in Chapter 2 of the "Notes." It is "always appealed to by rulers when they wish to impose burdens or carry unpopular points," as numerous examples in English and French history demonstrate.[62]

Madison was no more satisfied with this proffered solution to the menace of political conquest and war than was Jean Jacques Rousseau. But neither was he at all in agreement with Rousseau's model of the confederal republic. In an "Abstract of Monsieur the Abbé de Saint-Pierre's Plan for Perpetual Peace," which was essentially an abridgement of the Abbé de Saint-Pierre's much longer work on perpetual peace, Rousseau criticized those who pretended there existed a "fraternity of the peoples of Europe," when in actuality, these nations shared "mutual animosity."[63] The "boasted balance of power in Europe" (or "vaunted equilibrium") had not been formally "established by anyone," Rousseau argued. Rather, it came about accidentally. If any of the princes who are accused of aspiring to universal monarchy have actually harbored such a ridiculous notion, they would find that there is no power in Europe capable of becoming master of another.[64] In this work, Rousseau presented a model of the "confederative government" that connects "[p]eoples by bonds similar to those which unite individuals," subjecting both to the authority of the laws; this confederal union "comprehends the advantages of large and small States at the same time."[65] Moreover, Rousseau imagined that in this society, mankind would be united by friendship and love. Indeed, it would be a "peaceful society of brothers, living in an eternal concord, all led by the same maxims, all happy with the common happiness."[66]

Despite Rousseau's insistence on the equality of republican citizens in his other writings, he abandoned this standard when it came to international politics and the desire for perpetual peace. In "Universal Peace," Madison criticized Rousseau's recommendation of a "confederation of sovereigns"

61 Buchan, for example, argues that the "state monopolization of violence" advanced by Hume and other philosophic historians was essentially "an inherently militaristic template of Enlightenment conceptions of civilization" ("Enlightened Histories," 4).

62 "Notes on Government," *MJM*, 130; *PJM*, 14:160–61.

63 Jean-Jacques Rousseau, "Abstract of Monsieur the Abbé de Saint-Pierre's Plan for Perpetual Peace," in *The Plan for Perpetual Peace, On the Government of Poland, and Other Writings on History and Politics*, trans. Judith Bush and Christopher Kelly, ed. Christopher Kelly, vol. 11 of *The Collected Writings of Rousseau*, eds. Roger D. Masters and Christopher Kelly (Hanover, NH: University Press of New England, 2005), 31.

64 Rousseau, "Plan for Perpetual Peace," 33.

65 Rousseau, "Plan for Perpetual Peace," 28–29.

66 Rousseau, "Plan for Perpetual Peace," 28.

because it did nothing to counteract the allurements to war and, in fact, would perpetuate existing arbitrary governments.[67] Rather than following through on the principles of republicanism and devising an international model based on governments whose wills are dependent on the will of their respective societies, Rousseau accepted and continued the "disease" of the "*hereditary*" domestic model of government, of which his international plan is "the offspring."[68]

Montesquieu, by contrast, had insisted that a federal republic should be entirely composed of republican states.[69] Furthermore, he indicated that the modern European commercial states would, in all probability, eventually be of the republican brand.[70] Still, Montesquieu's envisioned "nation composed of many nations" lacked a constitutional unifying power;[71] it was not based on the sovereignty of the public, and if it united nations in some respects, it did not unite individuals or citizens. Conversely, Rousseau's international model, based on the European geopolitical reality of predominantly hereditary monarchical governments, did not unite nations by the same ties that unite republican citizens. In the recommendation of a relatively powerful central government over these states, Rousseau thought he could achieve a unity and equilibrium in international politics that replicated the domestic republican model of politics. "The Powers of Europe form a sort of system among themselves," Rousseau wrote, "which unites them by one single religion, the same international law, morals, literature, commerce, and a sort of equilibrium that is the necessary effect of all this."[72] The problem with Rousseau's model as well as with that of Montesquieu and the philosophical historians was that they did not provide a way in which the will of the government could be "made subordinate to, or rather the same with, the will of the community."[73] In the absence of this, these prototypes lacked a means to "regenerate" republicanism. Were a nation to impose such republican requirements on itself, Madison declared, "avarice would be sure to calculate the expences

[67] "Universal Peace," *MJM*, 251–53; *PJM*, 14:206–09. Rousseau's list of the major European players consisted of the Emperor of the Romans, the Emperor of Russia, the King of France, the King of Spain, the King of England, the Estates General, the King of Denmark, Sweden, Poland, the King of Portugal, the Sovereign of Rome, the King of Prussia, the Elector of Bavaria and his coassociates, the Palatine Elector and his coassociates, the Swiss and their coassociates, the Ecclesiastical Electors and their associates, the Republic of Venice and its coassociates, the King of Naples, and the King of Sardinia (Rousseau, "Perpetual Peace," 39).

[68] "Universal Peace," *MJM*, 251–53; *PJM*, 14:206–09. "Universal Peace" was published in the *National Gazette* on February 2, 1792; as one of the essays Madison wrote for Freneau's newspaper, it was included in the reference to "Freneau's National Gazette" articles at the very end of the "Notes on Government."

[69] Montesquieu, *SOL*, 19:3, 127; 19:6, 138.

[70] Montesquieu, *SOL*, 20:2, 316.

[71] Montesquieu, *Reflections on Universal Monarchy in Europe*, XVIII.

[72] Rousseau, "Plan for Perpetual Peace," 28–29.

[73] "Universal Peace," *MJM*, 252; *PJM*, 14:207.

of ambition," and "in the equipoise of these passions, reason would be free to decide for the public good."[74]

In the subsequent section of the "Notes," Madison further explicates his view that the only genuinely free and republican government is based on the will of the society, which in turn must be grounded in the reason of the society. To accomplish his goal, he believed, he must explain how a large territory can be hospitable to the feeling of individual significance and favorable to individual liberty. Furthermore, he needed to demonstrate how, in the equipoise of the passions and interests of society, a public opinion is formed that is more than a mere aggregation of sentiments and views. Instead, it must be transformed to become the "reason of the society" – or, in other words, impartial decisions about the public good.

STAGE OF SOCIETY

Subsequent to Montesquieu's presentation of a theory of the stages of society, French economist Anne Robert Jacques Turgot as well as a number of Scottish historians, including William Robertson, Adam Ferguson, Adam Smith, and John Millar, expanded on the theory of economic and social stages of societal development.[75] Robertson's presentation of a stadial view of history in his lengthy preface to *The History of the Reign of Charles V*, titled *A View of the Progress of Society in Europe From the Subversion of the Roman Empire to the Beginning of the Sixteenth Century* (1769),[76] became something of a template to others interested in the stages of societal development in Europe, including Jacques Peuchet and Condorcet in France. (Robertson's work was translated into French by Jean-Baptiste-Antoine Suard and widely read on the continent.)

Madison's chapter heading "Influence of the stage of Society on Government" in the "Notes" refers to the eighteenth-century stadial view of history. In *Federalist* 10 and in his letter of October 24, 1787, to Jefferson (both cited in this section of the "Notes"), Madison briefly addressed the issue of "civilized Societies." Criticizing the views of "theoretical politicians" and "theoretical writers" who believe that a republic must be limited to a small area (because only within narrow bounds can the people be "perfectly equalized, and assimilated in their possessions, their opinions, and their passions"), Madison countered that only in the "savage State" is there anything even

74 "Universal Peace," *MJM*, 253; *PJM*, 14:208.

75 Despite the widely held view that it was Turgot who introduced the theory of societal stages, Paul A. Rahe demonstrates that this theory was already present in Montesquieu's writings and that it had a substantial impact on subsequent thought. See *Montesquieu and the Logic of Liberty*, 310n8. See also Istvan Hont's discussion of Samuel von Pufendorf on societal stages in *Jealousy of Trade: International Competition and the Nation State in Historical Perspective* (Cambridge, MA: Belknap Press of Harvard University Press, 2005), 46.

76 William Robertson, *The History of the Reign of the Emperor Charles V*, vol. I (Philadelphia: J. B. Lippincott, [1769] 1895).

approaching homogeneity.[77] (Madison explicitly pointed to Plato as a theoretical writer in the "Notes," although one can easily imagine that he also intended to include Rousseau in this general category.) The legislators of all other societies – "all civilized Societies" – need to recognize that distinctions accompany all civilized life and that these have a tremendous impact on the formation of different and opposing interests and views in the society. "Civilized Societies," as the term is used by Madison, is not synonymous with modern commercial republics – at least not if what is meant by this is manufacturing or industrialized states. In fact, all nonsavage states are more or less civilized, according to Madison. The relevant consideration is not so much whether the society is civilized but what particular stage of civilization characterizes it, including the distinction between predominantly agricultural societies and manufacturing nations.[78]

The philosophic historians sought to unearth the historical forces that moved Europe from barbarism to an advanced stage of civilization and, in particular, to demonstrate how the states of Europe had developed with respect to customs, manners, mores, and the climate of opinion (both secular and religious). In contrast to the traditional concentration on governments and laws or on mere erudition, they also studied how the arts, commerce, manners, and opinions affected historical change and contributed to a new phase of society.[79] Hume argued, for example, that a confederation of a number of states with an active commerce of arts and goods serves to limit the authority and power of the governments. "Their mutual jealousy" serves to keep them

> from receiving too lightly the law from each other. ... The contagion of popular opinion spreads not so easily from one place to another. It readily receives a check in some state or other, where it concurs not with the prevailing prejudices. And nothing but nature and reason, or, at least, what bears them a strong resemblance, can force its way through all obstacles, and unite the most rival nations into an esteem and admiration of it.[80]

For Hume, the historical progress in taste and reasoning were linked together with the establishment of a political balance of power among commercial

[77] Madison to Jefferson, October 24, 1787, *MJM*, 220; *PJM*, 10:212.

[78] See, for example, the title of Chapter 3 of the "Notes" as well as Madison's use of the term "different stages of civilization" during his Constitutional Convention speech of July 11, 1787 (*PJM*, 10:99); see also Madison's letter to Jefferson, October 24, 1787 (*MJM*, 220–21; *PJM*, 10:212–13). The issue of the changes wrought throughout the different stages of civilized society was of great concern to Madison throughout his life, particularly with respect to the changing population and greater discrepancies of wealth among the citizens of the United States that he anticipated in future years. See Drew McCoy's fine study of this issue in *The Last of the Fathers*, 194–207. Cf. "Address to the Agricultural Society of Albermarle, Virginia," May 12, 1818, *Retirement Series*, *PJM*, 1:257–59.

[79] Carhart and Robertson, "The Enlightenments of J. G. A. Pocock," 123–51, 146–47; Mark Salber Phillips, *Society and Sentiment: Genres of Historical Writing in Britain, 1740–1820* (Princeton, NJ: Princeton University Press, 2000), 6, 15–17.

[80] Hume, "Of the Rise and Progress of the Arts and Sciences," *Essays*, 120.

nations, which had the effect of "resisting the torrent of popular opinion" and encouraging instead a more stable climate of opinion and manners.[81]

This was important, Hume believed, because all governments rest on opinion. Robertson agreed with Hume regarding the critical role of opinion in political life.[82] Following the approach taken in *The Spirit of Laws*, the philosophic historians combined the study of politics and society; they examined the interaction between constitutional structures and "the dominant spirits or general manners of the times" to understand the prevailing climate of opinion and to discover how this might resolve the problems posed by political and religious conquests for dominion.[83] For them, as for Montesquieu, the history of commerce was the history of the "communication of people."[84] "Commerce," Robertson wrote, "tends to wear off those prejudices which maintain distinction and animosity between nations. It softens and polishes the manners of men. It unites them, by one of the strongest of all ties, the desire of supplying their mutual wants. It disposes them to peace."[85]

The philosophic historians did not believe that the "progress" from barbarism to civilization was an inevitable historical process nor did they think that the advancement of civilization was an unmixed blessing. New inventions in military technology, the displacement of militias with professional armies, and the growth of large, centralized states had indeed made the ferociousness of the citizen-soldier a thing of the past. Modern warfare, conducted by paid soldiers with guns and cannons aimed from a distance rather than man-to-man combat with bloody swords flaying through human hearts, meant that the hyper-manly spiritedness and violent passions of the Roman warrior were no longer necessary to the preservation of a republic. But it also meant that citizens were no longer citizens in the classical republican sense; the safeguarding of men's families, their lands and possessions, and their honor were no longer inextricably tied to their country or to a willingness to sacrifice themselves in defense of it. The new citizen could now envision himself and his interests as distinct – perhaps even separate – from the state. The irrelevance of the citizen-soldier and the emergence of the merchant and manufacturer ushered in a radically new prospect for peace – but at a cost. It meant the loss of civic virtue (in the

81 Hume, "Of the Rise and Progress of the Arts and Sciences," *Essays*, 122; cf. Ameida, "What Republicans Tell Us About International Society," 25.

82 See Karen O'Brien's discussion of the importance of public opinion in Robertson's thought in "Robertson's Place in the Development of Eighteenth-Century Narrative History," in *William Robertson and the Expansion of Empire*, ed. Stewart J. Brown (New York: Cambridge University Press, 1997), 82–83. "Despite occasional acknowledgments, particularly in the *History of Charles V*, of the dynamic creativity of popular opinion and protest," O'Brien argues, "Robertson accorded only to the narrower band of educated opinion the key functions of defining and legitimating the nation's political arrangements and cultural self-image."

83 Almeida, "What Republicans Tell Us About International Society," 33.

84 Montesquieu, *SOL*, 21:5, 334.

85 Robertson, *The History of the Reign of Emperor Charles V*, I:89.

classical sense of love of one's fatherland) as the defining element of republican government. To counteract this loss, the philosophic historians advanced a new conception of ethics befitting the modern commercial era: the ethics of "manners" or "politeness." In this, they again followed the great sage Montesquieu.[86] This redefinition of the republican ethos was grounded in a model of political and social interaction in which considerations of interest were primary to matters of moral or religious conscience.[87]

EXPANDING ON THE POLITICAL WISDOM OF THE GREAT ORACLES

Despite the attention given by Montesquieu, Robertson, Gibbon, and Hume to the factors of territorial size, external danger, stage of society, and confederal alliance, and their presumed advancement beyond the classical republican model, Madison did not think they had thought through the political problem far enough. In a short essay that is not part of the notebook outline but is evidently directly related to the material of the "Notes on Government," Madison summarized the thrust of the first three chapters of the "Notes" and connected them with the remaining chapters of Section 1:

> In estimating the tendency of Governme[n]t to the increase or the relaxation of their powers[,] particular causes distinct from their respective structures, but of powerful influence on their operation, seem to have been overlooked or little heeded by the great oracles of political wisdom. In the discussions produced by the establishment and revisions of the new forms of Govt. in the U. S. and especially of their General Govt. some of these causes have engaged particular attention. (See the *Federalist* No. 10.) A Govt. of the same structure, would operate very differently within a very small territory and a very extensive one: over a people homogeneous in their opinions & pursuits, and over a people consisting of adverse sects in religion, or attached to adverse theories of Govt: over a Society composed wholly of tenants of the soil aspiring and hoping for an enlargement of their possessions and a Society divided into a rich or independent class, and a more numerous class without property and hopeless of acquiring a permanent interest in maintaining its rights: over a nation secure agst. foreign enemies, and over one in the midst of formidable neighbours.[88]

The founding and maintenance of a polity require that certain powerful influences on government "distinct from their respective structures" be given careful

[86] Again, they followed Montesquieu's lead in this, albeit expanding substantially on his discussion. See *SOL*, 19, especially Chapter 16, 300–01.

[87] Pocock, "Edward Gibbon in History," 18–21; Buchan, "Enlightened Histories: Civilization, War and the Scottish Enlightenment," 181. Cf. Daniele Francesconi, "William Robertson on Historical Causation and Unintended Consequences," *Cromohs* 4 (1999): 1–18, www.cromohs.unifi.it/4_99/francesconi.html.

[88] "Notes on the Influence of Extent of Territory on Government," *PJM*, 14:132.

scrutiny. The "great oracles of political wisdom" neglected or little heeded the effect of territorial size on the other influences on government, including external danger, the stage of society, public opinion, religion, and so forth. Indeed, "the influence of extent of territory seems to have been least understood or attended to," Madison wrote, "yet admits of the most satisfactory illustrations." Madison's purpose in returning to the subject of *Federalist* 10 in the "Notes" was to add to the analysis of political philosophers and to consider more fully the *interactive effect* of the factor of territorial size/population, particularly its influence on "the facility of popular combinations and the force of public opinion." He sought to demonstrate how this correlative relationship could achieve the political dynamic and outcome that had so long been sought by the true friends of republican government.[89]

Although he does not name the "great oracles of political wisdom" in this fragment, Madison was apparently referring to the classical political authors he cited in the "Notes" (Plato and Aristotle) as well as to Montesquieu. The two ancient oracles of political wisdom neglected these factors entirely, while Montesquieu did not heed them sufficiently enough to see the way in which a genuinely republican solution to the problem of political power could be achieved.[90]

With respect to the most neglected factor of territorial size, Madison underscored its political benefits, but he also recognized a peculiar problem associated with it. If the extension of the territory increases respect for the nation, it also diminishes the importance felt by each individual, making him more submissive to the general will. This is the danger Tocqueville would later emphasize in his discussion of the omnipotence of the majority in popular governments in *Democracy in America*. If a republic is too extensive, Madison believed, the people will feel the same stultifying lack of confidence and tendency toward submissiveness that they do in absolute monarchies and tyrannies. Accordingly, he sought to avoid this by constructing an environment that not only prevented the people from uniting too easily, but also provided the conditions for the ultimate formation of an effective public voice. In addition to the actual size of the territory, Madison explored a number of other factors that, due to their influence on the formation and influence of public opinion, act as equivalents to the contraction or expansion of a nation's size. "Whatever facilitates a general intercommunication of sentiments & ideas among the body of the people," he argued,

[89] "Notes on the Influence of the Extent of Territory on Government," *PJM*, 14:132.

[90] In Chapter 1 of his "Notes on Government," titled "Influence of the Size of Nation on Government," to which this fragment titled "Notes on the Influence of Extent of Territory on Government" is clearly related, Madison opens with the following: "Plato limits the number of Citizens to five thousand and forty. Montesquieu tom. II c. 16, 17." Additionally, in *Federalist* 47, Madison writes that "the oracle who is always consulted and cited on this subject is the celebrated Montesquieu" (269).

[such] as a free press, compact situation, good roads, interior commerce &c, is equivalent to a contraction of the orbit within wch. the Govt. is to act; and may favor liberty in a nation too large for free Govt. or hasten its violent death in one too small & so vice versa.[91]

In this portion of the "Notes," Madison moved beyond his earlier discussion of preventing injustice through hampering or encouraging an association of the people. Here, he added his concern for the political significance of the individual and the security of the citizen's liberty. This concern went hand in hand with his repeated emphasis on the issue of the ease or difficulty of forming "combination(s) of the people," which he identified as the salient factor in determining the proper size of a nation. Madison thus indicated the significance of territorial size within the larger context of the purpose of his investigation: What are the geographical conditions (or their equivalents) that allow for a sufficiently ready combination of the people, such that they are able to unite to prevent governmental oppression and sustain their liberty as citizens and at the same time deter them from pursuing oppressive aims?

In both the "Notes on Government" and in his fragment on "the Influence of Extent of Territory," Madison took up the issue of the relationship among the size of a territory, the nature of its union, and the ability of its inhabitants to communicate effectively. If the European states formed one society, or if England were spread across a territory ten times its size and public communication were obstructed, Madison mused, the people would be unable to unite against oppression or govern themselves, and the result would be tyranny.[92] Conversely, imagine England shrunk to the size of London and freed from foreign threats, in which case the monarchy would be unable to support itself against the power of the House of Commons. In this circumstance, the people could easily unite and transform the country into a simple democracy, and the ease of communication would "hasten [the] violent death" of liberty.[93] Madison's discussion here shows that to the degree that England is free, it is partially owing to its size; it is not so large as to impede a combination of the people against the oppression of the monarch nor is it so compact that the people can all too readily unite and substitute democracy for its present form. In Chapter 4 of the "Notes," however, Madison will qualify the allegedly beneficial impact of its size on the preservation of its constitution. Although England is large enough to prevent the people from effortlessly uniting, it is not large enough to prevent them, if they wished, from tipping the delicate balance and destroying the constitutional equilibrium. Thus, while the nation is small

[91] "Notes on Government," *MJM*, 127; *PJM*, 14:159; see also the Party Press Essay "Public Opinion," *MJM*, 245; *PJM*, 14:170.

[92] See also "Notes on the Influence of Extent of Territory on Government," *PJM*, 14:132–33.

[93] "Notes on the Influence of Extent of Territory on Government," *PJM*, 14:132–33.

enough for the public voice to form and be effective, it is not large enough to prevent the formation and rule of a factious majority.

In contrast to Rousseau, Montesquieu, and the philosophic historians, Madison sought to explore how the circumstantial influences of size of territory, external danger, and stage of society might be employed for the benefit of the liberty of the citizen in such a way as to affect the formation of public opinion and sustain the spirit of a genuinely republican government. He believed that stable and free republican government could be established over a very great extent of territory – indeed, over a territory much larger than the moderately sized nations of England, France, or Spain. The success of this new model primarily depended not on a balance of power among sovereign states or on the free flow of passions and interests in a commercial nation, but rather on a "modification of the sovereignty."

Learning from the philosophic historians' insights concerning the stages of civilization and the problem of external danger in the modern world, Madison rethought the question of territorial size in an age of commerce and communication and charted a substantially different philosophic and political course. Refusing to accept the Montesquieuian premise they endorsed, he denied that the rise of the spirit of commerce necessarily meant the atomization of citizenship and the rather happy acceptance of a world in which nations are united but individuals are divided.[94] Instead, he sought an alternative way to think through the problem and to reclaim an age-old hope for a new republican land. In his voyage to the classical world, Madison discovered how the commerce of ideas could maintain and reinvigorate the spirit of genuine republicanism. He believed that he had also discovered how the politics of public opinion was capable of uniting individuals and making them fellow citizens.

[94] Montesquieu, *SOL*, 20:2, 338. Montesquieu writes here: "But if the spirit of commerce unites nations, it does not unite individuals." According to Ralph Lerner: "For Montesquieu, a regime dedicated to commerce partook less of a union of fellow citizens, bound together by ties of friendship, than of an alliance of contracting parties, intent on maximizing their freedom of choice through a confederation of convenience. It was in this character of an alliance that men found themselves cut off from one another or, rather, linked to one another principally through a market mechanism. It was a world in which everything had its price ..." ("Commerce and Character: The Anglo-American as New-Model Man," *William and Mary Quarterly* 36, no. 1 [1979]: 21). When Montesquieu remarked in Chapter 13 of the eleventh book (on the commercial republic of England) that "one can never leave the Romans ... ," he indicated that his abandonment of the classical political task was not a glib move on his part. Nonetheless, as Lerner points out, Montesquieu looked upon ancient pretensions as "in some respects admirable, in other respects astonishing, in most respects consequential, but at bottom absurd" ("Commerce and Character: The Anglo-American as New-Model Man," 5). Indeed, Montesquieu believed that the classical reliance "on virtue as the support of popular government displayed an equal disregard for how men are. Political thinkers of his own time, in contrast, 'speak to us only of manufacture, commerce, finance, opulence, and even of luxury' (*SOL*, 21:20; 3:3). This was not a change that Montesquieu regretted" (12).

3

The power and authority of public opinion

Chapter 4 of the "Notes on Government," titled "Influence of public opinion on Government," contains the central argument of Section 1 of the "Notes" and is the pivotal thesis of the entire work. In the opening salvo, Madison emphatically declared: "Public opinion sets bounds to every government, and is the real sovereign in every free one."[1] In this chapter of the "Notes" and in the Party Press Essay "Public Opinion" based on it, Madison argued that the degree of respect due to public opinion depends on whether it is in flux or settled. When public opinion is not settled, government may influence it; when it is settled, government must obey it. The formation of a settled public opinion is contingent on two factors: the existence of a common view among the citizenry and the opportunity for them to communicate and coalesce on the basis of a shared view.

THE INFLUENCE OF PUBLIC OPINION ON THE BRITISH GOVERNMENT

Building on his examination of the influences of territorial size, stage of society, and external danger on the formation of popular majorities, Madison is now ready to apply his analysis to a particular case and offer some conclusions. Choosing the vaunted British government, he argued that given Britain's moderate size, advanced stage of civilization, and insulation from foreign danger, the force of public opinion is decisive in this nation. Madison's scrutiny of the British model reveals his disagreement with such men as John Adams and Montesquieu – the former of whom attributed the stability and longevity of

[1] Madison included portions of this chapter in the Party Press Essays "Public Opinion" and "British Government"; see *MJM*, 245 and 250; *PJM*, 14:170 and 14:201–02.

its constitution primarily to the balance of three rival governmental powers, while the latter based his praise of the English constitution on the distribution of its powers and the stability that resulted from the competition and clash of rival parties in society.[2] In Madison's view, these conflict-driven models of politics overlooked the critical significance of the influence of public opinion on the British government. If public opinion in Britain favored absolute monarchy, Madison argued, the representatives would soon surrender the public liberty. If it favored republicanism, the monarch could not resist the people's will. If public opinion were neutral, "the ambition of the House of Commons would easily strip the Prince of his prerogatives."[3] Although the King can, to some extent, counteract the power of the House by the practice of corruption, he is nonetheless ultimately dependent on the civil list[4] granted him by the representative branch – and this branch, in turn, depends on public opinion.

Like Montesquieu, David Hume wrote about the nexus between partisan rivalry and the longevity and stability of the British government, but Hume also saw in English political history a role that public opinion played in the preservation of the constitution. Accordingly, Madison's implied criticism of Montesquieu and Adams in these passages is simultaneously an agreement – at least in part – with Hume. He undoubtedly had in mind – and perhaps even borrowed a good portion of his argument here – from Hume's political essays "Of the First Principles of Government," "Independency of Parliament," and "Whether the British Government Inclines More to Absolute Monarchy, or to a Republic," and from his longer work: *The History of England*.[5] In the first of these essays, Hume argued that "governors have nothing to support them but

[2] As many scholars have noted, Montesquieu's praise of the British model is not without qualification. Montesquieu indicated in *The Spirit of Laws* that England may not be the model par excellence for a regime dedicated to the end of liberty; at the close of his critical chapter on the English constitution (*SOL*, 11:6), he remarked: "It is not my business to examine whether the English actually enjoy this liberty or not" (162). Both Montesquieu and Adams identified and admired the British government's grounding in the separation of the powers of government, including a bicameral legislature and an executive in possession of a veto on legislative measures. Adams, however, also advocated mixed, balanced government (i.e., mixing and balancing the one, the few, and the many in the legislative power of government), albeit of a modern variant that also included the principle of representation and a recognition and respect for natural rights. In contrast, Montesquieu's admiration of the British model had much less to do with the mixture and balancing of the few and many in government than with the interested, partisan competition between Court and Country within society. Adams appears to have believed that the best way to achieve the security of the citizen via the superiority of the rule of law – which of course Montesquieu famously argued for in *The Spirit of Laws* – was by taking Montesquieu's thought further and instituting mixed, balanced government. See C. Bradley Thompson, *John Adams and the Spirit of Liberty* (Lawrence: University of Kansas Press, 1988), 213–22.

[3] "Notes on Government," *MJM*, 134; *PJM*, 14:162–63; cf. "British Government," *MJM*, 250; *PJM*, 14:202.

[4] See *MJM*, 134; 250.

[5] Hume, *Essays*, 32–36, 42–46, 47–53.

opinion" and it "is therefore, on opinion only that government is founded,"[6] an idea that is generally thought to be the source of Madison's famous declaration in *Federalist* 49 that "all governments rest on opinion."[7] Subsequently, in "Of the First Principles of Government," Hume demonstrated that it is not primarily due to a balance of power and property in government that the British constitution has endured for so long (as was Harrington's view), but rather to the power of opinion. In *The History of England*, he argued against those who claimed that the current mixed constitution is of ancient origin, demonstrating that there were at least two – and probably five – stages of development in English constitutional history.[8] In Gothic and feudal times, the government was not mixed and balanced; following the Glorious Revolution, a system of constitutional mixture and equilibrium between the King and the House of Commons was established. "In each of these successive alterations, the only rule of government, which is intelligible or carries any authority with it, is the established practice of the age, and the maxims of administration, which are at that time prevalent, and universally assented to," Hume asserted. Nonetheless, there are "those who, from a pretended respect to antiquity, appeal at every turn to an original plan of the constitution, only cover their turbulent spirit and their private ambition under the appearance of venerable forms; and whatever period they pitch on for their model, they may still be carried back to a more ancient period, where they will find the measures of power entirely different."[9]

In "Of the Independency of Parliament," Hume argued that in the present era (that is, in the mid-eighteenth century), the equilibrium of the British constitution is not primarily due to the skillful distribution of power, for there is actually a significantly greater portion of power allotted to the House of Commons (particularly in terms of the exclusive right of the House of Commons to appropriate monies). Accordingly, "how easy... it would it be for that

[6] Hume, "Of the First Principles of Government," 32.

[7] *Federalist* 49:282. See also Madison's Party Press Essay "Charters," in which he argued that "All power has been traced up to opinion. The stability of all governments and security of all rights may be traced to the same source. The most arbitrary government is controuled where the public opinion is fixed" (*MJM*, 247–48; *PJM*, 14:192).

[8] Eugene F. Miller, "Hume on English Liberty," *The Political Science Reviewer* XVI (Fall, 1986): 127–83. See also Phillips, *Society and Sentiment*, 5–6. According to Phillips, Hume demonstrated that "the settled liberties of England after the expulsion of the Stuarts were primarily an indirect consequence of the House of Common's struggle to wrest powers from the Crown, not – as the Whigs contended – a direct consequence of their defense of traditional powers guaranteed by an 'ancient constitution'" (6).

[9] David Hume, *The History of England From the Invasion of Julius Caesar to the Revolution in 1688*, Foreword by William B. Todd (Indianapolis: Liberty Fund, 1983), II:439. Cf. Inuzuka Hajime, "David Hume's Politics: Inheritance and Renewal of the Traditional Political Thought," Institute of Social Science, no. F-113 (March 2004), www.iss.u-tokyo.ac.jp/publishments/dpf/pdf/f-113.pdf.

house to wrest from the crown all the powers."[10] How, then, is the House of Commons maintained within its proper limits and the balance maintained? By the Crown's practice of influence or corruption, Hume contended.[11] However, this practice could not preserve the constitutional equilibrium if public opinion did not at times throw its weight behind the monarchy. Contrary to those writers who suppose that the House of Commons is supported by the total weight of the common people, there are instances when the people have supported the Crown against the House.[12] If this were not the case, "at the least shock or convulsion," the ties of corrupt interest would be broken to pieces and "the royal power, being no longer supported by the settled principles and opinions of men, [would] immediately dissolve."[13] Clearly following Hume's analysis and argument in these essays – and even adopting some of his phraseology – Madison wrote in an essay based on Chapter 4 of the "Notes": "Were the public opinion neutral only, and the public voice silent, ambition in the House of commons could wrest from him his prerogatives, or the avarice of its members, might sell to him its privileges."[14]

Against those who attribute the equilibrium and longevity of the British model to the balance of property and power via the institutions of government, Hume claimed that the universal assent of the public to the prevailing maxims and practices of the age (or what he called elsewhere the "opinion of the public") is primarily responsible for maintaining the British system in both ancient and modern times.[15] Opinion, Hume taught, is of two kinds: opinion of interest and opinion of right, with the latter subdivided into opinion of right to power and opinion of right to property. Opinion of right to power is tantamount to the attachment people have to their ancient government and is manifested as a reverence or veneration of the established government. Whatever prevalence this kind of opinion may have over mankind, he argued, during the past fifty years, "there has been a sudden and sensible change in the opinions of men ... by the progress of learning and liberty" and "most people, in this island, have divested themselves of all superstitious reverence to names and authority."[16] In the present situation, the opinion of the people is more susceptible to other influences, and their spirit is "frequently ... rouzed [*sic*] in order to curb the ambition of the court."[17] It can also be roused to prevent usurpations by the House of Commons. This is accomplished particularly

[10] Hume, "Of the Independency of Parliament," *Essays*, 43–44.

[11] Hume, "Of the Independency of Parliament," *Essays*, 44–45.

[12] Hume, "Of the First Principles of Government," *Essays*, 35.

[13] Hume, "Whether the British Government Inclines More to Absolute Monarchy, or to a Republic," *Essays*, 51.

[14] "British Government," *MJM*, 250; *PJM*, 14:201.

[15] Hume, *The History of England*, II:276.

[16] Hume, "Whether the British Government Inclines More to Absolute Monarchy, or to a Republic," *Essays*, 51. Cf. "Of the First Principles of Government," *Essays*, 33.

[17] Hume, "Of the Liberty of the Press," *Essays*, 12.

through the channels of a free press. These channels of public communication encourage a "watchfulness and jealousy" in the people over the various parts of their government. Accordingly, Hume demonstrated that via the means of public communication in a free society, the opinion of the public takes on a politically active and censorial quality that goes beyond the citizens' attachment to or veneration of the government. Although interest is the primary motive governing men, Hume remarked, "yet even interest itself, and all human affairs, are entirely governed by opinion."[18]

Subsequent to Hume's publication of his political and moral essays in the 1740s, Montesquieu identified the emergence of a new "master" in the modern era – that is, a "universal master" that serves as the teacher in the school of the world.[19] Montesquieu's identification of this new master, which subsumes the place of families and public schools, is akin to a notion of the opinion of the world or public opinion. Despite Montesquieu's recognition of the force of opinion and *moeurs*, he did not develop a theory of the politics of public opinion. Instead, he relied on a separation of governmental powers as well as the competition among diverse interests and passions in a modern commercial society to render them politically harmless. In contrast, Hume explicitly emphasized the power of opinion in maintaining the equilibrium of the British government. However, while his insights into the effects of communication and the power of public opinion in the modern world moved him beyond a merely mechanistic theory of government, it did not inspire him to develop a theory of public opinion, as French writers on the subject would later do. Rather, it reinforced his fears of popular government, leading him to advocate strengthening the monarchical element of the British constitution in order to achieve a genuine balance between the King and the House of Commons. While Hume did go so far as to encourage "Men of Letters" to form a league with the conversable world via the vehicle of the public presses, his vision of a civic educative role for the literati fell largely within the confines of maintaining an equilibrium within the government. As Eugene Miller perceptively noted, Hume's intended role for the literati was "to moderate Britain's party disputes, support salutary institutions, favor practicable policies, and undermine pernicious ideas."[20]

[18] Hume, "Whether the British Government Inclines More to Absolute Monarchy, or to a Republic," *Essays*, 51. Hamilton would later include this view in prepared notes for his famous speech of July 18, 1787, at the Constitutional Convention.

[19] *SOL*, 4:2, 31.

[20] Remarks by the late Eugene Miller in correspondence, December 20, 2004. I am indebted to Professor Miller for both his unsurpassed work on David Hume and for a number of conversations over the years that have helped me to develop my understanding of Hume's political philosophy. If I have erred in interpreting Hume, the errors are, of course, mine alone.

ARISTOTLE'S VIEW OF THE POWER OF PUBLIC OPINION

In the Party Press Essay "British Government," Madison left the argument regarding the stability and longevity of political orders at a comparison between the distribution of governmental powers on the one hand and the force of public opinion on the other. In the "Notes on Government," he took a substantial and dramatic step beyond this focus on the British constitution. In the "Notes," he immediately connected this inquiry with the classical analysis of the problem of faction, or stasis, and the theory of the natural cycle of regimes. "Theoretical writers," such as Plato (in the *Republic*), and "more practical ones," such as Jonathan Swift, have argued that there is "a natural rotation in Government from the abuses of Monarchy to Aristocracy, from the oppression of aristocracy to democracy, and from the licentiousness of Democracy back to Monarchy," Madison wrote. However, he continued, "it appears from Aristotle that under the influence of public opinion, the rotation was very different in some of the States of Greece." Madison then wrote: "See Arist: Repub. B. 5 c. 12."[21]

Madison no doubt had in mind John Adams' volumes of the *Defence* when he penned this chapter of the "Notes." Adams emphatically attributed the liberty, stability, and longevity of the British constitution to its distribution and balance of powers. Furthermore, he claimed that the essential cause of the downfall of classical republics was due to the increased power of the people and the destruction of the constitutional equilibrium.[22] According to Adams, Plato

[21] "Notes on Government," *MJM*, 135; *PJM*, 14:162. Madison's specific reference here is to Book V, Chapter 12, of the *Politics*, where Aristotle criticizes Plato's theory in the *Republic*, Book VIII. In Plato's account in Book VIII of the *Republic*, the natural rotation of regimes ends in tyranny; it does not return back to monarchy. However, in Polybius' summary of Plato's theory of regime change, the rotation is brought full circle back to monarchy. In Book 6 of *The Histories*, Polybius comments on "the cycle of political revolution [and] the course appointed by nature in which constitutions change, disappear, and finally return to the point from which they started" (Polybius, *The Histories*, Vol. III: Bks 5–8, W. R. Paton, trans. [Loeb Classical Library; Cambridge: Harvard University Press, 2011], 315). In the *Defence*, Adams devotes Letter XXXI to the rotation of governments set forth by Plato and Polybius. He concluded that in this "rotation of governments … [and] order of nature," governments are "changed, transformed, and return to the same point of the circle" (Adams, *Defence*, vol. 1, *WJA*, 4:443). Cf. Gilbert Chinard, "Polybius and the American Constitution," *Journal of the History of Ideas* 1, no. 1 (January 1940): 38–58.

[22] An example of this, Adams said, could be seen in the actions of Aristides, who gave way to the "furious ambition of the people" and paved the way for a "democratical ascendancy," which led to the final loss of Greek liberty – an event in which Madison showed particular interest in the "Notes." See Adams, *Defence*, vol. 3, *WJA*, 6:101 and 101n. In later years, during the Madison administration, Adams repeated this assertion and summarized the connection between an overbalance of democracy and the final loss of Greek liberty: "When Solon's balance was destroyed by Aristides, and the preponderance given to the multitude, for which he was rewarded with the title of Just, when he ought to have been punished with the ostracism, the Athenians grew more and more democratic. I need not enumerate to you the foolish wars into which the people forced their wisest men and ablest generals against their own judgments, by

and Swift also identified the cause of political destruction and regime rotation as the lack of balance in the constitution. So, too, did Aristotle. Even Aristotle's criticisms of Plato's theory of the cycle of regimes at *Politics* V:12, Adams asserted, strengthen his own claim of "the necessity of mixtures of different orders and decisive balances" to avoid revolution and constitutional destruction. In Letter XLV on Corinth in the first volume of the *Defence*, Adams devoted his intellectual energies to understanding Aristotle's analysis at *Politics* V:12. Paraphrasing Aristotle, he wrote:

> Cypselus ... had long been the head of the popular party, and was deservedly a popular character, possessed of the confidence and affection of his fellow-citizens to a great degree, or he never could have refused the guard which was offered him for the protection of his person against the attempts of the defeated oligarchy. His moderation and clemency are allowed by all; yet he is universally called by the Grecian writers Tyrant of Corinth, and his government a Tyranny. Aristotle, 1. v. c. 12,[23] informs us that his tyranny continued thirty years, because he was a popular man, and governed without guards. Periander, one of the seven wise men, his son and successor, reigned forty-four years, because he was an able general. Psampsneticus, the son of Gorgias, succeeded, but his reign was short; yet this space of seventy-seven years is thought by Aristotle one of the longest examples of a tyranny or an oligarchy.[24]

And "here we find the usual circle," Adams wrote. Monarchy degenerates into aristocracy/oligarchy, then into democracy, and then back to monarchy. But "the new idol's posterity grow insolent; and the people finally think of introducing a mixture of three regular branches of power, in the one, the few, and the many, to controul one another, to be guardians in turn to the laws, and secure equal liberty to all."[25]

According to Adams, "Aristotle, in this chapter, censures some parts of the eighth book of Plato," arguing that "in general, when governments alter, they change into the contrary species to what they before were, and not into one like the former: and this reasoning holds true of other changes." Nonetheless, "[w]hether these observations of Aristotle upon Plato be all just or not, they only serve to strengthen our argument, by shewing the mutability of simple governments in a fuller light." Thus, according to Adams, Aristotle did not deny the natural pattern of revolutions in Plato's theory; rather, he enumerated "a multitude of other changes to which such governments are liable." In sum, Aristotle demonstrated "the greater necessity of mixtures of different orders,

which the state was finally ruined, and Philip and Alexander became their masters" (Adams, "Letters to John Taylor, of Caroline, Virginia, in Reply to His Strictures on Some Parts of the Defence of the American Constitutions," *WJA*, 6:485). For Madison's attention to Aristides and the consequences of his actions, see "Notes on Government," *MJM*, 140–42; *PJM*, 14:164, including the citations to Aristotle, Plutarch, and *Voyage* I:147–48 (French ed.); cf. *Voyage* I:140 (English trans.). See also "Notes on Government," *MJM*, 147; *PJM*, 14:165.

23 The reference here is to Aristotle, *Politics*, V:12.

24 *Defence*, vol. 1, *WJA*, 4:507.

25 *Defence*, vol. 1, *WJA*, 4:507–08.

and decisive balances, to preserve mankind from those horrible calamities which revolutions always bring with them."[26]

From Madison's perspective, Adams missed the point of Aristotle's criticism of Plato's theory of regime rotation in Book V, Chapter 12, of the *Politics*. Adams did not comprehend Aristotle's view of the importance of public opinion to regime stability and preservation. So enamored was he by the mechanical model of a three-way political scale representing balanced government that Adams did not see that the achievement of stability – and liberty – depends substantially and primarily on the opinions and mores of the citizens. Adams' praise of the British government, implicated in both Chapter 4 of the "Notes on Government" and the Party Press Essay "British Government," represented to Madison a kind of superficial analysis that reduces politics to the collision of governmental powers. Although Adams called himself a republican, his version of republicanism was not grounded in Madison's conception of popular sovereignty. In order to achieve the governmental balance he sought, Adams assigned merely a portion – or what he called an "essential share" – of sovereignty to the people.[27] Indeed, for Adams, sovereignty rested in the government – more specifically, in the legislature – in which the people were to possess one-third of the sovereign authority.[28] With this tenet of Adams' version of republicanism in mind, Madison intended in the "Notes" to show that something much more than an equilibrium in the powers of government was needed to secure a free republic.

What was also needed, Madison believed, was "an equilibrium in the interests & passions of the Society." Like Montesquieu, Madison sought to render the various passions and claims of men and groups unable to destabilize the political order. Departing from Montesquieu's analysis, however, Madison envisioned the idea of an equilibrium in the passions and interests within society not merely for the sake of preventing any single particular interest or party from concentrating political power in its hands, but he also intended this equilibrium to serve as a political and social environment in which public opinion could form and provide the primary stabilizing element of the political order. Moreover, this environment would allow for the refinement and enlargement of

[26] *Defence*, vol. 1, *WJA*, 4:508–09.

[27] Writing to Samuel Adams on October 18, 1790, John Adams remarked: "Whenever I use the word republic with approbation, I mean a government in which the people have collectively, or by representation, an essential share in the sovereignty" (*WJA*, 6:415). Cf. Gordon Wood, *The Creation of the American Republic, 1776–1787* (Chapel Hill: University of North Carolina Press, 1969), 585.

[28] See Madison's discussion in "Parties," *MJM*, 249; *PJM*, 14:197–99, which is apparently directed at Adams' theory of balanced orders in government; cf. Madison's discussion of parties in Chapter 1 of the "Notes of Government," on which this *National Gazette* essay is based (*MJM*, 129; *PJM*, 14:160).

the public views, thereby reclaiming for public opinion its rightful place as the sovereign authority in republican government.[29]

In Aristotle's *Politics* and in Barthélemy's commentary on Aristotle's *Politics*, Madison identified support for his understanding of the overarching influence of public opinion on the preservation of political orders. Barthélemy devoted an entire and lengthy chapter to the subject of regime preservation and destruction in *Voyage* (Volume 5, Chapter 62), within which he focused almost exclusively on Aristotle's discussion of the issue. Summarizing Aristotle's analysis, he discussed the influence of territorial size, foreign danger, public opinion, laws, customs, and mores (including education, religion, slavery, and dependent territories) on the stability of government and the liberty of the citizens. Barthélemy's attention to the causes of regime preservation and destruction reflects an approach to politics that follows Aristotle's practical treatment in Books IV–VI of the *Politics*. Madison deliberately adopted this same practical approach in the "Notes." "On the basis of the regimes collected together," Aristotle wrote,

> let us attempt to contemplate what sorts of things preserve and destroy cities, what sorts of things do so for each of the regimes, and through what causes some regimes are governed nobly, others in the contrary way. For once these matters have been contemplated, we might perhaps understand better also what sort of regime is best, and how each regime has been ordered, and by making use of what laws and customs.[30]

In contrast to Aristotle's discussion of the best regime in the *Politics*, his treatment of political phenomena in Books IV–VI places the initial emphasis on stability and regime preservation. The consideration of justice in these books emerges within the context of the concern for political stability, pointing to the explication of political justice as a combination of natural and conventional right as set forth in Book V of the *Nicomachean Ethics*.[31] Regimes that act contrary – or appear to act contrary – to the laws, mores, and customs of the people tend to be unstable and short lived, while those that cultivate the favor of public opinion are generally more stable and longer lasting.

Book V of the *Politics* takes up the subject of the destruction and preservation of regimes generally, inquiring into the causes of stasis in each type and

[29] "Notes on Government," *MJM*, 127; 134; *PJM*, 14:158–59; 161.

[30] Aristotle, *Nicomachean Ethics*, trans. Robert C. Bartlett and Susan D. Collins (Chicago: University of Chicago Press, 2011), X:9, 234–35.

[31] In *Thomism and Aristotelianism* (Chicago: University of Chicago Press, 1952), Harry V. Jaffa writes: "We refer, first, to Aristotle's statement at the end of Book IV [*NE*, 1128b22], concerning shame: the good man will defer to the standard of common opinion, even if it be wide of the truth. And, as to changing the constitution, we may quote a passage from the *Politics*, concerning revolutions: 'And of all men those who excel in virtue would most justifiably stir up faction, *though they are the least given to doing so*.' [*Politics*, 1301a40] Aristotle does not, of course, say that good men never revolt, but it is apparent that they would never do so except in extreme cases" (181–82).

their particular effects on regime change as well as the factors that engender stability or instability that are common to all governmental forms. In the passage at V:12 specifically cited by Madison, Aristotle took issue with Socrates' theory of the cycles of regimes (as presented in Book VIII of Plato's *Republic*), arguing instead that there are numerous causes of stasis in government and, thus, there is no fixed pattern of regime rotation. According to Madison's reading of this passage of the *Politics*, Aristotle demonstrated how regime alteration was different in some of the states of ancient Greece as a result of the influence of public opinion.

Madison may have come to this conclusion as a result of his own independent reading of Aristotle's *Politics* or he may have adopted or felt supported in this interpretation after reading Barthélemy's account in *Voyage*. Regarding Aristotle's claim that tyrannical governments tend to be short lived but that there are historical examples of such political orders enduring for some time – namely, the tyrannies of Sicyon, Corinth, Athens, and Syracuse – Barthélemy interprets Aristotle to argue that tyranny has maintained its authority at Sicyon and Corinth for a substantial period of time due to the esteem and confidence of the people in the cities' rulers. In other words, the cause of these tyrannies' relative longevity was the favorable influence of public opinion.[32] Whereas tyrants generally seek to instill modest thoughts in and distrust among their subjects, rendering them incapable of concerted action, in the longer-lived tyrannies, the rulers sought "popularity with the many" and so were able to extend their rule.[33] Thus, we learn in Book V, Chapter 11, of the *Politics* that with regard to the primary *practical* question of political stability, the most important consideration must be the climate of public opinion and the substantial influence it has on the preservation or destruction of political orders.[34]

Aristotle continued to develop this theme at *Politics* V:12, claiming that there are a number of examples of stasis that do not follow the Socratic/Platonic theory of the cycle of regimes. In the oligarchic regime of Carthage, for example, one might expect it to have undergone a revolution into a democratic government. But it did not, for Carthage was a "well-organized regime" in which "the people voluntarily acquiesce in the arrangement of the regime." In Carthage, the rulers "acquired the friendship of the people" and there was no significant "factional conflict."[35] Moreover, despite the fact that Carthage and

[32] *Voyage*, 5:233; cf. *Voyage*, 5:230–33. At *Voyage* 5:233, Barthélemy writes: "The sovereigns who governed those two states obtained the esteem or the confidence of their people, some by their military talents, others by their affability, and others by the respect which, on certain occasions, they paid to the laws. Every where else tyranny has subsisted a longer or a shorter time, according as it has more or less neglected to conceal itself."

[33] Aristotle, *Politics*, V:11, 175–78.

[34] See, for example, *Politics*, III:14, 109; IV:10, 133; V:10. See the thoughtful discussion of this subject by Mary P. Nichols in her excellent work *Citizens and Statesmen: A Study of Aristotle's Politics* (Savage, MD: Rowman & Littlefield, 1991), 105–14.

[35] Aristotle, *Politics*, II:11, 81; VI:5, 190.

Sparta were two very different types of regimes, Aristotle drew a resemblance between them based on the significance of the force of public opinion, thereby adding complexity and nuance to his earlier regime classification.[36]

A set of notes Madison wrote in preparation for the Virginia Ratifying Convention of 1788, which is designated by the editors of *The Papers of James Madison* as "Additional Memorandums on Ancient and Modern Confederacies" but which Madison titled "Memorandums for the Convention of Virginia in 1788 on the federal Constitution,"[37] illustrates Madison's attention to Aristotle's discussion of the causes of destruction and preservation of regimes three years prior to his composition of the "Notes on Government" (and at least two years before he studied Barthélemy's account of Aristotle's republican theory in *Voyage*).[38] In these notes, Madison cited Aristotle's *Politics* and stressed the discussion of the longevity and lack of factional conflict or tyranny experienced by the Carthaginian regime for a period of 500 years (discussed at *Politics* II:11). He included an examination of the durable regimes of Sparta (again citing Aristotle's commentary) and Rome. Interestingly, this portion of the "Memorandums for the Convention of Virginia in 1788" is not devoted to the subject of ancient or modern confederacies at all; Sparta, Carthage, and Rome were not confederacies. Madison's concern in this section of these notes is with the division of authority in each political order, the existence and makeup of the senate as a representative institution, and its election by and degree of accountability to the people. These themes are linked to the capacity of a political order to avoid revolution and maintain its constitution. In *Federalist* 14 and 63 and in the "Notes on Government," Madison again addressed these themes. In the "Notes," he explicitly set forth and developed more fully what is implicit in his earlier writings – namely, the correlation between representative accountability and the force of public opinion and the effect of public opinion on governmental stability and longevity.

In Barthélemy's discussion at *Voyage* 5:62, Anacharsis elaborated on the relationship between the power of public opinion and regime preservation that he learned from Aristotle's political treatise. The central importance of Aristotle's *Politics* to Anacharsis' understanding of political phenomena is revealed in the exaggerated literary conceit Barthélemy employed in this chapter: Anacharsis not only engaged in discussions about politics with Aristotle directly, but he also allegedly received from him an advance copy of the *Politics*, which he closely studied and from which he composed a précis. "The most absolute authority becomes lawful if the subjects consent to establish or support it," Anacharsis wrote.[39] At Politics V:12, Aristotle taught that by gaining the "confidence of their people," some tyrants have maintained their rule longer

[36] Aristotle, *Politics*, II:11, 80. [37] *PJM*, 10:273–83.

[38] "Memorandums for the Convention of Virginia in 1788 on the federal Constitution," *MJM*, 205–13; *PJM*, 10:274–83.

[39] *Voyage*, 5:62, 225.

than is usually the case with tyrannical government.[40] Most governments, however, are combined primarily of democratic and oligarchic elements and are characterized by a factious rivalry between the people and the nobles. These "divisions have almost everywhere corrupted the primitive constitution," as the examples of Megara and the Italian republics demonstrate (which Madison argued in the first chapter of the "Notes," citing Barthélemy and the authority of Aristotle).[41]

According to Aristotle, in their simple forms, neither oligarchy nor democracy is stable or long lasting.[42] The most stable governmental type is the mixed regime that inclines more toward popular rule. There is less factional conflict in regimes "inclining more toward the multitude" because the majority of citizens are equal and more content.[43] The crux of Aristotle's argument is that the great virtue of the democratic polity is the support it is given by the greater part of the citizenry – or, in other words, by public opinion. "The part of the city that wants the regime to continue must be superior to the part not wanting it."[44]

Contrary to those who interpreted the classical mixed constitution or polity as rooted in class rivalry, Barthélemy understood Aristotle to seek, as much as possible, to "stifle in [the citizens'] hearts that odious rivalry which has been the destruction of the greater part of the republics of Greece." Even better than reconciling the claims of the few rich and many poor is to favor the "middle estate" and to render it as powerful as possible. Those of a moderate competency neither feel the "contemptuous pride" of the rich nor the "low envy" of the poor. A political order composed of a large middle class will be less subject to faction than any other, for the preponderance of this estate will secure it against the designs of injustice of the rich and the poor. Moreover, the majority of the citizens will exhibit a strong attachment to the republic, thereby exerting all their efforts to ensure its preservation and duration, "which is the first element and best proof of a good constitution."[45]

Barthélemy thus described Aristotle's conception of the best practicable regime as one in which public opinion acts as a safeguard against the deleterious effects of faction and the problem of regime degeneration. Characterized by the active political participation of the citizens, this regime derives an unparalleled advantage from the support of public opinion and constitutes the most stable and free type of political order. Moreover, it achieves a high degree of

[40] *Voyage*, 5:62, 233.

[41] Barthélemy went on to discuss constitutions that are better organized and have achieved greater stability and longevity, offering Sparta, Carthage, and Crete as examples of aristocratic/oligarchic governments that have enjoyed longevity. Despite its advantages, the Carthaginian constitution also contained vices that ultimately led to its destruction, which Aristotle predicted but did not witness. Barthélemy also noted that Polybius considered usurpations of authority by the people to be the chief cause of its decline – precisely the assessment Madison made in both the "Additional Memorandums" and the "Notes on Government."

[42] Aristotle, *Politics*, V:1, 148–49.

[43] Aristotle, *Politics*, V:7, 160; V:1, 149.

[44] Aristotle, *Politics*, IV:12, 136.

[45] *Voyage*, 5:62, 267–68.

justice and actually surpasses the theoretically best regime in its capacity for self-renewal and durability. In Aristotle's illustration of the best practicable polity, Barthélemy and Madison discovered the way in which the power of public opinion alters the conventional rotation of regimes.

Drawing from his study of Aristotle and the Classics, Barthélemy concluded that the "unanimous decision of legislators and philosophers, of all the Greeks, and perhaps of all nations" was that "the solid foundations of the tranquility and happiness of states" are to be found in "the institutions which form the citizens, and give activity to their minds" and in "the public voice when it makes an exact distribution of contempt and esteem." Impotent in and of themselves, the laws are empowered only by the force of public morality. The "difference in the *moeurs* of a people is sufficient to destroy the best of constitutions, or to rectify the most defective," Barthélemy argued, for *moeurs* "restrain the citizen by the fear of the public opinion."[46]

Like Montesquieu, Barthélemy understood that the central task Aristotle had assigned to students of politics was "to penetrate to the spirit of the laws, and to follow them in their effects." He did not, however, adopt Montesquieu's reformulation of the Aristotelian task. According to Barthélemy, Aristotle taught (at *Politics* IV:8) that the principle of the democratic regime is liberty – specifically, the liberty of the citizen. To prevent the degeneration of this principle into licentiousness and to perpetuate a popular constitution, the legislator must "ascend to first principles."[47] Barthélemy thus delineated Aristotle's account of the best popular government, giving due consideration to the size of the territory, the population, the various occupations of the citizens, and their dispositions. "Liberty does not consist in doing what one wants, as is maintained in certain democracies," he wrote, citing Book V of Aristotle's *Politics*, "but only in doing what the laws enjoin, which secure the independence of each individual."[48] The phraseology Barthélemy used in this passage was clearly intended to bring to readers' minds the passage in Book 11, Chapter 3, of Montesquieu's *The Spirit of Laws*. There, Montesquieu wrote that even though "in democracies the people seem to act as they please, … political liberty does not consist in an unlimited freedom." Rather, "in societies directed by laws, liberty can consist only in being able to do what we ought to will, and in not being coerced to do what we ought not to will."[49] Montesquieu

[46] *Voyage*, 5:277. I have retained Barthélemy's word *moeurs* rather than the translator's "manners" here because it conveys a moral depth to this phenomenon, which the English word "manners" tends to lack.

[47] *Voyage*, 5:253. [48] See Aristotle, *Politics*, V:9, 167.

[49] Montesquieu, *SOL*, 11:3, 150. Nugent translates the last part of this phrase as "liberty can consist only in the power of doing what we ought to will"; I have altered this to reflect Montesquieu's contextual use of *pouvoir* as an infinitive and not as a noun. I am grateful to Paul A. Rahe for pointing this out to me. In the forthcoming translation of *The Spirit of the Laws* by William B. Allen, the translation is consistent with Rahe's observation: "It is true that, in democracies, the people appear to do whatever they wish, but political liberty does not consist of

then distinguished between liberty and independence, declaring that "liberty is the right to do everything the laws permit."[50] Although Barthélemy's passage is clearly imitative of Montesquieu's and despite citations to *The Spirit of Laws* elsewhere in this chapter and throughout the *Voyage*, Barthélemy did not cite Montesquieu's text at this juncture of his work. Instead, he restored the classical import of the dictum, which taught that all citizens should enjoy equal liberty, that they "shall participate in the sovereign authority," and that their freedom will be in proportion to their virtue.[51]

Barthélemy's subtle strategy in this section of Chapter 62 is to remind readers of Montesquieu's definition of liberty and at the same time mimic the clever strategy of displacement the author of *The Spirit of Laws* employed in Book 11, Chapter 3. Here, Montesquieu's discussion would remind attentive readers about Aristotle's definition of liberty and its relationship to law at *Politics* V:9. But instead of adopting Aristotle's manner of thinking about liberty, Montesquieu supplanted it with a radically new formulation. Montesquieu's redefinition of liberty represents the abandonment of the core of Aristotle's teaching regarding citizenship and participation in the ruling authority of the regime. In imitating Montesquieu's artful stratagem, Barthélemy displaced the Baron's new conception of liberty and restored the classical one.

Like Barthélemy, Madison rejected the views of those who employed the language of "republicanism" but were willing to give up the classical notion of a genuinely participatory and free citizenry. Rather, he believed that the authority of public opinion, which Aristotle had identified as a principal source of stability and freedom in the classical polity, must be reclaimed and reconfigured to fit the realities of the modern world. In essence, he believed he had discovered a way to achieve political liberty in a large republic. Specifically, he sought to achieve what Montesquieu called "liberty in relation to the constitution," which consists of protection against the abuse of power and is achieved by the separation of powers and the rule of law. He also sought to achieve what Montesquieu termed "liberty in relation to the subject" or citizen, which

doing whatever one wishes. In a state – that is, in a society in which there are laws – liberty can only consist in being able to do that which one ought to wish and in not being coerced to do that which one ought not to wish." I have also substituted Allen's translation of "constraint" as "coerced" rather than Nugent's translation of "constrained" in this passage.

50 Barthélemy wrote at *Voyage* 5:62: "… la liberté ne consiste pas à faire tout ce que l'on veut, comme on le soutient dans certaines démocraties; mais à ne faire que ce que veulent les lois qui assurent l'indépendance de chaque particulier." Compare this with Montesquieu, *L'Esprit des Lois* 11:3: "… dans les démocraties le peuple paroît faire ce qu'il veut; mais la liberté politique ne consiste point à faire ce que l'on veut. Dans un État, c'est-à-dire dans une société où il y a des lois, la liberté ne peut consister qu'à pouvoir faire ce que l'on doit vouloir, et à n'être point contraint de faire ce que l'on ne doit pas vouloir. Il faut se mettre dans l'esprit ce que c'est que l'indépendance, et ce que c'est que la liberté. La liberté est le droit de faire tout ce que les lois permettent."

51 *Voyage*, 5:261.

consists in security or the opinion of security – or, in other words, the sense that one is not subject to the arbitrary power of another.[52] However, Madison did not reduce the idea of the liberty of the citizen merely to security or the opinion of security. Instead, he added to Montesquieu's idea of liberty-as-security the older notion of the citizen's liberty, which is manifest in the citizen's active participation in the sovereignty. Thus, rather than following Montesquieu in modifying the meaning of the citizen's liberty to fit a new account of republicanism, Madison modified the size of the republic to fit a full account of the citizen's liberty. He did this by making the republic *even larger* than Montesquieu had prescribed in order to accommodate an older version of liberty as collective self-government and to reclaim the guiding principle and spirit of republicanism.

SPIRIT OF GOVERNMENTS

Madison took up the central theme of Montesquieu's *The Spirit of Laws* in the Party Press Essay titled "Spirit of Governments."[53] He agreed with Montesquieu that the spirit of each governmental type is critical to understanding political phenomena. While "no government is perhaps reducible to a sole principle of operation" because most include a mixture of heterogeneous principles that influence their administration, as Montesquieu taught, it is still useful to analyze the various types of government and to "characterize them by the spirit which predominates in each," Madison argued.

Madison paid tribute to Montesquieu's recovery of a conception of politics that recognizes that the stability and character of a government depend, in the final analysis, on the general spirit of the nation. When the laws are in accord with the manners, mores, and customs of a nation, "the spirit engendered among the people will be the guiding spirit of that society, and it can be expected to preserve the people from harm."[54]

In *The Spirit of Laws*, Montesquieu divided governments into three major types – despotism, monarchy, and republic – based on the principles of fear, honor, and virtue, respectively.[55] He then proceeded to identify a new type of republic, which he illustrated by way of the British constitutional model. "The portion of truth blended with the ingenuity" of Montesquieu's system of regime classification, Madison wrote, "sufficiently justifies the admiration bestowed on [him]."[56]

In "Spirit of Governments," Madison also took up the project of classifying the chief political archetypes. He also offered three main types of government,

[52] Montesquieu, *SOL*, 11:4, 150; 12:2, 183–84.

[53] "Spirit of Governments," *MJM*, 256–257; *PJM*, 14:233–34.

[54] Ira O. Wade, *The Structure and Form of the French Enlightenment* (Princeton: Princeton University Press, 1977), I:435–36.

[55] Montesquieu, *SOL*, 3:1, 19–28.

[56] "Spirit of Governments," *MJM*, 256; *PJM*, 14:233.

but his classification is not the same as Montesquieu's. Why and in what respect did he disagree with Montesquieu's classification of regime types? Indeed, why was this divergence of views of such importance to Madison that he wrote and published an essay highlighting his quarrel with Montesquieu?

Madison's first type of government operates by a "permanent military force"; it is based on coercion and characterized by a spirit of submission in the people. The second type of government substitutes "the motive of private interest in place of public duty"; by corruption and bribery as well as the "power of the sword," it accommodates the avarice of the few rather than "the benefit of the whole." This government is an imposter and its boasted liberty of the many is but a ruse. Although Madison did not name Great Britain explicitly, he clearly implicated the English model in this description, registering his disagreement with Montesquieu's praise of the British constitution and his categorization of it as a republic.[57] In contrast, he presented his third governmental type – the genuine republic – which derives "its energy from the will of the society, and operat[es] by the reason of its measures, on the understanding and interest of the society."[58]

As Madison repeatedly argued throughout the founding period, in a genuine republic, the will of the government is dependent on the will of the society – and the will of the society is dependent on the reason of the society. In *Federalist* 51, for example, he claimed that the extent and structure of the government of the United States make it dependent on the will of the society; in *Federalist* 49, he declared that it is the reason of the public that ought to sit in judgment on public measures. In the "Notes on Government" and the Party Press Essays, he placed this motif at center stage, encapsulating it in the idea of the sovereignty of public opinion.

Derived from the will of the society, public opinion is the result of a process of public communication and deliberation that refines, enlarges, and transforms public views into the reason of the society. In turn, the reason of the society operates on the understanding and interest of the society. In Madison's conception, public opinion is not, as is generally thought today, a mere aggregate of the popular and fleeting views of the people. Rather, it is the result of the

57 Montesquieu, *SOL*, 19:27. With respect to the political-military nexus, Robert J. Morgan cites Montesquieu to demonstrate that the aim of modern warfare is the profit of ministers and merchants, accomplished via a symbiotic relationship between the political and military establishment on the one hand and commercial elites on the other, leaving "only the façade of liberty to cover the new prosperity." Morgan also cites here *WJM*, VI:94, 193 ("'Time Hath Found Us': The Jeffersonian Revolutionary Vision," *Journal of Politics* 38, no. 3 [1976]: 30–31). Cf. Morgan's penetrating discussion with respect to Madison's and Jefferson's belief that this dynamic of "imperialism and industrialization" characterized the British political system; the alternative model they advocated, Morgan argues, was founded on the political and economic independence of individuals and nations, resulting in a popular participatory government grounded in public opinion (30–35).

58 "Spirit of Governments," *MJM*, 257; *PJM*, 14:234.

"communication of their opinions"[59] through a political process designed to moderate the claims of citizen-participants and instill in them a sense of the conditions of freedom. Public opinion is the expression of a particular view of justice held by the community; it is made tangible in the way of life of a people. Public opinion manifests itself in the predominant spirit of the society, which links the way of life of a people to the animating idea or principle of their political order. To the extent that public opinion accords with the principle of the regime, it provides support and stability to the political order. As such, public opinion is, as Aristotle recognized, a particularly powerful influence on the preservation or destruction of the constitution.

In "Spirit of Governments," Madison acknowledged Montesquieu's significant contribution to the science of politics, albeit declaring Montesquieu's second-tier status in the pantheon of political wisdom. Montesquieu was neither a Newton nor a Locke – "who established immortal systems, the one in matter, the other in mind." Rather, in political science, he was more akin to what Bacon was in "universal science." "He lifted the veil from the venerable errors that enslaved opinion and pointed the way to those luminous truths of which he had but a glimpse himself."[60] Like Locke (whose contribution to epistemology, not politics, is lauded by Madison), Montesquieu wrote during a period before the principles of liberty and governmental structure "were illuminated by the events and discussions which distinguish a very recent period."[61] Indeed, according to the comte de Mirabeau: "It had been Montesquieu's fate to write his great book just ten years before the dawn of science. Consequently, Montesquieu had overlooked the key to what went on in public life – the root both of the resistance to change and of its motive force – opinion."[62] Moreover, Madison claimed that, like Locke, Montesquieu was "warped by a regard to the particular government of England" and that the Frenchman's admiration bordered on "idolatry."[63] In *The Federalist*, Madison had made a similar claim regarding Montesquieu's overzealous admiration of England's government, claiming that for Montesquieu, the British constitution was "what Homer has been to the didactic writers on epic poetry." Just as "the latter have considered the work of the immortal bard as the perfect model from which the principles and rules of the epic art were to be drawn, and by which all similar works were to be judged," so too, apparently, did Montesquieu view "the Constitution of England as the standard, or to use his own expression, as the mirror of political liberty."[64]

59 "Property," *MJM*, 263; *PJM*, 14:266.

60 "Spirit of Governments," *MJM*, 256; *PJM*, 14:233.

61 "Helvedius No. I," *PJM*, 15:68.

62 Quoted in J. A. W. Gun, *Queen of the World: Opinion in the Public Life of France From the Renaissance to the Revolution* (Oxford: Voltaire Foundation, 1995), 263.

63 "Helvedius No. I," *PJM*, 15:68.

64 *Federalist* 47:269–70. According to Paul A. Rahe, the conclusion that Montesquieu profoundly admired the British government was in accord with a commonly accepted opinion of his time.

According to Montesquieu, the English model – or at least this government as he creatively imagined it as the archetype of modern republicanism – provided an alternative to the classical republican model, for it offered a new way to conceptualize a solution to the political problem of the opposing claims to rule.[65] In Montesquieu's original tripartite regime classification, he also named a principle for each governmental type, although he substituted a predominant passion (or "spring") for a ruling opinion. As such, Montesquieu does not classify governments in terms of a substantive principle or opinion about justice held by the predominant part of the political order. Furthermore, when he delineated the foundations of his new republic, he deliberately avoided identifying its principle and challenged his readers to understand his reasons for the omission. "But we must not always exhaust a subject, so as to leave no work at all for the reader," Montesquieu wrote. "My business is not to make people read, but to make them think."[66]

Accordingly, we are not told what principle informs the British constitution. However, in Book 11, Chapter 5, of *The Spirit of Laws*, Montesquieu evocatively pronounces that the British constitution is the only one that has liberty as its *direct object*. Madison understood Montesquieu to teach that the basis for this accomplishment is the separation of the powers of government, which, by juxtaposing and checking the interests and ambitions of men in government, prevents the concentration of political power and preserves liberty in relation to the constitution. In Book 19, Chapter 27, of *The Spirit of Laws*, he discussed the "two visible powers" in this nation – the legislative and the executive powers – to which men attach themselves and form parties, albeit fluctuating attachments due to the dynamics of holding political office. This relentless two-party competition, which Montesquieu witnessed during his stay in England, was the Court-Country party rivalry that Hume discussed at some length in his *Essays*.[67] The result of this partisan conflict and general social restlessness, Montesquieu taught, was a kind of political equipoise that contributes to the security (or opinion of security) of the individual. In effect,

Montesquieu's support for the English system, however, was not unequivocal; while the English constitution, as a type, had great potential for liberty, Montesquieu did not necessarily think this potential was a reality actualized in England at the time (*Montesquieu and the Logic of Liberty*, 41–42, 96–100).

[65] For Aristotle, the principle that informs each type of regime is manifested in a claim to rule (i.e., an opinion) based on a particular conception of justice. For example, the principle or aspiration of aristocracy is excellence; of oligarchy, it is wealth. Liberty is the principle of democracy, which is generally couched in terms of numerical equality and the requirement of popular participation and rule (Aristotle, *Politics*, VI:2, 183).

[66] Montesquieu, *SOL*, 11:20, 182.

[67] See, for example, Michael A. Mosher's discussion of Montesquieu's treatment of the Court and Country party rivalry: "Monarchy's Paradox: Honor in the Face of Sovereign Power," in *Montesquieu's Science of Politics: Essays on The Spirit of Laws*, eds. David W. Carrithers, Michael A. Mosher, and Paul A. Rahe (Lanham, MD: Rowman & Littlefield, 2001), 183–85.

Montesquieu advanced this conflict model of politics in order to fragment governmental power and deter the formation of any single predominating opinion in the political order, thereby substituting the rule of impartial law for the arbitrary rule of men.

By this method, Montesquieu was able to dispense with the traditional primary task of republican self-government – at least as self-government was understood by the Classics. The new republic need not engage in the educative task of shaping the minds and mores of the citizenry, which in fact had rarely succeeded in producing stable, long-lasting polities in the ancient world. The classical polities had failed largely because of the predominantly self-interested character of men and their tendency to divide into political groups along these lines. In contrast to the classical model, Montesquieu's republic would allow all the passions, prejudices, and interests of men to flow freely. This republican nation would achieve its object of liberty, deriving benefit from the free and active expression of unmodified and even mistaken opinions. "In a free nation," Montesquieu wrote, "it is very often a matter of indifference whether individuals reason well or ill; it is sufficient that they do reason: hence springs that liberty which is a security from the effects of these reasonings."[68]

According to William B. Allen, Montesquieu believed that there is no way to resolve the constitution-destroying conflict between the rich and the poor in a government based on the rule of men. Hence, Montesquieu conceptualized a new kind of republic whose end is the liberty of all, achieved by a constitutional structure that functionally separates the powers of government, thereby dispersing power in such a way that no single man or group of men possess the sole ability to rule. The functional separation of powers has the effect of opposing will against will and raw power against raw power, thereby moderating and limiting the impact of power on individuals.[69] Although Montesquieu grounded his political theory in a conception of human nature that involves the freedom of the human soul and the concomitant moral requirements of self-government, he did not take the subsequent step of assigning a role to virtue, as the classical philosophers did.[70] Instead of the teleological perspective of the Classics, in which self-government consists in making choices directed to the end of virtuous activity, Montesquieu conceived of self-government as simply self-directed activity. The necessary condition for self-government is the individual's opinion of security; in turn, the fundamental criterion for the opinion

[68] Montesquieu, *SOL*, 19:27, 315.

[69] As William B. Allen notes in his thoughtful and provocative essay "Translating Power: Commentary on *Spirit of the Laws*" (unpublished manuscript), Print, 16, 32–35, Montesquieu "translates" or modifies the effects of power. Raw power, or *pouvoir*, is declawed, becoming *puissant*, or constitutionally prescribed authority whose exercise is beneficial to liberty and individual security (or, at least, the perception of security).

[70] Allen, "Translating Power," 11–12. At *SOL* 11:6, 154, Montesquieu wrote: "As in a country of liberty, every man who is supposed a free agent ought to be his own governor."

of security is the capacity to limit the power of government, which is attained by a deliberate constitutional design. As such, Montesquieu did not argue, as the Classics did, that natural justice constitutes the standard of well-constituted regimes. Consequently, although Montesquieu grounded his conception of self-government in the nature of man, he arrived at its meaning and its place in political life "in a very non-Aristotelian way."[71] In sum, Montesquieu's liberal, nonteleological conception of liberty and self-government embodied his vision of *political* excellence, which is achieved not by education in singular institutions or a common regime principle but by deliberate institutional arrangements that protect individuals against the abuse of power.

Despite Montesquieu's rejection of a teleological conception of liberty, he did not reduce the human condition or political aspirations to formulaic political theory, as some other modern thinkers had done before him. Indeed, Montesquieu learned from the Classics the paramount importance of the spirit of the regime. But the problem for Montesquieu was that the spirit of the government was a manifestation of the predominant opinion about justice in any given political order, and the predominant view of justice in most types of government tends to favor some individuals and leads to the oppression of others.

Montesquieu's sociology of politics followed classical political philosophy in recognizing that the spirit of a political order results from the things that form opinion – for example, *moeurs*, manners, religion, laws, and the maxims of government. However, Montesquieu sharply departed from the Classics in positing a dynamic, jarring constitutional and societal environment that simultaneously secures liberty and enervates political opinion, rendering the warring passions and interests of men harmless. This was a new and quite radical way to conceptualize the achievement of a spirit of moderation in the nation.

Madison rightly understood the various principles of governments in Montesquieu's classification scheme (including in the new republic) to be manifestations of human passions. Indeed, Montesquieu had made this explicit in *The Spirit of Laws*:

> There is this difference between the nature and principle of government, that the former is that by which it is constituted, the latter that by which it is made to act. One is its particular structure, and the other the human passions which set it in motion.[72]

Madison believed that Montesquieu had attempted to solve the problem of the destructive conflict between the opposing views of justice in the political order, especially the age-old battle between the oligarchs and democrats that had destroyed many an ancient polity, by replacing it with a new template

[71] Allen, "Translating Power," 41, 53. See also Thomas L. Pangle, *Montesquieu's Philosophy of Liberalism: A Commentary on The Spirit of the Laws* (Chicago: University of Chicago Press, 1989), especially Chapters 4 and 5.

[72] Montesquieu, *SOL*, 3:1, 19.

for political science based on Newton's discoveries. In essence, Montesquieu applied Newton's theory of material physical action and reaction to the political and social realm.[73] Montesquieu thus sought to solve the problem of instability caused by the conflicting opinions, passions, and interests of men by setting them against each other in order to cancel out their powerful and all-too-often destructive effects. He saw in the English system something of a template for his vision of Newtonian mechanics applied to politics; the British model replicated Newtonian harmonics through dissonance in both the operation of its constitutional institutions and the clash and competition of social interests and passions within the nation.[74] Montesquieu's aim, then, was not to resolve the *inquiétude* caused by the rival interests and warring passions and parties that characterized the English system but rather to recognize, accept, and take advantage of it.[75]

It is on the basis of this understanding of politics, I believe, that Montesquieu did not identify the principle of the British political order; there are many diverse and even rival passions and interests at play in this nation. In contrast to the regimes that are each dominated by a single, unique principle, which Montesquieu discussed in the original tripartite classification he presented in Book 3 of *The Spirit of Laws*, we learn that the new republic is constituted by "principles."[76] In other words, there is no single dominant, operative principle in Montesquieu's new republic.

[73] See Montesquieu, *SOL*, 5:1, 40, where Montesquieu argues that political motion is similar to physical motion: "And thus it is in mechanics, that action is always followed by reaction." Ana Samuel points out that Montesquieu's discussion here concerns the predictable activity that results from the relationship between the laws and the principles in the three archetypal governmental forms; in the English republican model or free regime, there is constant "internal agitation" that "is marked by an almost chaotic, unpredictable 'changeableness' of its government" ("The Design of Montesquieu's *The Spirit of the Laws*," 310).

[74] According to R. L. Nadeau, R. Aron argued that "Montesquieu's essential idea is not the separation of powers in the judicial sense but what might be called the *equilibrium of social forces* as a condition of political freedom" (*The Environmental Endgame: Mainstream Economics, Ecological Disaster, and Human Disaster* [Piscataway, NJ: Rutgers University Press, 2006], 85).

[75] In *Considerations*, Montesquieu wrote: "What is called union in a body politic is a very equivocal thing. The true kind is a union of harmony, whereby all the parts, however opposed they may appear, cooperate for the general good of society – as dissonances in music cooperate in producing overall concord. In a state where we seem to see nothing but commotion there can be union – that is, a harmony resulting in happiness, which alone is true peace. It is as with the parts of the universe, eternally linked together by the action of some and the reaction of others" (*Considerations on the Decline of the Romans*, 93–94). According to Alan Macfarlane, Montesquieu set forth the "idea of a productive tension, a harmony created through dissonance, a balanced and dynamic equilibrium of forces" (*Montesquieu and the Making of the Modern World* [CreateSpace Independent Publishing Platform, 2013], www.alanmacfarlane.com/TEXTS/Montesquieu_final.pdf). Originally published in Alan Macfarlane, *The Riddle of the Modern World: Of Liberty, Wealth, and Equality* (New York: Palgrave Macmillan, 2000).

[76] In *The Spirit of Laws*, Montesquieu wrote in Book 11, Chapter 5 (156), that "We shall presently examine the *principles* on which this liberty is founded; if they are sound, liberty will appear in its highest perfection" [emphasis added]. In Book 19, Chapter 27 (325), he remarked: "I have

In Madison's view, Montesquieu failed to see the way in which the *end* of liberty can be achieved in a government in which the *operative principle* is liberty. As a consequence, Montesquieu sacrificed the *principle* and *spirit* of republicanism, and he substituted in their place a constitutional structure that channels private interests and jealous passions to achieve the *end* of liberty. Montesquieu's *new spirit* of republicanism seeks to achieve liberty without being informed by the particular idea or principle of justice that defines republican liberty. The new spirit of republicanism, then, is not the manifestation of a common opinion; it is, rather, characterized by a restless attentiveness (*inquiétude*) that accompanies the conflict-ridden action and reaction of self-interested individuals and partisan groups in free societies. Over and above this political dissonance, there is a general spirit of moderation and cooperation "for the general good" that might be called "the spirit of laws." Indeed, one could say that in Montesquieu's science of politics, the classical conception of the spirit of republican citizens is replaced by the general spirit of laws and, thus, the very apropos title of his great work.[77]

Madison understood Montesquieu to advance a political design that secures liberty by pitting interest against interest, passion against passion, and ambition against ambition. Madison adopted this dissonant Newtonian politics of conflict that he found in the pages of *The Spirit of Laws*, but he did so as a means to establish the necessary but not sufficient conditions for republican liberty and self-government. Unlike Montesquieu, he did not regard as possible or choiceworthy the substitution of the spirit of laws for the vital human spirit of republican citizens. Madison believed that Montesquieu had contributed greatly to thinking through the political questions in the changed economic and social conditions of the modern era, but he judged his provisions for the attainment of liberty deficient and his conception of self-government defective when measured against what he considered the true standards of republicanism. His aspiration to recapture the classical idea of the spirit of

spoken in the eleventh book of a free people, and have given the *principles* of their constitution" [emphasis added]. See Ana J. Samuel's discussion of this in "The Design of Montesquieu's *The Spirit of the Laws*," 310. Paul A. Rahe and William B. Allen read Montesquieu differently on this point, with each concluding that Montesquieu's republic is driven by a different overarching single principle. According to Allen, liberty is the principle of Montesquieu's modern republic. In Rahe's view, "partisanship" constitutes the principle of the English constitution (*Montesquieu and the Logic of Liberty*, 99–117, and *passim*). See also Diana Schaub's review of Rahe's *Montesquieu and the Logic of Liberty*, in which she argues that her own hunch is that Montesquieu was suggesting that the new republic could "dispense with a regime-specific motive force." Rather, "the free flow of man's self-interested passions channeled through the proper institutions is sufficient" (*Claremont Review of Books* (Spring 2010), http://claremont.org/index.php?act=crbArticle&id=500#.U8s4-vldWSp).

[77] As Paul Carrese has deftly put it, instead of seeking a principle or "law of the human spirit," as Aristotle did, Montesquieu followed in the steps of Newton and analyzed "a spirit of laws" (Carrese, "Montesquieu's Complex Natural Right and Moderate Liberalism: The Roots of American Moderation," *Polity* 36, no. 2 [2004]: 227–50, 234).

republicanism, however, did not mean that he desired to institute the kind of harsh regulations and singular institutions that Lycurgus or the Romans employed to train the citizens in virtue. In fact, he was as firmly committed as Montesquieu was to the creation of a political order in which individual conscience and the freedom of the individual are recognized and respected. Still, Madison did believe that political legitimacy and political excellence are grounded in natural justice and the moral principles that constitute it. Moreover, he sought to construct the political architecture of republican government with a purpose substantially beyond liberal pluralism; in this latter objective, he departed consciously and significantly from Montesquieu.

Madison believed that the political order, like the individual human soul, is answerable to a standard of reason and natural right, and he framed the unique political challenge as that of placing power and right on the same side.[78] He certainly rejected the view that it does not matter whether republican citizens reason well or reason badly.[79] Madison's notion of "the reason of the public" is not a mere aggregate of the selfish interests and prejudicial passions of the people, that, in canceling each other out, results in a public decision that is merely an epiphenomenon of the sense of the community. That is why communication and the effects of communicative activity occupy such a central position in his political theory. His main criticism of Montesquieu in the Party Press Essay "Spirit of Governments," in fact, is the French theorist's neglect (or conscious abandonment) of the concern to cultivate the central principle and spirit of republican government. This, Madison believed, could only be accomplished by educating public opinion in the moral principles of republicanism, thereby establishing a political system in which the will of the society is based on the reason of the society.

Thus, unlike Montesquieu, Madison was not content simply to counteract the effects of partial interests and prejudicial passions, but he sought, to the extent possible, to refine and unite the sentiments and opinions of a republican people via a political process erected on the basis of the active sovereignty of the citizens. In a free society, the primary responsibility for the "defence of public liberty" does not depend on institutions but rather on the soundness of public opinion. This requires, at least in critical times, the people to make a "common cause" in spite "of circumstantial and artificial distinctions."[80]

In Madison's typology of government, he described the first type of government as one based on military force, the second type as grounded in

[78] This natural moral hierarchy is analogous for the Christian believer to the theological hierarchy discussed by Madison in his "Memorial and Remonstrance," which makes human beings accountable for their actions to their Creator. In the exercise of his free will, an individual is answerable to reason and conscience. See *PJM*, 8:298–304; see also Madison's discussion of power and right in "Vices of the Political System of the United States," *MJM*, 196–204; *PJM*, 9:350–51.

[79] Montesquieu, *SOL*, 19:27, 315.

[80] "A Candid State of Parties," *MJM*, 268; *PJM*, 14:372.

self-interest, and the third type as based on deliberate public opinion. Madison's schematic is a rejection of Montesquieu's substitution of passion for opinion as the determinative principle of classification. In this, Madison followed Hume in sustaining the classical view of the centrality of opinion in regime analysis. According to Hume, even in a despotic government, fear is not the primary principle, for even the despot must depend on the voluntary support of his military. "No man would have any reason to *fear* the fury of a tyrant," Hume wrote, "if he had no authority over any but from fear; since, as a single man, his bodily force can reach but a small way, and all the farther power he possesses must be founded either on our own opinion, or on the presumed opinion of others."[81] In the first type of government, Madison argued that oppressive military regimes breed a spirit of submission in the people. In the second category (Madison's description of the British model), private interest, partisanship, bribery, and corruption spawn a spirit of selfishness and avidity. The liberty that supposedly infuses it is merely a false liberty; it is not a government of the people, but one dominated by the few. As for republics truly worthy of the name, Madison contrasted the untempered power and self-serving ends of the pseudo-republican model of the second governmental type with his third type, which he described as a government based on the will of the society, whose will is subjected to the reason of the society. In "Republican Distribution of Citizens" (the essay immediately following "Spirit of Governments" in the *National Gazette*), Madison paints for his reader a portrait of the character and spirit of the genuine republican citizen.[82]

"Spirit of Governments" is a severe rebuke to those who would make partisan conflict and the rule of law a surrogate for the genuine liberty of the citizen and the sovereignty of public opinion. Madison's title ("Spirit of Governments") is a corrective to Montesquieu's title ("Spirit of Laws"), recovering the connection between the essential vitality of the regime that is actually embodied in the ruling authority. Montesquieu's attempt to apply Newtonian physics to solve the problem of raw power and its effect on regime destabilization – by reducing the problem to the motion and countermotion of the

[81] Hume, "Of the First Principles of Government," *Essays*, 34. Madison's regime classification in "Spirit of Governments" is an amplification of his claim in *Federalist* 49 that "all governments rest on opinion." See *Federalist* 49:282. In *Federalist* 49, Madison wrote: "If it be true that all governments rest on opinion ..." The conditional clause that starts the sentence has led some scholars to raise the question of whether Madison actually believed that all governments rest on opinion. I do not think Madison was undecided on the issue, as is clear in his discussion of the foundations of government in the Party Press Essays, particularly "Charters." In "Charters," Madison claimed: "All power has been traced up to opinion. The stability of all governments and security of all rights may be traced to the same source. The most arbitrary government is controuled where the public opinion is fixed" (*MJM*, 247–48; *PJM*, 14:192). Cf. "Vices of the Political System of the United States," *MJM*, 196–204; *PJM*, 9:345–58; "Public Opinion," *MJM*, 245; *PJM*, 14:170.

[82] The character and spirit of Madison's republican citizen is discussed on pp. 258–59 herein.

passions and interests to achieve moderation – meant abandoning the classical concern for educating the citizens and shaping their character. If Montesquieu adopted Newtonian dissonance as his standard, Madison used the idea of a societal equilibrium of the passions and interests as a means to create an environment hospitable to the refinement of public opinion. For Madison, raw power was not only to be modified in its effects, but in the properly constituted republic, the raw power of the majority was to be educated and modified in its substance, thereby meeting the fundamental challenge he had identified in "Vices of the Political System of the United States" – that of positioning power on the side of right. Deliberately moving beyond Montesquieu, Madison conceived of the active liberty of the citizens and the expression of the "reason of the public" as the manifestation of an opinion of republican right.

Indeed, according to Aristotle, "[t]he greatest of all the things that have been mentioned with a view to making regimes lasting... is education relative to the regimes."[83] "For there is no benefit in the most beneficial laws, even when these have been approved by all those engaging in politics, if they are not going to be habituated and educated in the regime." This requires attention to the spirit of the polity, Aristotle taught. "If the laws are popular, [the citizens must be educated and habituated] in a popular spirit, if oligarchic, in an oligarchic spirit." This is the case because all laws depend on the regime – that is, on the principle that manifests itself in the spirit that permeates the political order and gives it its particular character (*êthos*). "Spirit" is the phenomenon that "links up" the "hypothesis" of a given regime with its "*êthos*."[84] It is, in essence, the vital power that gives life and movement to the regime principle and manifests itself in the way of life of the polity.[85] Political analyses that proffer the rule of law as the solution to the political problem, based on a

[83] Aristotle, *Politics*, V:9, 167.

[84] See Aristotle, *Politics*, VIII:1; cf. Strauss, "Lectures on Aristotle's *Politics*," XVI:7–8. What we would today speak of as "personality," as in democratic or authoritarian personality, Strauss argued, Aristotle would have designated "*êthos*" or "character" (see *Politics*, VIII:1, 229). Earlier in Book VI of the *Politics*, Aristotle spoke of something similar, but not identical to, this notion when he discussed the "hypothesis" or originating principle. The hypothesis "is not identical with the ethos [*êthos*]," Strauss contended, "but there is a connection between the two. Aristotle did not deign to elaborate that, and we would have to do that. The word 'spirit' used by [Ernest Barker] in the translation is a kind of bridge between the two things. The hypothesis of democracy, we have learned, is freedom, and freedom has since a complicated meaning as stated in Book VI. There is a democratic ethos [*êthos*]. What links the two things we would call the democratic spirit. Aristotle does not have such a word." In commenting on the importance Aristotle attached to what is "distinctive and hence controversial" to each regime, Strauss remarked that "in our language we would say the spirit differs. ... Where we speak of spirit, Aristotle would say the end pursuit differs" (Lecture VII:6).

[85] See Aristotle, *Politics*, VIII:1, 229; cf. Strauss, "Lectures on Aristotle," XVI:7–8. Cf. my discussion of "spirit" as a linking phenomenon in *James Madison and the Spirit of Republican Self-Government*, xvi–xix; 156–75.

conception of politics in which reasonable laws rule – even though the individuals and groups that make up the state are not reasonable – evade the central issue: laws never simply rule. In every political order, law is the product of human legislators. In each regime, the rulers have a particular view of justice – whether the oligarchic view, the democratic view, a blend of these views, and so forth. The question of the fundamental opinion on which the society rests is always primary.[86] In every political order, there is an operative opinion about justice that is anterior to the laws and that is a manifestation of the spirit of the polity.

Barthélemy also read Aristotle's *Politics* to posit the idea of a particular spirit of each constitution; this spirit creates an "empire of *moeurs*" much more powerful than the force of the laws. Because the institutions that form the *moeurs* of the citizenry and "give activity to their minds" are more powerful than the laws, the citizens must be educated "in the principles which ... regulate their virtues, their opinions, their sentiments, and their behaviour"; they must be reared in the "spirit and love of the constitution."[87]

Madison reclaimed the classical perspective that in every political order, the laws are the product of the opinion of the human being or the group of human beings who possess the supreme political authority. Even in a government in which the rule of law is considered supreme, it is nonetheless men who make the law. Madison learned this, in fact, in his classes at the College of New Jersey from his mentor: Dr. John Witherspoon. In his lecture on the "Different Forms of Government," Witherspoon showed his indebtedness to Montesquieu by devoting significant time to a discussion of his political theory, including the need for the separation and distribution of powers in government. In his

[86] See Leo Strauss' analysis of the regime question in classical political philosophy in *Liberalism Ancient and Modern* (Chicago: University of Chicago Press, 1968), x; "Lectures on Aristotle's *Politics*," VII:3, VIII:7–8, IX:3, X:3. Cf. Harvey Mansfield's discussion of the distinction between the classical idea of regime and the notion of the impersonal modern state (*Machiavelli's Virtue* [Chicago: University of Chicago Press, 1988], 281–94). According to Mansfield, the modern impersonal state was an abstraction from personal to impersonal rule; it did not develop within the republican tradition but rather arose from an attitude of neutrality toward classical republicanism, which required a transformation of the republican spirit.

[87] *Voyage*, 5:277. See also Jean Jacques Barthélemy's *A Treatise on Morals*, in which, explicitly following Xenophon, Barthélemy spoke of that "sublime and luminous principle – *that virtue should be the habit of man*" (*Carite and Polydorus, to Which Is Prefixed, A Treatise on Morals* [London: Otridge and Sons et al., 1799], 2). Implicitly, Barthélemy invoked Montesquieu's analysis, arguing that "it is said that the love of one's country prevails most in a republic, and a sentiment of honour in a monarchy; *but it has never been asserted*, that under this last form of government it would not be advantageous to inspire youth with an enlightened love of their country. This passion, united in the same breast with a sentiment of honour, would produce the greatest achievements, accompanied with a manner that would render them the more illustrious: the two principles might even tend to perfect each other; the sentiment of honour might be freed from its prejudices, sometimes so hurtful to the state, and the love of one's country, of that ferocity which is not less injurious" (30–31).

summary, however, the professor set forth a chief point that was very much at odds with Montesquieu's teachings. Dr. Witherspoon lectured:

> ... [I]n every government there is a *supreme irresistible power* lodged somewhere in *king, senate*, or *people*. To this power is the *final appeal* in all questions. *Beyond* this we cannot go. How *far* does this authority extend? We answer, as far as authority in a social state *can extend*; it is not *accountable* to any other tribunal.[88]

That in every government there is a human tribunal that possesses supreme power is simply another way of saying that in every government there is an opinion about justice that is authoritative and that this opinion of right is manifest in the spirit of the government. In tyrannical government, one sees this in the arrogant and reprehensible spirit of might that the tyrant exudes, which weighs heavily and oppressively over the lives of his silenced subjects and their bleak existence. The opinion of right that prevails in republican government is revealed not only in the laws but in the vibrant spirit of freedom and the activity of the minds, mores, and manners of the citizenry.

Madison concurred with Aristotle's argument at *Politics* V:12 that public opinion is a powerful factor in determining the stability of the political order.[89] He also agreed that in small republics, public opinion tends to be constituted by the factious views of the majority, and he acknowledged that in large territories, it had historically been impossible for the people to discover a common opinion and act on it. In response to this problem, Madison rethought the question of public opinion within a new historical context in which the means of communication had been dramatically improved. In the modern age, scientific and technological discoveries had made possible the communication of views and opinions over a large swath of territory. In turn, this advance in communications offered the possibility of modifying the public sentiments and views via a process that Madison termed "the commerce of ideas" (or, in Barthélemy's

[88] John Witherspoon, *Lectures on Moral Philosophy* (Philadelphia: William W. Woodward, 1822), 116.

[89] In his introduction to William Ellis' translation of Aristotle's *Treatise on Government*, A. D. Lindsay emphasized the importance of public opinion to the Classics: "In an early dialogue of Plato's, the Protagoras, Socrates asks Protagoras why it is not easy to find teachers of virtue as it is to find teachers of swordsmanship, riding, or any other art. Protagoras' answer is that there are no special teachers of virtue, because virtue is taught by the whole community. Plato and Aristotle both accept the view of moral education implied in this answer. ... No private education can hold out against the irresistible force of public opinion and the ordinary moral standards of society" (Aristotle, *Politics*, trans. William Ellis, with an introduction by A. D. Lindsay [London: J. M. Dent & Sons, 1912], vii). See also David W. Minar's brief discussion of Aristotle's conception of public opinion as "the vehicle of the spirit and continuity of the life of the organic community," which "carries the enduring wisdom of the social organism and reflects that wisdom on particular, immediate actions of government" ("Public Opinion in the Perspective of Political Theory," *The Western Political Science Quarterly* 13, no. 1 (1960): 31–44, 38–39); cf. Carroll J. Glynn, Susan Herbst, Garrett J. O'Keefe, and Robert Y. Shapiro, *Public Opinion* (Boulder, CO: Westview Press), 35.

phraseology, "le commerce des idées"[90]) throughout an extensive territory, thereby supplying an environment for the quarantining of factions *and* the refinement and enlargement of public opinion in a republic.

Accordingly, Madison sought to remedy Aristotle's problem of republican stasis with a two-part solution. First, he sought to establish a large and populous republic and institute a system of representation, separation of powers, and governmental checks. These checks would diminish the likelihood of a common factious impulse in a majority at the same time or reduce the likelihood of the opportunity to act on such an impulse. Second, within this new, extensive republic, he sought to apply the classical idea of shaping public opinion via an education in the principle and spirit of the regime, albeit largely through political and social avenues rather than governmental means. In formulating and applying this innovative political and social approach, Madison conceived of the cultivation of the spirit of republicanism to involve the marrying of a respect for individual liberty with the moral requisites of natural right.

Madison conceived of public opinion as the tangible manifestation of the spirit of the polity and the link that connects the principle of the regime with its way of life. He believed that, especially in a free polity, public opinion is a force that cannot be ignored by government. It pervades the minds and *moeurs* of the citizens and reshapes public morality; in reforming and changing public morality, public opinion reconstructs majorities and rewrites the laws. The influence of public opinion on the preservation or destruction of the constitution and government is immense and inimitable. It is a power that destroys or revitalizes the central idea of the polity in the minds and hearts of the citizens. It is the vital spirit that gives life to an idea and stamps the essential character of a people onto its land. The politics of public opinion in a large, populous territory makes possible the education and moderation of the sentiments and views of the citizenry and provides a real opportunity for the flourishing of the great experiment in self-government. This is "the government," Madison triumphantly declared, "for which philosophy has been searching, and humanity been sighing, from the most remote ages. Such are the republican governments which it is the glory of America to have invented, and her unrivalled happiness to possess."[91]

Reclaiming the Aristotelian perspective that public opinion was a central factor in determining the stability of the political order and that its operative power characterizes the republican form of government, Madison then turned his attention in the "Notes on Government" to the factors that influence public opinion. In particular, his concern was with the various institutions of society

[90] Jean Jacques Barthélemy, *Voyage du Jeune Anacharsis en Grèce dans le Milieu du Quatrième Siècle Avant l'Ère Vulgaire* (Paris, 1988), I:234; see also "Réception de M. l'Abbé Barthélemy, Discours Prononcé dans la Séance Publique, Le 25 Août 1789, Paris, Le Louvre," www.academie-francaise.fr/reponse-au-discours-de-reception-de-jean-jacques-barthelemy.

[91] "Spirit of Governments," *MJM*, 257; *PJM*, 14:234.

that shape public morality and thus have a considerable impact on the substantive content of public opinion. Although Madison certainly does not neglect the role that laws and representatives play in forming public opinion, he believed that public opinion is largely shaped through private nongovernmental institutions that compose much of the moral fabric of civic society.

THE INFLUENCE OF MORES ON PUBLIC OPINION

At the conclusion of Chapter 4 of the "Notes on Government," Madison indicated the subject that would immediately follow: "In proportion as Government is influenced by opinion, must it be so by whatever influences opinion." Accordingly, the next four chapters of the "Notes" concern phenomena that directly affect the attitudes and beliefs of the populace, in contrast to the circumstantial influences on public opinion discussed in the first three chapters. The factors that have a direct impact on the views and sentiments of the people include education, religion, slavery, and dependent dominions. These are constitutive elements of public morality; such institutions affect the content of public opinion, but they do not compose its sum. Madison's conception of the relationship between public morality and public opinion in the modern world of advanced communications is similar to that presented by Jacques Peuchet in the *Encyclopédie Méthodique*.[92] In the small polities of ancient times, political communication was for the most part oral and unmediated, and thus the beliefs and views that composed public morality and were voiced in the assembly translated directly and immediately into the ruling opinion of the city. In modern times, with much larger and more populous nations and the advent of circulating newspapers, public morality is not simply tantamount to public opinion. Rather, public opinion is formed over time and undergoes a process of refinement and enlargement via the influence of various intermediary institutions. Like Barthélemy, Peuchet consciously built on Montesquieu's analysis of the relationship between *moeurs* and laws in modern communicative societies; ultimately, however, he moved beyond Montesquieu in developing a dynamic view of the politics of public opinion in the modern age. Madison went even further than Barthélemy's and Peuchet's theory of public opinion by conceptualizing the dramatic results that could be achieved by launching the politics of public opinion in an extended republic.

Although Madison recorded no information under the heading of "Influence of Education on Government," his discussion of the topic elsewhere in the "Notes" suggests at least some of the ground he intended to cover with respect to this subject. In Chapter 4, for example, he indicated how representatives and the free circulation of newspapers throughout a vast land can contribute to educating and refining the public views. In addition, as we shall see in the final

[92] See Peuchet, "Discours Préliminaire," *passim*.

chapter of the "Notes," he placed significant emphasis on the responsibility of the literati to shape the minds and manners of republican citizens, presumably to a large extent via the public print media he had previously discussed. Madison's conception of civic education thus comprised both intellectual and moral learning – the teachers of which included statesmen and private men of letters.[93] These direct influences on the citizens' mores and views are part of a dynamic process that molds public opinion in a large, politically communicative republic. However, this mentoring activity is only part of an even broader communicative process that takes place among the citizenry at large. As important as the representatives and the literati are in forming the reason of the public, they are ultimately facilitators of the "general intercourse of sentiments ... *through the entire body of the people*," which constitutes the overarching enterprise of the "commerce of ideas" in a large republic.[94]

Madison also looked to the laws to serve as schoolmasters in a republic. Over time, he argued, the laws acquire an influence over public sentiment and opinion and may have a beneficial effect on the citizens' self-restraint. In fact, he claimed this as a decisive factor in his ultimate support for a bill of rights. "The political truths declared in that solemn manner acquire by degrees the character of fundamental maxims of free Government, and as they become incorporated with the national sentiment, counteract the impulses of interest and passion."[95]

[93] As Washington and Jefferson had done before him during their respective tenures as President of the United States, during his presidency, Madison also sought to establish the idea of civic education in practice by the institution of a national university. In his Seventh Annual Message to Congress (December 5, 1815), Madison argued that a national university deserves the public patronage, for it is "a monument of their solicitude for the advancement of knowledge, without which the blessings of liberty can not be fully enjoyed or long preserved; as a model instructive in the formation of other seminaries; as a nursery of enlightened preceptors, and as a central resort of youth and genius from every part of their country, diffusing on their return examples of those national feelings, those liberal sentiments, and those congenial manners which contribute cement to our Union and strength to the great political fabric of which that is the foundation" (James Madison, *State of the Union Addresses* [New York: Kensington Publishing, 2004], 44). Unsuccessful in persuading Congress to establish a national university, Jefferson and Madison continued their efforts to promote higher education in America by working together to establish the University of Virginia, the purpose of which was "to form the statesmen, legislators and judges, on whom public prosperity and individual happiness are so much to depend"; "to develop the reasoning faculties of our youth, enlarge their minds, cultivate their morals, and instill into them the precepts of virtue and order"; and "to form them to habits of reflection and correct action, rendering them examples of virtue to others and of happiness within themselves" (*James Madison, 1751–1836*, ed. Ian Elliot [Dobbs Ferry, New York: Oceana Publications, 1969], 108). After Jefferson's death, Madison became rector of the University of Virginia, devoting much of his retirement years to realizing in practice the task of civic education he had promoted in the 1790s.

[94] "Public Opinion," *MJM*, 245; *PJM*, 14:170; "Notes on Government," *MJM*, 165; *PJM*, 14:168.

[95] "Notes on Government," *MJM*, 123–65; *PJM*, 14:162–63; cf. Madison to Jefferson, October 17, 1788, *PJM*, 11:298–99; "Amendments to the Constitution," *PJM*, 12:204; and "Public Opinion," *MJM*, 245; *PJM*, 14:170.

According to Martin Diamond, Madison's conception of the pedagogical influence of a bill of rights contributes to an interpretation of the founding as "more than an arrangement of the passions and interests." A bill of rights "can serve as an ethical admonition to the people, teaching them to subdue dangerous impulses of passion and interest. This goes far in the direction of genuine republican virtue."[96] Madison's discussion of this topic within the context of the education of public opinion in the "Notes on Government" – writings Diamond does not reference – strengthens and confirms Diamond's passing concession that Madison's conception of republicanism may have been more grounded in the concern for the moral education of republican citizens than Diamond's analysis otherwise indicates.

In the classical age, the established religion of a polity had a tremendous influence on the character and unity of public opinion within the city as well as on the respect citizens paid to the laws. This phenomenon was naturally given serious attention by the founders and rulers of ancient polities; to be sure, religion was sometimes artfully used to bolster popular support for the regime. In Crete, for example, the lawgiver Minos claimed to have received divine sanction for the laws at the Cave of Jupiter, a detail of classical politics that Madison satirically recorded in the "Notes." The context of Madison's notation may have been Adams' or Barthélemy's discussion of the artifice at the Cave of Jupiter in their respective works.[97] Given Madison's strenuous and

[96] Martin Diamond, "Ethics and Politics: The American Way," in *The Moral Foundations of the American Republic*, 3rd edn., ed. Robert H. Horwitz (Charlottesville: University Press of Virginia, 1986), 107.

[97] This is one point on which Madison was in full agreement with John Adams. See Madison's mention of Minos in *Federalist* 38:199–200. In the Preface to the *Defence*, Adams wrote: "It was a tradition in antiquity that the laws of Crete were dictated to Minos by the inspiration of Jupiter. This legislator, and his brother Rhadamanthus, were both his sons: once in nine years they went to converse with their father, to propose questions concerning the wants of the people; and his answers were recorded as laws for their government. . . . [N]othing can be inferred from it more than this, that the multitude have always been credulous, and the few artful. The United States of America have exhibited, perhaps, the first example of governments erected on the simple principles of nature: and if men are now sufficiently enlightened to disabuse themselves of artifice, imposture, hypocrisy, and superstition, they will consider this event as an æra in their history" (*Defence*, vol. I, *WJA*, 4:291–92; cf. 4:505–06). See also Barthélemy's discussion of Minos' pretense of divine sanction of the laws at the Cave of Jupiter at *Voyage* 6:214. Regarding "le trône de Jupiter," Barthélemy wrote that "On prétend en effet que Minos, Epiménide et Pythagore, voulant donner une sanction divine à leurs lois ou à leurs dogmes, descendirent dans la caverne, et s'y tinrent plus ou moins de temps renfermés." ["It is claimed, in fact, that Minos, Epimenides, and Pythagoras, when they wished to give a divine sanction to their laws or their opinions, descended into the cave, and remained more or less sequestered in it for a time."] Robert J. Morgan sees a connection between this reference to the Cave of Jupiter in Madison's "Notes" and the Party Press Essay "Who Are the Best Keepers of the People's Liberties?" in which Madison discusses the "science of the stars" and the "mysteries of government" (*James Madison on the Constitution and the Bill of Rights* [Westport, CT: Greenwood Press, 1988], 150–51). I think it is more likely, however, that in this Party Press Essay, Madison had in mind

sustained commitment to religious freedom, the ruse by Minos symbolized for him the notorious lack of freedom of conscience in the ancient world. But Madison's notation also indicated his recognition of the immense importance of religious attachments to civic unity. What is particularly interesting within the context of the "Notes" is Madison's acknowledgement of the significance of religion in the formation of public morality and public opinion. While we know from earlier writings that he rejected a reliance on moral and religious motives to restrain a majority faction once it is formed, we see definitively in the "Notes" that he believed that public morality and widely held religious views encourage or restrain the people in the demands they place on government. Despite the altered perspective on the relationship between law and piety in the modern era, Madison believed that the influence of religion on public opinion was an important consideration in modern as well as in ancient times. As such, it would be as foolish to ignore the impact of religious opinions on public morality, as it would be inappropriate to attempt to shape such opinions by governmental means. In the final chapter of the "Notes on Government" and the Party Press Essay based on it, Madison specifically addressed this concern. Religious "divines" are critical, he argued, in forming the moral character of a republican people and teaching the art of living and the path to happiness.[98]

Just as government-mandated religious belief is a form of tyranny over the minds of men, slavery and dependent territories represent another kind of tyranny – in this case, physical, economic, and psychological. In all societies in which slavery is prevalent, Madison argued in Chapter 7 of the "Notes," although they may be democratic in name, in reality, they are aristocratic. All popular governments of ancient times, with their strict qualifications for citizenship and their dependence on slavery, were actually aristocracies. Moreover, he noted, in ancient democracies, a majority of people were slaves. "Of the residue[,] a part were in the Country and did not attend the assemblies, a part were poor and tho in the city, could not spare the time to attend." As a consequence, the exercise of power was the province of "the rich and easy."[99] Based on his reading of Aristotle's *Politics*, Madison observed that "a Citizen or member of the sovereignty" is defined as "one who is sufficiently free from all private cares, to devote himself exclusively to the service of his Country."[100]

Adams' discussion of the "mystery of a commonwealth" and the "centripetal and centrifugal forces by which the heavenly bodies are continued in their orbits, instead of rushing to the sun, or flying off in tangents among comets and fixed starts impelled or drawn by different forces in different directions, they are blessings to their own inhabitants. ..." (*Defence*, vol. 1, *WJA*, 4:390–91).

[98] "Notes on Government," *MJM*, 136; *PJM*, 14:168; "Republican Distribution of Citizens," *MJM*, 258–59; *PJM*, 14:246.

[99] "Notes on Government," *MJM*, 138; *PJM*, 14:163.

[100] See Aristotle, *Politics*, III:5, 92–94. See also Barthélemy's discussion of Aristotle's conception of the citizen at *Voyage* 5:258 as one who is free to dedicate "himself solely to the service of his country" and to participate "in the sovereign authority."

In the ancient world, the institution of (non-race-based) slavery was defended on the basis of economic necessity. The dilemma resulted from the mundane fact that provisions for the necessities of life required so much time and physical human labor that, if there were to be a political community, it had to be limited to the few who possessed sufficient leisure to participate in public affairs. In Book I of the *Politics*, Aristotle demonstrated that he fully recognized the artificiality and injustice of most forms of slavery (the exception was the natural slave, i.e., a person incapable of governing himself), but he could find no way out of the dilemma caused by economic necessity. He also saw slavery as problematic from a practical standpoint; it posed a potential danger to the stability of the regime by incorporating a large group of people who had no attachment to the political order and no interest in perpetuating it.[101]

Madison did not confine his republican criticism of slavery to the ancient practice. The southern states of America, he lamented, are, in reality, aristocratic rather than democratic governments. As Drew McCoy has pointed out, Madison's discussion of slavery here should be linked to his previous remark in Chapter 1 concerning the oppressive nature of "the case of Black slaves in Modern times." According to McCoy:

> Madison saw clearly the relevance of slavery to his political theory and to the political complexion of the United States. He was fully prepared – privately, at least – to integrate slavery into his analysis of both republicanism and American society. [The "Notes on Government"] also indicate that Madison saw just as clearly what some recent scholars have seen: that by reducing the potential for challenge and insurgency from the lower ranks of society, slavery crucially affected the political posture and vision of republican elites. ... Madison's reflections on slavery and republicanism convey the measure of his intellectual integrity. Racism could not obscure for him a central truth of American politics. ... [B]lack slaves had to be considered people in any meaningful analysis of the character of modern governments.[102]

Madison's criticism of slavery in America in the "Notes" is explicit and harsh; he saw it as a flagrant contradiction of republicanism and anathema to his political principles. Governments in which slavery exists are neither truly popular nor free. They are governed by the opinion of a part rather than the opinion of the whole; such governments are a negation of the rightful sovereignty of public opinion.[103]

Madison's discussion of the contradiction between slavery and free government illustrates his plain acknowledgement of the severe tension between the principles and practices of the American polity. Like Aristotle before him, he recognized both the injustice of conventional slavery and the practical threat

[101] See also Montesquieu's discussion of this subject in *SOL*, 15:13, 243.

[102] McCoy, *The Last of the Fathers*, 235.

[103] Allen, "Justice and the General Good," 135.

that it posed to the security of the body politic. In fact, the practical danger in America was not so unlike that which confronted the Greek city-states, in which slaves and nonfreemen greatly outnumbered citizens. The majority in Virginia, for example, was composed of slaves and nonfreeholders, who made up approximately 75% of the population.[104] As a result, raw power resided in the hands of those with the least affection for or interest in maintaining the constitutional order.

Madison's condemnation of slavery in the "Notes" was not accompanied by any practical plan to end the institution in America – at least not more than the inference that what was needed was the gradual formation of a more reasonable and just public opinion. While he did work to end the practice of slavery in his native Virginia and the United States, it would seem that he could have done more to end the despicable institution in his state and country, and certainly at his own home at Montpelier.[105] As a matter of prudence and constitutionalism, however, Madison's reliance on civic education and the gradual alteration of public opinion in the direction of republican principles was perhaps not as meager a response to the grave injustice of the horrific institution as it might appear at first glance. It was, after all, the cornerstone of Lincoln's strategy to end slavery in the American republic. "Our government rests in public opinion. Whoever can change public opinion, can change the government, practically just so much," Lincoln said in Chicago in 1856. The sixteenth President of the United States continued:

> Public opinion, on any subject, always has a "*central idea*," from which all its minor thoughts radiate. That "central idea" in our political public opinion at the beginning was, and until recently has continued to be, "the equality of men." And although it was always submitted patiently to whatever of inequality there seemed to be as matter of actual necessity, its constant working has been a steady progress towards the practical equality of all men.[106]

As both Madison and Lincoln well understood, however, changing public views on the issue of slavery was an especially arduous task because the practice itself obstructs the moral clarity of those engaged in it.

104 "Notes on Government," *MJM*, 139; *PJM*, 14:163.

105 While there exists no in-depth scholarly study of James Madison and slavery, there are several works on James Madison that delve into the issue at some length or that offer important insights into the discussion. See Scott Kester, *The Haunted Philosophe: James Madison, Republicanism, and Slavery* (Lanham, MD: Rowman & Littlefield, 2008), and McCoy, *The Last of the Fathers*, 4–5, 230–35, 308–22. There is also a recent book about one of Madison's slaves; see Elizabeth Dowling Taylor, *A Slave in the White House: Paul Jennings and the Madisons* (New York: Palgrave Macmillan, 2012). See also C-SPAN's special, *James Madison's Slaves* (www.c-span.org/video/?304765-1/james-madisons-slaves).

106 Abraham Lincoln, "Speech at a Republican Banquet," in *The Collected Works of Abraham Lincoln*, ed. Roy P. Basler (New Brunswick, NJ: Rutgers University Press, 1955), 2:385.

This is also the case with nations in dependent economic relations with a "mother" country. The relationship between dependent dominions and the superior nation is not akin to children and parent, as commonly described, Madison argued; rather, it is analogous to "slaves and Master." The establishment of dependent colonies has a decisive influence on the interests, passions, opinions, and character of all the parties involved. It causes the master or "superior" to "cherish pride, luxury, and vanity."[107] Like slavery, it makes "the labor of one part tributary to the enjoyment of another."

Madison divided dependent territories into two types: those in which the superior state establishes a monopoly over its useful productions and provides a market for the superfluities, and those in which the profits gained by individuals of the superior state increase the wealth of that nation. The British West Indies are an example of the first type; the British East Indies are an example of the second. Regarding the British practice, Scottish professor of rhetoric and logic William Barron, in his 1777 essay, "The History of the Colonization of the Free States of Antiquity, Applied to the Present Contest Between Great Britain and Her American Colonies," argued that the British practice of taxing her colonies was justified by the historical precedents set by the Greeks, Romans, and Carthaginians.[108] Immediately after referencing this essay in the "Notes," Madison cited John Symonds' published critical assessment of Barron. Symonds, a professor of history at Cambridge, argued that there is a radical difference between the ancient cases and the British example. After the battle at Plataea, the free states of the Greek confederation voluntarily taxed themselves for the purpose of carrying on a war against their mutual foe, the Persians, whereas Britain unilaterally imposed taxes on her American colonies in order to raise revenue for the parent state. The original contract between Athens and her equal confederates, however, was ultimately succeeded by a policy built on iniquity. First, the treasury was moved from Delos to Athens on the pretext that it was not safe in Delos. Next, the tribute was increased, and it was no longer marked for a specific purpose; instead, it was considered by the Athenians a tax due to them for which they were not required to account. Pericles then spent the bulk of the proceeds on buildings to decorate Athens. "These were indeed the pride and ornament of that city," Symonds wrote, "and their remains afford us a genuine idea of the splendor of ancient Greece; but as they were erected on the ruins of liberty, they are an eternal reproach to the memory of Pericles."[109]

107 "Notes on Government," *MJM*, 145; *PJM*, 14:164.

108 For a study of the relationship between colonies and superiors in the ancient world, see A. J. Graham, *Colony and Mother City in Ancient Greece* (Manchester, UK: Manchester University Press, 1964).

109 John Symonds, *Remarks Upon an Essay Intituled* [sic], *The History of the Colonization of the Free States of Antiquity, Applied to the Present Contest Between Great Britain and Her American Colonies* (London: J. Nichols, 1778), 42–43.

In another set of writings Madison seems to have composed a number of years later, probably after his retirement from the presidency, he returned to the theme of the influences on government. These "Additional Notes on Government" contain a table of contents and four chapters, two of which concern the commerce between nations and two others devoted to the related topics of emigration and the impact of a national debt. These "Additional Notes" essentially pick up where Madison left off in Section 1 of the "Notes." In the chapters on the influence of slavery and dependent dominions on government, Madison is scathingly critical of policies of economic inequity between individuals and between nations; in the "Additional Notes," he clearly implied his decided preference for economic liberty and the advancement of an international system of free trade. Whether domestically or internationally, he believed that the servile dependence of one man or one state on another was destructive of the political, economic, and psychological independence that is the hallmark of free citizens and free nations and on which the formation of republican mores and a just public opinion depends.

THE COMMERCE OF IDEAS

Madison's presentation of the politics of public opinion in the "Notes on Government" and the "Additional Notes on Government" is a delineation of the influences on public opinion in ancient polities as well as of the more complex, dynamic process of opinion formation that characterizes the modern world. His discussion of new modes that could vindicate age-old republican aspirations in these "Notes" was a direct response to the challenge Aristotle articulated and Montesquieu reformulated.

Madison accepted the terms of Aristotle's challenge and Barthélemy's reiteration of it. He also embraced their conclusion that the character of each political order is fundamentally determined by the opinion and spirit of the citizens – or of the greater part of the citizens – who constitute it. Indeed, Madison's enchantment with Anacharsis is a conscious replication of Anacharsis' enchantment with the aspirations of classical republicanism.

Nonetheless, Madison believed that Aristotle did not succeed in meeting the terms of the challenge he had articulated. In classical times, the means of communication within society were essentially limited to the spoken word, thereby confining the operation of public opinion in a republic to a small territory. As a result, the ease of communication made the problem of stasis or faction an ever present danger. Aristotle's response to the problem lacked the institutional precautions Montesquieu would later recommend. Conversely, Madison believed that Montesquieu's solution failed to attend to the fact that there is always a prevailing opinion in free societies and that liberty cannot be achieved or maintained by a primary dependence on political mechanics. It is in the interstice between these two theories that Madison developed his own unique contribution to the theory of republican government. He employed

Montesquieu's method for the preservation of liberty in relation to the constitution, and at the same time he reclaimed the Aristotelian concern for the active liberty of the citizen and the need for civic education. He accomplished this by rethinking the question of the size of the territory and population in a new age of communication, thereby demonstrating the conditions in the modern world that made possible the achievement of a deliberative public opinion in republican government.

4

The federal republican polity

Chapters 9 through 12 of the "Notes on Government" are concerned with checks on political power, the separation and distribution of powers, and the structure of federal governments. As Madison indicated earlier in the "Notes," in terms of the preservation of the political order, institutional arrangements are certainly not to be neglected, although they are secondary in importance to the proper formation of public opinion in republican government.

We recall that the weakness of the classical republican polity was that it could not match the strength of an empire. In addition, unless there existed a large middle class, the problem of the rivalry between the rich and the poor generally led to the destruction of governments in ancient times. In Section 1 of the "Notes," Madison demonstrated how representative government in a large territory contributes to solving the problems associated with popular government. External strength is achieved by sufficient size. Internal stability is gained by (1) the exclusion of the direct participation of the people in government and the obstacles to the formation of majority faction that accompany the extension of the territory and (2) participatory politics and the attachment of republican citizens to their political order and its principles. However, Madison also pointed to the danger that an extended republic presents: The citizens of a large, representative republic might refrain from participation due to a sense of insignificance. Because public opinion is the real sovereign in all free governments, Madison sought to establish equivalents to the contraction of the territory in order to encourage civic participation and make effective the communication of ideas. In this second section of the "Notes," Madison added to his analysis of how the operation of public opinion in a large nation can remedy the problems associated with popular governments. Separation of powers, intergovernmental checks, and federalism are prudential devices that contribute to the prevention of demagogic seduction and majority tyranny *and* serve as equivalents to territorial contraction and the formation of an effectual public voice over a large republic.

CHECKS ON DEMOCRATIC GOVERNMENTS

In Chapter 9 of the "Notes," Madison returned once more to the classical antidotes for the problems that tend to plague popular government. In ancient democracies, he noted, popular assemblies were often unduly influenced by a single orator.[1] Distrusting the power of popular demagogues, the Classics devised a series of checks to curtail their activity and influence. Among the methods used to keep public orators in check in the Athenian democracy or ancient Italian republics were age requirements, character examinations, frightful imprecations, ostracism, petalism (temporary banishment), and death. In the Italian republic of Locris, for example, whoever proposed a new law or urged the alteration or repeal of an old one had to do so with a rope around his neck.[2] If he should be unsuccessful, the constitution called for his immediate execution. "What ignorance & susceptibility of delusion in the people of Locris, is [impl]ied by such a precaution!"[3] Madison commented. Even though he shared with the ancients an unwillingness to flatter democrats, Madison believed there were means much better adapted to the genius of a free people than many of those employed by classical republics. Superior to the noose or ostracism, for example, was the institution of a senate. In Athens, the senate-like institution of the Aeropagus served as a check on the people's authority, as did the Augurs and College of Heralds instituted by Numa in Rome. Over time, however, these institutions were not able to maintain their authority against the force of public opinion.[4]

In Chapter 10 of the "Notes," Madison scripted a curious heading: "True Reasons for Keeping Great Departments of Power Separate."[5] Unfortunately,

[1] See *Federalist* 58:328; "Notes of Government," *MJM*, 147–52; *PJM*, 14:165–66.

[2] Madison may have taken examples of these practices from Aristotle's *Politics* or perhaps from Barthélemy's summary of Aristotle's discussion of ancient practices. See Aristotle, *Politics*, IV:13, 137–38; V:8, 162; V:8, 164; *Voyage*, 5:268, 276. Adams also mentioned some of these practices in his account of ancient republics in the *Defence*, vol. I, *WJA*, 4:377, 384–85.

[3] "Notes on Government," *MJM*, 152; *PJM*, 14:166.

[4] Madison's argument that the British government – despite its distribution of powers – would be unable to maintain itself against the power of public opinion was grounded in what he learned from his study of ancient history, as exemplified in his commentary in this portion of the "Notes." (Compare "Influence of public opinion on Government" in the "Notes," *MJM*, 134–36; *PJM*, 14:161–63 and the Party Press Essay "British Government," *MJM*, 250; *PJM*, 14:170).

[5] There exists an undated note in Madison's hand that may be related to this chapter heading. It concerns "Judicial Precedents Expounding the Law on Erroneous Inferences" and possible limitations on "that authority to questions of law, as distinct from const[itutiona]l questions." Madison continued: "It may be proper, being therefore drawn into this subject to state briefly my view of the relation between the great Departments of Govt." Following this brief note, there is a line added at another time and apparently by another hand: "See the paper on this subject"

he did not elaborate on the meaning of this intriguing title. Among the possible explanations for this heading is that he intended to return to his own earlier arguments in *The Federalist*, implying that his explanation for separation of powers offered there was not true, or at least not the whole truth. Or he might have been referring to the classical idea of separation of the deliberative and magisterial offices of government, which was not for the purpose of protecting individual liberty. Another possibility is that he intended to criticize Turgot's, Condorcet's, and the physiocrats' rejection of the doctrine of separation of powers.[6] Or perhaps Madison was alluding here to the flawed theory (in his view) of mixed government advocated by such thinkers as John Adams and Polybius. Or he may have intended to treat what he perceived as the deficiencies of Montesquieu's notion of the separation of powers. Finally, he may have meant to treat the doctrine of separation of powers in an historically and philosophically comprehensive manner.

While we cannot be certain what Madison intended to discuss here, it may nonetheless be helpful to consider the subject in context, particularly with respect to the immediately preceding chapter as well as Chapter 4 on public opinion. The checks devised in ancient democracies were, he contended, marks of popular "self-distrust." The provisions discussed in *Federalist* 10 and 51 represent the American republic's modern counterpart for ancient contrivances of self-distrust. In *Federalist* 51, the doctrine of separation of powers appears to be set forth within the context of the problem of governmental tyranny. However, in this essay, he offered only a partial explanation of the doctrine, declaring that his discussion does not comprehend "a full development of this important idea." In a letter to Jefferson on October 17, 1788, he again remarked on the unfinished nature of this inquiry:

> The invasion of private rights is *chiefly* to be apprehended, not from acts of Government contrary to the sense of its constituents, but from acts in which the Government is the mere instrument of the major number of the constituents. This is a truth of great importance, but not yet sufficiently attended to.[7]

The checks devised in ancient polities indicating self-distrust were created particularly with the problem of the popular demagogue in mind. The danger posed by the demagogue was not that he promoted measures contrary to the

(James Madison, "Note, Departments of the Government," Series 1, From February 10, 1833 to Undated, Image 1160, *The James Madison Papers*, LOC, http://hdl.loc.gov/loc.mss/mjm.24_1160_1160).

[6] See Keith Michael Baker, *Condorcet: From Natural Philosophy to Social Mathematics* (Chicago: Chicago University Press, 1975), 260, 265; Condorcet, *Selected Writings*, ed. Keith Michael Baker (Indianapolis: Macmillan, 1976), 155–56, 178; Anne Robert Jacques Turgot, "Letter from A. Turgot," in *The Correspondence of Richard Price*, eds. W. Bernard Peach and D. O. Thomas (Durham, NC: Duke University Press, 1999), 2:13. Cf. Sheehan, *James Madison and the Spirit of Republican Self-Government*, 33–35, 82.

[7] Madison to Jefferson, October 17, 1788, *PJM*, 11:298.

demands of the people, but that he pandered to them in order to gain personal popularity. Thus, despite the various checks on popular orators, including the establishment of a senate or other institutions to check the demands of the multitude, the people often became an overmatch for the senate and were able to seize all the powers of government into their own hands.

The problem of controlling and moderating the demands of the people was not solved by the classical contrivances employed to check their power. Madison's references to senates or their equivalents in Chapter 9 implied a similar argument as that in the section on classical republics in his "Memorandums for the Convention of Virginia in 1788 on the federal Constitution."[8] Madison relied on this portion of the "Memorandums for the Convention of Virginia" to write *Federalist* 63, in which he briefly explored the application of the representative principle in classical polities. Unlike the American republic, none of the classical republics excluded the people from government in their direct, collective capacity. In *Federalist* 63, Madison underscored the idea of responsibility and its twofold meaning. In general, the Antifederalists conceived of responsibility in terms of the representatives' responsiveness to the interests and demands of their constituents, while many of the Federalists considered the representatives' responsibility to be a kind of aristocratic trust that involved a minimal degree of responsiveness and accountability to the people. In contrast, Madison argued that responsibility consists of both responsiveness to the interests and opinions of the people as well as the duty of representatives to abide by the Constitution and seek the common good and general welfare.[9] In the first case, representatives are responsible *to* the public; in the second, they are responsible *for* the public good, as delineated in the Constitution and the principles it embodies. When the two senses of responsibility are in conflict, Madison advocated that the higher responsibility of representatives is to protect the people against their own temporary errors and illicit passions until the authority of reason and justice can be reestablished in the public mind. In both instances, however, government is responsible to public opinion. On the one hand, the representatives are responsive to ordinary public opinion. On the other hand, they are responsible to the sovereign opinion of the public that is embedded in the Constitution, which was consented to and authorized by the people.

Madison showed through his examples of Sparta, Carthage, and Rome in the "Memorandums for the Convention of Virginia in 1788 on the federal Constitution" and *Federalist* 63 (as well as Athens and Crete in the latter) that the principle of representation was indeed known to the ancients. Although different regime types, all these ancient polities attempted to combine some

[8] *MJM*, 205–13, especially 210–13; *PJM*, 10:273–83, especially 278–81; Cf. Madison's speech at the Virginia Ratifying Convention of June 7, 1788, relating to the weaknesses of confederate governments, *PJM*, 11:90–99.

[9] *Federalist* 63:351.

degree of popular power with a representative institution tasked with looking after the long-term interests of the city. According to Aristotle, Sparta, Crete, and, especially, Carthage exhibited certain characteristics of the well-organized regime. In particular, they were supported by public opinion and, as a result, were relatively long-lived polities. As Madison noted, however, none of them excluded the people in their direct collective capacity; ultimately, all were unable to resist the popular current and maintain their constitutional form.[10] The essential distinction between the classical republics and the American republic, Madison contended, consists in the exclusion of the direct participation of the people in government in the United States – or, in other words, the full application of the principle of representation.

The theme of responsibility explored in the "Memorandums for the Convention of Virginia in 1788 on the federal Constitution" and emphasized in *The Federalist* is also taken up by Madison in the chapter on public opinion in the "Notes on Government." His discussion concerning the respect government owes to the people in the "Notes" is a restatement of the twofold sense of responsibility he set forth in *The Federalist*. On the one hand, the representatives of free governments are responsible and accountable *to* public opinion. This is the case when public opinion has a fixed and settled quality. On the other hand, the representatives are responsible *for* informing the popular views and contributing to the construction of public opinion. This is their duty when public opinion is not settled or is contrary to the Constitution and the principles of republican justice. As we have seen, the size of the territory makes communicative activity and the formation of a united opinion more difficult. However, representation acts as an equivalent to a contraction of the size of the territory by actively contributing to the formation of a public voice.

According to Madison, some of the ancient republics made use of the principle of representation and some placed checks on the power of the people;[11] they were nonetheless unable to maintain their constitutions. The territories were

[10] By the phrase "total exclusion of the people, in their collective capacity, from any share in [the American governments]" in *Federalist* 63, I do not take Madison to mean the total exclusion of the people from any share or any significant share in their governments. Rather, I believe Madison was referring to the difference between the American and the ancient popular governments. In ancient democracies, the collective body of the people ruled – they *were* the government – whereas in the U.S. government, the representatives of the people, and not the people as a collective body, are tasked with making public policy. In this, Madison may have had in mind Montesquieu's juxtaposition of representative government with classical direct democracy: "The great advantage of representatives," Montesquieu wrote, "is that they are able to discuss public affairs. The people are not at all appropriate [collectively fit] for such discussions; this forms one of the great drawbacks [inconveniences] of democracy" (*SOL*, 11:6, 159). For a contrasting interpretation of this passage in *Federalist* 63, see Thomas L. Pangle, *The Spirit of Modern Republicanism: The Moral Vision of the American Founders and the Philosophy of Locke* (Chicago: University of Chicago Press, 1990), 96.

[11] See *Federalist* 63:355; see Chapter 9, "Checks devised in democracies marking self-distrust," in the "Notes on Government," *MJM*, 147–52.

simply too small to cultivate a sustained sense of popular responsibility in the midst of powerfully engaging popular demagogues whose rhetorical skills were often an overmatch for any show of calm and reasonable deliberation in the assembly. Such demagogues were masters at exacerbating the most passionate demands of the majority, which often translated into schemes of minority oppression. The advantage America derives from the principle of representation, Madison instructed his readers of *The Federalist*, can only be understood when it is combined with the extension of territory.[12] Furthermore, separation of powers is a particularly necessary prudential device in representative governments that are grounded in popular sovereignty. Madison endorsed Montesquieu's theory of the functional separation of powers and checks and balances in order to prevent governmental *and* majority tyranny, thereby promoting the dual sense of responsibility that he believed defined the contours of free government.

As we have seen, Montesquieu's purpose in devising his theory of the separation of powers was for protection against governmental oppression, which is always a threat when any single person or group can accumulate all power into the same set of hands. Turgot, Condorcet, and Mazzei rejected Montesquieu's and the American doctrine of bicameralism (as well as the executive veto). They believed such a division and checking of the legislative power encourages rather than quells class conflict and undercuts the authority of the nation – or, in other words, the authority of public opinion. Madison believed that those who rejected bicameralism and its attendant checks failed to give sufficient attention to the idea of what Montesquieu called "liberty in relation to the constitution" or the protection against arbitrary power and the safeguarding of individual liberties.

Nonetheless, Madison believed that Turgot and his followers were correct in their criticisms of Montesquieu's inattention to the force of public opinion and its rightful claim as the ruling authority in free polities. In all free governments, there is "one centre," as Turgot put it, which constitutes the sovereign body of the nation.[13] In Madison's view (and in the view of many French writers post-Montesquieu), the vaunted British model denied the public its sovereign authority by splitting up and balancing the government in such a way that the people constituted only a portion of the sovereignty. Montesquieu and Adams feared the existence of a predominant principle or ruling opinion in the political order because they failed to recognize how public opinion can be refined and enlarged in a large republic. If Madison intended to treat the doctrine of separation of powers comprehensively in the "Notes," he would likely have linked this doctrine to his twofold notion of responsibility. He would have demonstrated

[12] *Federalist* 63:355.

[13] Anne Robert Jacques Turgot to Dr. Price, March 22, 1778, in *Observations on the Importance of the American Revolution, and the Means of Making It a Benefit to the World* (1784), The Online Library of Liberty, http://oll.libertyfund.org/titles/1788.

that the duty of government to secure the constitutional rights and liberties of individuals constitutes one form of responsibility, as Montesquieu understood. The duty of government to obey the modified and settled opinion of the public constitutes another and equally important sense of responsibility. Madison would thus have conceived of this chapter as a fleshing out and completion of his prior remarks in Chapter 4 concerning the respect government owes to public opinion.

FEDERALISM AND THE REPUBLICAN EMPIRE

In Chapter 11 of the "Notes," Madison again returned to the studies he had engaged in regarding ancient and modern confederations.[14] This chapter represents the accumulated knowledge of the greatest student of federalism. Here, his purpose was to examine a number of confederal alliances or unions, including the Greek cantons and the Boetian, Aphyctionic, Thessalian, Calmarian, Saxon Heptarchic, Etolian, Acarnanian, Achæan, Elisian, Arcadian, Argivian, Asiatic Greek, Hanseatic, Germanic, and Belgian confederacies.[15] He also included an examination of the confederation of the four New England colonies, the federation proposed by Benjamin Franklin in his Albany Plan of Union, and the structure of union set forth by Thomas Pownall in *The Administration of the Colonies* (1764).

Of course, Madison had extensively researched and written about confederal/federal (the terms were generally used interchangeably in the eighteenth century) governments in prior notes, in letters, and in *The Federalist*. So why would he spend time penning new notes on this subject in the "Notes on Government," including returning to an examination of many of the confederacies he had already studied? I suspect he had three reasons for doing so. First, he planned to connect his arguments from the first three chapters of the "Notes" to the subject of federal governments, thereby expanding on his analysis of the subjects of size of the territory, external danger, and stage of society in the first section of the "Notes." Second, he intended the "Notes" as a comprehensive inquiry into the central questions of government – and republican government in particular – and he intended to situate the principle of federalism within a broader and fuller discussion of republicanism than he had

[14] Although it would have been in some ways a smoother transition for Madison to take up the subject of federal structure immediately following the first three chapters, he left the subject for a later analysis because he intended a logical progression from the influence of external factors on public opinion to the subject of public opinion itself; in turn, the direct influences on public opinion naturally follows in these outline notes. Next, the additional factors that serve virtually to modify the territory and actually to contribute to the modification of public opinion are treated.

[15] Madison was building on the work he had done previously on ancient and modern confederacies here in the "Notes on Government." See *MJM*, 175–95.

previously done in *The Federalist*. Third, although he had lost his bid for the negative on state laws at the Constitutional Convention, he did not yet consider the issue closed – at least as a theoretical argument regarding the importance of the constitutional negative to federal republics.

We recall that in the first section of the "Notes," Madison emphasized the "received opinion" that overgrown territories (that is, empires) are inimical to republicanism. Taking up where he left off in Section 1 and adding to his criticism of an overreliance on balancing political powers in Chapter 4,[16] in Chapter 11 of the "Notes," he presented his alternative solution for achieving stability and liberty in the domestic and international political arenas.[17] Like Montesquieu and the philosophic historians, his objective was to meet the exigencies of the modern age. Madison, however, thought he had succeeded where he believed they had not. He believed he had discovered a solution consistent with the form and spirit of genuine republicanism. Such a remedy had to take into account the scientific and technological developments in modern times, including the growth of commerce and communication, the increased diversification of occupations, and the growth of the territorial size and population of the nation-state.

All these factors were given serious consideration by the philosophic historians and, to a significant extent, by Montesquieu as well. Their analyses led them to conclude that in the modern age, nations can and should be so interdependent and interconnected that the accommodation of mutual political and economic interests replaces the desire for territorial expansion and war. To this end, Montesquieu and the philosophic historians promoted commercial cooperation, arguing that the mutual economic benefits of modern commercial nations were proving to be more advantageous to nations than territorial conquest. They saw this "nation composed of many nations"[18] growing out of an international system of sovereign states based on a balance of power and policy of mutual deterrence, which, similar to the Utrecht system (and unlike

[16] At some point later in his life, Madison changed his mind on the constitutional negative. In his unfinished sketch of a preface to the "Notes of Debates in the federal Convention of 1787," he wrote: "The feature in the letter which vested in the general Authy. a negative on the laws of the States, was suggested by the negative in the head of the British Empire, which prevented collisions between the parts & the whole, and between the parts themselves. It was supposed that the substitution, of an elective and responsible authority for an hereditary and irresponsible one, would avoid the appearance even of a departure from the principle of Republicanism. But altho' the subject was so viewed in the Convention, and the votes on it were more than once equally divided, it was finally & justly abandoned" (James Madison, *Notes of Debates*, 16).

[17] In the Party Press Essay "Government," Madison explicitly connected the arguments in Chapters 1 and 2 of the "Notes" with the discussion of federalism in Chapter 11.

[18] Montesquieu, *Reflections on Universal Monarchy in Europe*, XVIII. See Henry C. Clark's fine discussion of this subject in *Compass of Society: Commerce and Absolutism in Old-Regime France* (Lanham, MD: Lexington Books, 2006), 89–95.

the unified military empire), helped to prevent any single sovereign from attaining empire and thus averted the threat of universal monarchy.[19]

Madison rejected the underlying assumption that fueled the fear of universal empire. He did not believe that a great extent of territory was *necessarily* a threat to individual liberty or a precursor to universal monarchy or despotism. Indeed, his analysis was unique and strikingly bold: He believed that *republican empire* was both possible and desirable.[20] The empire he envisioned was a federation of states – but not of sovereign states sustained by balancing the power of one against another (or others). Moreover, although Madison did seek to use economic self-interest and narrow passions when they could not be adjusted by the deliberative process, he did not rely on these lower human motives as a substitute for the formation of a public opinion grounded in republican principles. Rather, he sought to establish a republican empire grounded in the sovereignty of public opinion and endowed with constitutional authority at its center. He also sought to establish a federal system of smaller states, which were integral to the formation of public opinion. Sovereignty, defined as constitutional authority, would be shared by the states and the general government. In its most fundamental sense as ultimate political authority, however, sovereignty was possessed by neither the states nor the federal government. It resides, Madison claimed, in the will of the whole society.[21]

Madison did not believe that the best model for a federal republic was to be found in Montesquieu's notion of "a society of societies that makes a new one," as set forth in the first three chapters of Book 9 of *The Spirit of Laws*. Montesquieu's model for the federal republic was Lycia; Madison, however, disparaged the Lycian league for being one of the examples of "mere confederacies."[22] In his pre-Convention "Notes on Ancient and Modern Confederacies," under the heading of "Lycian Confederacy," he wrote:

[19] See, for example, J. G. A. Pocock's discussion of Gibbon's contrast between the unified military empire and a plurality of confederate states, which, like William Robertson's prior *View of the Progress of Society*, justified the concert of Europe ("Edward Gibbon in History," 23). Subsequently, after the American founding, Pocock argues, the problem of republic and empire arose in a new form.

[20] It is beyond the scope of this study to investigate the etymology and uses of the term *empire*, although I suspect that this examination is necessary to an even fuller exposition of Madison's ideas than I am able to provide here. The excellent study by Anthony Pagden, *Lords of all the World* (New Haven: Yale University Press, 1995), will be essential to this investigation.

[21] James Wilson of Pennsylvania also emphasized this view of sovereignty at the Constitutional Convention and throughout his life.

[22] "Memorandums for the Convention of Virginia in 1788 on the Federal Constitution," *MJM*, 206; *PJM*, 10:274. In these notes, under the first heading of "Examples Shewing Defect of Mere Confederacies," Madison listed the Lycian confederacy. According to J. G. A. Pocock, Montesquieu took "an important step in transferring the meaning of 'federative' power from that of an attribute of sovereignty, essential to the being of a 'state,' to that of an authority common to an association of 'states,' but he left it unclear whether the common authority of the *république federative* owed its existence to anything more than a pact or *foedus* between 'states,' which

In this confederacy the number of votes allotted to each member was proportioned to its pecuniary contributions. The Judges and Town magistrates were elected by the general authority in like proportion.

— See Montesquieu who prefers this mode.

The name of a federal republic may be refused to Lycia which Montesquieu cites as an example in which the importance of the members determined the proportion of their votes in the general Councils. The Gryson League is a juster example. Code de l'Hum. – Confederation[23]

Whether Madison understood Montesquieu's idea of the federal republic accurately might be disputed by some contemporary scholars who claim that the Lycian league was a much more unified association than most federal governments prior to that of the United States.[24]

Indeed, according to Montesquieu, voting in the common council of the Lycian league was proportionate to the relative size of each of the twenty-three towns; in addition, the common council elected the judges and magistrates of the various towns, thus showing the very high degree of authority of the central government in the internal administration of the towns. In *Federalist* 9, Hamilton discussed at some length Montesquieu's thoughts on the confederate republic. The Antifederalist view was that in a confederacy, the local units must be represented equally in the general assembly; furthermore, the confederal form requires that there be no involvement of the general government in the internal administration of the local units. Hamilton argued that this was proved

would retain the sovereignty of which the 'federative power' was an attribute." Despite Pocock's claim of some ambiguity in Montesquieu's stance, he nonetheless concludes that "by many criteria," the examples of federative republics Montesquieu offers show that "these confederations were not states but leagues of states" ("States, Republics, and Empires: The American Founding in Early Modern Perspective," in *Conceptual Change and the Constitution*, eds. Terrence Ball and J. G. A. Pocock [Lawrence: University of Kansas Press, 1988], 67).

23 "Notes on Ancient and Modern Confederacies," *MJM*, 175; *PJM*, 9:4.

24 See, for example, Long, "The 'Anti-Hobbes?' Montesquieu's Contribution to International Relations Theory." Long argues that "if there remains a debate over the level of integration Montesquieu saw in a federation of republics (he uses both the term 'federation' and 'confederation' as synonyms), he did consider that if each unit maintains the right to secede, there is also a right of interference for each part in the affairs of the other parts. Indeed, not only do the republics exercise their federative power collectively, they also surrender part of their domestic sovereignty since their fellow confederates can intervene in their internal affairs if there is a risk of corruption and despotism. ... In fact, the Lycian league which he pronounced to be his favourite, shared taxation; had a federal court responsible for dealing with disputes among the members of the league; controlled communal land and trade rights; dealt with religious and economic questions as well as certain aspects of civil life" (99–100). James W. Muller claims that the Lycian confederacy served as a model for the American federal union. First, "it was a model of a federal union the strength of whose parts in the national councils was proportionate to their size. Second, it showed the possibility of popular government that was representative. Thirdly, it offered the example of a strong national government with its own strong officers and the power to make laws that applied directly to individual citizens." See James W. Muller, "The Political Economy of Republicanism," in *Montesquieu and the Spirit of Modernity*, eds. David W. Carrithers and Patrick Coleman (Oxford: Voltaire Foundation, 2002), 61–75.

false by Montesquieu in his discussion of Lycia – the authorial source the Antifederalists generally appealed to on this subject. Madison had made the former argument in response to Mr. Oliver Ellsworth on June 30, 1787, at the Constitutional Convention:

Mr. E. had also erred in saying that no instance had existed in which confederated States had not retained to themselves a perfect equality of suffrage. Passing over the German system in which the K. of Prussia has nine voices, he reminded Mr. E. of the Lycian Confederacy, in which the component members had votes proportioned to their importance, and which Montesquieu recommends as the fittest model for that form of Government.[25]

With regard to Lycia, however, neither Montesquieu nor Hamilton addressed the Antifederalist view that a confederate republic must be restricted in its operation "to the members in their collective capacities, without reaching to the individuals of whom they are composed."[26] As strong and united as the town of the Lycian alliance might have been, the confederation apparently did not operate directly on individuals, as was the case in the federal republic of the United States under the new Constitution.[27]

In contrast to the Lycian confederacy, Madison claimed – or at least cited Fortuné de Barthélemy Félice as claiming in *Code de l'Humanité* – that "the Gryson League is a juster example" of a "federal republic."[28] The Grisons, or

[25] Madison, *Notes of Debates in the Federal Convention of 1787*, 223–24. See also Madison's *Federalist* 45:258 and Hamilton's *Federalist* 9:44 and *Federalist* 16:81.

[26] *Federalist* 9:43.

[27] See, for example, James Wilson of Pennsylvania on this issue in James Wilson, *Works of James Wilson*, ed. James DeWitt Andrews (Chicago: Callaghan and Co., 1896), 1:285–86n1.

[28] *Code de l'Humanité, ou la Législation Universelle, Naturelle, Civile et Politique*, 13 vols. (Yverdon, Switzerland, 1778); "Notes on Ancient and Modern Confederacies," *MJM*, 175; *PJM*, 9:4. Note the difference between Madison's initial summary of the Lycian confederacy as one in which "the Judges and Town magistrates were elected by the general authority in like proportion" (which matches Hamilton's claim in *Federalist* 9) with Madison's passage following this in his "Notes on Ancient and Modern Confederacies": "Strabo [Lib. xiv, cap. iii], moreover, mentions the lack of laws of the Lycians: concerning which we will add a little to what he says. – There were twenty-three cities, divided into three classes, according to their power. To the first class belonged the six largest, to the second those of intermediate rank, the number of which is uncertain, to the third all the rest, whose importance was very small. *And each of these cities took care of its affairs at home, and had its own magistrates and its own system of civil government*, but all, uniting, formed one joint republic, and had one deliberative assembly, a greater senate, as it were" [emphasis added; James Madison, "Notes on Ancient and Modern Confederacies," *MJM*, 175–76; *PJM*, 9:4]. See Christopher Wolfe on this issue of the Lycian confederation and the election of local magistrates as discussed by Strabo and Montesquieu, in "The Confederate Republic of Montesquieu," *Polity* 9, no. 4 (1977): 427–45. According to Wolfe, "Strabo probably does not say that the common council names the magistrates and judges of the cities." Rather, he says that the "judges and magistrates are elected according to the proportion of the number of votes belonging to each city" (433). Thus, either Montesquieu misread Strabo, or he deliberately and purposively misstated him. It is possible that Madison's notes citing the two conflicting accounts of the election of local magistrates in the Lycian

Graubünden (the Grey League), was a federation of three cantons situated in the Swiss Alps. Each member of the League had its own laws and customs and was independent in all municipal matters that did not affect the federation as a whole. The federation, or Bund, established a diet, consisting of sixty-three deputies based proportionately on the population of each league, which met annually to discuss and decide on general affairs of the confederation. The Grey League sent twenty-seven deputies to this diet, the Cade sent twenty-two, and the Ten Jurisdictions sent fourteen. These representatives were elected in each of the communes on the basis of universal manhood suffrage. The Grison confederation was known especially for the principle of popular sovereignty on which it was based as well as for the high degree of responsibility of the diet's representatives to their constituents in their respective local communities. In fact, the ultimate constitutional authority resided not in the diet but in the people of the several communities.[29]

While both the Grey League and Lycia were based on proportional representation, the former differed from the latter confederacy in that (1) the towns retained control of municipal elections and matters not affecting the league as a whole, (2) the central government operated directly on individuals instead of merely on the municipal units, and (3) it was rooted in popular sovereignty rather than state/town sovereignty. Accordingly, like the United States under the Constitution of 1787, the character of the Grison union was federal with regard to the limited extent of the powers of the central government; it was national with regard to the operation of its powers on individuals. Like representation in the U.S. House of Representatives (but not as in the Senate), the Grison diet manifested a national character due to its basis in proportional representation, but it was a mixture of national and federal features with respect to the location of supreme and ultimate authority in the people of the communities at large rather than in the diet or in each canton. Unlike the U.S. government, however, in its enthusiasm for democratic processes, the Grison League apparently implemented the practice of the "instruction" of it representatives in the diet by their various constituencies.[30]

As Lance Banning has persuasively argued, Madison's study of ancient and modern confederacies led him to discover the advantages of a "middle ground"

Confederacy (essentially, one right after the other) indicate that Madison believed that Montesquieu (and, following him, Hamilton) had misstated Strabo on this point.

29 See William Coxe, *Travels in Switzerland, in a Series of Letters to William Melmoth, Esq. From William Coxe* (London: T. Cadell, 1789), 3:227, and *passim.*

30 See Coxe, *Travels in Switzerland*, 3:227. See also Adams' discussion of the government of the Grison League in the section on democratic republics in the *Defence*. Adams was critical not only of the League's location of sovereignty in all the people but was also particularly derisive about the instruction of representatives by their constituents in the diet. It also appears that if Madison considered the Grison League superior to the Lycian Confederacy, it was not intended as unqualified praise. There are a number of instances in Madison's writings and speeches in which he is critical of the government of the Swiss cantons.

between a national consolidated government and a confederacy of sovereign states.[31] In following Madison's argument in the "Notes on Government," one sees that the "middle course" is in fact a wholly new kind of federal arrangement and that the nuances of this novel theory are critical to understanding how the processes of republicanism can maintain the principles of free government. The conception of federal republicanism Madison sets forth in some detail in his letter to Jefferson of October 24, 1787 (cited in Chapter 1 of the "Notes") is particularly helpful in following his line of reasoning on the subject.

Interestingly, in this letter, Madison bestowed circumscribed approval on the feudal model of the Middle Ages, claiming that it is superior to that of the Articles of Confederation. He considered it inferior, however, to the type of political system he had hoped to secure by establishing a constitutional negative over state legislation. The distinctions Madison made in this letter and elsewhere actually amount to a more subtle classification of governments than the threefold one generally presented in contemporary political science – that is, a confederation of sovereign states versus a national (or consolidated) government, with a federal government in between. Madison saw the ground between confederalism and nationalism as more complex. In the "Notes," he identified three political arrangements within the confederal/federal types of government that are neither confederations composed of sovereign states nor simple consolidated governments. One of these is the feudal system, another is a specific interpretation of the British Empire and her colonies, and the last is exemplified by the U.S. federal government – the subject of Chapter 12 of the "Notes."

Madison's partial praise of the feudal system stemmed from its theoretical superiority over confederal/federal government.[32] Technically, the feudal model was more than a mere confederation of sovereign states that could secede at will. The vassals owed allegiance to the King, who reigned as sovereign over the land. In reality, however, the King had to share power with the

[31] Banning, *Sacred Fire of Liberty*, 119, 163–64.

[32] Madison may have been spurred in his thinking about feudal institutions by Gabriel Bonnot de Mably's commentary on the extensive empire under Charlemagne. "[H]owever vast an empire may be," Mably wrote in *De la Legislation* (1773), "neither the number nor the extent of its provinces amount to insurmountable obstacles to its policies, whether one wants to reform it or simply to maintain good order.... All that is required to succeed in this enterprise is to decompose, so to speak, a state and turn all its provinces into as many federated republics. Their union will be their strength abroad and the small size of their territory will be their security at home. ... [Charlemagne] began by dividing the lands of his dominions into a hundred different provinces. His secret was to give them individual assemblies open to every order of citizen.... By way of this division, each province acquired the movement that could be imprinted upon it and the whole Empire acquired a new spirit and new manners" (quoted in Johnson Kent Wright, "The Idea of Republican Constitution in the Old Régime France," in *Republicanism: A Shared European Heritage*, eds. Martin Van Gelderen and Quentin Skinner [Cambridge: Cambridge University Press, 2002], 2:279–80).

barons, whose power served to limit and often match – or overmatch – his.[33] As Hamilton noted in *Federalist* 17, although the feudal system was not "strictly speaking" a confederacy, it nonetheless "partook of the nature of that species of association." It consisted of

> a common head, chieftain, or sovereign, whose authority extended over the whole nation; and a number of subordinate vassals, or feudatories, who had large portions of land allotted to them, and numerous trains of INFERIOR vassals or retainers, who occupied and cultivated that land upon the tenure of fealty or obedience, to the persons of whom they held it. Each principal vassal was a kind of sovereign, within his particular demesnes. The consequences of this situation were a continual opposition to authority of the sovereign, and frequent wars between the great barons or chief feudatories themselves. ... In those instances in which the monarch finally prevailed over his vassals, his success was chiefly owing to the tyranny of those vassals over their dependents. ...[34]

According to Madison, the feudal system was characterized by "a continual struggle between the head and the inferior members, until a final victory has been gained in some instances by one, in others, by the other of them."[35]

In *Federalist* 19, Madison expanded on this claim, offering specific examples. Charlemagne and his immediate descendants possessed both the emblems and the reality of imperial power, but gradually, the chief vassals who composed the national diets were able to accumulate power and attain independence and "sovereign jurisdiction." Thus, in the eleventh century, the emperors possessed absolute sovereignty, but by the fifteenth, they "had little more than the symbols and decorations of power."[36] The feudal system, Madison argued, "has itself many of the important features of a confederacy." The federal system of the Germanic Empire, for example, is an outgrowth of it. Powers are there vested in a national diet, which represents the members of the confederacy, and the emperor possesses numerous prerogatives – among them the exclusive right to propose measures to the diet and to negate its decrees. "From such a parade of constitutional powers in the representatives and head of this Confederacy," Madison wrote, "the natural supposition would be that it must form an exception to the general character which belongs to its kindred systems" – but "nothing would be further from the reality." The Germanic confederacy is grounded in the principle that "empire is a community of sovereigns." The diet is composed of sovereigns and the laws of the empire are addressed to sovereigns. The empire is in truth "a nerveless body, incapable of regulating

[33] Madison discussed this problem in *The Federalist*. In the absence of external danger to enforce the internal unity of the feudal system, and especially if the barons had "possessed the affections of the people, the great kingdoms in Europe would at this time consist of as many independent princes as there were formerly feudatory barons" (*Federalist* 45:287).

[34] *Federalist* 17:88–89.

[35] Madison to Jefferson, October 24, 1787, *MJM*, 218; *PJM*, 10:210.

[36] *Federalist* 19:97.

its own members, insecure against external dangers, and agitated with unceasing fermentations in its own bowels."[37]

In this discussion of the Germanic Empire, Madison identified both the central problem of confederacies of the past and pointed to his proposed alternative model. He summarized the problem in the conclusion of the next *Federalist* essay and in his letter to Jefferson: "a sovereignty over sovereigns ... is a solecism in theory," and "in practice it is subversive of the order and ends of civil polity." It is "the evil of imperia in imperio."[38] Madison's solution was to institute more than an empty parade of constitutional powers in the head of a confederacy. He sought to establish one ultimate and final sovereign authority with constitutional prerogative power.

The example of the British royal prerogative over legislation in the American colonies (prior to the war for independence) helped Madison achieve this solution. Albeit with important and substantive variations, this was the model for his proposed negative over state legislation at the Constitutional Convention; it continued to be a subject of concern in his analysis of federal governments in the "Notes on Government." In the years leading up to the American Revolution, a number of men, including Thomas Jefferson, Benjamin Franklin, and Thomas Pownall (the royal governor of Massachusetts), argued against the claim of parliamentary supremacy. Instead, they asserted, the colonies possess the supreme legislative power, albeit united by the sovereign authority of the Crown and subject to the royal negative, exercised by the King-in-Council (that is, the Privy Council). In the 1754 Albany Plan of Union, Franklin argued that the American colonies shall be administered by a Grand Council "chosen by the representatives of the people of the several Colonies" and subject only to the royal negative. The laws made by the Grand Council, Franklin argued,

> shall not be repugnant but as near as may be agreeable to the Laws of England, and Shall be transmitted to the King in Council for Approbation, as Soon as may be after their Passing and if not disapproved within Three years after Presentation, to remain in Force.[39]

Pownall also argued for jurisdictional legislative sovereignty in the American colonies – at least as time wore on. In the first edition of his work *The*

[37] See Hamilton's speech of June 18, 1787, at the Constitutional Convention, in which, according to Madison's "Notes of Debates," Hamilton argued that "[t]he authority of Charlemagne seemed to be as great as could be necessary. The great feudal chiefs however, exercising their local sovereignties, soon felt the spirit & found the means of, encroachments, which reduced the imperial authority to a nominal sovereignty. The Diet has succeeded, which tho' aided by a Prince at its head, of great authority independently of his imperial attributes, is a striking illustration of the weakness of Confederated Governments" (*Notes of Debates*, 132).

[38] Madison to Jefferson, October 24, 1787, *MJM*, 217; *PJM*, 10:209; cf. *Federalist* 20:106.

[39] Benjamin Franklin, *A Benjamin Franklin Reader*, ed. Walter Isaacson (New York: Simon & Schuster, 2005), 165.

Administration of the Colonies, he attacked the view that the colonies were a mere "dependent appendix of the demesnes of the crown" and argued instead that they are "members and parts of the realm" and "essential parts of a one organized whole."[40] In the fifth edition, Pownall argued that the government in the colonies was "free and sovereign ... within the limits of its own jurisdiction," although it was not "national and independent." Beyond these limits, Great Britain possessed sovereign power, as evidenced in the royal negative exercised by the King through his representatives in the Privy Council.[41]

Madison's references to Franklin's Albany Plan and Pownall's *Administration of the Colonies* in the "Notes" may have been based on research he did earlier when formulating his thoughts on the constitutional negative prior to the Constitutional Convention. Franklin's and Pownall's views on the political status of the colonies within the British Empire emphasized two main points with which Madison agreed in the 1780s and which continued to occupy his thoughts in the 1790s. First, the colonies were not mere dependent territories whose citizens could be taxed without representation and whose resources and products could be monopolized by the mother country, as William Barron claimed. Indeed, the American colonial government possessed constitutional standing and legislative jurisdiction in the colonies. Second, there was one ultimate sovereign authority in the empire that unified the system. This interpretation made a place for the American colonies within the British political system that was more akin to the feudal-federal model of empire than to a merely confederal or imperial one. "If the supremacy of the British Parliament is not necessary as has been contended, for the harmony of that Empire," Madison wrote to Jefferson, "it is evident I think that without the royal negative or some equivalent controul, the unity of the system would be destroyed."[42]

Just as Madison viewed the royal negative or some corresponding power necessary to the harmony and unity of the British Empire during the founding era, he also believed "some equivalent controul" essential to the unity and harmony of the American republic. While he modeled his idea of the negative on state laws on the royal prerogative exercised by the King's Council in colonial America, he clearly did not intend it to be a royal prerogative or executive prerogative. In the United States, it was to be vested in the national legislature – but on the understanding that the national legislature would be sufficiently controlled from making decisions adverse to the whole society. In preparation for the Constitutional Convention in spring 1787, Madison wrote

40 Thomas Pownall, *The Administration of the Colonies* (London, 1764), 65, 130–31. Cf. G. H. Guttridge, "Thomas Pownall's *The Administration of the Colonies:* The Six Editions," *William and Mary Quarterly* 26, no. 1 (1969): 35–36.

41 Thomas Pownall, *The Administration of the Colonies*, 5th edn., 35–37; see also the 1st edn. (1764), 44. Cf. Guttridge, "Thomas Pownall's *The Administration of the Colonies*," 45.

42 Madison to Jefferson, October 24, 1787, *MJM*, 217; *PJM*, 10:210.

Washington a long and thoughtful letter explaining his goal of achieving some "middle ground" between state sovereignty and consolidation and, within this context, the need for a negative on state laws. Madison's aim was to establish a "*due* supremacy of the national authority" – one which would "be the least possible encroachment on the State jurisdictions."[43] On June 28, at the Constitutional Convention, Madison argued that "the highest prerogative of supremacy is proposed to be vested in the National Gov[ernmen]t"; the "negative proposed on the State laws" will assimilate the national government within the individual states by making it "an essential branch of the State Legislatures."[44] Despite his failure to attain passage of the constitutional negative at the Convention, Madison did not concede an inch of ground as to its necessity in the months following the work at Philadelphia. In his October 24, 1787, letter to Jefferson, he argued for its necessity in a federal system that was neither composed of sovereign members nor was a consolidated nation. He also reiterated the argument he had made to Washington the previous spring: "The great desideratum in Government is so to modify the sovereignty as that it may be sufficiently neutral between different parts of the society to control one part from invading the rights of another, and at the same time sufficiently controlled itself from setting up an interest adverse to that of the entire society."[45]

As a number of scholars have argued, the constitutional negative Madison envisioned was not a positive power.[46] Only a particular state had the authority to propose legislation within its own jurisdiction. Like the governor of each state, the national legislature would serve as another check on state legislation, negating state laws that did not accord with the U.S. Constitution or were

[43] Madison to Washington, April 16, 1787, *PJM*, 9:383; emphasis added.

[44] Speech at Constitutional Convention, June 28, 1787, *PJM*, 10:80.

[45] Madison to Jefferson, October 24, 1787, *MJM*, 222; *PJM*, 10:209. In this letter, Madison listed five possible positions on the partition of power between the general and state governments: (1) the complete abolition of the states, (2) a Congress possessing indefinite power and a negative over state legislation, (3) a Congress possessing indefinite power without a negative over state legislation, (4) a Congress with limited powers and a negative over state legislation (Madison's position), and (5) a Congress with limited power and without a negative over state legislation (the view that prevailed at the Constitutional Convention). In Madison's view, none of the first three options were acceptable; all represented forms of unlimited and consolidated government. He favored retaining the state governments, defining and limiting the powers of the general government, creating better safeguards for individual rights (which he believed had been notoriously trampled on by the states under the Articles of Confederation), and preventing a collision between state and federal laws before the former have passed constitutional muster rather than after the fact, when an appeal to force might be considered the solution by some.

[46] Charles F. Hobson, "The Negative on State Laws: James Madison, the Constitution, and the Crisis of Republican Government," *William and Mary Quarterly* 36, no. 2 (April 1979), 221, and *passim*. See also Michael P. Zuckert, "Federalism and the Founding: Toward a Reinterpretation of the Constitutional Convention," *Review of Politics* 48, no. 2 (1986): 166–210, 196; and Banning, *Sacred Fire of Liberty*, 112–21.

contrary to individual rights or the general good. Still, the prerogative over state laws would be possessed by the federal or national legislature. And, indeed, the remedy Madison proposed is often referred to as the *national* negative, although to my knowledge, Madison never referred to it precisely as such. Madison's advocacy of the negative on state laws has been cited by many scholars as evidence that he was a "nationalist" and that his stance in the 1790s, particularly his support of "intervention" in the Virginia Resolutions, represents an abandonment of his earlier nationalism and a change of mind. Once the stage has been set by this apparently powerful evidence, then other examples of Madison's inconsistency seem to fall neatly into place. For example, he is viewed as inconsistent in advocating for the multiplicity and fragmentation of interests and views at the Constitutional Convention (and in his writings as Publius), and then calling for a "consolidation" of public opinion a few years later. In sum, the conclusion many scholars have reached is that Madison was a nationalist and skeptic of popular rule in the 1780s, and a Jeffersonian states' righter and man of faith in the people in the 1790s.

If we follow the line of reasoning on the constitutional negative that Madison outlined in the "Notes on Government," however, I believe that the alleged demonstration of Madison's inconsistency is not so clear cut or persuasive and that the case can reasonably be made that his conception of federal republicanism was erected on a constant attachment to the principle of popular sovereignty and the aspiration for self-government. Madison's continued investigation into the structure of the British American colonies prior to the American Revolution – in particular, his attention to the negative on colonial laws – was spurred by his desire to find a middle ground between a confederation composed of individual sovereign states and a consolidated government. Just as he believed that a sovereignty over sovereign entities was a theoretical solecism and had in fact been the cause of the downfall of most confederacies in history, he also eschewed the notion of "overgrown" empire. As we have seen, with respect to the latter, Madison taught that a nation is too large if combinations of the people cannot be formed to prevent governmental oppression. This is the natural result in a large territory that lacks effective local organs of government, without which public opinion cannot be collected and brought to bear on the general government.[47] In a large territory, consolidated government is self-directed government; in an extensive nation, a federal structure is necessary to sustain the processes of republican government. Federalism contributes to enlarging the practicable sphere of republican government, in the absence of which even a good administration does not have the needed information to make policy directed to justice and the general good. A bad administration simply has a clear road to executive aggrandizement and tyranny.[48]

[47] "Consolidation," *MJM*, 235; *PJM*, 14:138. Cf. *Federalist* 46; *PJM*, 17:247.

[48] "Consolidation," *MJM*, 235–36; *PJM*, 14:138–39.

These were not concerns that Alexander Hamilton spent late nights mulling over, but James Madison did. Charles Hobson's claim that "in 1787, Madison was scarcely less a consolidationist than Hamilton"[49] fails to account for the importance Madison attached to the federal structure in order to prevent governmental oppression and sustain the processes of republicanism. Madison's "nationalism" – if this is the appropriate term – was not tantamount to consolidation, which lacks an interior structure capable of supporting the effective expression of public opinion. Madison's brand of "nationalism" – no less than his conception of federalism – was a logical corollary of his commitment to *republicanism* and *union*. Like Hamilton, he did not think any alliance of sovereign governments was adequate to stymie the propensity to disunion. But he disagreed with Hamilton's view that a good administration (even – and especially – in a large territory) could make economic interest an adequate force of stability and guardian of liberty, thereby dispensing with the need to depend on a majority combination of the people to limit and control the government.

The negative Madison envisioned to achieve a "disinterested and dispassionate umpire" was indeed a "national prerogative" – to be exercised by Congress over the states. The "modification" Madison spoke of in "Vices of the Political System" and in his letters to Washington and Jefferson is clearly a modification of the old confederal system of state sovereignty, but it is not merely or most fundamentally a modification of state sovereignty by national sovereignty. He did not envision his stated objective of achieving a "disinterested and dispassionate umpire" as answered by a national legislature composed of better sorts of men who, for all practical intents and purposes, would be independent of the will of the society. This is because, in his mind, the problem was not one that could simply be solved by the proper distribution of governmental powers or, in the final analysis, by any government per se.[50]

[49] Hobson, "The Negative on State Laws," 218.

[50] Madison decisively stated in *Federalist* 46: "The adversaries of the Constitution seem to have lost sight of the people altogether in their reasonings on this subject: and to have viewed these different establishments not only as mutual rivals and enemies, but as uncontrolled by any common superior in their efforts to usurp the authorities of each other. These gentlemen must here be reminded of their error. They must be told that the ultimate authority, wherever the derivative may be found, resides in the people alone...." (291). See Gordon Wood's treatment of the question of Madison's "nationalism" and of his republican vision in his essay "Is There a James Madison Problem?" in *Revolutionary Characters: What Made the Founders Different* (New York: Penguin Press, 2006), 141–72. Wood claims that while Madison was a nationalist, his brand of nationalism was very different from Hamilton's modern perspective, which was intimately connected with the idea of building a modern state with a powerful executive.

In contrast, Madison's "strange" vision of nationalism harkened back to a traditionalist and idealistic conception of politics. His goal was to evade popular majoritarian rule in the states by creating a dispassionate and disinterested umpire at the national level, which would be achieved by elevating the few enlightened and virtuous sorts to positions of national political power and, in a system that neutralizes the effects of interest group politics, essentially gives the elite a free hand to rule. Accordingly, Wood believes that the inconsistency many scholars find in Madison's

In fact, as Madison conceived of the prerogative power in republican government, it resides most fundamentally in the will of the society.

At the outset of the legislative session under the new Constitution, Madison declared that "*the highest prerogative of power … [is] not found in either the executive or legislative departments of government, but in the body of the people, operating by the majority.* …"[51] In this, Madison disagreed with John Adams' view of the executive as an "impartial mediator" who would achieve the "great desideratum in a government" by disinterestedly rising above and balancing the interests of the few against the many.[52] Madison also disagreed with both Montesquieu and Aristotle, the former of whom believed that disinterestedness would be the result of political decisions in a constitutional government of separated powers. The latter conceived of disinterestedness as

political theory stems from the erroneous view that in the 1780s, and especially in the tenth *Federalist*, Madison was committed to a pluralist model of interest group conflict and resolution. However, this conflict was merely the necessary condition for creating a political environment in which the better sorts rule. Moreover, Wood argues, when one studies Madison properly within the historical context in which he formed his ideas, one sees that he resembles the country Whigs who feared the consolidation of political and military power in the hands of a powerful monarch unresponsive to the popular will, and whose policies of increasing the public debt, levying heavy taxes, and establishing standing armies enabled him to wage wars and generally engage in modern state-building.

In response, Madison followed opposition political thinkers in promoting modern commercial republicanism, which united the economic interests of nations and created a world of peace and prosperity. Madison's "ideal," Wood claims, "was to have the world become republican, that is, composed of states whose governments were identical with the will of the people." While Wood has correctly identified Madison's agreement with those who wrote and worked to oppose universal monarchy in modern Europe (although Montesquieu's lead in this deserves mention), Wood's Madison ultimately emerges with a new problem of inconsistency. If Madison's brand of nationalism relegates political rule to the few aristocratic types of men, how do we square this with his vision of a world constituted by republican governments whose wills are "identical with the will of the people"?

In this interpretation, we are still left with a serious "Madison problem." A close study of the "Notes on Government," however, shows us that Madison's support for the constitutional negative as well as his conception of a world composed of republican states was grounded in a vision of federal union that did not place ultimate reliance on either rule by an aristocratic elite or on the effects of merely interest-based commerce among nations. Rather, Madison intended representation in the national legislature and economic commercialism (both domestic and international) to contribute substantially to the creation of a political environment in which the will of the government of each state/nation is dependent on the will of the society and, in turn, the will of the society is rooted in the reason of the society.

51 In Congress, June 8, 1789, *PJM*, 12:204; emphasis added.

52 Compare Madison's language of "great desideratum in Government," "disinterested & dispassionate umpire," and "impartial" judge, with Adams' language cited above. See Madison to Washington, April 16, 1787, *PJM*, 9:384; "Vices of the Political System of the United States," *MJM*, 203; *PJM*, 9:357; Madison to Jefferson, October 24, 1787, *MJM*, 222; *PJM*, 10:214; cf. Sheehan, *James Madison and the Spirit of Republican Self-Government*, 92–94, and notes. See also the *Defence*, *WJA*, 6:396, 5:473; cf. 5:585; Thompson, *John Adams and the Spirit of Liberty*, 221.

resulting optimally from either an enlightened monarch or a polity composed chiefly of the middle class. In this ancient polity, there existed no political space between the direct, collective political capacity of the people and the considered will of the society. In Madison's republic, the will of the society is not identical to the will of the government, as it necessarily was in the classical small republics. Rather, Madison conceptualized the will of the society as achieved only by much effort, including the communication of views and the refinement of ideas that are required to achieve a common opinion in a large and populous nation. The will of the government should be dependent on the will of the society – the latter of which is the embodiment of the greatest political power and the highest political authority.

To view the issue of the constitutional negative in terms of the supremacy of the national over the state governments is not an erroneous formulation, but it is incomplete and inadequate to understanding Madison's republican theory. Madison did advocate making the national government the arbiter of state laws, but his reasoning for this was tied to the differences he perceived between the procedural formation and substantive character of majority opinion at the two distinct levels of government. The dangers to republicanism at these two levels were not precisely the same. At the state or micro level, the problem was less that the government would tyrannize over the people than that the majority, operating through the legislature, would oppress the minority. This is due to the ease of forming combinations of the people in smaller territories with less population. At the macro level, it is much more difficult for a majority to unite in a common oppressive demand; nevertheless, the power of the legislature vis-à-vis the other branches of government is as predominant at the national level as it is at the state level. Consequently, the means for uniting the people in defensive measures against governmental oppression are of prime importance at the national level. As Madison explained to Jefferson:

> As in too small a sphere oppressive combinations may be too easily formed agst. the weaker party; so in too extensive a one, a defensive concert may be rendered too difficult against the oppression of those entrusted with the administration.[53]

Thus, while the national legislature would serve well the purpose of providing "a pretty even balance between the parties of particular States," Madison continued, with respect to national issues, it must be "sufficiently restrained by its dependence on the community, from betraying its general interests." The prerogative power of the national legislature, then, must be a manifestation of the will of the society – or, in other words, of the constitutional majority. "The General Government would hold a pretty even balance between the parties of

[53] Madison to Jefferson, October 24, 1787, *MJM*, 222; *PJM*, 10:214.

particular States, and be at the same time sufficiently restrained by its dependence on the community, from betraying its general interests."

In addition to the idea of prerogative as the discretionary power to act for the public good where the laws are silent, the term also refers to the special preeminence that is a consequence of sovereignty. It was in this latter sense that Madison equated a constitutional negative with the national prerogative. In the British government, a battle between the King and Parliament over who possessed the preeminent power of sovereignty had been fought for many years. In the United States, however, Madison taught, no government or governmental branch possesses sovereignty. In America,

> [t]he people, not the government, possess the absolute sovereignty. The legislature, no less than the executive, is under limitations of power. Encroachments are regarded as possible from the one as well as from the other. Hence, in the United States, the great and essential rights of the people are secured against legislative as well as against executive ambition. They are secured, not by laws paramount to prerogative, but by constitutions paramount to laws.[54]

The term *sovereignty*, like *prerogative*, was used by Madison in two different senses: In one sense, the word *sovereignty* connotes governmental power; in another sense, it refers to the most fundamental authority in the polity.[55] In *The Federalist*, for example, Madison used the term *sovereignty* (and its cognates) in both ways. He claimed that the states are sovereign *and* that a sovereignty over sovereigns (that is, divided sovereignty) is an oxymoron.

With some careful exegesis, one can tease out the two different uses of the word in Madison's writings, but fortunately, this is unnecessary because Madison himself, in his later years, took pains to draft an essay on the very subject.[56] Madison's distinction hinges on the difference between sovereignty as "supreme power" and the "attributes" of sovereignty. In the former case, there can only be one supreme power in a state; in the latter, the powers granted by the sovereign can be divided and distributed among different governments and the branches of government. In the United States, the "supreme power" is identified with "the sovereignty of the people of the States." The people can, and, in fact, have, according to the Constitution, divided the attributes of sovereign power between the states and the general government. Government can never be sovereign in the supreme and absolute sense of the term, Madison

[54] "Virginia Report of 1800," in *Mind of the Founder*, ed. Marvin Meyers, 257.

[55] With regard to the idea of the national prerogative, see Madison's speech of June 28, 1787, at the Constitutional Convention, in which he stated: "By the plan proposed[,] ... the highest prerogative of supremacy is proposed to be vested in the National Govt. ... The negative proposed on the State laws, will make it an essential branch of the State Legislatures & of course will require that it should be exercised by a body established on like principles with the other branches of those Legislatures" ("Rule of Representation in the First Branch of the Legislature," *PJM*, 10:80).

[56] "Sovereignty," 1835, *WJM*, 9:568–73.

taught. All just and free governments are founded in compact, and their powers are derivative from the natural right of individuals to form political societies, which to them shall be deemed conducive to their safety and happiness. The compact created by these individuals is established by a moral power, which in turn arms the governments they establish with a moral power. They cannot transfer power they do not morally or rightfully possess; they cannot, for example, imbue the majority or the government with rights that cannot be alienated by human beings, such as the right of conscience.

The next question, Madison wrote, "is how far the will of a majority of the society, by virtue of its identity with the will of the society, can divide, modify, or dispose of the sovereignty of the society."[57] Just as it has been admitted that a majority can divide the society itself into distinct and sovereign entities (as, for example, has occurred in the separation of Kentucky from the state of Virginia and Maine from Massachusetts), a majority can also divide the attributes of sovereign power between the general and the state governments. In this sense, then, the idea of "divided sovereignty" is perfectly legitimate and the consequence of the act of a "supreme power" of sovereignty derived from social compact. Indeed, because they are created by a "supreme power" of sovereignty based on compact, state governments and the general government are equally sovereign in their respective spheres and the equivalent of moral persons. However, once individuals have entered into such a social compact and formed a constitutional and moral being, Madison warned, they cannot separate on constitutional grounds.

Clearly, Madison was not a nationalist in the sense of wanting to endow the central government or even the national legislature with supreme sovereign authority. Within the context of the argument of the "Notes," federalism is a structural device that contributes to the formation of public opinion and the actualization of its role as the operational and moral sovereign in the polity. In Chapter 12 of the "Notes," Madison summarized the arguments of the three preceding chapters and presented the U.S. government as the example of a properly structured federal republic. Citing *Federalist* 51, he claimed that the government of America derives a double security from the separation of powers between the general and state governments and from the separation of the departments of governmental power at each level. By a "judicious modification and mixture of the *federal principle*," the practicable sphere of the territory is enlarged, thereby contributing to the means for achieving the "*republican cause*." In *The Federalist* and in his reference to this work in his "Notes," Madison thus elevates the structural device of federalism to a principle of republican government.

Madison's discussion of checks on democratic government, separation of powers, and federalism is intended to show how the structural and institutional

[57] "Sovereignty," *WJM*, 9:571.

mechanisms that interface with the large territory and the principle of representation contribute to safeguard individual liberty and to achieve governmental dependency on public opinion. In the Party Press Essay "Consolidation," Madison discussed more specifically the way in which a well-organized federal republic gives efficacy to public opinion in a large nation. There, he argued that state and local governments are absolutely essential to collecting and expressing the public voice. Without the "local organs" of government, the large extent of the territory Madison had in mind would make it impossible for the people to communicate effectively over a great distance. Absent government at the level of the states and local communities, the people could not form a united voice to control the government. Conversely, Madison argued that "the most arbitrary government is controuled where the public opinion is fixed."[58] In Madison's view, federalism is an indispensable element to securing a responsible dependency of the will of the government on the will of the society. Federalism is thus more than a structural device; it is a necessary principle to the formation of a united and effectual voice and to the union of a sovereign people in an extensive territory.

In contrast to Montesquieu and his followers, who called for a federative system that limited the military and political power of several sovereign states by elevating the rivalry of economic interests and jealous passions over civic attachments, Madison envisioned a republican empire composed of fellow citizens united by "one harmonious interest." Whereas Montesquieu concluded that the new spirit of commerce among peoples "unites nations, [but] it does not in the same manner unite individuals,"[59] Madison concluded that improved communications made possible an exchange of "ideas throughout the society." This "commerce of ideas" opened the way to the achievement of a "consolidation" in the "interests and affections" of the society and "throughout the great body of the people."[60] In a genuine republic, the "general harmony" of republican citizens is promoted, "wherever [they] resid[e], or however [they are] employed."[61]

In the "Notes on Government," Madison responded to the view of the federative republic predominant in his age with an entirely new analysis of republican government. The strength of empire is not antithetical to the freedom of the polis, he contended. Rather, if properly modified by the federal principle, it is the means to protect and perfect freedom. Grounded in the sovereignty of the people at every level of political association, he envisioned an association of states *and citizens* that merited the name "polity." Recalculating the aptitude of empire for liberty, he sought to promote "the *republican cause*" by way of "a judicious modification and mixture of the *federal principle*."

58 "Consolidation," *MJM*, 247–48; *PJM*, 14:138; cf. *Federalist* 46.

59 Montesquieu, *SOL*, 20:2, 316–17.

60 "Consolidation," *MJM*, 235–36; *PJM*, 14:138.

61 "A Candid State of Parties," *MJM*, 268; *PJM*, 14:372.

He coined the political order he envisioned a "compound of Fed[era]l & Repub [lican] polity."[62]

The federal republican polity was Madison's blueprint for America, but it was not limited to America. Such a polity, Madison declared, is "susceptible of … indefinite extents of space, by … combinations of its attributes: by a pyramid of Federal systems." Indeed, it is capable of "practical extension over the globe." Madison thus responded to the ancient paradox of republican polity versus empire and the vexing British problem of colonial dependency versus federal union by creating an entirely new order for the ages: the federal republican empire.[63] Suppose all the world under one government, "provinces of one empire," Madison mused in preparation for one of his first speeches in Congress.[64] Stability and freedom are not preserved by a system of sovereign states whose rulers possess the power of the sword and maintain their strength by the profits of commercial discrimination and monopoly but by "universal intercourse," which abolishes "the causes of external violence" and makes it the "interest of all to maintain the peace of all." Accordingly, free trade supplies the wants of mankind by making the superfluous products of every nation and every individual mutually contributory of every other. In sum, Madison declared: "Universal freedom presents the most noble spectacle, [it] unites all nations – makes <every man> a citizen of the whole society of mankind – and perfects the good aimed at by the Social union & Civil Govt."

THE REPUBLICAN WAY OF LIFE

The concluding chapter of the "Notes" is titled "Best distribution of people in [a] Republic."[65] Although a "perfect Theory on this subject" cannot "be reduced to practice by any plan of legislation," Madison argued that it is nonetheless "useful … [as] a model to which successive spontaneous improvements might approximate the condition of the Society."[66] Madison's republican archetype is based on the ends of the best polity, which he identified as the security, health, competency, liberty, virtue (or "health of the soul"[67]), and intelligence of the citizens.

[62] Cf. *Federalist* 51:293; James Madison, "Notes – Social Compact.," Series 1, From February 10, 1833 to Undated, Image 1188, *The James Madison Papers*, LOC, http://hdl.loc.gov/loc.mss/mjm.24_1188_1188. Cf. *WJM*, 9:216–17, 290, 430–31n.

[63] For a finely wrought study of the problem of colonial dependency, federation, and empire, see Pagden, *Lords of All the World, passim.*

[64] "Notes for Speech in Congress," ca. April 9, 1789, *PJM*, 12:68–69.

[65] See Madison's earlier discussion of this subject in the letter to Jefferson of June 19, 1786, *PJM*, 9:76–77.

[66] "Notes on Government," *MJM*, 164; *PJM*, 14:168.

[67] "Republican Distribution of Citizens," *MJM*, 258; *PJM*, 14:245.

First and foremost, Madison listed agriculture as the livelihood most conducive to the health and happiness of the individual and the society.[68] The greater number of people engaged in farming, he argued, the more free, independent, and happy is the society itself.[69] The manufacturer of the necessities and useful products of life is next in Madison's hierarchical ordering of occupations. Preferably, this manufacturing occurs at home, taken up by the hands not needed to work the farm. Less conducive to the internal and external goods of life is the manufacturing of nonessentials and luxury products outside the home, particularly employment in city factories. In his ideas on this, Madison anticipated the critical assessment of urban factory life set forth by Charles Dickens and Karl Marx, as well as recognized earlier by Adam Smith.

Such occupations are detrimental to the health of the body, mind, and soul of the worker. In cities, men are crowded upon one another and breathe putrid air;[70] the division of labor often means that one's narrow task is repetitive and mind-numbing. Those employed in the manufacture of superfluities also precariously depend on the demands and tastes of others. In the Party Press Essay "Fashion," Madison recounts the story of the humble buckle manufacturers of England, whose very livelihood was at stake when the fashion for slippers and shoestrings made buckles passé – despite the directive to their subjects to wear buckles by the Duke of York and the dandy Prince of Wales (later to become George IV). In an uncharacteristically contemptuous tone, Madison wrote:

> AN humble address has been lately presented to the Prince of Wales by the BUCKLE MANUFACTURERS of Birmingham, Wassal, Wolverhampton, and their environs, stating that the BUCKLE TRADE gives employment to more than TWENTY THOUSAND persons, numbers of whom, in consequence of the prevailing fashion of SHOESTRINGS & SLIPPERS, are at present without employ, almost destitute of bread, and exposed to the horrors of want at the most inclement season; that to the manufactures of BUCKLES and BUTTONS, Birmingham owes its important figure on the map of England; that it is to no purpose to address FASHION herself, she being void of feeling and deaf to argument, but fortunately accustomed to listen to his voice, and to obey his commands: and finally, IMPLORING his Royal Highness to consider the deplorable condition of

68 Compare Madison's praise of the way of life of the yeoman farmer as the backbone of republican virtue with Aristotle's discussion of the best kind of democracy at *Politics* VI:4, 186: "The best people is the farming sort, so that it is possible also to create [the best] democracy wherever the multitude lives from farming or herding." According to Aristotle, because the life of the farmer lacks leisure, he cannot often meet at the assembly; he does not covet his neighbor's goods nor is he envious of the respectable and notable men who occupy the political offices but who are restrained from ruling unjustly by the fact that the multitude of farmers have "authority over the audits" (*Politics*, VI:4, 186–87). Also see Aristotle's discussion of the inferior types of democracy, which are constituted by men whose occupations do not involve virtue, such as the merchants, artisans, wage earners, etc., at *Politics* VI:4, 187, 210.

69 "Republican Distribution of Citizens," *MJM*, 259; *PJM*, 14:246; cf. "Notes on Government," *MJM*, 164; *PJM*, 14:168.

70 Madison treats this subject more extensively in his "Address to the Agricultural Society of Albermarle, Virginia," May 12, 1818, *Retirement Series*, *PJM*, 1:257–59.

their trade, which is in danger of being ruined by the *mutability of fashion*, and to give that direction to the *public taste*, which will insure the lasting gratitude of the petitioners.[71]

In vivid contrast to the independent yeoman farmer, the producers of luxury goods depend on the fancy and caprice of such men as the notoriously self-indulgent Prince of Wales. In these and like circumstances, Madison argued, the dependence of a man "sinks to the lowest point of servility." Indeed, "*[t]wenty thousand* persons are to get or go without their bread, as a wanton youth, may fancy to wear his shoes with or without straps, or to fasten his straps with strings or with buckles," Madison satirically observed. "Can any despotism be more cruel than a situation, in which the existence of thousands depends on one will, and that will on the most slight and fickle of all motives, a mere whim of the imagination."[72]

Vying with the manufacturer of luxury goods for the lowest kind of human occupation is the sailor. The seaman's lot is not as dependent as is the former on the whims of others, but it is even more lacking in the mores and manners that form a part of human civilization. In fact, it is the least conducive to the health of the body and mind, Madison contended. While sea travel contributes to the intercourse that enlightens nations, refines manners, and extends the safety of the political community, the lifestyle of the sailor is confined and crude, and his existence is precarious. "His virtue, at no time aided, is occasionally exposed to every scene that can poison it. His mind, like his body, is imprisoned within the bark that transports him."[73] He is often without even the necessities of life, living on little more than "a bare sustenance," but "if his ultimate prospects do not embitter the present moment, it is because he never looks beyond it."

After these dreary portraits of crude and servile human existence, Madison offered an account of the more "elevated" professions. He included in this category "the merchant, the lawyer, the physician, the philosopher, [and] the divine." The most educated of this class form the "literati," who are no less necessary in the scale of human civilization than any other. Indeed, they are

the cultivators of the human mind – the manufacturers of useful knowledge – the agents of the commerce of ideas – the censors of public manners – the teachers of the arts of life and the means of happiness.[74]

As "the agents of the commerce of ideas," the literati perform an essential task in the extended, deliberative, modern republic. At the apex of the occupations that are not necessary for the physical survival of the community but are the most important to the quality of life of individuals and their polity, Madison listed the philosopher and the divine. They are tasked with the civic

[71] "Fashion," *MJM*, 260; *PJM*, 14:258. [72] "Fashion," *MJM*, 260–61; *PJM*, 14:258.

[73] "Republican Distribution of Citizens," *MJM*, 258; *PJM*, 14:245.

[74] "Notes on Government," *MJM*, 165; *PJM*, 14:168. Cf. "Republican Distribution of Citizens," *MJM*, 259; *PJM*, 14:246.

responsibility of looking after the minds and souls of their fellow citizens. They are the teachers of the teachers, on whose intellectual and moral guidance the character of a civilization significantly depends.

It is clear in this essay that the character of the republican citizen is uppermost in Madison's mind. To advance the conditions that form the character and spirit of the citizenry is the first duty of republican statesmen, albeit without impinging on individual freedom or the rights of property. In "Spirit of Governments," he described the character and spirit that typifies human beings in such pseudo-republican regimes as Great Britain: The people are mercenary, petty, and partisan and depend on the wealthy few for the spoils the corrupt system discharges. In "Republican Distribution of Citizens" and the associated notes, he presents a starkly different model of the genuine republican citizen, whose hardy independence, no nonsense manner, and common man's pride are a portrait of the American spirit and character we have all come to know. He is Horatio Alger who pulls himself up by his bootstraps. He is Robert Frost's New England farmer who thrusts his hoe into the ground decisively, "blade-end up and five feet tall," before he strides to the stone wall for a friendly chat with his approaching neighbor.[75] She is Rosa Parks, whose courage stemmed from her uncompromising sense of justice and human dignity. They are the crew of the Challenger Seven, pioneers who possessed a "special spirit" – the kind that welcome a challenge and meet it with joy, even on that hoary day when "they prepared for their journey and waved goodbye and 'slipped the surly bonds of earth' to 'touch the face of God.'"[76]

[75] See Robert Frost, "A Time to Talk," in *Robert Frost's Poems*, Introduction and Commentary by Louis Untermeyer (New York: St. Martin's Press, 2002), 172.

[76] Ronald Reagan, "Speech on the Challenger Disaster," January 28, 1986, http://teachingamericanhistory.org/library/document/speech-on-the-challenger-disaster.

5

Postscript

At the very end of the "Notes on Government," Madison referred to his published *National Gazette* essays. Assuming that he added this line some time after composing the "Notes," as the editors of *The Papers of James Madison* reasonably suggest (and as the difference in ink and handwriting indicate), the question of why he would have done so admits of two possible explanations. Either he added the note simply for purposes of clarification, probably much later in his life when he was putting his papers in order for posterity, or he appended this citation sometime after 1792, when he returned – or because he meant to return at some later time – to his unfinished work. Because he would have already polished and published some of the arguments from the "Notes" as newspaper essays, he could then include the discussion and analysis of the *National Gazette* articles as part of the notebook project rather than rewrite the passages he may have been specifically interested in including. If this were the case, however, then one wonders whether, later in his life, Madison intended (or perhaps had always intended) to use his "Notes" as the basis for some project other than the Party Press Essays. There exists, for example, a brief composition that is based on the first three chapters of the "Notes," but the date of its composition and its purpose are unknown.[1] The composition certainly appears, however, like an introductory statement to an essay or discourse on the subject of government.[2]

[1] See *PJM*, 14:172.

[2] This essay, titled by the editors of *The Papers of James Madison* as "Notes on the Influence of Extent of Territory on Government" (*PJM*, 14:132–33), is almost as polished as Madison's other Party Press Essays and, with the exception of a few abbreviations, seems ready for publication. This leads one to suspect that it might have been published in another newspaper about the time of the publication of the *National Gazette* essays or perhaps at an earlier or later date. As such, it would not have been included in the bound copy of the *National Gazette* essays that Madison

Moreover, sometime subsequent to the War of 1812 and most likely after he left the presidency and retired to Montpelier,[3] Madison resumed work on the subject of the various influences on government. (See Chapter 7: "Additional Notes on Government.") This set of notes consists of four separate headings that pertain to the subjects of emigration and the fiscal influences on government: "Exceptions to the maxim that commerce should be free," "Influence of foreign commerce on Government," "Emigration," and "Influence of a large public debt on Government."[4] Given the headings and their theme, one reasonably wonders whether Madison may have intended these notes as a

initialed. (The initialed, bound notebook does not include all of Madison's *National Gazette* essays; "Dependent Territories" was not included in the list.) If it was published elsewhere, however, I have not been able to locate it. It is also possible that this piece was intended as the opening salvo to a comprehensive work based on his research in the "Notes on Government." Following is the brief essay:

In estimating the tendency of Governme[n]t to the increase or the relaxation of their powers[,] particular causes distinct from their respective structures, but of powerful influence on their operation, seem to have been overlooked or little heeded by the great oracles of political wisdom. In the discussions produced by the establishment and revisions of the new forms of Govt. in the U. S. and especially of their General Govt. some of these causes have engaged particular attention. (See the *Federalist* No. 10.) A Govt. of the same structure, would operate very differently within a very small territory and a very extensive one: over a people homogeneous in their opinions & pursuits, and over a people consisting of adverse sects in religion, or attached to adverse theories of Govt: over a Society composed wholly of tenants of the soil aspiring and hoping for an enlargement of their possessions and a Society divided into a rich or independent class, and a more numerous class without property and hopeless of acquiring a permanent interest in maintaining its rights: over a nation secure agst. foreign enemies, and over one in the midst of formidable neighbours.

The influence of the extent of territory seems to have been least understood or attended to; and yet admits of the most satisfactory illustrations. Were the British Govt. limited in its exercise to the City of London and freed from all external dangers, is it not certain that the facility of popular combinations and the force of public opinion & feeling, would give the law to the monarch with all his splendid prerogatives and to the peers with all their titled wealth, and be able at any moment to transform the Govt. into a simple democracy. Reverse the supposition, and let the Island be enlarged to the dimensions of China, and it is equally evident, that the difficulty of concerting popular plans & movements, with [the] facility possessed by veiling its designs from distant eyes, and of turning the prejudices and interests real or imaginary of the parts agst each other, and the necessity of multiplying the prerogatives of the Ex., as a substitute for the minute & diversified legislation called for, would gradually enable the Executive branch of the Govt. to overwhelm the others, and convert the Govt. into an absolute monarchy.

[3] See the reference to the War of 1812 in "Exceptions to the maxim that commerce should be free," at #10 of Madison's listing. In addition, at #7 in this listing, Madison discussed the "machinations" of Great Britain against the American cotton and glass manufacturers, which probably referred to the British policy of shipping large quantities of goods to the United States, particularly glass and cotton, after the war ended and a commercial nondiscrimination agreement was signed by the two countries in 1815. See *MJM*, 167–68.

[4] John C. Payne, the executor of Madison's estate, believed that these notes on "Emigration" may have constituted the original sketch for Madison's Party Press Essay "Population and Emigration."

continuum of his 1791 "Notes on Government" and in particular to the first section of the "Notes" focused on the "Influence(s) ... on Government."[5] We recall that in the 1791 "Notes," Madison consulted and cited at length Barthélemy's *Voyage of Anacharsis*; in the "Additional Notes," he returned to *Voyage*, citing specific examples and page numbers on the subject of colonization and commerce from Barthélemy's work.

Be that as it may, we know for a fact that Madison did write on the subject of commerce in his retirement years. On October 30, 1828, Madison wrote his fellow Virginian (and cofounder of the University of Virginia) Joseph C. Cabell a letter that, together with a letter to the same of September 18, 1828, was subsequently published in the *National Intelligencer* on December 22, 23, and 25, 1828.[6] The first letter addressed the issue of the constitutionality of the tariff, and the second set forth exceptions to the free trade doctrine. According to Marvin Meyers, although Madison requested that the letters not be published until after the presidential election (which was complied with), the letters nonetheless "raised a political storm in Washington and Richmond."[7] What is particularly interesting with regard to the "Additional Notes on Government," however, is that the arguments in Madison's second letter are clearly related to (and probably based on) the entry in this notebook titled "Exceptions to the maxim that commerce should be free."

Commercial policy was only one of the political and philosophic subjects Madison studied during his leisure hours at Montpelier after returning in 1817. According to his own account in his autobiographical sketch, when he retired from the presidency, he "devoted himself to his farm & his books," although perhaps not to the extent he wished, for much of his time was taken up by the "extensive and often laborious correspondence" demanded of him as an ex-president and lifelong public servant.[8] In addition to his correspondence with many of his contemporaries on constitutional and political subjects, Madison notes that he also left behind "sundry letters and papers on Constitutional and other subjects never printed."[9]

[5] In Madison's notes for a speech in Congress of April 9, 1789 (*PJM*, 12:68–69), on the theme of the principles of and exceptions to a free system of commerce, Madison outlined his general theory of the influence of commerce on government and then noted the various exceptions to this theory. On the back of this page, he wrote (perhaps at a later date): "Head. for a discourse." The editors of *The Papers of James Madison* transcribe Madison's note on the verso: "Heads for a discourse," but I believe that "Head." may be an abbreviation for "Heading," thus signifying "Heading for a discourse."

[6] These letters are reprinted in Meyers, *Mind of the Founder*, 370–89.

[7] Meyers, *Mind of the Founder*, 269–70.

[8] "Autobiography," 1830, http://rotunda.upress.virginia.edu/founders/default.xqy?keys=FOEA-print-02-02-02-2226.

[9] Douglass Adair, "James Madison's Autobiography," *William and Mary Quarterly* 2, no. 2 (1945): 191–209, 207.

Madison's intent to resume his scholarly habits after leaving the presidency is borne out by his confidante, Jefferson. On June 22, 1817, Jefferson wrote to Madison:

> When here an observation fell from you once or twice which did not strike me at the time, but reflection afterwards led me to hope it had meaning: and that you thought of applying your retirement to the best use possible, to a work which we have both long wished to see well done, and which we thought at one time would have been done.[10]

In this letter, Jefferson referred to his hope that Madison would write a history of the Republican Party to offset John Marshall's *Life of Washington* and its proffered vindication of the principles and policies of the Federalist Party.

A few years later, in January 1823, Judge William Johnson, who was working on a history of American political parties and believed that Madison might also have been engaged in writing on the same subject, asked Jefferson about this. Jefferson relayed the query to Madison. In response, Madison asked Jefferson to correct the error of Judge Johnson, remarking:

> I hope you will find an occasion for correcting the error of the Judge in supposing that I am at work on the same ground as will be occupied by his historical view of parties, and for *animating* him to the completion of what he has begun on that subject.[11]

Madison implied in this letter that the Judge (and perhaps also Jefferson to some degree) had misunderstood the project he was working on. He also intimated that he was working on a project of some significance but that his work was on a *different ground* than the Judge's work on the *history* of parties. That Madison was not working on the "same ground" as the Judge leads one to think that he was working on a related subject, but perhaps with a different focus or approach to it. It is at least conceivable that the ground of approach Madison alluded to was a philosophical rather than an historical treatment of parties in the early America republic, or perhaps it was an analysis of republicanism in general, with emphasis on the American model. It is also possible that the scholarly project he was working on in 1823 was the work he had mentioned to Jefferson in 1817 and had planned for some time to pursue. Clearly, his friends and associates believed he was engaged in a substantial scholarly project in the years following the conclusion of his tenure as president, as Judge Johnson's letter reveals.[12]

[10] James Morton Smith, ed., *The Republic of Letters: The Correspondence Between Thomas Jefferson and James Madison, 1776–1826* (New York: W. W. Norton & Company, 1995), 3:1786.

[11] Madison to Jefferson, January 15, 1823, in *The Republic of Letters*, ed. James Morton Smith (New York: W.W. Norton & Company, 1995), 3:1855.

[12] Jefferson's response of March 4, 1823, to Judge Johnson strengthens the claim that Madison was indeed working on some project other than the *historical* account of parties in America. After encouraging the Judge to finish his history of American parties, Jefferson wrote: "Mr. Madison will probably leave something, but, I believe, *only particular passages of our history*, and these

If Madison was at this time engaged in a theoretical analysis of republican government, which included examining additional influences on government that he had not covered in his 1791 "Notes on Government," or if he was working on some other scholarly project in his retirement, then either he did not follow through on his intentions beyond the notes he composed sometime after 1812 on demographic and economic considerations, or this work has been lost or destroyed.

Unfortunately, the collection of Madison's papers housed in the Library of Congress is far from complete. Shortly after Madison's death in 1836, his widow found herself reduced to near poverty due to the extravagant spending habits and gambling debts of her grown son, John Payne Todd. To cover his debts, Dolley Madison was forced to sell some of her husband's papers to the federal Congress in 1837; in 1848, she sold to Congress what she considered the remainder of his unpublished writings. Many of these papers were then loaned to Madison's first biographer, William Cabell Rives, who ultimately returned only a portion of what he had borrowed. In addition, the collection Mrs. Madison sold to the federal government was not complete in the first

chiefly confined to the period between the dissolution of the old, and commencement of the new government; which is peculiarly within his knolege [*sic*]. [A]fter he joined me in the administration he had no leisure to write" (Thomas Jefferson to William Johnson, March 4, 1823, Series 1, From February 14, 1822 to September 18, 1823, Image 750, *The Thomas Jefferson Papers*, LOC, http://hdl.loc.gov/loc.mss/mtj.mtjbib024584; emphasis added). Jefferson may have been referring here to Madison's brief (albeit unfinished) historical account of the constitutional framing period in his preface to the *Notes of Debates in the Federal Convention of 1787*. Whatever project or projects Madison was working on, it clearly seemed to occupy his retirement for quite some time. In 1820, for example, Dolley Madison complained to her cousin and good friend Sally Coles Stevenson that she had been confined to Montpelier for the past three winters because her husband had been working on the arrangement of his papers. Dolley wrote: "I have just now recd. by post your welcome letter my ever dear cousin, and cannot express my anxiety to embrace you once more! But a spell rests upon me and withholds me from those I love best in this world – not a mile can I go from home – and in no way can I account for it, but that my Husband is also, fixed there. This is the third winter in which he has been engaged in the arrangement of papers, and the <…> appears to accumulate as he proceeds – so that I calculate its out-lasting my patience and yet I cannot press him to forsake a duty so important, or find it in my heart to leave him during its fulfillment" (Dolley Payne Todd Madison to Sarah (Sally) Coles Stevenson, ca. February 1820, Letter, *The Dolley Madison Digital Edition*, edited by Holly C. Shulman, University of Virginia Press, http://rotunda.upress.virginia.edu:8080/dmde/dolley-details.xqy?letter=/dmde/DPM0649.xml&return=toc_chron). And, indeed, four years later, on November 27, 1824, Dolley again remarked about the fact that she and her husband had not budged from Montpelier: "Mr. Madison & myself have been favored with fine health since our residence at Montpelleir [*sic*], … tho we have not been far from home within 8 years" (Dolley Madison to John George Jackson, *The Dolley Madison Digital Edition*, http://rotunda.upress.virginia.edu:8080/dmde/dolley-details.xqy?letter=/dmde/DPM0613.xml&return=toc_chron). As Dolley noted, Madison was engaged in arranging his papers for posterity during this period. However, his work on his papers may have well included much more than corrections and cataloguing. It may have included, as Judge Johnson and others suspected, a larger and more scholarly endeavor.

place; her wastrel of a son had pilfered a substantial amount of the material, which, after passing through another set of hands, was widely dispersed at public auction.[13]

Some of this was perhaps James Madison's own fault, or at least the fault of a loving husband and generous stepfather. John Payne Todd's irresponsible spending and gambling habits had been a pattern for years, landing him twice in debtors' prison. While Madison was alive, however, he paid off Payne Todd's creditors and covered his debts time and time again. And he did this more often than not without his wife's knowledge.[14] He knew the grief that Dolley's son had caused her, and to the extent he was able, he wished to spare her additional pain.

It is perhaps an irony of history that the story of the founding scholar, whose vision of America was that of a land of self-government, may remain unfinished in the archives of the American mind because of a stepson whose life was the antithesis of that vision. Be that as it may, as Madison knew, the virtue of the republican citizen cannot be forced. The responsible exercise of freedom must be willed – and to be willed, it must be part of a man's or woman's understanding and habits. Such is the eternal challenge but yet abiding hope of the age-old experiment in self-government.

Whether or not Madison returned to the project of the "Notes" with the intention of completing his outline, or even perhaps of writing a polished commentary on government, fortunately, he did leave for posterity an outline that is rich in context and comprehensive in scope. The "Notes on Government" reveal the workings of the mind of Madison, confirming that he was indeed a man who blended together the qualities of the republican statesman and profound philosophical scholar.

[13] See Library of Congress, http://lcweb2.loc.gov/ammem/collections/madison_papers/mjmabout2.html.

[14] Ralph Ketcham, *James Madison: A Biography* (Charlottesville: University of Virginia Press, 1990), 615–16.

PART II

6

Notes on Government[1]

The articles in this volume were written after the commencement of the new government, as is proved, among other circumstances, by frequent references to "Travels of Anacharsis," first published in 1789. ——[2]

[1] James Madison, "Notes on Federal Governments, 1789," Series 6, Notes on Federal Governments. 1789, Image 1771, *The James Madison Papers*, LOC, http://hdl.loc.gov/loc.mss/mjm.28_1771_1794, *PJM*, 14:157–69. Generally, the citations to Barthélemy's *Voyage* first list Madison's citation to the 2nd French edition (which he was working with) and then, for the ease of English readers, in parentheses to the English translation of 1806: Jean Jacques Barthélemy, *Travels of Anacharsis the Younger in Greece During the Middle of the Fourth Century Before the Christian Aera*, 4th edn., 7 vols. and an eighth in quarto (London, 1806). When only the English is cited, the reference is in parenthesis. Passages reprinted from *Voyage* include Barthélemy's reference notes. These citations are abbreviated throughout *Voyage*; herein, the first reference to a particular source is written in full. Four loose sets of papers are interleaved in the "Notes on Government" notebook: (1) a paper which includes information on "Washington. Highways," a note reading "Some critics whose disaffection to our form of govmt have lost them the public confidence, preferring every thing to insignificance have in their despair talked of a dissolution of the Union. These however are so few that our madhouses will hold them should should [*sic*] acts follow their words of insanity," an "Agenda," and some mathematical calculations; (2) a letter from Lt. Horace C. Story to Madison, April 8, 1822; (3) "notes for calculating interest"; (4) and "Books sent by Mr. Jefferson for Dr. Curry" (this is likely Dr. James Currie). According to the editors of *The Papers of James Madison*, the first and third of these items are in Jefferson's hand, while the fourth item is in Madison's hand (*PJM*, 14:168).

[2] Madison added this sentence at some later date – probably sometime after his retirement from public life in 1817, when he organized his papers for posterity. The "Xs" and underlining on this page are also in a lighter ink and appear to have been added at a later date.

(1)[3]

INFLUENCE OF THE SIZE OF A NATION ON GOVERNMENT

Plato limits the number of Citizens to five thousand and forty. Montesquieu tom. II c. 16, 17[4] L'experience a fait voir que le nombre des hommes en etat de porter les armes, ne doit être ici [dans une republique sagement reglee] ni fort au dessus, ni fort au dessous de vingt mille. Anach: vol. [II] p: 117 & citation.[5]

See Convention Notes[6] – letter to Mr. Jefferson on a federal negative on State laws[7] Federalists No. X et alia: – Case of popular confiscation in Switzerland, mentioned in Encyclop: Method:[8] Plunder of rich Citizens by democracy of Megara.

[3] Madison wrote "(1)" in the upper corner of the page to indicate that this is page 1 of his notebook. He numbered some of the pages of this notebook and left others blank.

[4] Montesquieu, *SOL*, 23:17, 11 nnm, n: "The politics of the Greeks were particularly employed in regulating the number of citizens. Plato fixes them at five thousand and forty,[a] and he would have them stop or encourage propagation, as was most convenient, by honors, shame, and the advice of the old men; he would even regulate the number of marriages in such a manner that the republic might be recruited without being overcharged.[b]"

---

[a] "Repub." lib. V.

[b] Ibid.

[5] Madison's citation of *Voyage* 2:117 is an error; the quotation he referred to is in *Voyage* 1, Introduction, Partie 2, Section 1 (111): "In a well regulated republic the number of inhabitants should neither be too great nor too inconsiderable.[a] Experience has shown that the number of men able to bear arms ought neither greatly to surpass nor fall much short of, twenty thousand.[b]"

---

[a] Plato. De Republic. lib. 4. t. ii. p. 423. Aristotle. De Republica Atheniensium. lib. 7. cap. 4. p. 430.

[b] Plat. in Crito. t. iii. p. 112. Demosthene in Aristogitonem. p. 836: Plutarch in Pericles. t. i. p. 172. Philochorus in Scholium Pindar, Olympian Odes 9. v. 67. Scholium Aristophanes in Vespae v. 716.

In the original French text, Barthélemy wrote: "Dans une république sagement réglée, il ne faut pas que le nombre des habitans soit trop grand ni trop petit. L'expérience a fait voir que le nombre des hommes en état de porter les armes, ne doit être ici ni fort au dessus, ni fort au dessous de vingt mille" (*Voyage du Jeune Anacharsis en Grèce dans le Milieu du Quartrième Siècle Avant l'Ère Vulgaire*) [Document électronique]. T. 1. [1] /, Introduction, Partie 2, Section 1, 52 [par l'Abbé J.-J. Barthélemy], *Gallica Classique*, http://gallica.bnf.fr/ark:/12148/bpt6k61716r/f72.image.r=.langEN.

[6] This reference may be either to the "Notes of Debates in the federal Convention" (*PJM*, 10, *passim*) and/or to Madison's notes in preparation for the Federal Convention, "Vices of the Political System of the United States" and "Notes on Ancient and Modern Confederacies" (*PJM*, 9:3–24); the reference may possibly also refer to Madison's "Additional Memorandums on Ancient and Modern Confederacies" (*PJM*, 10:274–83).

[7] Madison to Jefferson, October 24, 1787, *PJM*, 10:205–20.

[8] Panckoucke, *Encyclopédie Méthodique*.

Anacharsis vol. 3. p. 409[9] instances of proscriptions of rich in Antient & Italian Republics – Exiles so numerous as to return sometimes and seize the Govt. Aristotle Repub. book 5. cap. 5.[10] Anacharsis vol. 5 page 268.[11]

(a) All overgrown empires have betrayed first tyranny – then impotency, as the Assyrian – Persian – Macedonian – Roman – that of Charlemagne –

In order to temper an aristocracy into a mild Govt. the state should like those of Switzerland be so small as to admit a ready combination of the people agst. oppression, as in order to temper a Republic, it ought to be so large, as to impede a combination of the people for the purpose of oppression. – See p. 10. – [12] See Anacharsis as to oligarchy of Rhodes. vol. 6 p. 240.[13]

9 *Voyage*, 3:409 (359–60): "Megara, which is the capital, was formerly joined to the harbour of Nisæa by two long walls, which the inhabitants thought proper to demolish about a century ago.[a] It was long governed by kings.[b] Democracy succeeded, and subsisted till the public orators, to please the multitude, invited them to share amongst them the spoils of the rich citizens. An oligarchical form was then established;[c] but in our time the people have resumed their authority.[d]"

---

[a] Thucydides lib. 4. cap. 109. Strabo lib. 7. p. 392.
[b] Pausanias lib. 1. cap. 39. p. 95; cap. 41. p. 99.
[c] Thucyd. lib. 4. cap. 74. Aristot. de Rep. lib. 5. cap. 3. t. ii. p. 388; cap. 5. p. 392.
[d] Diodorus Siculus lib. 15. p. 357.

10 Aristotle, *Politics*, V:5, 155: "The democracy in Megara was also overthrown in a similar way. The popular leaders, in order to be in a position to confiscate their goods, expelled many of the notables, until they had created many exiles, who then returned, defeated the people in battle, and established an oligarchy."

11 *Voyage*, 5:268 (247–48): "Almost all our governments, under whatever form they may be established, contain within themselves many seeds of destruction. As the greater part of the Grecian republics are confined within the narrow limits of a city, or a district, the divisions of individuals, which become the divisions of the state, the misfortunes of a war which seems to leave no resource, the inveterate and perpetually-renewed jealousy of the different classes of citizens, or a rapid succession of unforeseen events, may in a moment shake to the foundations or overturn the constitution. We have seen the democracy abolished in the city of Thebes by the loss of a battle,[a] and in those of Heraclea, Cumæ, and Megara, by the return of some principal citizens, whom the people had proscribed to enrich the public treasury with their spoils.[b] We have seen the form of government changed at Syracuse by a love-intrigue;[c] in the city of Eretria, by an insult offered to an individual;[d] at Epidaurus, by a fine imposed on another individual:[e] and how many seditions have there been which have not originated from more important causes, and which gradually spreading have at last occasioned the most destructive wars!"

---

[a] Aristot. de Rep. lib. 5. cap. 3. p. 388.
[b] Id. ibid. cap. 5. p. 392.
[c] Aristot. de Rep. lib. 5. cap. 4. p. 390.
[d] Id. ibid. cap. 6. p. 395.
[e] Id. ibid. cap. 6. p. 391.

12 See *MJM*, 131, where Madison wrote: "In *small* states external danger tends to aristocracy (see p. 1) . . ."

13 *Voyage*, 6:240 (210–11):

The supreme authority [in Rhodes] had always been in the hands of the people, but it was wrested from them some years since by a faction in the interest of Mausolus king of Caria,[a] and

---

For the extent of antient republics & confederacies – see Encyclopae. Ant: Geograp: Anacharsis with the Maps ——[14]

---

they in vain implored the assistance of Athens.[b] The rich, who had before been ill treated by the people, took more care of their interests than they had done themselves. They ordered distributions of corn to be made among them, from time to time; and appointed certain officers to supply the necessities of the poorer class, and especially of those employed in the fleets and arsenals.[c]

Such prudent measures will no doubt perpetuate the oligarchy;[d] and, so long as the principles of the constitution shall remain uncorrupted, other states will ever seek the alliance of a people, the leaders of whom are distinguished by consummate prudence, and the soldiers by intrepid courage.[e] But these alliances will never be frequent.[f] The Rhodians will remain as much as possible in an armed neutrality. They will have fleets always ready to protect their commerce; by commerce they will amass riches; and the riches will enable them to maintain their fleets.

Their laws inspire them with an ardent love for liberty, and their superb monuments impress their minds with the ideas and sentiments of grandeur. They preserve hope in the most calamitous reverses of fortune, and the ancient simplicity of their fathers in the midst of opulence.* Their manners have sometimes been endangered; but they are so attached to certain forms of order and decency, that such attacks have on them only a transient influence. They appear in public in modest habits, and with a grave demeanour. They are never seen running in the streets, and hurrying over each other. They are present at the public shows in silence; and in those entertainments in which mirth and the confidence of friendship reign, they forget not the respect they owe to themselves.[g]

[a] Aristot. De Rep. lib. 5. cap. 3. t.ii. p. 388; et cap. 5. p. 392. Theopompus Historicus in Athenæi Deipnosophistarum lib. 10. cap. 12. p. 444. Demosth. On the Liberty of the Rhodians. p. 144, 145. Libanius. Argument to Demosthene, Ibid. p. 143. Ulpianus in Demosth. p. 149.

[b] Demosth. de Libert, Rhod. p. 143.

[c] Strab. lib. 14. p. 652.

[d] The oligarchy established at Rhodes in the time of Aristotle still subsisted in the time of Strabo.

[e] Polybius. lib. 5. p. 428. Id. Excerpt. Legat. O. 924. Diod. Sic. lib. 20. p. 820. Hist. de Bell. Alexandr. cap. 15.

[f] Diod. Sic. lib. 20. p. 809.

See note IX. at the end of the volume.

[g] Dionis Chrysostomi. Orationes. 31. p. 359; orat. 32. p. 377.

**Voyage* 6 (441): Note IX. chap LXXIII, 211: *On the Rhodians*

The character which I give of the Rhodians is founded on a number of passages in ancient authors, particularly on the testimonies of esteem they received from Alexander;[a] on the famous siege which they sustained, with so much courage, against Demetrius Poliorcetes, thirty-eight years after the time when I suppose Anacharsis to have visited their island;[b] on the powerful succours which they furnished to the Romans; and on the marks of gratitude which they, in consequence, received from the republic of Rome.

---

[a] Diod. Sic. 20. p. 809.

[b] Id. ibid. p. 810. Plut. in Demetrius p. 898.

[c] Livii (Titi), Historiæ lib. 51. cap. 15; lib. 37. cap. 12. Auli Gelli, Noctes Atticæ lib. 7. cap. 3.

[14] Madison referred here to the "General Map of Greece and the Grecian Colonies" in the eighth volume of *Voyage*. In the English 1806 edition cited herein, however, the translator was unable to include this particular map. The atlas was the work of M. Barbié du Bocage; in the corrected

---

The best provision for a stable and free Govt. is not a balance in the powers of the Govt. tho' that is not to be neglected, but an equilibrium in the interests & passions of the Society itself, which can not be attained in a small Society. Much has been said on the first. The last[15] deserves a thorough investigation. (see p 2. (a))[16]

The larger a community, the more respectable the whole & the less the share of importance felt by each member, the more submissive consequently each individual to the general will.

Whatever facilitates a general intercommunication of sentiments & ideas among the body of the people, as a free press, compact situation, good roads, interior commerce &c. is equivalent to a contraction of the orbit within wch. the Govt. is to act: and may favor liberty in a nation too large for free Govt. or hasten its violent death in one too small & so vice versa. Could the people of G. Britain be contracted into one of its Counties it would be scarcely possible for the monarchical branch to support itself agst. the popular branch. Could they be spread over 10 times the present area, or the communion of sentiments be obstructed by an abolition of the press &c. the reverse would happen. The extent of France & heterogeneousness of its component provinces have been among the principal causes of the monarchical usurpation. See Robertson's Chs. V. notes.[17]

---

edition of *Voyage*, which this English translation is based on, the new, large map of Greece and the Grecian colonies had not yet been published in France (VII:7; cf. I:xi–xiii).

15 Above "the last" is written "has been." Madison usually indicates where such additions should be inserted, but in this case he did not, and it is not clear from the context where it should appear.

16 See *MJM*, 129, where Madison is referring to the subsequent passage that begins: "see p. 1 – (Natural divisions exist in all political societies . . .)"

17 Robertson, *The History of the Reign of the Emperor Charles V*. See especially the prefatory essay titled "A View of the Progress of Society in Europe From the Subversion of the Roman Empire to the Beginning of the Sixteenth Century," which is also available at www.eliohs.unifi.it/testi/700/robertson/section-2.htm. In his lengthy preface, Robertson traced the history of monarchical usurpations in France, providing a summary of the subject in the opening of Section II:

> Such are the events and institutions which, by their powerful operation, contributed gradually to introduce regular government and polished manners in the various nations of Europe. When we survey the state of society, or the character of individuals, at the opening of the fifteenth century, and then turn back to view the condition of both at the time when the barbarous tribes which overturned the Roman power completed their settlement in their new conquests, the progress which mankind had made towards order and refinement will appear immense.
>
> Government, however, was still far from having attained that state in which extensive monarchies act with the united vigour of the whole community, or carry on great undertakings with perseverance and success. Small tribes or communities, even in their rudest state, may operate in concert and exert their utmost force. They are excited to act, not by the distant objects or the refined speculations which interest or affect men in polished societies, but by their present feelings. The insults of an enemy kindle resentment; the success of a rival tribe awakens emulation: these passions communicate from breast to breast, and all the members of the community, with united ardor, rush into the field in order to gratify their revenge or to acquire distinction. But in widely-extended states, such as the great kingdoms of Europe at the beginning of the fifteenth century, where there is little intercourse between the

---

The Roman Empire was more than 2,000 miles from N. to S. & [more] than 3000 from W to E. Its population about 120,000[,]000 including slaves (who amounted to about one half) – this more than the population of all Europe. See Gibbon[18]

---

distant members of the community, and where every great enterprise requires previous concert and long preparation, nothing can rouse and call forth their united strength but the absolute command of a despot or the powerful influence of regular policy. Of the former, the vast empires in the East are an example: the irresistible mandate of the sovereign reaches the most remote provinces of his dominions, and compels whatever number of his subjects he is pleased to summon to follow his standard. The kingdoms of Europe, in the present age, are an instance of the latter: the prince, by the less violent but no less effectual operation of laws and a well-regulated government, is enabled to avail himself of the whole force of his state, and to employ it in enterprises which require strenuous and persevering efforts (72–73).

[18] Edward Gibbon, *The History of the Decline and Fall of the Roman Empire*, ed. J. B. Bury, (New York: Fred de Fau and Co., 1906), http://oll.libertyfund.org/titles/1681:

> But the temper, as well as knowledge, of a modern historian require a more sober and accurate language. He may impress a juster image of the greatness of Rome by observing that the empire was above two thousand miles in breadth, from the wall of Antoninus and the northern limits of Dacia to Mount Atlas and the tropic of Cancer; that it extended in length more than three thousand miles, from the Western Ocean to the Euphrates; that it was situated in the finest part of the Temperate Zone, between the twenty-fourth and fifty-sixth degrees of northern latitude; and that it was supposed to contain above sixteen hundred thousand square miles, for the most part of fertile and well-cultivated land ("The Extent of the Empire in the Age of the Antoinines," 1:55).
>
> ...The number of subjects who acknowledged the laws of Rome, of citizens, of provincials, and of slaves, cannot now be fixed with such a degree of accuracy as the importance of the object would deserve. We are informed that, when the emperor Claudius exercised the office of censor, he took an account of six millions nine hundred and forty-five thousand Roman citizens, who, with the proportion of women and children, must have amounted to about twenty millions of souls. The multitude of subjects of an inferior rank was uncertain and fluctuating. But, after weighing with attention every circumstance which could influence the balance, it seems probable that there existed, in the time of Claudius, about twice as many provincials as there were citizens, of either sex and of every age; and that the slaves were at least equal in number to the free inhabitants of the Roman world. The total amount of this imperfect calculation would rise to about one hundred and twenty millions of persons: a degree of population which possibly exceeds that of modern Europe, and forms the most numerous society that has ever been united under the same system of government ("The Internal Prosperity in the Age of the Antoinines," 1:63–64).

As the editors of the *PJM* (14:168–69n8) accurately note, Madison drew the information cited here from his earlier "Memorandums for the Convention of Virginia in 1788 on the federal Constitution" (*MJM*, 205–13; *PJM* 10). In the "Memorandums," Madison wrote:

> Roman Empire more than 2000 M. from N. to. S. more than 3000 from W. to. E. Gibbon population of do. abt. 120 Million including slaves who abt. ½. this more than in Europe. Id.

Spain 700 by 500 Miles	Engd. 360 by 300
France 600 by 500	Scotd. 300 by –150
Italy – – 600 by 500	
Germany 600 by 500	Denmark 240 by 180
Poland 700 by 680	Norway 1000 by 900.
Sweeden 800 by 500	

In monarchies, the danger is twofold. 1. that the eyes of a good prince cannot see all that he ought to know. 2 that the hands of a bad one cannot be sufficiently tied by the fear of easy combinations against him. Both these considerations prove, contrary to the received opinion, that a very great extent of Country is not suited to that form of Government: In a Representative Republic the eyes of the Government see every thing; and the danger arising cheifly [*sic*] from easy combinations under the impulse of misinformed or corrupt passions. it appears on the other hand, equally agst. the received opinion, that such a form of Govt. may be extended over a great Country, and cannot succeed in a small one.

The influence of this circumstance, is strongly enforced by attending to the extremes of size – Among 3 men in a Wilderness, two would never obey one – nor perhaps the one escape the oppression of the two should any real or fancied interest unite them agst. him. On the other hand, were all Europe formed into one society, the mighty mass, being unable to govern themselves wd be necessaryly [*sic*] governed by a few or one, and being also incapable of uniting agst. oppression, would be sure to be oppressed by their Governors.

(2

(a) see p 1. – [Natural divisions exist in all political societies, which should be made mutual checks on each other. But it does not follow that artificial distinctions, as kings & nobles, should be created, and then formed into checks and balances with each other & with the people. This reasoning in politics, would be as inadmissible as it would be in Ethics, to say that new vices ought be promoted that they may control each other, because this use may be made of existing vices – avarice and vanity – cowardice & malice – &c]

The danger of oppression to the minority from unjust combinations of the majority, and which is the disease of small States is illustrated by various instances.

By the case of Debtors & Creditors in Rome & Athens
By that of the Patricians & Plebeians & the Rich & poor, in the latter, in Florence & the other free Cities of Italy
By the Spartans & Helots
By the case of Black slaves in Modern times
By religious persecutions every where
By the tender & other unjust laws in U. S.
By the law of St. Marino which requires its Judges to be foreigners
By the law de medietate[19] in England
By the law agst. admitting a member of Corporation to be on a jury where the Corporation is party.

[19] *De medietate linguæ* was an English common law practice signifying a mixed (or, literally, "half tongue") jury. The practice was used when one party in a lawsuit was a non-English-speaking foreigner; the jury was composed of half Englishmen and half natives of the foreigner's country.

The danger is still greater where geographical distinctions enforce the others, as appears

By the conduct of Carthage towards Sicily &c –
of Athens towards her colonies
of Genoa towards Corsica
of Holland towards her colonies
of Rome towards her provinces
of G. B towards Ireland
of do towards America.

(10

INFLUENCE OF EXTERNAL DANGER ON GOVERNMENT

Fear & hatred of other nations, the greatest cement, always appealed to by rulers when they wish to impose burdens or carry unpopular points. Examples in Engd. & France abound. – See Federalist No. VII[20] & XXX.[21] Roman: Senate quelled popular commotions by exciting foreign wars –

See (a) under the preceding head page 1.[22] Extensive Governments have fallen to pieces not more from the inadequacy of Govt. to the Extent – than from the security agst. external danger.

---

[20] Hamilton's conclusion in *Federalist* 7 is that "America, if not connected at all, or only by the feeble tie of a simple league, offensive and defensive, would, by the operation of such jarring alliances, be gradually entangled in all the pernicious labyrinths of European politics and wars; and by the destructive contentions of the parts into which she was divided, would be likely to become a prey to the artifices and machinations of powers equally the enemies of them all. *Divide et impera* must be the motto of every nation that either hates or fears us" (33–34).

[21] Madison is referring here to Hamilton's argument in *Federalist* 30 regarding the national government's power of taxation. Specifically, he is citing Hamilton's reference to the possibility of using foreign wars in the future in order to justify this power, and to carry this probably none-too-popular point with many of his readers. In this essay, Hamilton wrote: "Let us attend to what would be the effects of this situation in the very first war in which we should happen to be engaged. We will presume, for argument's sake, that the revenue arising from the impost duties answers the purposes of a provision for the public debt and of a peace establishment for the Union. Thus circumstanced, a war breaks out. What would be the probable conduct of the government in such an emergency? Taught by experience that proper dependence could not be placed on the success of requisitions, unable by its own authority to lay hold of fresh resources, and urged by considerations of national danger, would it not be driven to the expedient of diverting the funds already appropriated from their proper objects to the defense of the State? It is not easy to see how a step of this kind could be avoided; and if it should be taken, it is evident that it would prove the destruction of public credit at the very moment that it was becoming essential to the public safety" (159–60).

[22] Madison is referring here to the following passage on p. 1 of the "Notes" (*MJM*, 125 herein):

(a) All overgrown empires have betrayed first tyranny – then impotency, as the Assyrian – Persian – Macedonian – Roman – that of Charlemagne –

Quere, if an insulated people be found on the Globe united under one Govt.? – However small the number, they must be divided into hostile nations, that mutual fear may support Govt. in each.

In small states external danger tends to aristocracy (see p. 1.) a concentration of the Public will being necessary, and that degree of concentration being sufficient. The many can not govern on acct. of the emergencies which require the constant vigilance & provisions of a few, but on account of the smallness of the Society the facility of the combinations of the many moderates the power of the few, & the few themselves oppose the usurpation of a single tyrant. In Thessaly, intersected by Mountainous barriers into a number of small cantons, the Governments were for the most part oligarchical – see Thucidides 1. 4. c. 78.[23] see Anachar: v: 3. p. 352.[24]

---

[23] Thucydides, *History of the Peloponnesian War*, trans. Charles Forster Smith (London: William Heinemann, 1920), II:347 (Book IV, Chapter 78, of Thucydides): "Indeed, Thessaly was not in any case an easy country to traverse without an escort, and especially with an armed force; and among all the Hellenes alike to traverse the territory of neighbours without their consent was looked on with suspicion. Besides, the common people of Thessaly had always been well disposed to the Athenians. If, therefore, the Thessalians had not been under the sway of a few powerful men, as is usual in that country, rather than under a free democracy, Brasidas would not have made headway..."

[24] *Voyage*, 3:352 (310–11):

> The Achæans, and Æolians, the Dorians, from whom descended the Lacedæmonians, and several other powerful states of Greece, derive their origin from Thessaly. The people who inhabit it at present are the Thessalians properly so called, the Œteans, the Phthiotians, the Malians, the Magnesians, the Perrhæbians, &c. These nations were formerly governed by kings, and afterwards experienced revolutions common to great and small states; at present they are for the most part subject to an oligarchy.[a]
>
> On certain occasions, the towns of each of these states send their deputies to a council in which their interests are discussed;[b] but the decrees of these assemblies are binding only on those who have subscribed to them. Thus not only are the states independent of each other, but this independence is extended to the towns of every state. For instance, the state of the Œteans being divided into fourteen districts,[c] the inhabitants of one may refuse to follow the others to war.[d] This excessive liberty diminishes the strength of each state, by preventing it from uniting its forces, and produces such languor in the public deliberations, that they often dispense with convening the assemblies.[e]
>
> The confederacy of the Thessalians properly so called is the most powerful of all, both from the number of towns appertaining to it, and from the accession of the Magnesians and Perrhæbians, whom it has almost brought under complete subjection.[f]
>
> We meet likewise with some free cities which seem unconnected with any of these states, and which, too weak singly to maintain their independence and command a proper respect, have formed an alliance with two or three other neighboring towns, detached and feeble like themselves.[g]
>
> ---
>
> [a] Thucyd. lib. 4. cap. 78.
> [b] Id. ibid. Liv. lib. 35. cap. 31; lib. 36. cap. 8; lib. 39. cap. 25; lib. 42. cap. 38.
> [c] Strab. lib. 9. p. 434.
> [d] Diod. Sic. lib. 18. p. 595.
> [e] Liv. lib. 34. cap. 51.
> [f] Theophilus in Athennæi Deipnosophistarum lib. 6. p. 265.
> [g] Strab. lib. 9. p. 437. Liv. lib. 42. cap. 53.

For the effect of the situation of Crete on its internal divisions – see Id. v. 6. p. 257.[25]

---

[25] *Voyage*, 6:257 (224–27):

Lycurgus borrowed from the Cretans the practice of repasts in common, the rigid rules of public education, and several other particulars which seem to establish a perfect conformity between his laws and those of Crete. Why then have the Cretans more early and more shamefully degenerated from their institutions than the Spartans? Unless I am mistaken, the following are the principle causes.

1) In a country surrounded by seas and mountains, which separate it from the neighboring regions, each people it contains must sacrifice one part of their liberty to preserve the other; and, for their mutual protection, unite their interests in one common center. Sparta having become, by the valour of its inhabitants, or the institutions of Lycurgus, the capital of Laconia, dissensions are rarely seen to arise within that country. But in Crete, the cities of Cnossus, Gortyna, Cydonia, Phæstus, Lyctos, and a number of others, form so many independent republics, who are jealous enemies, and constantly at war with each other. When a rupture takes place between the people of Cnossus and Gortyna her rival, the island is distracted with factions; and when they are united, it is in danger of being reduced to slavery.[a]

2) At the head of each of these republics ten magistrates, named Cosmi,[b,c] are charged with the administration of the government, and the command of the armies. They consult with the senate; and lay the decrees, which they draw up in concert with that body, before the assembly of the people, which only possesses the privilege of confirming them.[d] This constitution has an essential defect. The cosmi are only chosen from a certain class of citizens; and as, after their year of office has expired, they possess the exclusive right of filling the vacant places in the senate, the consequence is, that a small number of families, invested with the whole authority of the state, refuse to obey the laws; exercise, by uniting, the most despotic power; or, by opposing each other, excite the most fatal seditions.[e]

3) The laws of Lycurgus establish equality of possessions among the citizens, and preserve it by prohibiting commerce and industry; but those of Crete permit every person to increase his property.[f] The former forbid all communication with foreign nations; but this stroke of genius escaped the legislators of Crete. That island is open to merchants and travellers from all countries, who import the contagion of riches and that of evil example. It appears that Lycurgus justly relied more on the purity of manners than on the excellence of laws. What has been the result? In no country have the laws been so respected as by the magistrates and citizens of Sparta. The Cretan legislators seem to have laid greater stress on the laws than on manners, and to have been more careful to punish than to prevent crimes: the consequence has been, injustice in the heads of state, and corruption in individuals.[g]

The law of syncretism, which enjoins all the inhabitants of the island to unite if a foreign power should attempt a descent, would be insufficient to defend them either against their internal dissensions or against the arms of an enemy;[h] because it would only suspend instead of extinguishing animosities, and would suffer too many individual interests to subsist in a general confederation.

---

[a] Strab. lib. 10. p. 478, 479. Polyb. lib. 4. p. 319.

[b] Chishull, Antiquitates Asiaticæ p. 108.

[c] This name, which is sometimes written in Greek Κόσμοι, and sometimes Κόσμιοι, may signify Regulators or Inspectors. (Chish. Antiq. Asiat. p. 123.) Ancient authors sometimes compare them to the Ephori at Lacedæmon.

[d] Aristot. lib. 2. cap. 10. t. ii. p. 333.

[e] Aristot. lib. 2. cap. 10. t. ii. p. 333. Polyb. lib. 6. p. 490.

Sicily, tho a part of a moderate Kingdom, always when free divided into separate & hostile communities see Thucidides[26] Livy[27] &c[28]

(16

INFLUENCE OF STAGE OF SOCIETY ON GOVERNMENT.

---

[f] Polyb, ibid. p. 489.

[g] Polyb, lib. 6. p. 490. Meursii Bibliotheca Græca et Attica in Creta lib. 4. cap. 10. p. 231.

[h] Aristot. de Rep. lib. 2. cap. 10. p. 333. Plut. De Fraterno Amore. t. ii. p. 490.

[26] Thucydides, *History of the Peloponnesian War*, II:313 (Book IV, Chapter 61; speech by Hermocrates to his fellow Sicilians): "And yet, if we are prudent, we ought, each of us in behalf of his own state, to call in allies and incur dangers only when we are seeking to win what does not belong to us and not when we imperil what is already ours; and we should remember that faction is the chief cause of ruin to states and indeed to Sicily, seeing that we her inhabitants, although we are all being plotted against, are disunited, each city by itself."

[27] Titus Livy, *The History of Rome*, IV:31.29: "The meeting of the Aetolian League which they call the Pan-Aetolium was to be held on a certain day. The king's envoys hastened their journey in order to be in time for it and Lucius Furius Purpurio was also present as representing the consul, as was also a deputation from Athens. The Macedonians were allowed to speak first, as the treaty with them was the latest that had been made. They said that as no new circumstances had arisen they had nothing new to urge in support of the existing treaty. The Aetolians, having learnt by experience how little they had to gain by alliance with the Romans, had made peace with Philip, and they were bound to keep it now that it was made. 'Would you prefer,' asked one of the envoys, 'to copy the unscrupulousness – or shall I call it the levity? – of the Romans? When your ambassadors were in Rome, the reply they received was 'Why do you come to us, Aetolians, after you have made peace with Philip without our consent?' And now the very same men insist upon your joining them in war against Philip. Formerly they pretended that they had taken up arms against him on your account and for your protection, now they forbid you to be at peace with Philip. In the first Punic war they went to Sicily, ostensibly to help Messana; in the second, to deliver Syracuse from Carthaginian tyranny and restore her freedom. Now Messana and Syracuse and in fact the whole of Sicily are tributary to them: they have reduced the island to a province in which they exercise absolute power of life and death. You imagine, I suppose, that the Sicilians enjoy the same rights as you, and that as you hold your council at Naupactus under your own laws, presided over by magistrates of your own choice, and with full power of forming alliances or declaring war as you please, so it is with the councils which meet in the cities of Sicily, in Syracuse or Messana or Lilybaeum. No: a Roman governor manages their meetings; it is at his summons that they have to assemble; they see him issuing his edicts from his lofty tribunal like a despot, and surrounded by his lictors; their backs are threatened with the rod, their necks with the axe, and every year they have a different master allotted them. Nor ought they, nor can they wonder at this when they see the cities of Italy, such as Regium, Tarentum and Capua, lying prostrate beneath the same tyranny, to say nothing of those close to Rome out of whose ruin she has grown to greatness. ..." [http://etext.virginia.edu/etcbin/toccer-new2?id=Liv4His.sgm&images=images/modeng&data=/texts/english/modeng/parsed&tag=public&part=260&division=div2]. I am grateful to Dr. Christopher Haas, Professor of Ancient History at Villanova University, for his help in locating this passage.

[28] According to Barthélemy, in his August 25, 1789, induction speech to the Académie Française in the ancient republics, the ignorant multitude decided the fate of the polity – often based on the eloquence or reputation of the orator – and thus it was that the young Alcibiades involved Athens in the fatal expedition to Sicily: "Dans ces anciennes républiques, où une multitude ignorante décidoit des plus grands intérêts sans les connoître, le sort de l'état dépendoit souvent de l'éloquence ou du crédit de l'orateur; c'est ainsi que le jeune Alcibiade entraîna follement les Athéniens à cette fatale expédition de Sicile. ..." ["In these ancient republics, where an ignorant multitude decided great interests without knowing them, the fate of the state often depended on the eloquence or credit of the orator; thus the young Alcibiades foolishly led the Athenians on this fatal expedition to Sicily. ..."] www.academie-francaise.fr/discours-de-reception-de-jean-jacques-barthelemy.

(22

INFLUENCE OF PUBLIC OPINION ON GOVERNMENT

Public opinion, sets bounds to every Government, and is the real sovereign in every free one.

As there are cases where the public opinion must be obeyed by the Government, so there are cases, where, not being fixed, it may be influenced by the Government. This distinction, if kept in view, would prevent or decide many debates on the respect due from the Government to the sentiments of the people.

If the British Government be as excellent as represented, it is less because so in itself, than because so in the public opinion. Its boasted equilibrium is preserved more by this cause, than by the distribution of its powers. If the nation favored absolute monarchy its representatives would at once surrender the public liberty; if republicanism, the monarchical branch could not maintain its independence. If the public opinion was neutral only, the ambition of the House of Commons would easily strip the Prince of his prerogatives. The provision to be made at every accession, for the Civil list, shews at once his dependence on the popular branch, and its dependence on the public opinion. Were the establishment to be from year to year instead of for life, the Monarchy would dwindle into a name. But the nation would in such a case take the side of the King agst. its own representatives. – Those who ascribe the character of the British Government to the form alone in which its powers are distributed & counterpoised, forget the changes which its form has undergone. Compare its primitive with its present form; a King at the head of 7 or 8 hundred Barons sitting together in their own right, or (admitting another Hypothesis) some in their own right, others as representatives, of a few lesser barons, but still sitting together as one House – & the Judges holding during the pleasure[29] of the King – with a King at the head of a Legislature consisting of two Houses, each jealous of the other, one sitting in their own right, the other representing the body of the people, and the Judges forming a distinct & independent department; in the first case the Judiciary united with the Executive, the legislature not divided into separate branches; in the latter, the Legislative Executive & Judiciary distinct, and the Legislature itself divided into rival parts. What can be more contrasted than these forms? If the one be self-balanced, the other could have no balance at all. Yet the one subsisted as well as the other, and lasted longer than the other has yet been tried. It was supported by the opinion of the times, like many of the intermediate forms thro' which, the B. Govt. has passed, and as the future forms will probably be supported, thro' which[30] changes of circumstances and opinions are yet to conduct it.[31]

[29] In the Party Press Essay "British Government" Madison wrote "& the Judges holding their offices during the pleasure..."

[30] There appears to be a & symbol after "which." Based on the context, this seems to be extraneous.

[31] Madison's critique of the heralded claim that the British government owes its longevity to its constitutional distribution of powers is at least in part based on his reading of Hume's political essays, particularly "Of the First Principles of Government," "Of the Independency of

Not only Theoretical writers as Plato (Republic), but more practical ones as Swift &c. remark that the natural rotation in Government is from the abuses of Monarchy to Aristocracy, from the oppression of aristocracy to democracy, and from the licentiousness of Democracy back to Monarchy.[32] Many examples, as well as the reason of the thing,[33] shew this tendency. Yet it appears from Aristotle that under the influence of public opinion, the rotation was very different in some of the States of Greece. See Arist: Repub. b. 5 c. 12.[34]

Parliament," and "Whether the British Government Inclines More to Absolute Monarchy, or to a Republic" (Hume, *Essays*, 32–36, 42–53).

[32] See the opening discussion in Book VIII of Plato's *Republic*; see Jonathan Swift, *Discourse of the Contests and Dissentions Between the Nobles and the Commons in Athens and Rome: With the Consequences They Had Upon Both Those States*, ed. Frank H. Ellis (Oxford: Oxford University Press, 1967); cf. Adams, *A Defence of the Constitutions of the United States*, Letter XIV on "Dr. Swift" (*Defence*, vol. 1, *WJA*, 4:383–89) and Letter XXXIII on "Plato" (*Defence*, vol. 1, *WJA*, 4:448–63).

[33] As anyone who has studied Madison's original papers knows, the task of transcribing his writing is extremely onerous. The editors of *The Papers of James Madison* deserve the highest praise for the very fine transcription work they have done in volume after volume of this series. With respect to this one word in "Notes on Government," Madison almost certainly wrote "thing" rather than "King," as indicated at *PJM*, 14:62. Upon close inspection of the word and letters at issue ("thing" or "King"), it assuredly appears to be a "th" rather than a "K." While Madison's capital "K" and "th" are quite similar in appearance, his "K" often has a break after it – almost as if printed in block letter rather than cursively written – and the writing here is in cursive style. In addition, reference to "the reason of the King" does not appear to make sense in this context of regime degeneration. In contrast, reference to historical examples on the one hand and to "the reason of the thing" on the other to demonstrate the degenerative tendency of regimes makes good sense. The juxtaposition of historical example or usage on the one hand and "the reason of the thing" on the other was also employed by Jefferson (Jefferson to Madison, May 25, 1788, *PJM*, 11:56) and Hamilton (*Federalist* 66:371). Cf. *Federalist* 78:436 and 82:462 as well as Blackstone (*Commentaries*, on "Punishment"), Grotius (*On the Rights of War and Peace*), etc.

[34] Aristotle, *Politics*, V:12, 178–81. In this chapter, Aristotle discusses various tyrannical and oligarchic regimes; these types of government are generally short lived, although some lasted longer than others due to their popularity with the people. He then commented on Plato's theory of regime revolution:

Now in the *Republic* there is a discussion of revolutions by Socrates, but he does not argue rightly. In the case of the regime that is best and first he does not speak of a revolution proper to it. He asserts the reason is that nothing is lasting, but everything undergoes revolution over a certain cycle. . . .

In addition to these things, what is the reason for its undergoing revolution in the direction of the Spartan regime? All regimes undergo revolution more frequently into their opposite than into a regime of a neighboring sort. The same argument also applies to the other revolutions. He asserts that from the Spartan regime there is a revolution in the direction of oligarchy, from this to democracy, and from democracy to tyranny. Yet revolution may also go the other way – from [rule of] the people to oligarchy, for example; and this [is more likely to happen] than revolution in the direction of monarchy. Further, in the case of tyranny he does not say either if there will be a revolution or, if there will not, what the reason is for this, or into which sort of regime. The reason for this is that it would not have been easy for him to say, as it is impossible to determine. According to him it should be in the direction of the first and best, for in this way there would be a continuous circle. But tyranny also undergoes revolution into tyranny, for example the one at Sicyon, where the tyranny of Myron [was replaced by] that of Cleisthenes; into oligarchy, like that of Antileon at Chalcis; into democracy, like that of Gelo and his family

In proportion as Government is influenced by opinion, must it be so by whatever influences opinion. This decides the question concerning a bill of rights, which acquires efficacy as time sanctifies and incorporates it with the public sentiment.[35]

(30

INFLUENCE OF EDUCATION ON GOVERNMENT

(35

INFLUENCE OF RELIGION ON GOVERNMENT.

For the cave of Jupiter in Crete where Minos, Epimenides & Pythagoras pretended to have recd. a divine sanction to their laws & see Anacharsis v. 6. p. 248.[36]

---

at Syracuse; and into aristocracy, like that of Charilaus in Lacedaemon, and at Carthage. There can also be revolution from oligarchy to tyranny, as happened with most of the ancient oligarchies in Sicily – to the tyranny of Panaetius at Leontini, to that of Cleander at Gela, to that of Anaxilaus at Rhegium, and similarly in many other cities.

It is also odd to suppose that there is a revolution in the direction of oligarchy because those holding the offices are greedy and involved in business, and not because those who are very preeminent by the fact of their property suppose it is not just for those possessing nothing to have a share in the city equal to that of the possessors. In many oligarchies, to engage in business is not permitted, and there are laws preventing this; on the other hand, at Carthage they engage in business although it is run timocratically, and have not yet undergone a revolution. It is also odd to assert that an oligarchic city is really two cities, of the wealthy and the poor. For why should it have this characteristic more than the Spartan or any other [sort of regime] where all do not possess equal things or are not good men in a similar way? Without anyone's becoming poorer than before, regimes can nonetheless undergo revolution from oligarchy to democracy, if the poor become a majority, or from [rule of] the people to oligarchy, if the well-off element is superior to the multitude and the latter neglect [politics] while the former put their minds to it.

Though there are many reasons for revolutions occurring [from oligarchy to democracy], he only speaks of one – their becoming poor by extravagant living and paying out interest on loans, the assumption being that all or most were wealthy from the beginning. But this is false. Rather, when certain of the leaders have squandered their properties, these engage in sedition, but in the case of others nothing terrible happens, and even if it should, revolutions would be no more likely to occur in the direction of [rule of] the people than in that of any other sort of regime. Further, [men] engage in factional conflict and effect revolution in regimes if they have no share in prerogatives or if they are treated unjustly or arrogantly, even where they have not consumed all their property on account of the license to do whatever they want, the cause of which he asserts is too much freedom. Although there are many sorts of oligarchies and democracies, Socrates speaks of the revolutions as if there were only one sort of each.

35 Page 23 is numbered, but nothing else appears on the page.

36 *Voyage*, 6:248 (217–18):

The road which leads to the cave of Jupiter is very pleasant: it is bordered by lofty trees; and has on each side of it charming meadows, and a grove of cypress trees of remarkable height and beauty: the grove is consecrated to the gods, as is also a temple at which we afterward arrived.[a]

At the entrance of the cavern a number of offerings are suspended. We were shown, as a singularity, one of those black poplars which bear fruit annually; and we were told that others grew in the environs, on the borders of the fountain Saurus.[b] The length of the cave may be about two hundred feet, and its breadth twenty.[c] At the bottom we saw a seat which is called the throne of Jupiter; and near it this inscription, in ancient characters: THIS IS THE TOMB OF ZAN.[d,e]

As it was believed that the god revealed himself in the sacred cavern to those who repaired thither to consult him, men of genius took advantage of this error to enlighten or mislead people. It is, in fact,

(40

INFLUENCE OF DOMESTIC SLAVERY ON GOVERNMENT

See proportion of slaves in Grecian & Roman Republics –

See private life of Romans by – [37]
do. of Athenians[38] & Lacedemonians in Anacharsis[39]

In Arcadia 300,000 slaves. Anacharsis. vol. 4. p. 298.[40]

---

affirmed that Minos,[f] Epimenides, and Pythagoras, when they wished to give divine sanction to their laws or their opinions, descended into this cave, and remained shut up in it for a certain time.[g]

---

[a] Plat. De Leges. lib. 1. t.ii. p.925.
[b] Theophrasti. Historia Plantarum. lib.3.cap.5 p.124.
[c] Benedetto Bordone. Isolario. p.49.
[d] Meursii in Creta lib.1.cap.4. p.78
[e] Zan is the same as Zήν, Jupiter. It appears, by a coin in the cabinet of the king of France, that the Cretans pronounced TAN. (Mémoirs de l'Académie Royale des Inscriptions et Belles-Lettres t.xxvi. p.546.) This inscription was not of very great antiquity.
[f] Homer. Odyssey. lib.19. v.179. Plat. In Minos t. ii. p.319.
[g] Diogenis Laërtii Vitæ Illustrium Philosophroum. lib.8. §3.

[37] Jean Rodolphe d'Arnay, *De la Vie Privée des Romains* (Lausanne, 1757): "They began to commit to slaves every toilsome business, and to reserve only what was agreeable, or what was reckoned honourable. Hence that multitude of slaves which were counted by thousands, and distinguished by nations. Some forced by day to labour the earth in chains, under inspectors, also slaves, and with no other nourishment than bread, and water, and salt, by night were shut up in subterraneous prisons which opened only at top. Others, treated with less hardship, were fixed to the house in town, and to the personal service of their masters, with offices and names till then unknown" (*The Private Life of the Romans*, 2nd edn., trans. M. D'Arnay [Edinburgh: A. Donaldson and J. Reid. For A. Donaldson, 1764], 9–10).

[38] Madison appears to have written an extra syllable in "Athenians." It is written "Atheniaians."

[39] See *Voyage*, (2:98): "Throughout almost all Greece the number of slaves infinitely exceeds that of the citizens.[a] Almost every where the utmost exertions are obliged continually to be made to keep them in subjection.[b] Lacedæmon, by having recourse to rigorous measures to force them to obedience, has often driven them to revolt. Athens, wishing to secure their fidelity by gentler methods, has made them insolent.[c]"

---

[a] Athenæi Deipnosophistarum. lib. 5. p. 272.
[b] Plat. de Leg. lib. 6. t. ii. p. 776.
[c] Xenophontis. De Republica Atheniensium. p. 693.

[40] *Voyage*, 4:298 (266–67): "Arcadia was anciently governed by kings, but afterwards divided into several republics, all of which have a right to send deputies to the general council.[a] Mantinea and Tegea are at the head of this confederation, which would be too formidable were all its forces united: for the country is extremely populous, and is reckoned to contain not less than three hundred thousand slaves.[b] But the jealousy of power continually occasions divisions between the great and lesser states. In our time, factions had become so numerous, that a plan was laid before the assembly of the nation, in which, among other regulations, it was proposed that the power of determining on peace and war should be confided to a body of ten thousand men.[c] This project, which the new

In proportion as slavery prevails in a State, the Government, however democratic in name, must be aristocratic in fact. The power lies in a part instead of the whole; in the hands of property, not of numbers. All the antient popular governments, were for this reason aristocracies. The majority were slaves. Of the residue a part were in the Country and did not attend the assemblies, a part were poor and tho in the city, could not spare the time to attend. The power, was exercised for the most part by the rich and easy. Aristotle [de rep: lib. 3. cap. 1 & 4.][41] defines a Citizen or member of the

troubles that is [*sic*] occasioned caused to be laid aside, was again revived with more vigour after the battle of Leuctra. Epaminondas, who, to restrain the Spartans, had just recalled the exiled inhabitants of Messenia, proposed to the Arcadians to destroy the small towns which were without defence, and transfer the inhabitants to a place of strength, to be built on the frontiers of Laconia. He furnished them with a thousand men to carry his plan into execution, and the foundations of Megalopolis were immediately laid.[d] This happened about fifteen years before our arrival."

[a] Xenoph. Historia Græca. lib. 6. p. 602.

[b] Theoph. ap. Athen. lib. 6. cap. 20. p. 271.

[c] Demosth., On the Falsa Legatione, p. 295. Diod. Sic lib. 15. p. 372.

[d] Pausan. lib. 4. cap. 27. p. 654.; lib. 9. cap. 114. p. 739.

41 Aristotle, *Politics*, III:1, 86–87: "We are seeking the citizen in an unqualified sense, one who has no defect of this sort requiring correction, since questions may be raised and resolved concerning such things in the case of those who have been deprived of [civic] prerogatives or exiled as well. The citizen in an unqualified sense is defined by no other thing so much as by sharing in decision and office.... Who the citizen is, then, is evident from these things. Whoever is entitled to participate in an office involving deliberation or decision is, we can now say, a citizen in this city; and the city is the multitude of such persons that is adequate with a view to a self-sufficient life, to speak simply." Aristotle, *Politics*, III:4, 91–92:

At the same time, the capacity to rule and be ruled is praised, and the virtue of a citizen of reputation is held to be the capacity to rule and be ruled finely. Now if we regard the virtue of the good man as being of a ruling sort, while that of the citizen is both [of a ruling and a ruled sort], they would not be praiseworthy to a similar extent. Since both [views] are sometime held – that the ruler and the ruled ought to learn different things and not the same, and that the citizen must know both sorts of things and share in both – the next step becomes visible. There is rule of a master, by which we mean that connected with the necessary things. It is not necessary for the ruler to know how to perform these, but only to use [those who do]; the other [sort of knowledge] is servile (by the other I mean the capacity to perform the subordinate tasks of a servant). Now we speak of several forms of slave; for the sorts of work are several. One sort is that done by menials: as the term itself indicates, these are persons who live by their hands; the vulgar artisan is among them. Hence among some peoples the craftsmen did not share in offices in former times, prior to the emergence of [rule of] the people in its extreme form. Now the works of those ruled in this way should not be learned by the good [man] or the political [ruler] or the good citizen, unless he does it for himself out of some need of his own (for then it does not result in one person becoming master and another slave).

But there is also a sort of rule in accordance with which one rules those who are similar in stock and free. For this is what we speak of as political rule, and the ruler learns it by being ruled – just as the cavalry commander learns by being commanded, the general by being led, and [similarly in the case of] the leader of a regiment or company. Hence this too has been rightly said – that it is not possible to rule well without having been ruled. Virtue in [each of] these cases is different, but the good citizen should know and have the capacity both to be ruled and to rule, and this very thing is the virtue of a citizen – knowledge of rule over free persons from both [points of view].

sovereignty, to be one who is sufficiently free from all private cares, to devote himself exclusively to the service of his Country – See also Anacharsis. vol. 5. p. 280/1. – [42] The Southern States of America, are, on the same principle aristocracies. In Virginia the aristocratic character is increased by the rule of suffrage, which requiring a freehold in land excludes nearly half the free inhabitants, and must exclude a greater proportion, as the population increases. At present the slaves and non-freeholders amount to nearly 3/4 of the State. The power is therefore in about 1/4. Were the slaves freed and the right of suffrage

[42] *Voyage*, 5:280–81 (257–59):

Before we proceed further, let us examine what are the rights, and what ought to be the dispositions, of the citizen.

In certain places, to be a citizen, it suffices to be born of a father and mother who were citizens; in others, a great number of degrees are required in the descent: but it thence follows, that the first who have assumed that privilege did not rightfully possess it, and how then could they transmit it to their children?[a]

It is not the inclosure of a city or a state which bestows this privilege on him who inhabits it; for if so, it might be claimed by the slave as well as by the freeman.[b] If the slave cannot be a citizen, neither can those who are in the service of others, or who, by exercising the mechanic arts, immediately depend on the favours of the public.[c] I know that in most republics, and especially in the extreme democracy, they are considered as such; but in a well-constituted state so noble a privilege ought not to be granted to them.

Who is then the real citizen? He who, free from every other care, dedicates himself solely to the service of his country, and may participate in its offices, dignities, and honours;[d] in a word, in the sovereign authority.

It hence follows, that this name agrees but imperfectly to children or decrepit old men, and cannot appertain to artisans, labourers, and freedman.[e] It also follows, that there are no citizens but in a republic;[f] though they there share this privilege with persons to whom, according to our principles, it ought to be denied.

In the city which you shall found, every occupation that may divert the attention which is exclusively due to the interests of the country shall be forbidden to the citizen; and this title shall only be given to those who in their youth shall bear arms in defence of the state, and who in a more advanced age shall instruct it by their knowledge and experience.[g]

Thus shall your citizens truly make a part of the city: their essential prerogative shall be, to be admitted to offices of magistracy, to judge in the affairs of individuals, and to vote in the senate or the general assembly;[h] this they shall possess by a fundamental law, because the law is a contract[i] which secures the rights of citizens. The first of their duties shall be, to place themselves in a situation to command and to obey;[j] and they shall fulfil it in virtue of their institution, because that alone can inspire them with the virtues of the citizen, or the love of their country.

---

[a] Aristot. de. Rep. lib. 3. cap. 2. p. 340.
[b] Id. ibid. cap. 1.
[c] Id. ibid. cap. 5. p. 343.
[d] Id. ibid. cap. 1. p. 338 et 339; cap. 4. p. 341.
[e] Aristot. de Rep. lib. 3. cap. 1 et 5; lib. 7. cap. 9. p. 435.
[f] Id. ibid. lib. 3. cap. 1. p. 339.
[g] Id. ibid. lib. 7. cap. 9. p. 435.
[h] Id. ibid. lib. 3. cap. 1. p. 339.
[i] Id. ibid. cap. 9. p. 348.
[j] Id. ibid. cap. 4. p. 342.

extended to all, the operation of the Government might be very different. – The slavery of the Southern States, throws the power much more into the hands of property, than in the Northern States. Hence the people of property in the former are much more contented with their establishd. Governments, than the people of property in the latter.

(46

INFLUENCE OF DEPENDENT DOMINIONS ON GOVERNMENT

Mais c'est principalement aux victoires que les Atheniens remporterent contre les Perses, qu'on doit attribuer la ruine de l'ancienne Constitution. [Arist: de rep: 1. 2. cap. 12.][43] Apres la bataille de Platée, on ordonna que le citoyens de derniers classes exclus par Solon de principales magistratures, auroient desormais le droit d'y parvenir. Le sage Aristides, qui presenta ce decret [Plut: in aris][44] donna le plus

[43] Aristotle, *Politics*, II:12, 83–84: "As for Solon, there are some who suppose him to have been an excellent legislator. For [they say] he dismantled an oligarchy that was too unmixed, put an end to the slavery of the people, and established the traditional democracy, under which the regime was finely mixed – the council of Areopagus being oligarchic, the element of elective offices being aristocratic, and the courts being popular. It would seem, though, that Solon found these things existing previously – the council and election to offices – and did not dismantle them, but established [rule of] the people by making the courts open to all. Thus there are also some who blame him for dissolving the other [elements of the existing regime] by giving authority to the court, which was to be chosen from all by lot. For once this had become strong, they tried to gratify the people as if it were a tyrant, and [altering] the regime established the current democracy. Ephialtes and Pericles cut back the council of the Areopagus, Pericles established pay for the courts, and in this manner each of the popular leaders proceeded by increasing [the power of the people] in the direction of the current democracy. Yet it appears to have happened coincidentally rather than in accordance with the intention of Solon. For because the people were the cause of [Athenian] naval supremacy during the Persian wars, they began to have high thoughts and to obtain mean persons as popular leaders when they were opposed politically by the respectable. Solon seems, at any rate, to have granted only the most necessary power to the people..."

[44] Plutarch, "Aristides," in *Plutarch's Lives: The Translation Called Dryden's.*, ed. A. H. Clough, (Boston: Little, Brown, and Company, 1885), II:308–11:

> Aristides perceived that the Athenians, after their return into the city, were eager for a democracy; and deeming the people to deserve consideration on account of their valiant behavior, as also that it was a matter of difficulty, they being well armed, powerful, and full of spirit with their victories, to oppose them by force, he brought forward a decree that every one might share in the government and the archons be chosen out of the whole body of the Athenians. And on Themistocles telling the people in assembly that he had some advice for them, which could not be given in public, but was most important for the advantage and security of the city, they appointed Aristides alone to hear and consider it with him. And on his acquainting Aristides that his intent was to set fire to the arsenal of the Greeks, for by that means should the Athenians become supreme masters of all Greece, Aristides, returning to the assembly, told them that nothing was more advantageous than what Themistocles designed, and nothing more unjust. The Athenians, hearing this, gave Themistocles order to desist; such was the love of justice felt by the people, and such the credit and confidence they reposed in Aristides.
>
> Being sent in joint commission with Cimon to the war, he took notice that Pausanias and the other Spartan captains made themselves offensive by imperiousness and harshness to the confederates; and by being himself gentle and considerate, with them and by the courtesy and

funeste des examples a ceux qui lui succederent dans le commandement. Il leur fallut d'abord flatter la multitude, et ensuite ramper devant elle. Anarch: vol. 1. p. 147/8[45]

---

disinterested temper which Cimon, after his example, manifested in the expeditions, he stole away the chief command from the Lacedæmonians, neither by weapons, ships, or horses, but by equity and wise policy. For the Athenians being endeared to the Greeks by the justice of Aristides and by Cimon's moderation, the tyranny and selfishness of Pausanias rendered them yet more desirable. He on all occasions treated the commanders of the confederates haughtily and roughly; and the common soldiers he punished with stripes, or standing under the iron anchor for a whole day together; neither was it permitted for any to provide straw for themselves to lie on, or forage for their horses, or to come near the springs to water before the Spartans were furnished, but servants with whips drove away such as approached. And when Aristides once was about to complain and expostulate with Pausanias, he told him, with an angry look, that he was not at leisure, and gave no attention to him. The consequence was that the sea captains and generals of the Greeks, in particular, the Chians, Samians, and Lesbians, came to Aristides and requested him to be their general, and to receive the confederates into his command, who had long desired to relinquish the Spartans and come over to the Athenians. But he answered, that he saw both equity and necessity in what they said, but their fidelity required the test of some action, the commission of which would make it impossible for the multitude to change their minds again. Upon which Uliades, the Samian, and Antagoras of Chios, conspiring together, ran in near Byzantium on Pausanias's galley, getting her between them as she was sailing before the rest. But when Pausanias, beholding them, rose up and furiously threatened soon to make them know that they had been endangering not his galley, but their own countries, they bid him go his way, and thank Fortune that fought for him at Platæa; for hitherto, in reverence to that, the Greeks had forborne from inflicting on him the punishment he deserved. In fine, they all went off and joined the Athenians. And here the magnanimity of the Lacedæmonians was wonderful. For when they perceived that their generals were becoming corrupted by the greatness of their authority, they voluntarily laid down the chief command, and left off sending any more of them to the wars, choosing rather to have citizens of moderation and consistent in the observance of their customs, than to possess the dominion of all Greece.

Even during the command of the Lacedæmonians, the Greeks paid a certain contribution towards the maintenance of the war; and being desirous to be rated city by city in their due proportion, they desired Aristides of the Athenians, and gave him command, surveying the country and revenue, to assess everyone according to their ability and what they were worth. But he, being so largely empowered, Greece as it were submitting all her affairs to his sole management, went out poor, and returned poorer; laying the tax not only without corruption and injustice, but to the satisfaction and convenience of all. For as the ancients celebrated the age of Saturn, so did the confederates of Athens Aristides's taxation; terming it the happy time of Greece; and that more especially, as the sum was in a short time doubled, and afterwards trebled. For the assessment which Aristides made, was four hundred and sixty talents. But to this Pericles added very near one third part more; for Thucydides says, in the beginning of the Peloponnesian war, the Athenians had coming in from their confederates six hundred talents. But after Pericles's death, the demagogues, increasing by little and little, raised it to the sum of thirteen hundred talents; not so much through the war's being so expensive and chargeable either by its length or ill success, as by their alluring the people to spend upon largesses and play-house allowances, and in erecting statues and temples. Aristides, therefore, having acquired a wonderful and great reputation by this levy of the tribute, Themistocles is said to have derided him, as if this had been not the commendation of a man, but a money-bag; a retaliation, though not in the same kind, for some free words which

---

See Hist: of Grecian Colonies[46] – Roman Provinces – dependencies in E. & W. Indies –

Aristides had used. For he, when Themistocles once was saying that he thought the highest virtue of a general was to understand and foreknow the measures the enemy would take, replied, "This, indeed, Themistocles, is simply necessary, but the excellent thing in a general is to keep his hands from taking money."

Aristides, moreover, made all the people of Greece swear to keep the league, and himself took the oath in the name of the Athenians, flinging wedges of red-hot iron into the sea, after curses against such as should make breach of their vow. But afterwards, it would seem, when things were in such a state as constrained them to govern with a stronger hand, he bade the Athenians to throw the perjury upon him, and manage affairs as convenience required. And, in general, Theophrastus tells us, that Aristides was, in his own private affairs, and those of his fellow-citizens, rigorously just, but that in public matters he acted often in accordance with his country's policy, which demanded, sometimes, not a little injustice. It is reported of him that he said in a debate, upon the motion of the Samians for removing the treasure from Delos to Athens, contrary to the league, that the thing indeed was not just but was expedient.

45 *Voyage*, 1:147–48 (140): "But it is principally to the victories gained by the Athenians over the Persians that we must attribute the destruction of the ancient constitution.[a] After the battle of Platæa it was enacted that the citizens of the lowest classes, excluded by Solon from the chief offices of the magistracy, should henceforward possess that privilege. The sage Aristides, who proposed this decree,[b] gave the most fatal of examples to his successors in command. It became necessary for them first to flatter, then servilely to crouch to the multitude."

---

[a] Arist. de Rep. lib. 2. cap. 12. p. 336.
[b] Plutarch in Aristides, p. 332.

46 John Gillies, *History of Ancient Greece, Its Colonies and Conquests, From the Earliest Accounts Till the Division of the Macedonian Empire in the East* (Philadelphia: Thomas Wardle, 1843), 150–53:

Here the glory of Pausanias, who still commanded the forces of the confederacy; a man whose fame would rival the most illustrious names of antiquity, had he fallen in the siege of Byzantium. The rich spoils of Platæa, of which the tenth was allotted to him, as general, raised him above the equality required by the republican institutions of his country. His recent conquest still farther augmented his wealth and his ambition; a continual flow of prosperity, which is dangerous to the best regulated minds, proved fatal to the aspiring temper of Pausanias. As he conceived himself too great to remain a subject, he was willing to become a sovereign, through the assistance of Xerxes, the inveterate enemy of his country. To this prince he made application, by means of Gongylus the Eretrian, a fit instrument for any kind of villany. To such an associate Pausanias had entrusted the noble Persians taken in Byzantium. This man escaped with his prisoners across the Bosphorus, and conveyed a letter to the great king, in which the Spartan general, having mentioned, as indubitable proof of his sincerity, the restoring his captive kinsmen, proposed to enter into strict amity with Xerxes, to take his daughter in marriage, to second his efforts in conquering Greece, and to hold that country as a dependent province of the Persian empire. The Persian is said to have highly relished these proposals, the subjugation of Greece being the great object of his reign. It is certain that he speedily sent Artabazus, a nobleman of confidence, to confer and co-operate with the traitor.

But Pausanias himself acted with the precipitancy and inconsistency of a man, who had either been deluded into treason by bad advice, or totally intoxicated by the dangerous vapours of

---

The principal part of the Revenues of Athens consisted of tributes from her dependencies Anacharsis Vol. 4. p. 429.[47]

---

ambition that floated in his distempered brain. Instead of dissembling his designs until they were ripe for execution, he assumed at once the tone of a master and the manners of a tyrant. . . .

This intolerable insolence disgusted and provoked the army in general, but especially the Ionians, who lamented that they had been no sooner delivered from the shackles of Persian despotism, than they were bent under the severer and more odious yoke of Sparta. By common consent, they repaired to the Athenian Aristides, and his colleague Cimon, the son of Miltiades, a youth of the fairest hopes, who had signaled his patriotism and valour in all the glorious scenes of the war. Their designs being approved by the Athenian admirals, Uliades and Antagoras, who respectively commanded the fleets of Samos and Chios, the bravest of all the maritime allies, seized the first opportunity to insult the galley of Pausanias; and when reproached and threatened by the Spartan, they desired him to thank Fortune, who had favoured him at Platæ, the memory of which victory alone saved him from the immediate punishment of his arrogance and cruelty. These words speedily re-echoed through the whole fleet, and served, as soon as they were heard, for the signal of general revolt. The different squadrons of Asia and the Hellespont sailed from their stations, joined the ships of Uliades and Antagoras, loudly declared against the insolent ambition of Pausanias, abjured the proud tyranny of Sparta, and forever ranged themselves under the victorious colours of Athens, whose generous magnanimity seemed best fitted to command the willing obedience of freemen.[a]

. . .The late punishment of this detestable traitor could not repair the ruinous effects of his misconduct and villany. Not only the Ionians, who had first begun the revolt, but the foreign confederates in general, loudly rejected the pretensions of Dorcus (*sic*) and other captains whom the Spartans appointed to command them. A few communities of Peloponnesus still followed the Lacedæmonian standard; but the islanders and Asiatics unanimously applied to Aristides, to whose approved wisdom and virtue they not only entrusted the operations of the combined armament, but voluntarily submitted their more particular concerns; and experience soon justified their prudent choice. Pay was not yet introduced into the Grecian service, because the character of *soldier* was not separated from that of *citizen*. It had been usual, however, to raise annually a certain proportion of supplies among the several confederates, in order to purchase arms, to equip and victual the galleys, and to provide such engines of war as proved requisite in storming the fortified towns belonging to the common enemy.[b] By unanimous suffrage, Aristides was appointed to new-model and apply this necessary tax, which had been imposed and exacted by the Spartans without sufficient attention to the respective faculties of the contributaries. The honest Athenian executed this delicate office with no less judgment than equity. The whole annual imposition amounted to four hundred and sixty talents, about ninety thousand pounds sterling; which was proportioned with such nice accuracy, that no state found the smallest reason to complain of partiality or injustice. The common treasure was kept in the central and sacred island of Delos; and, though entrusted to the personal discretion of the Athenian commander, was soon conceived to lie at the disposition of his republic.[c]

[a] Nepos in Pausan. Plutarch. in Aristid.
[b] Plut. in Aristid. p. 532 et. seq.
[c] Ibid. p. 534. Thucyd. I. 1. c. xcvi. Diodor, p. 440.

47 *Voyage*, 4:429 (377–79):

The second and principal branch of the revenues of the state consists in tributes which are paid by a number of cities and islands dependent on it.[a] Its claims of this kind are founded on the abuse of power. After the battle of Platæa,[b] the conquerors having resolved to revenge on Persia the insults offered to Greece, the inhabitants of the islands who had entered into the league agreed to set apart every year a considerable sum to defray the expences of the war. The Athenians, who were to receive the money, collected, in different places, found hundred and sixty talents,[c] which they kept untouched so long as they had not a decided superiority;

Dependent Colonies are to the superior State, not in the relation of Children and parent according to the common language, but in that of slaves and Master; and have the same effect with slavery on the character of the Superior.

---

but when their power increased, they challenged the gratuitous contributions of the allied cities into an humiliating exaction, imposing on some the obligation to furnish ships whenever they should be called on,[d] and demanding of others the annual tribute to which they had formerly subjected themselves. They taxed their new conquests in the same manner; and the sum total of the foreign contributions amounted, at the beginning of the Peloponnesian war, to six hundred talents,[e,f] and towards the middle of the same war to twelve or thirteen hundred.[g] During my stay in Greece the conquests of Philip had reduced this sum to four hundred talents, but the Athenians flattered themselves they should again be able one day to advance it to twelve hundred.[h,i]

These revenues, considerable as they are, are not sufficient to defray the expences of the states; recourse is frequently obliged to be had to free gifts and forced contributions.[j]

---

[a] Aristoph. in Vesp. p. 705.

[b] Thucyd. lib. 1. cap. 19 et 96. Plut. in Aristides. t. i. p. 333. Nepos in Aristid. cap. 3. Pausan. lib. 8. p. 705.

[c] 2,484,000 livres (£. 103,500).

[d] Thucyd. lib. 6. cap. 85; lib. 7. cap. 57.

[e] Id. lib. 2. cap. 13. Plut. in Aristid. t. i. p. 333.

[f] 3,240,000 livres (£. 135,000).

[g] Andocides de Mysteriis et de Pace, Oratores Græciæ. p. 24. Plut. ibid.

[h] Plut. t. ii. p. 842.

[i] 6,480,000 livres (£. 270,000). See note XVII at the end of this volume.*

[j] Demosth. in Against Timocrates. p. 788.

* Note XVII, 501–502: *On the Contributions which the Athenians drew from their Allies.*

The four hundred and sixty talents which were drawn annually from the states leagued against the Persians, and which the Athenians deposited in the citadel, at first amounted to the sum of ten thousand talents,[k] according to Isocrates;[l] or nine thousand seven hundred,[m] according to Thucydides.[n] Pericles, during his administration, had laid up eight thousand;[o] but having expended three thousand seven hundred, either in the embellishment of the city, or the first expences of the siege of Potidæa, the nine thousand seven hundred were reduced to six thousand[p] at the beginning of the Peloponnesian war.[q]

This war was suspended by a truce which the Athenians entered into with Lacedæmon. The contributions which they had then received amounted to twelve or thirteen hundred talents; and, during the seven years which the truce lasted, they placed seven thousand talents[r] in the public treasury.[s]

---

[k] 54,000,000 livres (2,250,000*l.*).

[l] Isocrates, de Pace. t. i. p. 395.

[m] 52,380,000 livres (2,182,500*l.*).

[n] Thucyd. lib. 2. cap. 13.

[o] Isocr. de Pac. t. i. p. 395.

[p] 32,400,000 livres (1,350,000*l.*).

[q] Isocr. de Pac. t. i. p. 395.

[r] 37,800,000 livres (1,575,000*l.*).

[s] Andocides de Mysterries et de Pace, p. 24. Plut. in Aristid. t. i. p. 333.

They cherish pride, luxury, and vanity. They make the labor of one part tributary to the enjoyment of another.

Dependent territories are of two kinds. 1 those which yield to the superior State at once a monopoly of their useful productions, and a market for its superfluities. These may excite & employ industry and may be a source of riches. The West-Indies are an example. 2. those which, tho yielding in some degree a monopoly and a market, are lucrative by the wealth which they administer to individuals and which is transported to the Superior State. Their wealth resembles that drawn not from industry, but from mines, and may produce like consequences. The East Indies are an example.

The influence of the E. & W. Indies & other dependencies belonging to G. Britain, on the side of the Crown, is an adventitious circumstance, which like the National debt, weighs much.

See "History of the Colonization of the free States of Antiquity applied to the present Contest between G. B. & her American Colonies. With reflections concerning the future settlement of these Colonies.["] London, printed for T. Cadell on the Strand. M.DCC.LXXVII.[48]

[48] This anonymous pamphlet was written by William Barron, a professor of logic and rhetoric at the University of St. Andrews. (See *PJM*, 14:169n14.) William Barron, *History of the Colonization of the Free States of Antiquity, Applied to the Present Contest Between Great Britain and Her American Colonies* (London: T. Cadell, 1777), 51: "The good conduct and ability of the Athenian commanders, Themisticles and Aristides, added to the zeal the people of Athens had exhibited, in the course of the Persian war, recommended them highly to all the states of the alliance. The Athenians[a], therefore, now claimed openly the precedency in the affairs of Greece, and their pretensions were received with more partiality and favour, on account of the treachery and unworthy behaviour of Pausanias[b], the Spartan general, who had condescended to accept money[c] from Artabasus the Persian commander, as a reward for betraying the interests of his country. Aristides seized this favourable opportunity, to propose a general tax, for the purposes of common defence against the future attacks of Persia; and to make the measure more acceptable, it was added, that the money should be deposited in the island of Delos, the most safe and sacred place in the dominions of Greece. The overture was universally approved, and, in compliment to the integrity and ability of Aristides, he was appointed, not only to determine the assessment, but to fix the contingents which should be paid by the several states. He named 460 talents[d] as the sum, and rated to discreetly the different allies, as to merit ever the appellation of *Just.*[e]"

---

[a] Cornelius Nepos. Aristides.
[b] Thucyd. lib. I cap. 96.
[c] Diod. lib. 1 cap. 44, Nep. Pausanias.
[d] Thucyd. I cap. 96.
[e] Æschines de falsa Legatione.

See Remarks on an essay entitled "The History &c &c. – and her Amr. Colonies." By John Symonds. LLD. Professor of Mod. Hist: in the Univy. of Cambridge. London: printed by J. Nichols, successor to W. Bowyer; and sold by T. Payne, Mewsgate; W. Owen [,] Temple. Bar P. Elmsly. Strand; T. Evans Pat: Nost: row; J. Woodyer Cambridg & J. Fletcher Oxford. 1778[49]

---

[49] John Symonds, L.L.D., was Professor of Modern History at the University of Cambridge. In his *Remarks Upon an Essay Intituled* [sic], *The History of the Colonization of the Free States of Antiquity*... * he sought to refute Barron's claim that the British taxation of the American colonies was justified by the historical examples set by the Greeks, Romans, and Carthaginians in taxing their colonies. Symonds wrote (41–43):

> The money, that was raised in consequence of the tribute, was deposited in the island of Delos[a]; which was esteemed a place so sacred and inviolable, that it was the Loretto of antient Greece. They destined the money for one single object, the revenging of themselves upon the Persians. Our Author [William Barron] affirms, *that it was proposed for the purposes of common defence against the future attacks of Persia* (p. 51); and quotes Thucydides in the same page; but this historian declares, that it was levied for an invasion of the Persians,[b]; which, in my humble apprehension, was an offensive, not a *defensive* war. No man could have extracted from the original, the sense which our Author has given it, unless he had written to serve a particular purpose. It is needless to observe, that, were we to grant that the tax was levied by the order of Athens, our Author's hypothesis would still be overturned; for it was done not with a view to raise a revenue for the support of the parent state, but for the sole purpose of carrying on a particular war.
>
> Such was the original contract between Athens, and her confederates: a charter of rights established in the most solemn manner; and ratified by oaths, through the influence of Aristides.[c] But ambition is not to be restrained by so feeble ties. The Athenians soon manifested their aspiring and wicked views; and endeavoured to give law to those, who had formed a league upon terms of equality; and even Aristides himself, who had hitherto proved so disinterested a statesman, gave into their plans; and took the guilt of perjury upon himself.[d] After this breach of public faith, we must necessarily be prepared for scenes of iniquity. One of the first steps taken was the removal of the treasury from Delos to Athens, and that by the consent of Aristides himself.[e] The Athenians pretended, that the money was not safe in Delos, on account of the irruptions of the Spartans,[f] and the Persians[g]; but the truth was, they wished to have the management of it in their own hands. The next step was the augmenting of the tribute to near 600 talents.[h] They considered it no longer as raised by the confederates for a certain purpose; but as a tax due to themselves, for which they were not accountable; and accordingly, Pericles expended the greatest part of it in the buildings, with which he decorated Athens. These were indeed the pride and ornament of that city, as late as the time of Plutarch[i]; and their remains afford us a genuine idea of the splendor of ancient Greece; but, as they were erected on the ruins of liberty, they are an eternal reproach to the memory of Pericles.

---

* Madison used Jefferson's copy of Symonds' work, which was bound together with Barron's pamphlet, to which it was a response. See *PJM*, 14:169n15; cf. Sowerby, *Catalogue of the Library of Thomas Jefferson*, III:215–16.

[a] The scholiast on Thycydides says that the treasury was fixed at Delos, L. i. c. 54.

[b] L. i. c. 54.

[c] Plut. vital Aristid. p. 322.

[d] Ibid.

[e] Ibid.

[f] Justin. L. iii. c. 6.

The money with which Pericles decorated Athens, was raised by Aristides on the confederates of Athens for common defence, and on pretext of danger at Delos which was the common depository, removed to Athens, where it was soon regarded as the tribute of inferiors instead of the common property of associates, and applied by Pericles accordingly. See Remarks by J. Symonds above, & authors there cited. p. 42.[50]

(49

CHECKS DEVISED IN DEMOCRACIES MARKING SELF-DISTRUST

In Athens all laws were to be agreed to in the Senate before they, could be deliberated in the popular assembly.

The first speakers in the assembly were to be 50 years of age at least. Æschines in Timarc.[51] Anachar: Vol. 1. p. 106[52]

---

[g] Plut. vit. Pericl. vol. I. p. 350.

[h] Thucyd. L. ii. c. 92.

[i] Vit. Pericl. p. 352.

50 Page 47 is numbered, but nothing else is written on the page.

51 *Voyage*, 1:106 (100–01): "Since all citizens have the right of being present at the assembly, they must possess that of giving their suffrages. But there would be reason to fear, that, after the report of the senate, inexperienced men might suddenly take possession of the rostrum, and mislead the multitude. The first impressions they are to receive, therefore, must be previously prepared; and hence it was regulated that the first suffrages should be given by men who had passed the fiftieth year of their age.[a]"

---

[a] Æschin. in Against Timarchus. p. 264.

52 Aeschines, *Against Timarchus* (346 BC). Aeschines (ca. 390–314 BC) rose from humble beginnings to become a noted Athenian orator and rival of Demosthenes. Although he originally opposed Philip II of Macedon, he later argued that resistance to Macedonian power was futile. In 348 BC, he and Demosthenes were members of the embassy to Philip, after which Demosthenes accused Aeschines of accepting Macedonian bribes and brought him to trial. Demosthenes' associate, Timarchus, apparently was to lead the prosecution against Aeschines. Aeschines responded by prosecuting Timarchus, arguing to a jury (and appealing to public opinion) that Timarchus was ineligible to hold public office under Athenian law because (when younger) he had engaged in homosexual prostitution. In his oration *Against Timarchus* (www.fordham.edu/halsall/pwh/aeschines.asp, [22–24]), Aeschines argued:

> This law was enacted concerning youths who recklessly sin against their own bodies. The laws relating to boys are those read to you a moment ago; but I am going to cite now laws that have to do with the citizens at large. For when the lawgiver had finished with these laws, he next turned to the question of the proper manner of conducting our deliberations concerning the most important matters, when we are met in public assembly. How does he begin? "Laws," he says, "concerning orderly conduct." He began with morality, thinking that that state will be best administered in which orderly conduct is most common. And how does he command the presiding officers to proceed? After the purifying sacrifice has been carried round and the herald has offered the traditional prayers, the presiding officers are

No orator was allowed to engage in public affairs, until he had undergone an examination relative to his character, and every Citizen was permitted to prosecute an Orator who had found means to withold the irregularity of his manners from the severity of this examination. Æschin: ibid[53] et Suid in ρὴτορ[54]

---

commanded to declare to be next in order the discussion of matters pertaining to the national religion, the reception of heralds and ambassadors, and the discussion of secular matters. The herald then asks, "Who of those above fifty years of age wishes to address the assembly?" When all these have spoken, he then invites any other Athenian to speak who wishes (provided such privileges belongs [*sic*] to him).

Consider, fellow citizens, the wisdom of this regulation. The lawgiver does not forget, I think, that the older men are at their best in the matter of judgment, but that courage is now beginning to fail them as a result of their experience of the vicissitudes of life. So, wishing to accustom those who are the wisest to speak on public affairs, and to make this obligatory upon them, since he cannot call on each one of them by name, he comprehends them all under the designation of the age-group as a whole, invites them to the platform, and urges them to address the people. At the same time he teaches the younger men to respect their elders, to yield precedence to them in every act, and to honor that old age to which we shall all come if our lives are spared.

53 Aeschines, *Against Timarchus*:

Now it is my desire, in addressing you on this occasion, to follow in my speech the same order which the lawgiver followed in his laws. For you shall hear first a review of the laws that have been laid down to govern the orderly conduct of your children, then the laws concerning the lads, and next those concerning the other ages in succession, including not only private citizens, but the public men as well. For so, I think, my argument will most easily be followed. And at the same time I wish, fellow citizens, first to describe to you in detail the laws of the state, and then in contrast with the laws to examine the character and habits of Timarchus. For you will find that the life he has lived has been contrary to all the laws.

... See now, fellow citizens, how unlike to Timarchus were Solon and those men of old whom I mentioned a moment ago. They were too modest to speak with the arm outside the cloak, but this man not long ago, yes, only the other day, in an assembly of the people threw off his cloak and leaped about like a gymnast, half naked, his body so reduced and befouled through drunkenness and lewdness that right-minded men, at least, covered their eyes, being ashamed for the city, that we should let such men as he be our advisers.

It was with such conduct as this in view that the lawgiver expressly prescribed who were to address the assembly, and who were not to be permitted to speak before the people. ... Who then are they who in the lawgiver's opinion are not to be permitted to speak? Those who have lived a shameful life; these men he forbids to address the people. Where does he show this? Under the heading "Scrutiny of public men" (www.fordham.edu/halsall/pwh/aeschines.asp, [8]).

54 *Suidæ Lexicon, Græce et Latine*, ed. Ludolf Kuster (Cambridge, 1705), III:258. Madison's reference is to the entry "*ῥητορικὴ γραφή*" in *Suidæ Lexicon*, which described the legal action that could be pleaded by or brought against an orator. In classical Greek, "*ῥήτωρ*" is the nominative singular and "*ῥήτορα*" the accusative singular of "orator" (in Latin, "oratorem"). Madison, however, wrote "*ρὴτορ*," which omits the mark over the "*ῥ*" and, depending on whether he meant to write the accusative singular or the nominative singular, either omits the alpha (*α*) or neglects to replace the omicron (*ο*) with an omega (*ω*). This confusion stems, most likely, from the erroneous way "*ῥήτορα*" was handwritten by the author of the "*ῥητορικὴ γραφή*" entry in the *Suidæ Lexicon*. For this clarification and explanation, I am indebted to Anastasia Alexander, my Greek friend and scholar of comparative literature.

The Areopagus for life &c.[55]

With The prayers at the commencement of public deliberations were mingled frightful imprecations agst. the Orator who shd. have recd presents, to deceive the people, or the Senate, or the Tribunal of the Heliastes.[56] – See Anacharsis – & the citations II, p. 281.[57] For other cautions agst. the undue influence of Orators – see id: p. 287.[58]

[55] The Areopagus was a council of elder statesmen composed of former archons; after a positive evaluation of their conduct while in office, they became lifetime members of this council.

[56] The *heliaia* was the supreme court of ancient Athens. This tribunal was composed of 6,000 members, chosen annually by lot from among male citizens older than 30.

[57] *Voyage*, 2:281 (249–50): "When every one is seated,[a] and the place in which the assembly meets purified by the blood of victims,[b] a herald rises up and repeats a form of invocation, which is pronounced also in the senate as often as they proceed to deliberation.[c] With these prayers, addressed to Heaven for the prosperity of the state, are intermingled dreadful imprecations against the orator who shall have received presents to deceive the people, the senate, or the tribunal of the heliastæ.[d] The subject for deliberation is next proposed to the assembly, which is generally contained in a preliminary decree of the senate, and is read with a loud voice.[e] The herald then proclaims: 'Let every citizen, who can give useful counsel to his country, ascend the rostrum, beginning with those who are more than fifty years of age.' For it was formerly necessary to have passed that age to be permitted to speak first on any subject under deliberation; but this regulation is now neglected,[f] as well as many others."

---

[a] Aristoph. In Equites. v. 751 et 782. Id. in Ecclesiazusae v. 165.
[b] Æschin. In Timarch. p. 263. Aristoph. in Acharnenses. v. 43. Schol. ad vers 44.
[c] Demosth. De Falsa Legatione. p. 304.
[d] Demosth. in Aristocr. p. 741. Dicæarchi Status Græcos in Aristog. p. 107.
[e] Demosth. de Fals. Leg. p. 299.
[f] Æschin. in Tim. p. 264. in Ctesiph. p. 428.

[58] *Voyage*, 2:287 (256–57): "The laws, foreseeing the empire that men at once so useful and so dangerous may assume over the minds of the people, have ordained that their abilities should not be called into exertion till ample testimony can be borne to their moral conduct. They exclude from the rostrum[a] the man who shall be proved to have struck his parents, or who has denied them the means of subsistence: for how can he feel the love of his country, whose heart is shut to the sentiments of nature? They exclude the citizen who has dissipated the inheritance of his father, since he would lavish the treasures of the state with still greater unconcern: the man also who has no legitimate offspring,[b] or possesses no property in Attica; for without these ties, his attachment to the republic can be at best but vague and doubtful, since it is not strengthened by private interest: whoever likewise has refused to take arms at the command of the general,[c] abandoned his shield in battle, or addicted himself to shameful pleasures, is not permitted to speak in the assembly, because cowardice and corruption, almost inseparable companions, would expose his mind to every species of treachery: besides that no man who is unable either to defend his country by his valour, or edify it by his example, can be worthy to instruct it by his counsel."

[a] Æschin. de Cor. p. 513.
[b] Din. adv. Demosth. in Oper. Demosth. p. 182.
[c] Æschin. adv. Timarch. p. 364.

Ostracism, Petalism,[59] Dictatorship, punishment of unsuccessful propositions of new laws.

In Athens death was decreed by the people to the Orator who should propose to apply to the public defence, the money destined to pay for the seats of the poor at the Spectacles. Anacharsis vol. 4. p. 430/1[60]

In the Republic of the Italian Locris, it was ordained by Zaleucus,[61] that whoever proposed a new law, or repeal or alteration of an old one, should do it

---

[59] Petalism was a form of temporary banishment (five years) practiced in ancient Syracuse, similar to the practice of ostracism of Athens. As ostracism occurred by etching the name of a person on an *ostrakon*, or pot shard ballots, petalism took place by writing the name of a person on olive leaves. Both practices were employed against individuals considered dangerous to the constitution.

[60] *Voyage*, 4:430–31 (386): "Every year considerable sums are deposited in a treasury superintended by particular officers, which are to be publicly distributed to enable the poorer citizens to pay for their places at the public shows.[a] The people will not suffer this money to be touched; and we have seen them, in our time, decree that the punishment of death should be inflicted on the orator who should propose to employ it in the service of the state when exhausted by a long war.[b] The annals of nations do not afford a second example of such madness."

---

[a] Harpocration in Θεως.

[b] Ulpianus in Olynthus. 1. p. 13. Libani Præludia Oratoria et Declamationes, Argum ejusd. Orat.

[61] In the seventh century BC, Zaleucus drew up a code of laws for the Republic of Locris, a Greek colony in southeastern Italy, which he claimed was communicated to him in a dream by Athena. His laws were few in number but harsh in their consequences for anyone who should disobey. Regarding the proposal to enact a new or alter an existing law, Zaleucus's code commanded: "If any one wishes to change some one of the established laws, or to introduce another law, let him, with a halter about his neck, speak of the subject of his wishes to the people. And if it shall appear from the suffrages, that the law already established should be dissolved, or that a new law should be introduced, let him not be punished. But if it should be thought that the preexisting law is better, or that the law which is intended to be introduced is unjust, let him who wishes to change an old, or to introduce a new law, be executed by the halter" (Thomas Taylor, ed. and trans., *Political Fragments of Archytas, Charondas, Zaleucus, and Other Ancient Pythagoreans* ... [London: C. Whittingham, 1822], 49–50). Madison may have copied this information from *Voyage* 5:276; Barthélemy writes: "Nothing is so dangerous likewise as to make frequent changes in the laws. Among the Locrians,[a] he who advised to abrogate or alter any law, must make the proposal with a halter round his neck, and forfeit his life if his advice were disapproved.*"

[a] Zaleuc. ap. Stob. Serm. 42. p. 280. Demosth. in Timoc. p. 794.

* See Note IX. at the end of the volume.

* Note IX. (V:484): *On a Law of the Locrians in Italy*, Demosthenes[a] tells us, that, during two centuries, no alteration was made in the laws of this people. According to one of these laws, he who struck out the eye of another was to lose one of his own. A Locrian having threatened to strike out the eye of a person who had but one, the latter represented, that his enemy, though he should undergo the punishment of retaliation inflicted by the law, would be no means suffer equally with himself. It was therefore resolved, that in such a case the offender should lose both his eyes.

[a] Demosth. in Timocr. p. 795.

with a rope about his neck, that if unsuccessful, he might be immediately executed.* Ubbo Emmius. tom 3. p. 353[62]

The Augurs in Rome – College of Heralds with Negative on war & peace, instituted by Numa. See Moyle on Rom: Govt. p. 46[63] – & Dionysius Halycarnassus.[64]

---

62 Ubbo Emmius, *Vetus Græce* (Leiden: Bonaventura Elzevier & Abraham Elzevier, 1626): "Of the laws of Zaleucas the most memorable was that which both Demosthenes and Polybius mention, provided in order to make the laws stable and long-lasting, whereby the legislator laid it down that anyone who wished to propose a new law for the future, or to abolish a law passed previously, or to change something in it, or to strive with anyone about the meaning of the law contrary to what was written, should go into a council of a thousand and give his speech with his neck stuffed into a noose. And to this end: that if he proved his thought and wish to the council, and showed that what he sought was useful, honorable, and in the public interest, he should depart safe; but that if not, instantly, and with the council present and looking on, he should end his life by the noose. In this way, Demosthenes says, it was brought about that for two hundred years (for that was the period between Zaleucas and Demosthenes) only one new law was added to the old ones."

I am grateful to my colleague Dr. Brian Satterfield for his translation of this passage from *Vetus Græce*.

63 Walter Moyle, *A Select Collection of Tracts, Eighteenth Century Collections Online*. Gale Group.* http://galenet.galegroup.com.ps2.villanova.edu/servlet, *ECCO*, 44–46:

> The people, by their original constitution, had a negative vote in the choice of their magistrates, in the passing of all laws, and in the resolution of peace and war.[a] The elections of the magistrates before the institution of the Comitia Centuriata, by Servius,[b] lay almost wholly in the power of the people, who out-voted the nobility by their numbers. But Numa, by an artful policy, curbed this mighty privilege of the commons[c]: for he instituted a college of augurs, or diviners, who were to consult the gods upon the creation of their officers[d]; and without the concurrence and authority of this college, all the public resolutions of the people were void...
>
> It is true, by the antient constitution of Rome, the kings had the sole right of proposing laws to the people, and consequently had no need of the augurs to put a negative upon any law. But Numa was too wise to hazard the affection of the people, by refusing to propose any popular laws, and rather chose to make use of the authority of the augurs upon a dead-lift, than expose his prerogative to the hatred of the people....
>
> [H]e [Numa] added to the unlimited jurisdiction of the augurs an institution of a college of heralds at arms, composed of the nobility, whose province was to judge and determine of the rights of war and peace, and were, in other words, the public casuists of the state; with such an unbounded authority, that though the three states and the augurs had concurred upon declaring war, yet the heralds, by virtue of their office, had power to reverse their resolutions, unless the causes of the war appeared to them to be just and honourable. This order was founded upon the same principle with the former: That if the people had resolved upon war, against his inclination, he might still have a reserve to apply to in order to prevent it.
>
> That these were the considerations upon which Numa founded the institution of the augurs is apparent from the authority of Cicero.

---

* Walter Moyle, *An Essay Upon the Roman Government* (Glasgow, 1750), is also available in *Two English Republican Tracts*, ed. Caroline Robbins (London: Cambridge University Press, 1969); see especially pp. 224–25. Cf. J. A. W. Gunn, *Beyond Liberty and Property: The Process of Self-Recognition in Eighteenth-Century Political Thought* (Kingston: McGill-Queen's University Press, 1983). According to Gunn, Moyle was particularly interested in the way in which political power rested on opinion (20). Indeed, earlier in Moyle's *An Essay Upon the Roman Government*, he declared that "authority built upon opinion is usually derived to the clergy, from a persuasion in the people of

*What ignorance & susceptibility of delusion in the people of Locris, is (impl)ied by such a precaution! J. M.

---

their divine mission and designation; or from a reverence to their mystic ceremonies and institutions; or for their pretended empire over the consciences of mankind" (*A Select Collection of Tracts, Eighteenth Century Collections Online*, 25; Robbins, ed., 217).

[a] Dionysius Periegeta. p. 65, 66.

[b] Polyb. p. 643

[c] Liv. l. I. c. 36

[d] Dionys. p. 6.

[64] Page 50 is numbered, but nothing else is written on the page. Dionysius, of Halicarnassus. *The Roman Antiquities of Dionysius Halicarnassensis, Translated Into English; With Notes and Dissertations. By Edward Spelman, Esq.* ... (London, 1758), I:355–59:

The seventh part of his [Numa's] religious institutions was allotted to the college of the *Feciales*: These may be called, in Greek, *Ειζηνοδιχαι*, *Judges in matters relating to peace*: They are chosen out of the best families, and exercise their holy office during life; Numa being the first, who instituted this holy magistracy, also, among the Romans: But, whether he took the example from those, called the Aequicoli, according to the opinion of some; or from the city of the Ardeates, as Gellius writes, I cannot say: It is sufficient for me to give notice that, before Numa's reign, the college of the Feciales was not in being among the Romans. It was instituted by Numa, when he was upon the point of making war with the Fidenates, who had made incursions into, and ravished, his territories, in order to try, whether they would come to an accommodation with him without entering into a war, which, being under a necessity, they submitted to. But, since the college of the Feciales is not in use among the Greeks, it is incumbent on me to relate how many, and how great affairs fall under its jurisdiction; to the end that those, who are unacquainted with the piety of the men of those times, may not be surprised to find that the event of all their wars, was most successful: For it will appear that the springs, and motives of them all were most pious; and, for this reason, chiefly, the gods were propitious to them in all the dangers, that attended them. The multiplicity of the affairs, that fall within the province of these Feciales, makes it no easy matter to enumerate them all; but the substance of them is, as follows: To take care that the Romans do not enter into an unjust war against any confederate city: And, if others begin the violation of their treaties, to go as embassadors, and demand justice, in the first place; but, if they refuse to comply with their demands, then, to give their sanction to the war. In like manner, if any, in alliance with the Romans, complain of having been injured by them, and demand justice, these men are to inquire whether they have suffered any thing in violation of their alliance; and, if they find their complaints well grounded, to seize the guilty, and deliver them up to the sufferers. They are, also, to take cognizance of the crimes committed against embassadors; to take care that treaties are, religiously, observed; to make peace; and, if they find it entered into, contrary to the holy laws, to set it aside; to inquire into, and expiate, the transgressions of the generals, as far as they relate to oaths, and treaties, concerning which I shall speak in a proper place. As to the function they perform in quality of heralds, when they go to demand justice of any city thought to have injured the Romans (for these things, also, are worthy of our knowledge, being transacted with great regard both to religion, and justice) I have received the following account. One of these Feciales, chosen by his colleagues, being clad in his robes, and bearing the ensigns of his holy dignity to distinguish him from others, proceeds towards the city, whose inhabitants have done the injury; and, standing on the confines, calls upon Jupiter, and the rest of the gods to witness that he is come to demand justice on the behalf of the Romans: After which, he takes an oath that he is going to a city, that has done an injury; and, having made the most dreadful imprecations against himself, and his country, if, what he averred was not true; he then, enters their confines: Afterwards, he calls to witness the first man he meets, whether he was an inhabitant of the country, or of the city; and, having repeated the same imprecations, he advances towards the latter; and, before he enters it, he

(55

TRUE REASONS FOR KEEPING GREAT DEPARTMENTS OF POWER SEPARATE

FEDERAL GOVERNMENTS (65

See Federalist Vol. 1. pg.

The Governments of the cantons of Greece were federal – composed of the Govts. of Towns, of which the principal usually gave law to the rest – see Anacharsis. vol. 4. p. 345[65]

For the Beotian Confederacy – see Anacharsis. vol. 3. p. 309.[66]

---

calls the keeper of the gate, or the first person he finds there to witness, in the same manner: Upon which, he proceeds to the market-place; and, being there, he informs the magistrates of the reasons of his coming, adding, every where, the same oaths, and imprecations. If they are disposed to make satisfaction by delivering up the guilty, he leads them away, and returns as from friends, he himself being now their friend: If they desire time to deliberate, he allows them ten days, after which he returns, and waits till they have asked this three times: But, after the expiration of the thirty days, if the city still persists in refusing to do him justice, he calls both the celestial and infernal gods to witness, and goes away, saying no more than this, that the Romans will deliberate concerning them at their leisure. After his return to Rome, he, together with the rest of the Feciales, make their report to the senate, that they had done every thing, that was ordained by the holy laws; and, if they thought proper to resolve upon a war, there was no obstacle on the part of the gods. But, if any of these things were omitted, neither the senate, nor the people had the power of resolving upon a war. This, therefore, is the account we have received concerning the Feciales.

65 *Voyage*, 4:345 (309–10): "The history of Greece presents us with more than one example of these dreadful emigrations, which ought not to excite our surprise. The greater part of the districts of Greece at first contained a number of independent republics, some subject to aristocracy, others governed by a democracy, and all of which easily obtained the protection and assistance of the neighbouring powers whose interest it was to divide them.[a] In vain they endeavoured to unite together, by a general confederation; the most powerful, after having subjected the weaker, disputed the sovereignty with each other, and not unfrequently one among them, raising itself above the rest, exercised a real despotism under the specious forms of liberty. Hence those ancient hatreds and national wars which for so long a time have laid waste Thessaly, Bœotia, Aracdia, and Argolis. These have never desolated Attica and Laconia; not the former, because its inhabitants live under the same laws, like citizens of the same city; nor the latter, because the people of that country have been ever held in subjection by the active vigilance of the magistrates of Sparta, and the known valour of the Spartans."

---

[a] Thucyd. lib. 1. cap. 35 et 40.

66 *Voyage*, 3:309 (274–75):

Thebes is not only the great fortress of Bœotia,[a] but may be said to be its capital. It is at the head of a powerful confederacy composed of the chief cities of Bœotia; all of which possess the right of sending deputies to the assembly, in which affairs of the state are finally determined, after having been discussed in four different councils.[b] At this assembly preside eleven chiefs, known by the name of Bœotarchs,[c] to which station they are elected by the assembly itself. They have great influence in all deliberations, and generally have the command of the armies.[d] Such a power would be dangerous were it permanent; but those invested with it must resign it at the end of the year, under pain of death, even were they at the head of a victorious army, and on the eve of obtaining the most signal advantages.[e]

(a) For the Amphyctionic do. see do. vol. 3. 336 & seq.[67]

All the Bœotian cities have claims and just titles to independence; but in despite of all their efforts, and those of the other nations of Greece, the Thebans have never suffered them to enjoy a complete state of freedom.[f] With respect to the cities they have founded, the Thebans assert the right which other countries exercise over their colonies:[g] to the others they oppose force,[h] too often the most valid title, or possession, which is the most indisputable of all. They have destroyed Thespiæ and Platæa for separating from the Bœotian league, the resolutions and operations of which are now entirely at their devotion,[i] and which can bring into the field twenty thousand men.[j]

---

[a] Diod. Sic. 15. p. 342.
[b] Thucyd. lib. 5. cap. 38. Diod. Sic. lib. 15. p. 389. Liv. lib. 36. cap. 6
[c] Thucyd. lib. 4. cap. 91.
[d] Diod. Sic. lib. 15. p. 368. Plut. in Pelopidas. t. i. p. 288.
[e] Plut. ibid. p. 290.
[f] Xenoph. Hist. Græc. lib. 6. p. 594. Diod. Sic. lib. 15. p. 355, 367, 381, &c.
[g] Thucyd. lib. 3. cap. 61 et 62.
[h] Xenoph. Hist. Græc. lib. 6. p. 579. Diod. Sic. lib. 11. p. 62.
[i] Xenoph. ibid. lib. 5. p. 558. Diod. Sic. lib. 15. p. 389.
[j] Xenoph. Memorabilia lib. 3. p. 767. Diod. Sic. lib. 12. p. 119.

[67] *Voyage*, 3:336 & seq. (299–302):

The league was ratified by an oath, the form of which is still retained. "We swear," said the associated states, "never to destroy the Amphictyonic towns, nor ever to divert, either in peace or war, the springs or streams necessary to supply their wants: if any power should dare to attempt it, we will march against that power and destroy its cities. Should impious men seize on the offerings in the temple of Apollo, we swear to employ our feet, out arms, our voices, and all our powers, against them and their accomplices."[a]

This tribunal still subsists, nearly in the same form in which it was originally instituted. Its jurisdiction has extended with the nations which left the northern parts of Greece, and which, remaining united to the Amphictyonic league, have carried with them the right of attending and voting at these assemblies to their adopted countries.[b] This is the case with the Lacedæmonians, who formerly inhabited Thessaly, and who, when they settled in Peloponnesus, retained one of the two suffrages to which the Dorians, of whom they formed a part, were originally entitled. In like manner, the double suffrage granted to the Iönians was, in process of time, divided between the Athenians and Iönian colonies of Asia Minor.[c] But, though the number of votes at this council can never exceed twenty-four, the number of deputies is not limited; the Athenians sometimes had three or four.[d]

The Amphictyonic council is held in the spring at Delphi, and in autumn at the town of Anthela.[e] It attracts a numerous concourse of spectators, and opens by sacrifices offered up for the tranquility and prosperity of Greece. Besides the objects specified in the oath, the assembly judges all differences between cities which claim the right of presiding at the sacrifices offered by several cities in conjunction,[f] or which after a battle gained, may attempt to appropriate exclusively to themselves honours that should be the portion of all.[g] Other causes, civil as well as criminal, are brought before the tribunal,[h] but more especially such offences as openly violate the law of nations.[i] The question is discussed by the deputies of the contending parties, and decided by the majority of voices. A fine is imposed on the offending nations or cities, which, if not paid before a stated time is followed by a second sentence, by which it is doubled.[j] If those against whom it is awarded still continue refractory, the assembly may call for assistance to support its decree, and arm against them the whole Amphictyonic body, consisting of a great part of Greece. It may also exclude them from the Amphictyonic league or common union of the temple.[k]

For the confederacies of Thessaly see Anacharsis vol. p. 352 & seq.[68]

For Union of Calmar see –[69]

But powerful nations do not always submit to its decrees. Of this we have an instance in the recent conduct of the Lacedæmonians, who having, in time of profound peace, taken possession of the citadel of Thebes, the magistrates of that city summoned them to the Amphictyonic council. The Lacedæmonians were first sentenced to pay five hundred talents, and afterwards a thousand, which they refused, alleging that the decision was unjust.[l]

The judgments pronounced against nations who profane the temple of Delphi are more tremendous. Their soldiers march with the more repugnance on such an enterprise, as they are punished with death, and deprived of sepulture, when taken in arms;[m] while those called on by the council to avenge the profanation of the altars are the more willing to obey, as every man who favours or tolerates the act is deemed a sharer in the impiety. On these occasions the guilty people, besides the anathemas thundered out against them, have to dread the policy of the neighbouring princes, who frequently find the means of gratifying their own ambition by espousing the cause of the gods.

---

[a] Æschin. de Fals. Leg. p. 413.
[b] Mem. de l'Acad. des Bell. Lettr. t. xxi. Hist. p. 237.
[c] Æschin. de Fals. Leg. p. 413.
[d] Id. in Ctesiph. p. 446.
[e] Strab. lib. 9. p. 420. Æschin. ibid.
[f] Demosth. de. Cor. p. 495. Plut. Rhet. Vit. t. ii. p. 850.
[g] Demosth. in Against Neæra. P. 877. Cicero. De inventione rhetorica. lib. 2. cap. 23. t. i. p. 96
[h] Mem. de l'Acad. des Bell. Lettr. t. v. p. 405.
[i] Plut. in Cimon. t. i. p. 483.
[j] Diod. Sic. lib. 15. p. 430.
[k] Plut. in Themistocles. t. i. p. 122. Pausan. lib. 10. cap. 8. p. 816. Æschin. de Fals. Leg. p. 413.
[l] Doid. Sic. lib. 16. p. 430.
[m] Id. ibid. p. 427 et 431.

68 *Voyage*, 3:352 & seq. (310–11):

The Achæans, and Æolians, the Dorians, from whom descended the Lacedæmonians, and several other powerful states of Greece, derive their origin from Thessaly. The people who inhabit it at present are the Thessalians properly so called, the Œteans, the Phthiotians, the Malians, the Magnesians, the Perrhæbians, &c. These nations were formerly governed by kings, and afterwards experienced revolutions common to great and small states; at present they are for the most part subject to an oligarchy.[a]

On certain occasions, the towns of each of these states send their deputies to a council in which their interests are discussed;[b] but the decrees of these assemblies are binding only on those who have subscribed them. Thus not only are the states independent of each other, but this independence is extended to the towns of every state. For instance, the state of the Œteans being divided into fourteen districts,[c] the inhabitants of one may refuse to follow the others to war.[d] This excessive liberty diminishes the strength of each state, by preventing it from uniting its forces, and produces such languor in the public deliberations, that they often dispense with convening the assemblies.[e]

The confederacy of the Thessalians properly so called is the most powerful of all, both from the number of towns appertaining to it, and from the accession of the Magnesians and Perrhæbians, whom it has almost brought under complete subjection.[f]

We meet likewise with some free cities which seem unconnected with any of these states, and which, too weak singly to maintain their independence and command a proper respect, have formed an alliance with two or three other neighbouring towns, detached and feeble like themselves.[g]

For Saxon Heptarchy see –[70]

For confederation of 4 N. England Colonies – see Hazard collection of papers –[71]

For the Etolian Confederacy see Anacharsis vol. 3 p. 405.[72]

---

[a] Thucyd. lib. 4. cap. 78.
[b] Id. ibid. Liv. lib. 35. cap. 31; lib. 36. cap. 8; lib. 39. cap. 25; lib. 42. cap. 38.
[c] Strab. lib. 9. p. 434.
[d] Diod. Sic. lib. 18. p. 595.
[e] Liv. lib. 34. cap. 51.
[f] Theoph. ap. Athen. lib. 6. p. 265.
[g] Strab. lib. 9. p. 437. Liv. lib. 42. cap. 53.

69 The Union of Calmar (1397) united the kingdoms of Denmark, Sweden, and Norway under one sovereign for the purpose of foreign affairs; each kingdom retained its own laws and independence.

70 The Anglo-Saxon heptarchy existed prior to 800 AD and consisted of seven main kingdoms: Northumbria, Mercia, East Anglia, Essex, Wessex, Sussex, and Kent. These kingdoms were constantly at war with each other; they later merged to form the kingdom of England.

71 Ebenezer Hazard, *Historical Collections; Consisting of State Papers, and Other Authentic Documents; Intended as Materials for an History of the United States of America.* 2 vols. (Philadelphia, 1792–1794), 1:583–90. *Eighteenth Century Collections Online.* Gale Group. Madison probably briefly examined the unpublished manuscript of this work while it was in Jefferson's possession in early 1791. See my discussion of this in Chapter 1 of this work.

72 *Voyage*, 3:405 (356–57):

After passing the mouth of the Acheloüs, we coasted during a whole day along the shores of Ætolia.[a] This country, in which there are fertile plains, is inhabited by a warlike nation,[b] divided into several tribes, in general of Greek origin, though some of them still retain relics of their ancient barbarism, by speaking a language very difficult to understand, living on raw flesh, and inhabiting defenceless villages.[c] These various tribes, uniting together, have formed a powerful association, similar to that of the Bœötians, Thessalians, and Acarnanians. They assemble yearly by deputies in the city of Thermus, to elect their chief.[d] The pomp displayed on the occasion, the games, festivals, and concourse of merchants and spectators, render this no less splendid than august assembly.[e]

The Ætolians regard neither alliance nor treaties. When war breaks out between their neighbours they suffer them mutually to enfeeble each other, then fall upon them, and carry off the spoils from the victors. This they call *pillaging amongst the pillage.*[f]

---

[a] Dicæarchi Status Græciæ. v. 63. p. 5. Scylacis Periplus p. 14.
[b] Strab. lib. 10. p. 450. Palmer. Antiq. p. 423.
[c] Thucyd. lib. 3. cap. 94.
[d] Strab. lib. 10. p. 463. Polyb. Excerpt. Legat. cap. 74. p. 895.
[e] Polyb. Excerpt. Legat. lib. 5. p. 357.
[f] Id. ibid. lib. 17. p. 746.

For Acarnanian do. see do. p. 404.[73]

For Achæan do. – see do. p. 463 –[74]

For the Confederacy of Elis[75] see do. p. 470. Of Messenia do.[76]

[73] *Voyage*, 3:404 (355–56): "Pursuing our course, we saw to the right the isles of Ithaca and Cephallenia, and to the left the coasts of Acarnania. In this province we meet with some considerable towns,[a] many small fortified places,[b] and several nations of different origins,[c] but associated in one general confederacy, and almost always at war with the Ætolians their neighbours, whose states are separated from theirs by the river Acheloüs. The Acarnanians are faithful to their promise, and extremely jealous of their liberty.[d]"

---

[a] Thucyd. lib. 2. cap. 102.
[b] Diod. Sic. lib. 19. p. 708.
[c] Strab. lib. 7. p. 321.
[d] Polyb. lib. 4. p. 299.

[74] *Voyage*, 3:463 (406–08):

Achaia, from the earliest times, was divided into twelve cities, each comprising seven or eight towns within its district.[a] All have the privilege of sending deputies to the ordinary assembly, which is held at the beginning of their year, or towards the middle of the spring.[b] There such regulations are made as circumstances may require: magistrates are nominated to carry them into execution, and invested likewise with the power of convoking an extraordinary assembly, in case of war, or the necessity of deliberating on an alliance.[c]

The government goes forward, if I may use the expression, by its own motion. It is a democracy, which owes its origin and continuance to peculiar circumstances. The country being poor, without commerce, and almost without industry, its inhabitants peaceably enjoy the liberty and equality afforded them by a wise legislation. As no ambitious and turbulent spirits have risen amongst them,[d] they are strangers to the desire of conquests; and as they have little connection with corrupt nations, they never employ fraud or falsehood, even against their enemies:[e] as all their cities, in fine, have the same laws and the same offices of magistracy, they form only one body and one state, and the harmony that reigns amongst them pervades every class of citizens.[f] The excellence of their constitution and the probity of their magistrates are so universally admitted, that the Greek cities of Italy, wearied with their dissensions, have been known to address themselves to this people to become their arbitrators, and some of them even formed a similar confederation. Nay, it is not long since the Lacedæmonians and Thebans, mutually claiming the victory at Leuctra, referred this dispute, in which their honour was so materially interested,[g] and which demanded the most impartial decision, to the determination of the Achæans.

---

[a] Herodoti Historiarum. lib. 1. cap. 145. Polyb. lib. 2. p. 128. Strab. ibid. p. 337 et 386.
[c] Polyb. lib. 4. p. 305; lib. 5. p. 350. Strab. ibid. p. 385.
[c] Polyb. Excerpt. Legat. p. 855.
[d] Polyb. lib. 2. p. 125.
[e] Id. lib. 13. p. 672.
[f] Justin. lib. 34. cap. 1.
[g] Polyb. lib. 2. p. 126. Strab. lib. 8. p. 381.

[75] *Voyage*, 3:470 (413–14): "After the monarchical government was abolished, the cities associated in a fœderal league; but that of Elis, more powerful than the rest, has insensibly brought them under subjection,[a] leaving them only the shadow of liberty. Together they form eight tribes,[b]

(a) neither Thucidides nor Xenophon's continuation of him make the least allusion to the Amphyctionic Council, altho' Athens & Lacedemon were under its Authority. That the Pelopponesian War, so distinguished for its duration its belligerent parties and its consequences, should have been carried on without any interference or mention of that institution is a remarkable proof of its insignificancy.

For the Arcadian Confederacy see Anacharsis vol. 4. page 298[77]

---

governed by a body of ninety senators, who hold their places for life, and by their influence fill up vacancies at their pleasure: hence it is that authority resides only in a very few persons, and that an oligarchy has been introduced within an oligarchy, which is one of the destructive vices of this government.[c] Attempts have therefore recently been made to establish a democracy.[d]"

[a] Herodot. lib. 4. cap. 148. Thucyd. lib. 5. cap. 31.
[b] Pausan. lib. 5. p.. 397.
[c] Aristot. de Rep. lib. 5. cap. 6. t. ii. p. 394.
[d] Xenoph. Hist. Græc. lib. 7. p. 635.

76 *Voyage*, 4 (31–33):

Banished from Greece, strangers to other nations, we are only connected with mankind by the fruitless pity which they sometimes deign to bestow on out sufferings.... The Messenians enjoyed, during many ages, an undisturbed tranquility, in a country which sufficed to supply all their wants, and beneath the mild influences of a sky perpetually serene. They were free; they had wise laws, simple manners, kings who loved their people,[a] and joyous festivals to relax them after their labours.

On a sudden the alliance by which they were united to the Lacedæmonians received a mortal wound. The two states mutually accused and irritated each other, and menaces succeeded to complaints. Ambition, till then enchained by the laws of Lycurgus, seized the moment to break his fetters, and, loudly calling injustice and violence to his aid, entered with these infernal attendants into the hearts of the Spartans, and incited them to swear on their altars never to lay down their arms till they had enslaved Messenia.[b]

[a] Pausan. lib. 4. cap. 3. p. 286.
[b] Justin. lib. 3. cap. 4.

77 *Voyage*, 4:298 (266–67): "Arcadia was anciently governed by kings, but afterwards divided into several republics, all of which have a right to send deputies to the general council.[a] Mantinea and Tegea are at the head of this confederation, which would be too formidable were all its forces united: for the country is extremely populous, and is reckoned to contain not less than three hundred thousand slaves.[b] But the jealousy of power continually occasions divisions between the great and lesser states. In our time, factions had become so numerous, that a plan was laid before the assembly of the nation, in which, among other regulations, it was proposed that the power of determining on peace and war should be confided to a body of ten thousand men.[c] This project, which the new troubles that is occasioned caused to be laid aside, was again revived with more vigour after the battle of Leuctra. Epaminondas, who, to restrain the Spartans, had just recalled the exiled inhabitants of Messenia, proposed to the Arcadians to destroy the small towns which were without defence, and transfer the inhabitants to a place of strength, to be built on the frontiers of Laconia. He furnished them with a

For the Argive do. see Strabo lib. 8[78] – Anacharsis vol. 4. p. 346.[79]

---

thousand men to carry his plan into execution, and the foundations of Megalopolis were immediately laid.[d] This happened about fifteen years before our arrival."

---

[a] Xenoph. Hist. Græc. lib. 6. p. 602.
[b] Theoph. ap. Athen. lib. 6. cap. 20. p. 271
[c] Demosth. de. Fals. Legat. p. 295. Diod. Sic lib. 15. p. 372.
[d] Pausan. lib. 4. cap. 27. p. 654.; lib. 9. cap. 14. p. 739.

[78] Strabo, *The Geography of Strabo*, eds. Horace Leonard Jones and John Robert Sitlington Sterrett (London and New York: G. P. Putnam's Sons and William Heinemann, 1933): "And in the first place let me mention in how many ways the term 'Argos' is used by the poet, not only by itself, but also with epithets, when he calls Argos 'Achaean,' or 'Iasian,' or 'hippian,' or 'Pelasgian,' or 'horse-pasturing.' For, in the first place, the city is called Argos: 'Argos and Sparta,' 'and those who held Argos and Tiryns.' And secondly the Peloponnesus: 'in our home in Argos,' for the city of Argos was not his home. And, thirdly, Greece as a whole; at any rate, he calls all Greeks Argives, just as he calls them Danaans and Achaeans [IV, 155]. ... Now the city of the Argives is for the most part situated in a plain, but it has for a citadel the place called Larisa, a hill that is fairly well fortified and contains a temple of Zeus" (IV:159).

[79] *Voyage*, 4:346 (297–99):

Argos is situate at the foot of a hill, on which stands the citadel.[a] It is one of the most ancient cities of Greece,[b] and from the earliest ages possessed such power and splendor that its name was sometimes given to the province, to the whole of Peloponnesus, and even to all Greece.[c] The house of the Pelopidæ having established itself at Mycanæ, that city eclipsed the glory of her rival.[d] Agamemnon reigned in the former city, and Diomedes and Sthenelus in the latter.[e] Some time after, Argost regained its rank,[f] which it never afterwards lost.

The sovereign power [in Argos] was at first confided to kings, who oppressed their subjects, and who were soon only left in possession of that title which they had abused.[g]

The title itself was afterwards abolished, and democracy has subsisted ever since.[h] The affairs of the state are discussed in the senate, before they are submitted to the decision of the people;[i] but as the senate cannot take on itself the executive power, eighty of its members continually watch over the safety of the state, with nearly the same functions as the prytanes of Athens.[j] More than once, and even in our time, the principal citizens have endeavoured to free themselves from the tyranny of the multitude by establishing an oligarchy; but these attempts have answered no other purpose than to occasion an effusion of blood.[k]

They still felt the effects of a fruitless attempt of this kind which they had made about fourteen years before. Wearied with the continual calamities and reproaches of the public orators, they engaged in a project to change the form of government. Their design was discovered, and many of them were apprehended. When brought to the torture, some killed themselves; and one of them accused thirty of his associates, who were put to death without further trial. Their property was confiscated; informations multiplied, and to be accused was to be found guilty. Sixteen hundred of the richest of the citizens were massacred; and as the orators, through fear of a new order of things, began to relax in their zeal, the people, conceiving they had deserted them, sacrificed them all their fury. No city of Greece had seen within its walls the example of such barbarity; and the Athenians, having heard the account of it in one of their assemblies, thought themselves so polluted by only listening to the horrid narrative, that they immediately had recourse to the ceremonies of expiation.[l]

---

[a] Strab. lib. 8 p. 370. Liv. lib. 32. cap. 25.
[b] Herodot. lib. 1 cap. 1. Diod. Sic. lib. 1 p. 24.

For the three confederacies of the Asiatic Greeks – see Id. vol. 6. p. 203/4[80] – 209/210[81]

---

[c] Strab. lib. 8 p. 369. Schol. Pind. in Isthm. od. 2 v. 17. Plut. Quæst. Roman. T. ii. P. 272. Apollod. lib. 2. p. 75.
[d] Strab. ibid. p. 372.
[e] Homer. Iliad. lib. 2. v. 564.
[f] Strab. Ibid.
[g] Plut. in Lycurgus. t. i. p. 43. Pausan. lib. 2. cap. 19. p. 152.
[h] Thucyd. lib. 5. cap. 28, 31, et 41.
[i] Herodot. lib. 7. cap. 148. Thucyd. ibid. cap. 37.
[j] Thucyd. lib. 5. cap. 47. Diod. Sic. lib. 19.
[k] Thucyd. ib. cap. 76, 81, 82. Diod. Sic. lib. 15. p. 372.
[l] Diod. Sic. lib. 15. p. 372. Plut. de Reip. Ger. Præc. t. ii. p. 804. Hellad ap. Phot. p. 1593.

80 *Voyage*, 6:203–04 (178–80):

The Æolians possess, on the continent, eleven cities, the deputies of which assemble on certain occasions in that of Cyme.[a] The confederation of the Iönians is formed between twelve principal cities. Their deputies meet annually at a temple of Neptune, situate in a sacred grove, beneath Mount Mycale, at a small distance from Ephesus. After a sacrifice which the other Iönians are not permitted to be present at, and at which a young man of Priene presides, the affairs of the province are deliberated on.[b] The Doric states assemble at the promontory Triopium; and the city of Cnidus, the isle of Cos, and the three cities of Rhodes, alone possess the right of sending deputies to them.[c]

Nearly in this manner was it that the general assemblies of the Asiatic Greeks were regulated in the earliest times. Tranquil in their new habitations, they cultivated in peace their fertile fields, and were invited by their situation to transport their commodities from coast to coast. Their commerce soon increased with their industry. They afterward were seen to settle in Egypt, to brave the Adriatic and Tyrrhene seas, to build a city in Corsica, and to extend their navigation even to the island of Tartessus, beyond the Pillars of Hercules.[d]

Their first success had, however, attracted the attention of a nation too near them not to be formidable. The kings of Lydia, of which Sardes was the capital, seized on some of their cities:[e] Crœsus conquered them all, and imposed on them a tribute.[f] Cyrus, before he attacked the latter prince, proposed to them to join their arms to his, which they refused.[g] After his victory, he disdained to receive their submission, and ordered one of his generals to march against them, who added them to the Persian empire by right of conquest.[h]

---

[a] Herodot. ibid. cap. 149. 157.
[b] Id. ibid. cap. 143. 148. 170. Strab. lib. 8. p. 384; lib. 14. p. 639. Diod. Sic. lib. 15. p. 364.
[c] Herodot. lib. 1. cap. 144. Dionysii Halicarnassensis Opera, Antiq. Roman. lib. 4. §25. t. ii. p. 702.
[d] Herodot. ibid. cap. 163. 165; lib. 2. cap. 178; lib. 3. cap. 26; lib. 4. cap. 152. Strab. lib. 7. p. 801.
[e] Herodot. ibid. cap. 14, 15, 16.
[f] Ib. ibid. cap. 6 et 27.
[g] Id. ibid. cap. 75.
[h] Herodot. lib. 1. cap. 141. Thucyd. lib. 1. cap. 16.

81 *Voyage*, 6:209–10 (183–85):

If we consider with proper attention the circumstance in which they [the Asiatic Greeks] were situated, we shall be convinced that it was impossible they should preserve complete liberty. The

---

For the Syncretism[82] of Crete. Id. vol. 6. p. 259.[83]

For the Albany project see Franklin's works[84] also Pownal's Colonies[85]

---

kingdom of Lydia, which afterward became one of the provinces of the Persian Empire, had for its natural boundary the Ægean Sea, the shores of which are peopled by Greek colonies. They occupy so narrow a space, that they must necessarily fall into the hands of the Lydians and Persians, unless they took proper measures for their defence. But by a defect which also subsists among the confederate republics of the continent of Greece, not only in Æolia, Iönia, and Doris, when threatened with invasion, did not unite their forces, but in each of the three provinces the decrees of the general assembly were not obligatory on all the states of the deputies of which it was composed. Thus we see, in the time of Cyrus, the inhabitants of Miletus made a separate peace with that prince, and delivered up the other cities to the fury of their enemies.[a]

When Greece consented to take arms in their defence, she drew on herself the innumerable armies of the Persians; and, but for prodigies of chance and valour, must have sunk beneath a foreign yoke. If, after disastrous wars, repeated through a whole century, she has at last renounced the ill-fated project of breaking the chains of the Iönians, it is because she has at length been convinced that their situation and circumstance oppose invincible obstacles to their emancipation. This the sage Bias of Priene expressly declared when Cyrus had rendered himself master of Lydia. "Stay not here," said he to the Iönians, "sink into an ignominious slavery; embark on board your ships, traverse the seas, and take possession of Sardinia and the neighbouring islands, where you may still enjoy liberty and peace.[b]"

Twice have these people had it in their power to throw off the Persian yoke, once by following the counsel of Bias, and a second time by accepting the proposals of the Lacedæmonians, who, after the termination of the Median war, offered to convey them back into Greece;[c] but they have always refused to forsake their habitations; and, if we may judge from their population and their riches, independence was not necessary to their happiness.

---

[a] Herodot. lib. 1. cap. 141. 169.

[b] Id. ibid. cap. 170.

[c] Id. lib. 9. cap. 106. Diod. Sic. lib. 11. p. 29.

82 Syncretism is the synthesis of different religions and of disparate practices and beliefs.

83 *Voyage*, 6:259 (227): "The law of syncretism, which enjoins all the inhabitants of the island to unite if a foreign power should attempt a descent, would be insufficient to defend them either against their internal dissensions or against the arms of an enemy;[a] because it would only suspend instead of extinguishing animosities, and would suffer too many individual interests to subsist in a general confederation."

---

[a] Aristot. de Rep. lib. 2. Cap. 10. P. 333. Plut. De Fraterno Amore t. ii. P. 490.

84 Benjamin Franklin, *Political, Miscellaneous, and Philosophical Pieces* (London: J. Johnson, 1779); this work is in Millicent Sowerby's *Catalogue of the Library of Thomas Jefferson*, III:240–41. Franklin was a delegate to the Albany Conference of 1754, at which he proposed a union of the northern British American colonies. In his proposed plan, the general government was responsible for national defense and territorial expansion, and each colonial government retained its political authority for local purposes. The British King-in-Council possessed the prerogative of approving or negating (but not proposing) colonial legislation within three years after its passage. Although the commissioners to the Albany Conference adopted a plan along the lines Franklin recommended, neither the colonial assemblies nor the British Parliament followed suit. "Its fate was singular," Franklin remarked in his autobiography, "the assemblies did not adopt it, as they all thought there

For Hanseatic League, see[86]

was too much prerogative in it, and in England it was judg'd to have too much of the democratic" (*The Autobiography of Benjamin Franklin* [Mineola, NY: Dover, 1996], 102–03). Madison was likely referring to the federal character of the association Franklin proposed, particularly the following sections of the Albany Plan in the cited collection of Franklin's works:

> That the assent of the President General be required to all acts of the Grand Council; and that it is to be his office and duty to cause them to be carried into execution. The assent of the President General to all acts of the grand council was made necessary, in order to give the crown its due share of influence in this government, and connect it with that of *Great Britain* [103–04].
>
> That for these purposes they [the colonies] have power to make laws, and lay and levy such general duties, imports, and taxes, as to them shall appear most equal and just ... The laws which the President General and grand council are impowered to make, *are such only* as shall be necessary for the government of the settlements [112].
>
> That the laws made by them for the purposes aforesaid shall not be repugnant, but, as near as may be, agreeable to the laws of *England*, and shall be transmitted to the King in council for approbation as soon as may be after their passing; and if not disapproved within three years after presentation, to remain in force [115].

85 Thomas Pownall, *The Administration of the Colonies* (London: J. Wilkie, 1764). This text is available at Early Canadiana Online at http://eco.canadiana.ca/view/oocihm.20379/3?r=0&s=1. Madison had a copy of this work with him in Philadelphia. (See Madison's list of books to be transported to Philadelphia [ca. August 1790], *PJM*, 13:286.) First published anonymously in 1764, *The Administration of the Colonies* went through six editions and substantial additions and alterations, although the general themes remained constant. (See Guttridge, "Thomas Pownall's *The Administration of the Colonies*," 31–46; the edition Madison had in his possession in 1790–1791 is not identified in his book list.)

Pownall came to America in 1753 to serve as private secretary to the royal governor of New York. The next year, he attended the Albany congress, where he met Benjamin Franklin, with whom he developed a lifelong friendship. In 1757, he was appointed governor of Massachusetts; he returned to England in 1760 and later became a member of Parliament. Pownall opposed parliamentary taxation of the American colonies, promoted the recognition of the equal constitutional rights of Americans with Englishman, and advocated a strong union between the colonies and the mother country based on mutual economic interest.

In *The Administration of the Colonies*, Pownall argued that the power of commerce had replaced the power of the sword and the power of religion in the modern world. He believed that Great Britain was poised to become the center of a great commercial empire that might extend across the globe. According to Guttridge, Pownall's "*spirit* of commerce" is a "force of nature" that moves "by its own laws, beyond the contraint of individual nations, even though they might attempt to control the trade of their own subjects. It would create commercial and colonial interests which could break through all the regulations of European states, 'dissolve the effect of all artificial connections which government would create, and form the natural connections under which these interests actually exist'" (Guttridge, 33; quoting Pownall, 8).

Pownall's theory of the natural and free course of trade was an assertion of "principles broader than the conventions of the old colonial system," although they were "short of free trade in its later sense" (Guttridge, 33).

For the Germanic Belgic & Achean see Meerman's prize discourse[87] belongg. to Mr. Jefferson.

With respect to the Crown's American and Atlantic possessions, Pownall asserted that if Great Britain attends to a proper administration of the colonies, it may create "appropriated and good customers," thereby increasing its manufactures and exports and extend its commerce and dominions (Pownall, 23). Pownall advocated that "the final external profits of the labour and produce of colonies should center in the mother country, – that the colonists are the appropriated special customers of the mother country, – that the colonies, in their government and trade, should be all united in communion with, and subordination to the government of the mother country, but ever disconnected and independent of each other by any other communion than what centers here [in Great Britain]" (35). Given the present differences in religious and economic interests among the colonies and their rivalships and jealousies, the "impracticability, if not the impossibility of reconciling and accommodating [their] incompatible ideas and claims" is beneficial to the authority of the center (34). Pownall devoted a significant portion of this work to the proper political relationship between the mother country and the colonies with respect to the royal prerogative and the suspending clause. He wrote: "It is a standing instruction, as a security of the dependance of the government of the colonies, on the mother country, that no acts wherein the Kings Rights, or the rights of the mother country can be affected, shall be enacted into a law without a clause suspending the effect thereof, till his Majesty's pleasure shall be known" (41). Over and above the colonial charters and commissions, the colonies had to send all of their legislative acts to England to be "confirmed or abrogated by the crown" (44). The colonists universally rejected the suspending clause, claiming that "the crown has already in its hands the power of fixing this point; by the effect of its negative given to its governor" (41).

Despite the constitutional points made by each side in this debate, Pownall argued, the real issue is "the absolute necessity there is of their [the laws] being determined by that part of government, which shall be found to have the right and power to determine them; and to be so determined, that while the rights, liberties, and even privileges of the colonies are preserved, the colonies may be retained in that true and constitutional dependance to the mother country, and to the government of the mother country, which may unite them to it as parts of one whole" (49–50).

Pownall's overall objective was to form an administration "that shall firmly, uniformly, and constitutionally govern the colonies, by that predominant power, which the mother country ought to hold over the colonies, as corporations united to the realm, [and that] the people would become conscientiously in every individual, and constitutionally in their respective governments, disposed to receive the legal impression of the supreme government of the mother country, and to communicate the same through all its powers, so as to form, not a dependant appendix to the demesnes of the crown, but a subordinate united part of a one whole, this great commercial dominion of Great Britain" (65).

In the final edition of *The Administration of the Colonies*, Pownall advocated that the government of the colonies and the British colonial government share in the sovereign power, with the former sovereign within its own jurisdiction and the latter otherwise supreme and sovereign. There was, however, a caveat: Any act of the internal government of the colonies not in accordance with the laws of Great Britain was subject to negation by the King via his colonial appointees (Guttridge 45).

86 The Hanseatic League was an alliance of merchant associations in northern Germany that established exclusive trade privileges and monopolies for its members. It began in the thirteenth century and lasted well into the seventeenth century. Essentially an economic rather than a political alliance, the league lacked a permanent military force or governing authority except for periodic diets. As a result, the league was ultimately unable to compete with the new and powerful nations that were forming throughout Europe.

(75

GOVERNMENT OF UNITED STATES –

See Federalist. passim – particularly No. 51.

Here is the most characteristic trait in the Govt. of the U. S. – The powers surrendered by the people of America, are divided into two parts, one for the State, the other for the Genl. Govt. & each subdivided into Legislative Ex. & Judiciary. As in a single Govt. the Legislative Ex. & Judicy. ought to be kept separate by defensive armour for each. So ought the two Govts. federal & State. If this should be found practicable, it must be a happy discovery for mankind. As far as the security agst. power lies in a division of it, the security must be increased, by a system which doubles the number of parts. It must be confessed that the difficulty of dividing power between two Govts. is greater than between the several departmts. of the same Govt. as well as the difficulty of maintaining the division. It is more easy to divide from each other the Legislative Executive & Judiciary powers, wch. are distinct in their nature, than to divide the legislative powers wch. are of the same nature, from each other – as well as do the same with the Executive & Judiciary powers.[88]

(82

BEST DISTRIBUTION[89] OF PEOPLE IN REPUBLIC

A perfect Theory on this subject would be useful, not because it could be reduced to practice by any plan of legislation; but because it would be a model to which successive spontaneous improvements might approximate the condition of the Society.

That is the best distribution, which would most favor health, virtue, intelligence, and competency of fortune in the Citizens; and best secure the Republic agst. external dangers.

The life of the husbandman is most, that of the seaman least favorable to the comfort & happiness of the individual.

Among manufacturers, those employed on necessaries, are first to be secured. The remaining classes to be decided on by the preceding criteria.

---

87 Johan de Meerman, *Discours qui a remporté le prix de l'Académie royale des inscriptions et belles-lettres de Paris sur la question proposée en 1782. Comparer ensemble la Lique des Achéens 280 avant J.C., celle des Suisses en 1307 ..., & la Ligue des Provinces-Unies en 1579* ... (La Haye, 1784). Jefferson possessed this piece by Meerman; see Sowerby, *Catalogue of the Library of Thomas Jefferson*, III:210.

88 Pages 78 and 81 are numbered, but nothing else is written on the pages.

89 Madison wrote "arrangement" above "distribution," but did not cross out "distribution."

The class of literati is not less necessary than any other. They are the cultivators of the human mind – the manufacturers of useful knowledge – the agents of the commerce of ideas – the censors of public manners – the teachers of the arts of life and the means of happiness.

See with the mark [J. M.] Freneau's National Gazette[90]

[90] Madison most likely added this sentence at a later time. He was referring to the bound volume of the *Gazette* articles (housed in the Library of Congress), which he initialed; this compilation does not include his published *National Gazette* essay "Dependent Territories."

7

Additional Notes on Government[1]

[1] James Madison, Series 6, James Madison's notes on natural history and foreign trade, Image 1844, *The James Madison Papers*, LOC. These "Additional Notes on Government" are part of a bound notebook that also includes notes on the "Symmetry of Nature," "Questions proposed by the Abbé Raynal," "Extent of the British line of communication in Canada," "Origin of language" (inserted page); an inserted envelope addressed to "His Excellency James Madison, President of the United States," with a note written at the bottom stating: "shows the early use of envelopes (1812)"; "Notes on Buffon" (smaller notebook inserted); and "Miscellanies." The notes on the "Origin of language" were written in or after 1813 and probably in 1819 or later, as evidenced by Madison's referral to "Gov. Clarke" (Madison erroneously spelled Clark's name with an "e") and Duponceau's work on Native American languages. William Clark (1770–1838, of Lewis and Clark fame) was appointed governor of the Missouri territory by President James Madison in 1813, a position in which he served until 1820, when Missouri became a state. Pierre Etienne Duponceau (1760–1844) was a member of the Historical and Literary Committee of the American Philosophical Society and renowned for his report to the committee on the structure of Indian languages in 1819, which paved the way for his later induction into the Académie des Inscriptions and receipt of the Volney Prize in France. Also, compare "Symmetry of Nature," "Notes on Buffon," and "Emigration" to Madison's "Address to the Agricultural Society of Albermarle, Virginia," which he delivered on May 12, 1818.

(1

EXCEPTIONS TO THE MAXIM THAT COMMERCE SHOULD BE FREE.[2]

1. In cases when other nations would not follow the example, or admit a reciprocity.
2. To procure safety at the expence of interest – as in naval resources & other means of defence
3. To secure the means of transporting articles of commerce agst. the contingency of wars among carrying nations which divert or raise the price & ensurance of foreign bottoms
4. Duties on commerce for more conveniently in some cases, raising revenue.
5. Where the encouragement tends not to divert hands from other preferable objects – but to attract foreigners for the work into the country. (a) turnover
6. To foster infant establishments & enterprizes of an expensive & complex nature untill they grow up & can support themselves – See Franklin's Pamphlet Canada[3]

See also Anderson Introduction p.xlix[4]

[2] Compare Madison's list of exceptions to free trade in "Exceptions to the maxim that commerce should be free" to his similar list of exceptions in his letter to Joseph C. Cabell of October 30, 1828, which was published in the *National Intelligencer* in December of that year – about the same time that Calhoun anonymously published the "South Carolina Exposition and Protest," defending nullification (Meyers, *The Mind of the Founder*, 380–89). Prior to publication of this letter, Madison wrote Cabell: "Adverting casually to my letter of Oct. 30 it struck me as not amiss to erase the paragraph numbered 7 relating to cases which might require a simultaneous & diffusive concurrence & Tho true in itself, it may be thought not sufficiently incontrovertible to be classed with the other exceptions, nor sufficiently precise for the use made of it. Be so good therefore as to blot it out" (James Madison to Joseph C. Cabell, November 10, 1828, Series 1, From October 21, 1827 to January 25, 1830, Image 618, *The James Madison Papers*, LOC, http://hdl.loc.gov/loc.mss/mjm.22_0618_0619). Unfortunately, only the first three pages of Madison's long October 30, 1828 letter to Cabell are in the LOC collection. For the partial letter, see James Madison to Joseph C. Cabell, October 30, 1828, Series 1, From October 21, 1827 to January 25, 1830, Image 610, *The James Madison Papers*, LOC, http://hdl.loc.gov/loc.mss/mjm.22_0610_0612.

[3] Madison is probably referring here to Benjamin Franklin's "Canada Pamphlet," in Franklin's *Political, Miscellaneous, and Philosophical Pieces* (London: J. Johnson, 1779), which Jefferson owned and which Madison referred to in the chapter on federal governments in the "Notes on Government."

[4] Adam Anderson, *An Historical and Chronological Deduction of the Origin of Commerce* (Dublin: P. Byrne, 1790), I:xlix: "Vassalage and servile tenures also, or the feudal system, from many purchases and grants, began to grow gradually into disuse, in England much earlier than in Scotland: and our King Henry VII.'s law, for enabling the nobility to split their baronies or manors, without paying fines for alienation, gradually brought much of the landed interest into the seale of the Commons, and greatly multiplied the number of freeholds; as did also the succeeding wild extravagance of our Kings, in squandering away their own numerous baronies and demesne lands, most happily for their subjects ... [b]y these and other preceding as well as succeeding alterations, the face of things, in almost all Europe, became strangely changed for the better. ..."

7. To counteract foreign machinations, as of G.B. agst. the Cotton & Glass manufactories in U.S.[5]
8. Where a successful change in the direction of industry or labor, depends on a general Union of efforts at the same time, which may not be attainable without the aid of public authority.
9. Where the inveteracy of general habit resists useful innovations – as in the refusal of the French laborers to use the american hoe & mall,[6] instead of their own awkward ones. It happens in many cases that business accustomed long to a channel, which if good at first, has become bad, continues in it until in some degree forced, or seduced into a better by an enlightened government.
10. Temporary prevention of export of Specie as a guard to Banks agst. measures of a foreign Govt. for undermi[ni]ng them & distressing the pub: operations as, in the time of the War of 1812[7]

(a) Manufactures have generally been transplanted by the actual transfer of Manufacturers – as into Italy on the fall of the Greek Empire – from Italy into Spain and Flanders by the loss of liberty in Florence &c – from Flanders & France into England by the persecutions of Philip & revocation of the Edict of Nantz – and from Europe into America, by the causes of emigration from the former into the latter.
In Reign of Chs. 2. Imports of French luxuries turned the ballance agst. England 1,330,000 £ St: The Parl[iamen]t prohib[ite]d & the Brit. manufactures grew up & trade balanced itself – In Js. 2. trade again opened & the ballance till

[5] Madison's reference to the "machinations" of Great Britain against the American cotton and glass manufacturers most probably refers to the high volume of British exports to the United States, particularly glass and cotton textiles, following the close of the War of 1812 and the 1815 British-American commercial treaty setting import nondiscrimination. Indeed, the British flooded the American market with low-cost items – even sometimes selling them at a loss. During the war, domestic manufacturing in the United States grew as a result of the embargo and protective economic policies. After the conclusion of the war, however, many domestic manufacturing industries in the United States experienced an acute depression, including particularly the glass industry in western Pennsylvania and the cotton textile industry in Massachusetts. (The protective tariffs established in 1816, 1824, and 1828 were responses to the financial panic that resulted from the severe postwar economic conditions.) Madison's reference to British machinations against American cotton and glass manufacturers makes it highly probable that the "Additional Notes on Government" were written in 1815 or later.

[6] A mall (or maul) is a heavy, long-handled tool used to split pieces of wood along the grain. One side of the mall head is identical to a sledgehammer and the other side is a wedge-shaped axe.

[7] There should be an "X" to the left of the underlined words. Compare this argument with that in a letter by Madison, subsequently published on February 5, 1820, in Hezekiah Niles' *Weekly Register*, that discussed the need of specie to meet the call on the vaults of the bank.

prohibition renewed, was 1,712,559:7-0. £ St: See Anderson[8] & pamphlet on Edens[9] Treaty p.7, 10.[10]

(10

INFLUENCE OF COMMERCE ON GOVERNMENT[11]

(40

EMIGRATION

(see Freneau article Population & Emigration of which this seems the original sketch J.C.P.)[12]

Both in the vegetable and animal Kingdoms every species derives from nature a reproductive faculty beyond the demand for merely keeping up its stock. The seed of a single plant is sufficient to multiply it an hundred fold. The animal offspring is never limited to the number of its parents.

This ordinance of nature is calculated in both instances for a twofold purpose. In both it secures the continuance of the species which, if the generative principle had not a multiplying energy, would be reduced in number by every casual destruction of individuals, and by degrees be necessarily extinguished altogether. In the vegetable species the surplus answers moreover the essential purpose of sustaining the graminivorous tribes of animals: as in the animal, the surplus serves the like purpose of aliment for the carnivorous tribes. A crop of wheat may be reproduced

8 Anderson, *An Historical and Chronological Deduction of the Origin of Commerce.*

9 The Eden Treaty was a commercial agreement signed by Great Britain and France in 1786, named after its English negotiator. It ended the long commercial war between the two countries – at least for a brief time. However, it almost wholly benefitted the British and harmed the French economy, and in short order, French public opinion opposed it. Signed under the ancién regime, the treaty is considered one of the grievances that led to the French Revolution.

10 *Treaty of Navigation and Commerce Between His Britannick Majesty and the Most Christian King.* Signed at Versailles, September 26, 1786 (London: J. Stockdale, 1786). The pages Madison cites (7, 10) contain Articles VIII and XXII–XXIII, declaring an end to imported merchandise inspection and confiscation while enumerating a select few exceptions: "[A]bsolute Freedom shall be allowed to the Buyer and Seller to bargain and fix the Price for the (merchandise) as they shall see good" (7). The next page is numbered 3 but is blank except for a line on the page.

11 See Madison's "Head. for a discourse" in *PJM*, 12:68–69, 69n, which may be related to this subject heading. Madison's statements in these notes focused on the influence of commerce on government, the theory and policy of free commerce, exceptions to free trade theory, and the bold idea of a global republic.

12 This note was added later by John C. Payne, Madison's brother-in-law. Payne helped correct, alter, and transcribe Madison's original "Notes of Debates in the federal Convention" while the latter was afflicted with illness late in life. It was this service that likely motivated Madison's bequest of "two hundred and forty acres of land" for Payne and his heirs. See James Madison, *The Debates in the Federal Convention of 1787*, eds. Galliard Hunt and James Brown Scott (New York: Oxford University Press, 1920), xxii.

by one tenth of itself. The remaining nine tenths can be spared for the animals which feed on it. A flock of sheep may be continued by [13] of its increase. The residue is the bounty of nature to the animals which prey on that species.

Man who preys both on the vegetable and animals species, is himself prey to death alone. He too possesses the reproductive principle far beyond the degree requisite for the bare continuance of a given number. What becomes of the surplus of human life

life[14] to which the multiplying energy is competent? It is either destroyed by infanticide, as among the Chinese Lacedaemonians &c, or is starved or prevented by the deficit of subsistence, as among other nations whose population is commensurate to its food, or it overflows by emigration to places where a surplus of aliment is attainable.

It follows that a country whose population is full, may annually spare a part of its crop of human life, like a Hive of bees its swarm[,] without any diminution of its numbers, nay that it must necessarily either spare it or destroy it, or prevent its coming into existence.

It follows moreover from this multiplying faculty that in a nation sparing or losing more than its surplus, the vacancy must soon be refilled by the internal resources of life.

No populous nation then has reason to restrain the emigration of its people, in ordinary cases, and within certain proportions. On the contrary, every nation is impelled by[15] humanity as well as required by the principles of liberty to allow the free exercise of this right.

[But there are cases where policy teaches the same lesson as powerfully as humanity & justice.

41

The commercial nations of Europe, particularly France, is interested not only in permitting, but promoting the migration of their people to vacant countries, and particularly to the U. States.]

[The more populous parts of the U.S. have a national interest in not discouraging emigrations to the less inhabited parts.]

What is the greatest ratio of increase of which the human race is susceptible? Where no check would arise from scantiness of food, from war, from adventitious disease or any other preternatural cause? —— It is not possible to solve this curious problem with precision.

---

[13] Madison left this space blank.

[14] Madison often copied the first word of the page in the lower-right corner of the previous page. Sometimes, he repeated a whole phrase or just a section of a word. In this case, as is shown, "life" is written twice. The editors of the PJM omit the repetition throughout, but I have included it herein.

[15] Madison inserted a superscript "x" here, and at the bottom of the page wrote: "ˣIn France about seven million of men women & children live on about 25 livres each per annum. Traité de moral bonheur. p. 30." The source for this quotation is Jean-Zacharie Paradis de Raymondis, *Traité Élémentaire de Morale et du Bonheur pour Server de Prolégoménes ou de Suite à la Collection des Moralists* (Lyons, 1784). Jefferson sent Madison a copy of this work in 1785 (*PTJ*, VIII:462).

The actual progress of population in the U.S. has demonstrated the possibility of an increase which doubles the number in twenty five or perhaps twenty years. This is equivalent to annual increase of [16] per Cent. As many circumstances have even here diminished the full effect of the generative powers, it may be safely laid down that the human race is capable of increasing at the rate of 5 per Cent per annum.

Such a nation as France then[,] containing 30 million [see Price's sermon on love of Country[17]] possesses within itself a natural principle of increase, equal to 1½ million a year; that is, such might be the excess of its yearly births over its yearly deaths. And that no. might be annually spared with[ou]t. diminishing the whole no. as 1 sheep might be annually sold from the no. of [18] with[ou]t. reducing it.

The actual medium excess in that kingdom is thus stated by Docr. Price [see appendix to the said sermon][19] –

"of births for 4 years to 1774	914,710 –	for six years to 1780	958,419
of Deaths ————	793,931 –	Deaths———	834,865
of Marriages————	192,180	Marriages———	228,170"

The medium increase per annum for these terms is then only 120,779 for the first, and 123,554 for the second, the medium of which is [20] per Ct. only on 30 million, or 1/ [21] only of the increase to which nature is equal.

From 1771 to 1780 inclusive Docr Price says the excess of births over deaths, proved an increase 1½ million. this is but 1/10 of the natural increase.[22]

Supposing then an increase to be needed in France, the greatest we see which circumstances permit, leaves a surplus capacity to produce a million & [23] per annum.

[16] Madison left this space blank.

[17] Richard Price, *A Discourse on the Love of Our Country, Delivered on Nov. 4, 1789, at the Meeting House in Old Jewry, to the Society for Commemorating the Revolution in Great Britain* (London: T. Cadell, 1790). Referring to the spread of liberty in France, Price wrote:

> I have lived to see a diffusion of knowledge, which has undermined superstition and error – I have lived to see the rights of men better understood than ever; and nations panting for liberty, which seemed to have lost the idea of it. – I have lived to see THIRTY MILLIONS of people, indignant and resolute, spurning at slavery, and demanding liberty with an irresistible voice; their king led in triumph, and an arbitrary monarch surrendering himself to his subjects [49].

See also Price's appendix, "Thirty Millions of People in France," 1–4.

[18] Madison left this space blank.

[19] Price, "Thirty Millions of People in France," 2.

[20] Madison left this space blank.

[21] Madison left this space blank.

[22] Price, "Thirty Millions of People in France," 2: "It should be observed, that in the ten years from 1771 to 1780, there was in FRANCE such an increase of the annual births, deaths, and marriages (produced by the excess of the births above the deaths), as evidently proved that the number of inhabitants had increased in those ten years near a million and a half."

[23] Madison left this space blank.

This surplus capacity of nature must either be defeated, or the quantity of life produced from it must be allowed to overflow to countries, which like the U.S are disposed to admit and able to support it.

Let us examine the tendency of the latter policy, & to make it the more striking, with a particular eye to France & the U. States.

1. — a million & half of additional births, allow[in]g. 4 only to a marriage, which is below the computed proportion, would produce

---

The colonies and colonies of Colonies among the antient Greeks are remarkable instances of the Swarms that may be spared without diminishing the stock in the hive – Miletum on the Asiatic Coast which was itself a colony established 75 or according to Pliny 80 colonies on the coast of the Hellespont, the Propontis & Euxine – Anach: v. 6. p 217.[24]

For the colonies of Rhodes see Id. v. 6. p: 237[25]

[24] In this passage, under the line break, Madison offered examples of the point he made on the previous page regarding a country with a full population, which, like a hive of bees, may spare part of its population without diminishing its numbers. (Miletum is also called Miletus.) He discussed this same topic in his Party Press Essay "Population and Emigration"; see *MJM*, 229–34. In both cases the citation is to *Voyage*, 6:217 (190–91):

> We next proceeded to Miletus, and surveyed with admiration its temples, festivals, manufactures, harbours, and the innumerable concourse of ships, mariners, and workmen, there perpetually in motion. The city is an abode of opulence, learning, and pleasure: it is the Athens of Iönia. Doris, daughter of the Ocean, had by Nereus fifty daughters, named Nereides, all distinguished by various charms.[a] Miletus has sent forth a still greater number of colonies, which perpetuate her glory on the coasts of the Hellespont, the Propontis, and the Euxine Sea.[b,*] Their metropolis gave birth to the first historians and the first philosophers, and boasts of having produced Aspasia, and the most beautiful and accomplished courtesans. On certain occasions the interests of her commerce have compelled her to prefer peace to war; on others she has laid down her arms without having disgraced them; and hence the proverb: The Milesians were valiant in times past.[c]
>
> [a] Hesiod. De Gener. Deor. V. 241.
> [b] Ephor. ap. Athen. lib. 12. p. 523. Strab. lib. 14. p. 635. Senec. de Consolat. ad. Helv. cap. 6. Plin. lib. 5. cap. 22. t.i. p. 278.
> *Seneca attributes to Miletus seventy-five colonies; Pliny more than eighty. See the citations.
> [c] Athen. lib. 12. p. 523. Aristoph. in Plut. v. 1003.

[25] *Voyage*, 6:237 (207–08):

> Before the aera of the Olympiads, the Rhodians applied themselves to maritime affairs.[a] Their island, by its happy situation,[b] invited ships to put in there in their passage from Egypt to Greece, or Greece to Egypt.[c] They successively formed settlements in the greater part of the places to which they were drawn by commerce. Among their numerous colonies we must reckon Parthenope* and Salapia in Italy, Agrigentum and Gela in Sicily, Rhodes** on the coast of Iberia, at the foot of the Pyrenees, &c.[d]
>
> [a] Diod. Sic. lib. 20. P. 811.
> [b] Strab. lib. 14. P. 652. Diod. Sic. lib. 19. p. 689. Pausan. lib. 4. cap. 31. p. 356. Aristid. Orat. Rhodiac. t. ii. p. 342. et 358. Dio Chrysost. orat. 31. p. 354.
> [c] Diod. Sic. lib. 5. p. 329. Demosth. adv. Dionnys. p. 1121, &c.
> *Naples.

(42

add near 400,000 marriages, and proportionally diminish in France the moral evils resulting from celibacy. But as this is the maximum, it s[houl]d. not be the ground of reasoning intended for real practice. Say then only that every 4 emigrants must have been produced by a marriage which wd. not have otherwise taken place, and that the evil of celibacy is diminished by the tendency of emigration.

2. The value of imports of the U.S. are at least in the proportion of a guinea or Louis d'or a head. The expence of luxury among the makers of imports is [26]. Every [27] emigrants into the U.S. consequently by their consumption support [28] persons in the countries producing or manufacturing the imports. In twenty years the increase from this first stock will support double the no. of the manufactures. The habits & prepossessions of the emigrants & their descendants will naturally prefer the articles brought from their former Country. It may not only be s[ai]d. then that emigrations from commercial countries to the U.S. do not diminish the no. left behind. It is equally true that the number left will be increased by it. G.B. is an irrefragable proof. Not less than 2 of the 3 millions who inhabit the U.S. are sprung from her loins. Her own population as well as prosperity have instead of suffering, been in part owing to this loss. Not less than ½ a million of British subjects subsist on emplymt. afforded by the U.S. Her navigation, her manufactures, her revenue, derive their best aliment from her extended intercourse with the U.S.

3. The emigrants by their example would diffuse among others the taste for the productions of their primitive Country.

One plant of Elecampane yields 3000 seeds

Of Spelt— ---2000 do.	}	See Stillingfleet p. 68[29]
Sunflower——4000		
Poppy———3,200		
Tobacco——40,320		

** Roses in Spain.

[d] Strab. lib. 14. p. 654. Meurs. Rhod. lib. 1. cap. 18.

[26] Madison left this space blank.

[27] Madison left this space blank.

[28] Madison left this space blank.

[29] Benjamin Stillingfleet (*Miscellaneous Tracts Relating to Natural History, Husband, and Physick*, 4th edn. [London, 1799], 66, 68), speaking of an unnamed president's "oration concerning the augmentation of the habitable earth," wrote: "He gives some instances of the surprising fertility of certain plans, v.g. the elecampane, one plant of which produced 3000 seeds, of spelt 2000, of the sunflower 4000, of the poppy 3200, of tobacco 40320."

One annual plant of 2 seeds only produces in 20 years 1,048,576 – see a work quoted by Id. Ibid.[30]

The Roe of 1 Cod fish contains contains [*sic*] about 1,000,000 Eggs & a Carp spawns about 20,000 – Bradley's Phil. acct. of Work of Nat[31]
Mites will multiply to 1000 in a day. Stillingfleet – p. 90[32]
Some viviparous flies bring forth 2000 young. Id. p.119.[33]

MISCELLANIES

There can not be a greater satire on Kings than the praise given them for concessions to the people, which the greatest barbarism & tyranny only could withhold.[34]

---

[30] Stillingfleet (*Miscellaneous Tracts*) wrote concerning plant fertility: "But supposing any annual plant producing yearly only two seeds, even of this after 20 years there would be 1,048,576 individuals. For they would increase yearly in a duple proportion, viz, 2, 4, 8, 16, 32, &c." (68).

[31] Richard Bradley, *A Philosophical Account of the Works of Nature*, 2nd edn. (London: J. Hodges, 1739), 85–86: "The *Roe* of the *Cod-Fish*, for Example, in the Space of a Cube of ½ of an Inch, contains 250 *Eggs*; and according to that Proportion, the whole must contain about 1,000,000. ... Nor are the *Fish* of the Rivers and lakes less prolific, considering their Proportion. A *Carp* does not spawn less than 20,000, and perhaps a *Tench* ½ as many. ..."

[32] Stillingfleet, *Miscellaneous Tracts*, 90: "*Mites*, and many other insects will multiply to a thousand within the compass of a very few days. While the *elephant* scarcely produces one young in two years."

[33] Stillingfleet, *Miscellaneous Tracts*, 119: "There are some viviparous *flies*, which bring forth 2000 young. These in a little time would fill the air, and like clouds intercept the rays of the sun, unless they were devoured by birds, spiders, and many other animals." Page 43 is numbered but blank.

[34] See the anonymous article on this subject (and note the very similar wording in the conclusion of this article) in the *National Gazette*, June 28, 1792, Issue 70, p. 280:

Dean Swift's CANDID CONFESSION.

DEAN SWIFT, who is well known to have been the principal champion of monarchy during the greater part of his life, was, in the latter part of it, compelled by his own experience to change his mind, and give his testimony in favor of republics. Having used some expressions in "*The Presbyterians' Plea of Merit*," written in 1731, which might seem to reflect on republican governments, he obviates such a construction by the following words: "I do not say this in *diminution or disgrace to commonwealths*, wherein I confess I have much altered many opinions under which I was educated, having been led by some observation, long experience, and a thorough detestation of the corruption of mankind: insomuch that I am now justly liable to the censure of Hobbs who complains that the youth of England imbibe ill opinions from reading the histories of ancient Greece and Rome, those renowned scenes of liberty and every virtue."

Such a confession, extorted by experience and observation from a man no less distinguished for his knowledge of the world than his profound genius, in contradiction to the prejudices of education, the pride of former opinions committed to the public in various works of his pen, and on an occasion where his religious animosities and personal interest conspired with other motives to favour his original impressions, is a severe satire *against the corruptions of kingly government*, and ought to be an antidote to all doctrines which tend to poison the republican character and constitutions of America.

June 25, 1792

8

Madison's Convention Notes and Letter to Thomas Jefferson of October 24, 1787

A. Notes on Ancient & Modern Confederacies

Ancient & Modern Confederacies[1]

I

LYCIAN CONFEDERACY

In this confederacy the number of votes allotted to each member was proportioned to its pecuniary contributions. The Judges and Town magistrates were elected by the general authority in like proportion.

— See Montesquieu who prefers this mode.

The name of a federal republic may be refused to Lycia which Montesquieu cites as an example in which the importance of the members determined the proportion of their votes in the general Councils. The Gryson League is a juster example. Code de l'Hum. – Confederation[2]

Lyciorum quoque εὐνομίαν celebrat Strabo: de quâ pauca libet heic subjungere. Fuêre eorum urbes XXIII, distinctae in classes trés pro modo virium. In primâ classe censebantur maximae sex, in alterâ mediae, numbero nobis

[1] James Madison, "Ancient & Modern Confederacies [April–June?]," May 1787, Series 1, From July 5, 1783 to August 31, 1787, Image 1036, *The James Madison Papers*, LOC, http://hdl.loc.gov/loc.mss/mjm.02_1036_1063. *PJM*, 9:3–24. There is a note above the title: "Copd."

[2] Fortuné Barthélemy De Félice, *Code de l'Humanité*. In a letter to Madison, Thomas Jefferson writes: "I mentioned to you in a former letter a very good dictionary of universal law called the Code d'humanité in 13. vols. 4to. Meeting by chance an opportunity of buying a copy, new, & well bound for 104. livres I purchased it for you" (March 18, 1785, *PJM*, 8:249).

incerto, in tertiâ reliquae omnes, quarum fortuna minima. Et singulae quidem urbes hae domi res suas curabant, magistratus suos, ordinemque civilem suum habebant: universae tamen in unum coëuntes unam communem rempublicam constituebant, concilioque utebantur uno, velut, senatu majore. In eo de bello, de pace, de fœderibus, denique de rerum Lyciacarum summâ deliberabant & statuebant. Coibant vero in concilium hoc ex singulis urbibus missi cum potestate ferendi suffragii: utebanturque eâ in re jure aequissimo. Nam quaelibet urbs primae classis habebat jus suffragiorum trium, secundae duorum, tertiae unius. Eademque proportione tributa quoque conferebant, et munia alia obibant. Quemadmodum enim ratio ipsa dictat, et poscit aequitas, ut plura qui possident, et caeteris ditiores sunt, plura etiam in usus communes, et reipublicae subsidia conferant, sic quoque eadem aequitatis regula postulat, ut in statuendo de re communi iidem

(2

iidem illi plus aliis possint: praesertim cum eorundem magis intersit rempublicam esse salvam quàm tenuiorum. Locum concilii hujus non habebant fixum & certum, sed, ex omnibus urbem deligebant, quae videbatur pro tempore commodissima. Concilio coacto primum designabant Lyciarcham principem totius Reipublicae, dein magistratus alios creabant, partes reipublicae administraturos, demum judicia publica constituebant. Atque haec omnia faciebant servatâ proportione eadem, ut nulla omninò urbs praeteriretur munerumve aut honorum horum non fieret particeps. Et hoc jus illibatum mansit Lyciis ad id usque tempus, quo Romani assumpto Asiae imperio magnâ ex parte sui arbitrii id fecerunt.

Ubbo Emmius de Republica Lyciorum in Asia.[3]

(3

AMPHYCTIONIC CONFEDERACY

instituted by Amphyction son of Deucalion King of Athens 1522 years Ant: Christ: Code De l'Humanité Seated first at Thermopylae, then at Delphos, afterwards at these places alternately. It met half yearly to wit in the Spring & Fall, besides extraordinary occasions. Id. In the latter meetings, all such of the Greeks as happened to be at Delphos on a religious errand were admitted to deliberate, but not to vote. Encyclopedie.[4]

---

[3] Ubbo Emmius, *Graecorum Respublicae*. Madison listed this text in his "Memorandum of Books," *PJM*, 13:65.

[4] Charles Joseph Panckoucke, *Encyclopédie Méthodique*. Madison listed this text in his "Report on Books for Congress," *PJM*, 6:65.

The number and names of the confederated Cities differently reported. The Union seems to have consisted originally of the Delphians and their neighbours only, and by degrees to have comprehended all Greece. 10, 11, 12 are the different numbers of original members mentioned by different Authors. Code de l'Humanité.

Each City sent two deputies one to attend particularly to Religious matters – the other to civil and criminal matters affecting individuals – both to decide on matters of a general nature. Id. Sometimes more than two were sent, but they had two votes only. Encyclop.

(4

The Amphyctions took an oath mutually to defend and protect the United Cities – to inflict vengeance on those who should sacrilegiously despoil the temple of Delphos – to punish the violators of this oath – and never to divert the water courses of any of the Amphyctionic Cities either in peace or in war.

Code de l'Hum.

Aeschines orat: vs Ctesiph.[5]

The Amphyctionic Council was instituted by way of defence and terror agst. the Barbarians. Dictre. de Trevoux.[6]

Fœderal authority –

The Amphyctions had full power to propose and resolve whatever they judged useful to Greece. Encyclop. Pol. Oecono.

1. They judged in the last resort all differences between the Amphyctionic Cities. Code de l'Hum.
2. mulcted the aggressors. Id
3. employed whole force of Greece agst. such as refused to execute its decrees. Id. & Plutarch, Cimon[7]
4. guarded the immense Riches of the Temple at Delphos, and decided controversies between the inhabitants and those who came to consult the oracle. Encyclop.
5. superintended the pythian games. Code de l'Hum.
6. exercised } right of admitting new members. see Decree admitting Philip, in Demosthenes on Crown.[8]

[5] *Aeschines Orationes.*

[6] *Dictionnaire Universel François et Latin*, also known as *Dictionnaire de Trévoux.*

[7] Plutarch, *Lives*, "Life of Cimon." Madison listed this text in his "Report on Books for Congress," *PJM*, 6:77.

[8] Madison listed "Demos[th]enes" in his "Memorandum of Books," *PJM*, 13:287. "On the Crown" is a famous ancient speech.

(5

7. Appointed General of the federal troops with full powers to carry their decrees into execution. Ibid.
8. declared & carried on war. Code de l'Human.

Strabo says that the Council of Amphyctions was dissolved in the time of Augustus: but Pausanias, who lived in the time of Antoninus Pius says it remained entire then, and that the number of Amphyctions was thirty. Potter's Gre. Ant: Vol. 1. p. 90.[9]

The institution declined on the admission of Phil and in the time of the Roman Emperors, the functions of the Council were reduced to the administration & police of the Temple. This limited authority expired only

(6

with the Pagan Religion. Code de l'Human.

Vices of the Constitution.

It happened but too often that the Deputies of the strongest Cities awed and corrupted those of the weaker, and that Judgment went in favor of the most powerful party. Id. see also

Plutarch's Themistocles.[10]

Greece was the victim of Philip. If her confederation had been stricter, & been persevered in, she would never have yielded to Macedon, and might have proved a Barrier to the vast projects of Rome. Code de l'Hum

Philip had two votes in the Council. Rawleigh Hist: World. lib 4. c. 1. Sec. 7[11]

The Execution of the Amphyctionic powers was very different from the Theory. Id. – did not restrain the parties from warring agst. each other. Athens & Sparta were members during their conflicts. Quer. whether Thucidides or Xenophon in their Histories ever allude to the Amphyctionic authority which ought to have kept the peace? –

See Gillies Hist: Greece – particularly Vol. II. p. 345[12]

8[13]

ACHÆAN CONFEDERACY

In 124 olympd. the Patrians & Dymaeans joined first in this league. Polyb. lib. 2. c. 3[14]

9 John Potter, *The Antiquities of Greece.* Madison listed "Potter's Grecian Antiquities" in his "Report on Books for Congress," *PJM*, 6:76.

10 Plutarch, "Life of Themistocles," in *Lives*. *PJM*, 6:77.

11 Sir Walter Raleigh, *The History of the World.* Madison listed this text in his "Report on Books for Congress," *PJM*, 6:73.

12 John Gillies, *The History of Ancient Greece: Its Colonies and Conquests.*

13 Page 7 is numbered, but the remainder of the page is blank.

14 Polybius, *General History of Polybius.* Polybius, *Historiarum* is in Sowerby's *Catalogue of the Library of Thomas Jefferson*, 1:25.

This League consisted at first of three small Cities. Aratus added Sicyon, and drew in many other Cities of Achæia & Peloponnesus. Of these he formed a Republic of a peculiar sort. Code de l'Human.

It consisted of twelve Cities, and was produced by the necessity of such a defence agst. the Etolians. Encyclo. Pol Oe. & Polyb. lib. 2.

The members enjoyed a perfect equality, each of them sending the number of deputies to the Senate. Id.

The Senate assembled in the Spring & Fall, and was also convened on extraordinary occasions by two Pretors charged with the administration during the recess, but who could execute nothing witht. the consent of ten Inspectors. Id.

Fœderal Authority

1. The Senate composed of the deputies made war & peace. D'Albon. I page 270[15]
2. Appointed a Captain General annually. Co. d'Hum
3. Transferred the power of deciding to ten Citizens taken from the deputies, the rest retaining a right of Consultation only. Id.
4. Sent and received Ambassadors. D'Albon. Ibid.

9[x16]

5. appointed a prime Minister. D'Albon. Ibid.
6. contracted foreign Alliances. Code de l'Hum.
7. Confederated Cities in a manner forced to receive the same laws & Customs weights & measures; Id. & Polyb. lib. 2 cap. 3
   yet considered as having each their independent police & magistrates. Encyclop. Pol. Oecon.
8. Penes hoc concilium erat summum rerum arbitrium, ex cujus decreto bella suscipiebantur, & finiebantur, pax conveniebat, fœdera feriebantur & solvebantur, leges fiebant ratae aut irritae. Hujus etiam erat Magistratus toti Societati communes eligere, legationes decernere &c. Regebant concilium praetor praecipue, si praesens esset, et Magistratus X alii, quos Achæi δημιουργοὺς nuncupabant. Ubbo. Emmius

Vices of the Constitution.

The defect of subjection in the members to the general authority ruined the whole Body. The Romans seduced the members from the League by representing that it violated their sovereignty.

Code de l'Human.

After the death of Alexander, this Union was dissolved by various dissensions raised chiefly thro' the arts of the Kings of Macedon. Every City was now

[15] Madison is probably referring to Claude Camille François, Conde d'Albon, *Discours sur l'Historie* . . .

[16] This "x" refers to the note Madison wrote at the bottom of the page which begins, "Hi numero."

engaged in a separate interest & no longer acted in concert. Polyb. lib. 2. cap. 3. After in 124 Olympd. they saw their error & began to think of returning to former State. This was the time that Pyrhus invaded Italy. Ibid.

---

xHi numero X erant suffragiis legitimi concilii, quod verno tempore habebatur, electi ex universa societate prudentiâ praecipui, quorum concilio potissimum praetor ex lege utebatur. Horum potestas & dignitas maxima erat post ipsum Praetorem, quos idcirco Livius, Polybium sequens, summum

(10

Achæorum magistratum, appellabat. Cum his igitur de negociis gravioribus in concilio agitandis Praetor praeconsultabat, nec de iis, nisi in id pars major consentiret, licebat ad Consilium referre. Id.

Ista vero imprimis memorabilis lex est, vinculum societatis Achaicæ maximè stringens, et concordiam muniens, quâ interdictum fuit, ne cui civitati Societatis hujus participi fas esset, seorsim ad exteros ullos mittere legatos, non ad Romanos, non ad alios. Et haec expressim inserta fuit pactis conventis Achæorum cum populo Romano. – Omnium autem laudatissima lex apud eos viguit &c. quâ vetitum, ne quis omnino, sive privatae conditionis, seu magistratum gerens, ullam ob causam quaecunque etiam sit, dona a rege aliquo caperet. Id.

(11

HELVETIC CONFEDERACY

Commenced in 1308 by the temporary, and in 1315 by the perpetual Union, of Uri, Switz & Underwald, for the defence of their liberties agst. the invasions of the House of Austria. In 1315 the Confederacy included 8 Cantons; and 1513 the number of 13 was compleated by the accession of appenzel. Code de l'Hum.

The General Diet representing the United Cantons is composed of two deputies from each. Some of their allies as the Abbé St. Gall &c. are allowed by long usage to attend by their deputies. Id

All general Diets are held at such time & place as Zurich which is first in rank & the depositary of the common archives shall name in a circular summons. But the occasion of annual conferences for the administration of their dependent bailages has fixed the same time, to wit the feast of St. John, for the General Diet. And the City of Frawenweld in Turgovia is now the place of Meeting. Formerly it was the City of Baden. Id

The Diet is opened by a Complimentary Address of the first Deputy of each Canton by turns, called the Helvetic Salutation. It consists in a congratulatory review of circumstances & events favorable to their common interest – and exhortations to Union and patriotism.

(12

The deputies of the first Canton Zurich propose the matters to be discussed. Questions are decided by plurality of voices. In case of division, the Bailiff of Turgovia has the casting one. The Session of the Diet continues about a Month. Id

After the objects of universal concern are despatched such of the deputies whose Constituents have no share in the dependent bailages, withdraw, and the Diet then becomes a representation of the Cantons to whom these bailages belong, and proceeds to the consideration of the buisness relating thereto. Id

Extraordinary Diets for incidental business or giving audience to foreign Ministers may be called at any time by any one of the Cantons, or by any foreign Minister who will defray the expence of meeting. Seldom a year without an extraordinary Diet. Stanyan's Switzerland[17]

There is an annual Diet of 12 Cantons by 1 Deputy from each for the affairs of the Ultramontane bailages.

Code de l'Human.

Particular Cantons also have their diets for their particular affairs the time & place for whose meeting are settled by their particular Treaties.

All public affairs are now treated not in Genl. Diet but in the particular Assemblies of Protestant & Catholic Cantons. D'Albon.

13

FŒDERAL AUTHORITY

The title of Republic and Sovereign State improperly given to this Confederacy, which has no concentered authority the Diets being only a Congress of Delegates from some or all of the Cantons, and having no fixt objects that are national.

Dictionaire de Suisse[18]

The 13 Cantons do not make one Commonwealth like the United Provinces, but are so many independent Commonwealths in strict alliance. There is not so much as any common instrument by which they are all reciprocally bound together; The 3 Primitive Cantons alone being each directly allied to the other twelve. The others in many instances are connected[x] indirectly only, as allies of Allies. In this mode any one Canton may draw in all the others to make a common cause in its defence. Stanyan By the Convention of Stantz, any

[17] Abraham Stanyan, *An Account of Switzerland: Written in the Year 1714*. Madison listed this text in his "Report on Books for Congress," *PJM*, 6:84.

[18] Madison is probably referring to *Dictionnaire Géographique, Historique et Politique de la Suisse* . . .

member attacked has a[x] direct claim on the succour of the whole Confederacy. Coxe p: 343[19]

The Confederacy has no common Treasury – no common troops – no common Coin – no common Judicatory nor any other common mark of Sovereignty. Id.[20]

The General Diet cannot terminate any interesting affair without special instructions, & powers, & the deputies accordingly take most matters proposed ad referendum. Code de l'Hum.

The Cantons individually exercise the right of sending & receiving ambassadors – making Treaties –

14

coining money – proscribing the money of one another – prohibing the importation and exportation of merchandize – furnishing troops to foreign States, and doing every thing else which does not wound the liberty of any other Canton. Excepting a few cases specified in the Alliances and which directly concern the Object of the league, no Canton is subject to the Resolutions of the plurality. Id.

The only establishment truly national is that of a federal army, as regulated in 1668, and which is no more than an eventual plan of defence adopted among so many allied States. Id

1. The League consists in a perpetual defensive engagement agst. external attacks, and internal troubles. It may be regarded as an Axiom in the Public Law of the Confederacy, that the federal engagements are precedent to all other political engagements of the Cantons. Id

2. Another axiom is that there are no particular or common possessions of the Cantons, for the defence of which the others are not bound as Guarantees or auxiliaries of Guarantees. Id

3. All disputes are to be submitted to Neutral Cantons who may employ force if necessary in execution of their

(15

decrees. Id. Each party to choose 2 Judges who may in case of disagreement chuse umpire, and these under oath of impartiality to pronounce definitive sentence, which all Cantons to enforce. D'Albon, & Stan.

4. No Canton ought to form new alliances without the consent of the others. [This was stipulated in consequence of an improper alliance in 1442 by Zurich with the House of Austria.] Id.

5. It is an essential Object of the League to preserve interior tranquility by the reciprocal protection of the form of Governmt. established in each Canton,

[19] William Coxe, *Sketches of the Natural, Civil, and Political State of Swisserland*. According to Sowerby, *Catalogue of the Library of Thomas Jefferson*, IV:116, Jefferson owned this text.

[20] The editors of the *PJM* note that this reference is to Stanyan, not Coxe.

so that each is armed with the force of the whole Corps for the suppression of rebellions & Revolts, and the History of Switzerland affords frequent instances of mutual succors for these purposes. Dictre: de Suisse.
6. The Cantons are bound not to give shelter to fugitives from Justice, in consequence of which each Canton can at this day banish malefactors from all the territories of the League. Id.
7. Tho' each Canton may prohibit the exportation & importation of Merchandize, it must allow it to pass thro' from one neighboring Canton to another without any augmentation of the tolls. Code de l'Hum.
8. In claiming succours agst. foreign powers, the 8 Elder Cantons have a more extensive right than

(16

the 5 Junior ones. The former may demand them [of one another][21] without explaining the motives of the quarrel. The latter cannot intermeddle but as mediators or auxiliaries; nor can they commence hostilities without the sanction of the Confederates: and if cited by their adversaries cannot refuse to accept the other Cantons for Arbiters or Judges. Dictre. de Suisse.

9. In general each Canton is to pay its own forces without compensation from the whole or the succoured party. But in case a seige is to be formed for the benefit of a particular Canton, this is to defray the expence of it, and if for the common benefit, each is to pay its just proportion. D Albon. On no pretext is a Canton to be forced to march its troops out of the limits of Switzerland. Stanyan
10. Foreign Ministers from different Nations reside in different Cantons. Such of them as have letters of Credence for the whole Confederacy address them to Zurich the chief Canton. – The Ambassador of France who has most to do with the Confederacy is complimented at his Quarters by deputies from the whole body.

(17

Vices of the Constitution

1. disparity in size of Cantons
2. different principles of Governmt. in difft. Cantons
3. intolerance in Religion
4. weakness of the Union. The Common bailages wch. served as a Cement, sometimes become occasions of quarrels. Dictre. de Suisse.

In a treaty in 1683, with Victor Amadaeus of

[21] This passage is above "may demand" and may come before or after. Madison usually writes a caret (ˆ) to indicate where to place the phrase. In this case, he did not. Brackets are added.

18

Savoy, it is stipulated, that he shall interpose as Mediator in disputes between the Cantons, and if necessary use force agst. the party refusing to submit to the sentence. Dictre. de Suisse – a striking proof of the want of authority in the whole over its parts.

BELGIC CONFEDERACY[22]

established in 1679 by the Treaty called the Union of Utrecht. Code de l'Humanité

The provinces came into this Union slowly. Guelderland the smallest of them made many difficulties. Even some of the Cities & towns pretended to annex conditions to their acceding. Id.

When the Union was originally established a Committee composed of deputies from each province was appointed to regulate affairs, and to convoke the provinces according to art: XIX of the Treaty. Out of this Committee grew the States General Id. – who strictly speaking are only the Representatives of the States General Who amount to 800 members. Temple p. 112.[23]

The number of Deputies to the States General from each province not limitted, but have only a Single voice. They amount commonly all together to 40 or 50. They hold their seats, some for life – some for 6, 3 & 1 years, & those of Groninguen & Overijssel during pleasure. They are paid, but very moderately, by their respective Constituents, and are amenable to their Tribunals only. Code de l'Hum. No military man is deputable to the States Genl. Id. Ambassrs. of Republic have session & deliberation but no suffrage in States Genl. Id. The grand Pensioner of Holland as ordinary deputy from Holland, attends always in the States Genl. & makes the propositions of that Province to States Gl. Id.

24

They sit constantly at the Hague since 1593, and every day in the week except Saturday & sunday. The States of Holland in granting this residence, reserve by way of protestation, the rights, the honors & prerogatives belonging to them as Sovereigns of the Province; yielding the States Genl. only a rank in certain public ceremonies. Id.

[22] This page and the next are not numbered by Madison. Page 19 is numbered, but nothing else is written on the page.

[23] William Temple, *The Works of Sir William Temple, Bart.* Madison listed "Temple's works" in his "Report on Books for Congress," *PJM*, 6:87. He is probably referring specifically to *Observations Upon the United Provinces of the Netherlands.*

[24] The next page begins here.

The eldest deputy from each province presides for a week by turns. The president receives letters &c. from the Ministers of the Republic at foreign Courts, and of foreign Ministers residing at the Hague, as well as of all petitions presented to the Assembly; all which he causes to be read by the Secretary. Id.

The Secretary besides correcting & recording the Resolutions prepares & despatches instructions to Ministers abroad – & letters to foreign powers. He assists also at conferences held with foreign Ministers & there gives his voice. He has a deputy when there is not a second Secretary. The Agent of the States Genl. is charged with the Archives and is also employed on occasions of receiving foreign Ministers or sending Messages to them. Id.

(20

Federal Authority.

The avowed objects of the Treaty of Union. 1. to fortify the Union – 2 to repel the Common enemy. Id

The Union is to be perpetual in the same manner as if the Confederates formed one province only, without prejudice however to the privileges & rights of each province & City. Id

Differences between provinces & between Cities are to be settled by the ordinary Judges – by arbitration – by amicable agreement, without the interference of other provinces otherwise than by way of accomodation. The Stadtholder is to decide such differences in the last resort. Id.

No change to be made in the articles of Union, without unanimous consent of the parties & every thing done contrary to them to be null & void. Id

States General, 1. execute, without consulting their Constituents, treaties & alliances already formed. Id.

2. take oaths from Generals & Governrs and appoint Field Deputies

(21[25]

3. The collection of duties on imports & exports and the expedition of Safe Conducts are in their name & by their officers. Id.
4. They superintend & examine accounts of the E. India Company. Id
5. inspect the Mint – appoint les Maitres de la monnoye – fix la taille & la valeur[26] of the Coin, having always regard to the regular rights of the provinces within their own Territories. Id.
6. Appoint a Treasurer General & Receiver General of the Quotas furnished by the Provinces. Id.
7. elect out of a double nomination, the fiscal & other officers within the departments of the Admiralties, except that

[25] There is a note above the page number, which reads "1787 May."

[26] "The Supervisor of the currency – set the rate & the value"

(22

the High officers of the fleet are appointed by the Admiral General, to whom the maritime provinces have ceded this right. Id. The Navy supported by duties on foreign trade, appropriated thereto by the maritime provinces, for the benefit of whole Republic. Id.

8. They govern as Sovereigns, the dependent territories, according to the several capitulations. Id.
9. They form Committees of their own body of a Member from each deputation, for foreign affairs – finances marine – & other matters. At all these conferences the Grand Pensioner of Holland & the Secretary of the States Genl. attend & have a deciding voice. Id.
10. appt. & receive Ambassrs – negociate wth. foreign powers – deliberate on war – peace alliances – the raising forces – care of fortifications – military affairs to a certain degree – the equipment of fleets – building of Ships – direction concerning money. Id. But they can neither make peace – nor war – nor truces – nor treaties – nor raise troops – nor impose taxes, nor do other acts requiring unanimity without consulting & obtaining the sanction of the Provinces. Id. Coining[27]

(23

money also requires unanimity & express sanction of provinces. Temple. repealing an old law on same footing. Burrish. Batav: illustrata.[28] In points not enumerated in this article plurality of voices decides. Cod. de l'Hum.

11. Composition & publication of edicts & proclamations relative both to the objects expressed in the Articles of Union and to the measures taken for the common good, are in the name of the States, and altho' they are addressed to the States of the Provinces who announce them with their sanction, still it is in the name of the States Genl. that obedience is required of all the inhabitants of the provinces. Cod. de l'hum.

The Provinces have reserved to themselves

1. their sovereignty within their own limits in general. Cod. de l'H.
2. the right of coining money as essential to Sovereignty: but agreed at the same time that the money which sd. be current throughout the Republic sd. have the sam[e] intrinsic value: To give effect to which regulation a min[t] is established at the Hague under a chamber which has the inspection of all money struck either in name of States Genl. or particular provinces, as also of foreign coin. Id. – Coining money not in provinces or Cities, but in the generality of Union by common agreement. Temple.

[27] There is a large "X" on the side of the paper, next to the text of number "10."

[28] Onslow Burrish, *Batavia Illustrata, or, A View of the Policy and Commerce of the United Provinces* ...

3. Every province raises what money & by what means it pleases, & sends its quota to Receiver General. Temple. The quotas were not settled without great difficulty. Id.

(24

4. the naming to Govermts. of Towns within themselves keeping keys & giving word to Magistrates – a power over troops in all things not military – conferring Cols. Commissions & inferior posts in such Regiments as are paid by the Provinces respectively – taking oath of fidelity – Concerning a revocation of all which the States Genl. are not permitted to deliberate. Id.

The Provinces are restricted

1. from entering into any foreign Treaties without consent of the rest. Cod. d'Hum.
2. from establishing imposts prejudicial to others without general consent. Id.
3. from charging their nei[gh]bours with higher duties than their own subjects. Id.

25

Council of State. – composed of deputies from the provinces in different proportions. 3 of them are for life. the rest generally for 3 years: they vote per capita. Temple

They are subordinate to the States General, who frequently however consult with them. In matters of war which require secrecy they act of themselves. Military & fiscal matters are the object of their administration. They vote

They execute the Resolutions of the States Genl. propose requisitions of men & money & superintend the fortifications &c. & the affairs revenues & Govts. of the conquered possessions. Temple.

Chamber of Accounts. was erected for the ease of the Council of State. It is subordinate to the States Genl. is composed of two deputies from each province who are changed triennially. They examine & state all accts. of the several Receivers – controul and register orders of Council of State disposing of the finances. Id.

(26

College of Admiralty established by States Genl. 1597 – is subdivided into five of whc. three are in Holland – one in Zealand – one in Friezland, each composed of 7 deputies, 4 appd. by the province where the Admiralty resides & 3 by the other provinces. The vice-Admiral presides in all of them when he is present. Temple.

They take final conuzance[29] of all crimes & prizes at sea
- - - - of all frauds in customs
provide quota of fleets resolved on by States Genl.
appt. Capts. & superior officers of each squadron
take final cognizance also of Civil matters within 600 florins – an appeal lying to States Genl. for matters beyond that sum.

Code de l'Hum. & Temple

The authority of States Genl. in Admiralty Departmt. is much limited by the influence & privileges of maritime provinces, & the jurisdiction herein is full of confusion & contradiction. Code de l'humanité.

Stadtholder who is now hereditary in his political capacity is authorized

1. to settle differences between provinces, provisionally till other methods can be agreed on, which havg never been this prerogative may be deemed a permanent one. Code de l'Hum.
2. assists at deliberations of States Genl. & their particular conferences, recommends & influences appointmt. of Ambassadors. Id.
3. has seat & suffrage in Council of State. Id.

(27

4. presiding in the Provincial Courts of Justice where his name is prefixed to all public Acts. Id.
5. supreme Curator of most of the Universities. Id.
6. As Stadtholder of the provinces has considerable rights partaking of the Sovereignty, as appointing town Magistrates on presentation made to him of a certain number Executing provincial decrees &c. Id. & Mably. Etud. de l'hist.[30]
7. gives audiences to Ambassadors & may have Agents with their Sovereigns for his private Affairs. Mab. Ibid
8. exercises power of Pardon. Temple.

in his military capacity as Capt: Genl.

1. commands forces – directs marches – provides for garrisons – & in general regulates military affairs. Code de l'Hum.
2. disposes of all appointmts. from Ensigns to Cols. The Council of State havg. surrendered to him the appointmts. within their disposal. Id. & the States Genl. appt. the higher grades on his recommendation. Id

[29] In English Common Law, "conuzance" and "cognizance" were interchangeable terms. For a court or judge to have "conuzance" or "congnizance" over a matter meant that the court or judge had jurisdiction over it – the power, authority, and ability to rule on the matter in question.

[30] Gabriel Bonnot de Mably, *De l'Étude de l'Histoire* ... Madison listed "Abbe Mably's public law of Europe – principles of Negociation – other political works" in his "Report on Books for Congress," *PJM*, 6:71.

3. disposes of the Govts. &c. of the fortified towns tho' the Commissions issue from the States Genl. Id.

in his Marine capacity, as Admiral General

1. superintends & directs every thing relative to naval forces & other affairs within Admiralty. Id

(28

2. presides in the Admiralties in person or by proxy. Id
3. Appoints Lieutts. Admirals & Officers under them. Id.
4. establishes Councils of war, whose sentences are in the name of the States Genl. & his Highness and are not executed till he approves. Id.

The Stadtholder has a general & secret influence on the great machine which cannot be defined. Id.
His Revenue from appointmts. amount to 300,000 florins, to which is to be added his extensive patrimonies. Id.

The standing army of the Republic 40,000 men.

Vices of the Constitution

The Union of Utrecht imports an authority in the States Genl. seemingly sufficient to secure harmony; but the Jealousy in each province of its Sovereignty renders the practice very different from the Theory. Code de l'Hum

It is clear that the delay occasioned by recurring to

(29

seven independent provinces including about 52 voting Cities &c. is a vice in the Belgic Republic which exposes it to the most fatal inconveniences. Accordingly the fathers of their Country have endeavored to remedy it in the extraordinary Assemblies of the States Genl. in [1584] 1651, 1716, 1717, but unhappily without effect. This vice is notwithstanding deplorable. Id. – Among other evils it gives foreign ministers the means of arresting the most important deliberations by gaining a single province or City. This was done by France in 1726. when the Treaty of Hanover was delayed a whole year. In 1688. the States concluded a Treaty of themselves but at the risk of their heads. Id [illegible]. It is the practice also in matters of contribution or subsidy to pass over this article of the Union, for where delay wd. be dangerous the consenting provinces furnish their quotas without waiting for the others, but by such means the Union is weakened and if often repeated must be dissolved. Id.

Foreign Ministers elude matters taken ad referendum by tampering with the provinces & Cities. Temple p. 116

Treaty of Union obliges each province to levy certain contributions. But this article never could & probably never will be executed because the inland provinces

[31]

provinces who have little commerce cannot pay an equal Quota. Burrish. Bat: illustrat:

Deputations from agreeing to disagreeing provinces frequent. Temple.

It is certain that so many independent Corps & interests could not be kept together without such a center of Union as the Stadtholdership, as has been allowed & repeated in so many solemn Acts. Code d'Hum

In the intermission of the Stadtholdership Holland by her Riches & Authority which drew the others into a sort of dependence, supplied the place. Temple.

With such a Governmt. the Union never cd. have subsisted, if in effect the provinces had not within themselves a spring capable of quicken[in]g their tardiness, and impelling them to the same way of thinking. This Spring is the Stadtholder. His prerogatives are immense. 1 &c. &c. – A strange effect of human contradictions. Men too jealous to confide their liberty to their representatives who are their equals, abandoned it to a Prince who might the more easily abuse it as the affairs of the Republic were important & had not them fixed themselves. Mably. Etude d'Hist. 205/6.

Grotius[32] has sd. that the hatred of his Countrymen agst. the H. of Austria kept them from being destroyed by the vices of their Constitution. Ibid.

[33]

The difficulty of procuring unanimity has produced a breach of fundamentals in several instances – Treaty of Westphalia was concluded without consent of Zealand &c. D'Albon & Temple – These tend to alter the constitution. D'Albon.

It appears by several articles of the Union that the Confederates had formed the design of establishing a Genl. tax [Impôt][34] to be administered by the States Genl. But this design so proper for bracing this happy Union has not been executed. Code de l'Hum.

(31

GERMANIC CONFEDERACY. – took its

present form in the year, Code de l'Hum

The Diet is to be convoked by the Emperor, or on his failure, by the Archbishop of Mentz with consent of Electors once in ten years at least from the last adjournment, and six months before the time of meeting. Ratisbon is the seat of the Diet since 1663.

---

[31] This page and the next are not numbered. The numbering resumes with 30, which is blank.

[32] Hugo Grotius. Madison listed "Grotius de rebus Belgicis" in his "Report on Books for Congress," *PJM*, 6:78.

[33] The next page begins here.

[34] An *impôt* is a tax – but a tax on persons rather than a tax on transactions.

The members amount to 285, and compose three Colleges, to wit, that of the Electors – of Princes – of Imperial Cities. The voices amount to 159, of which 153 are individual, & 6 collective. The latter are particular to the College of princes and are formed out of 39 prelates &c, and 93 Counts &c. The individual voices are common to the three Colleges, and are given by 9 Electors – 94 princes, 33 of the ecclesiastical & 61 of the Secular Bench. – & 50 Imperial Cities. 13 of the Rhenish, & 37 of Suabian Bench. – The K. of Prussia has nine voices in as many differt. capacities. Id

The three Colleges assemble in the same House but in different apartments. Id

The Emperor as head of the Germanic body is presidt. of the Diet. He & others are represented by proxies at present. Id

The deliberations are groundd. on propositions from Emperor & commence in the College of Electors, from whence they pass to that of the Princes, & thence to that of the Imperial Cities. They are not resolutions till they have been passed in each. When the Electors & Princes cannot agree, they confer; but do not confer with the Imperial Cities. Plurality of voices decide in each College, except in matters of Religion & a few reserved cases, in which according to the Treaty of Westphalia, and the Imperial Capitulations the Empire

(32

the Empire is divided into the Catholic & Evangelic Corps. Id.

After the Resolutions have passed the three Colleges, they are presented to the Representative of the Emperor, without whose ratification they are null. Id They are called placita after passing the three colleges – conclusa after ratification by Emperor. Id.

The Collection of Acts of one Diet is called the Recess, which cannot be made up & have the force of law, till the Close of the Diet. The subsisting diet has not been closed for more than a hundred years. Of course it has furnished no effective Resolution though a great number of Interesting ones have passed. This delay proceeds from the Imperial Court who refuse to grant a Recess, notwithstanding the frequent & pressing applications made for one. Id

Fœderal authority.

The powers as well as the organization of the Diet have varied at different times. Antiently it elected as a Corps, the Emperors, and judged of their Conduct. The Golden Bull gives this right to the Electors alone. Antiently it regulated tolls. At present the Electors alone do this. Id

The Treaty of Westphalia & the Capitulations of the Emperors from Charles V downwards, define the present powers of the Diet. These concern – 1. Legislation of the Empire – 2. war & peace & alliances – 3. raising troops – 4. Contributions – 5 construction of fortresses – 6 Money – 7. Ban of the Empire

(33

8. admission of New Princes – 9. the supreme tribunals 10. disposition of Grand feifs & grand Charges – In all these points the Emperor & Diet must Concur. Id

The Ban of the Empire is a sort of proscription by which the disturbers of the Public peace are punished. The offenders life & goods are at the Mercy of every one. Formerly the Emperors themselves pronounced the ban agst. those who offended them. It has been since regulated that no one shall be exposed to the Ban without the examination & consent of the Diet. Encyclop.

By the Ban the party is outlawed – degraded from all his federal rights – his subjects absolved from their allegiance – and his possessions forfeited. Code de l'Hum.

The Ban is incurred when the Emperor or one of the Supreme Tribunals address an order to any one, on pain in case of disobedience, of being proscribed ipso facto. Id.

The Circles formerly were in number 6 only. There are now ten. They were instituted for the more effectual preservation of the Public peace, and the execution of decrees of Diet & supreme Tribunals – – – – – – – against contumacious members, for which purposes they have their particular diets, with the Chief prince of the Circle at their head, have particular officers for commanding the forces of the Circle, levy contributions, see that Justice is duly administered – that the Coin is not

(34

debased – that the customs are not unduly raised. Savage vol. 2 p. 35.[35]

If a Circle fail to send its due succours, it is to pay damages suffered therefrom to its neighbours. If a member of the circle refuse, the Col. of the Circle is to admonish, & if this be insufficient, the delinquent party is to be compelled under a sentence from the Imperial Chamber. Id.

(2.) Aulic Council – [established by Diet in 1512. Encyclop.] composed of members appointed by the Emperor. Code. de l'Hum.

Its cognizance is restrained to matters above 2000 Crowns, is concurrent with the jurisdiction of the Imperial Chamber in controversies between the States – also in those of subjects of the Empire by way of appeal from subaltern Tribunals of the Empire, and from sovereign Tribunals of princes. Id. – arms are to be used for carrying its decrees into execution, as was done 1718 by the troops of the Circle of Upper Rhine in a Controversy between Landgrave of Hesse Cassel & Prince of Hesse of Rhinfitz. Id.

(1) Imperial Chamber, established in 1495. by the Diet as a means of public peace, by deciding controversies between members of the Empire. Code de l'Hum.

[35] John Savage, *A Compleat History of Germany* ...

This is the first Tribunal of the Empire. It has an appellate jurisdiction in all Civil, and fiscal causes or where the public peace may be concerned. It has a concurrent jurisdiction with the Aulic Council; and causes cannot be

(35

removed from one to the other. Id.

The Judges of this Tribunal are appointed partly by the Emperor – partly by Electors – partly by Circles, are supported by all the States of the Empire, excepting the Emperor. They are badly paid, though great salaries are annexed to their offices. Id.

In every action real or personal – the Diet – Imperial-Chamber and Aulic Council are so many supreme Courts to which none of the States can demur. The jurisprudence, by which they govern themselves, are according to the subject matter – 1. the Provincial laws of Germany 2. the Scripture – 3 the law of nature – 4 law of Nations 5 the Roman law – 6 the Canon law – 7 the fœdal law of the Lombards. Id.

Members of Diet as such are subject in all public affairs to be judged by Emperor & Diet. – as individuals in private capacity are subject to Aulic Council & Imperial Chamber. Id.

The Members have reserved to themselves the right
1. to enter into war & peace with foreign powers 2 to enter into alliances with foreign powers and with one another, Not prejudicial to their engagements to the Empire Code d'Hum
– 3 to make laws, levy taxes, raise troops, to determine on

(36

life & death. Savage. 4. Coin money. Id. 5. exert territorial Sovereignty within their limits in their own name. Code de l'Hum
6. to grant Pardons. Savage. p. 44.
7. to furnish their quotas of troops, equipped mounted & armed & to provide for sustenance of them, as if they served at home. Cod. d'Hum

Members of Empire restricted

1. from entering into confederacies prejudicial to the Empire
2. from laying tolls or Customs upon bridges, rivers, or passages to which strangers are subject, without consent of the Emperor in full Diet.
3. cannot give any other value to Money, nor make any other kind of money that [*sic*] what is allowed by the Empire. Savage Vol. 2. p. 4.
4. (by edict of 1548 particularly) from taking arms one agst. another, from doing themselves injustice – from affording retreat, much more, assistance to infractors of the Public peace; the ban of the Empire being denounced

agst. the transgressors of these prohibitions, besides a fine of 2000 marks of gold & loss of regalities. Cod. d'Hum.

(37

Emperor. – has the prerogative 1. of exclusively making propositions to the Diet – 2 presiding in all Assemblies & Tribunals of the Empire when he chuses – 3 of giving suffrage in all affairs treated in the diet – 4 of negativing their resolutions – 5 of issuing them in his own name – 6. of watching over the safety of the Empire – 7 of naming Ambassadors to negociate within the Empire as well as at foreign Courts – affairs concerning the Germanic Corps. 8. of re-establishing in good fame, persons, dishonored by Council of war & civil Tribunal Cod. d'Hum. – 9 of giving investiture of the principal immediate fiefs of the Empire, wch. is not indeed of much consequence – 10. of conferring vacant electorates – 11 of preventing subjects from being withdrawn from the jurisdiction of their proper Judge – 12 of conferring charges of the Empire – 13 of conferring dignities & titles, as of Kings &c. – 14 of instituting military orders – 15. of granting the dernier resort – 16. of judging differences & controversies touching tolls – 17. of deciding contests between Catholic & Protestant States touching precedence &c. Id. – 18. of founding Universities within the lands of the States, so faras [*sic*] to make the person endowed with Academic honors therein be regarded as such throughout Germany. – 19 of granting all sorts of privileges not injurious to the States of the Empire – 20 of establishing great fairs. 21 of receiving the droit des Postes generals – 22 of striking money, but without augmenting or diminishing its value. 23 of permitting – Strangers to enlist soldiers, conformably to Recess of 1654. Id. 24. of receiving & applying Revenues of Empire. Savage, p.

(38

He cannot make war or peace, nor laws – nor levy taxes nor alter the denomination of money – nor weights or measures.

Savage v. 2. p. 35.

The Emperor as such does not properly possess any territory within the Empire, nor derives any Revenue for his support

Cod. d'Hum.

Vices of the Constitution.

1. The Quotas are complained of & supplied very irregularly & defectively. Cod. d'Hum. Provision is made by decree of diet for enforcing them, but it is a delicate matter to execute it agst. the powerful members. Id.

2. The establishmt. of the Imperial Chamber has not been found an efficacious remedy agst. Civil wars. It has committed faults. The Resortissans have not always been docile. Id.

3. Altho' the establishmt. of Imperial Chamber &c give a more regular form to the police of the feifs, it is not to be supposed they are capable of giving a certain force to the laws and maintaining the peace of the Empire

(39

if the House of Austria had not acquired power eno' to maintain itself on the imperial Throne, to make itself respected, & to give orders which it might be imprudent to despise, as the laws were theretofore despised. Mabley. Etude d'hist. p. 180

[Jealousy of the Imperial authority, seems to have been a great cement of the confederacy]

(41[36]

GRYSON CONFEDERACY

[36] Page 40 is blank, and this is all that is written on 41.

B. Notes on Vices of the Political System of the United States

April: 1787.[37]

Vices of the Political system of the U. States

Observations by J. M. (a copy taken by permission by Danl. Carroll & sent to Chs Carroll of Carrollton)

1. Failure of the States to comply with the Constitutional requisitions.

1. This evil has been so fully experienced both during the war and since the peace, results so naturally from the number and independent[38] authority of the States and has been so uniformly examplified in every similar Confederacy, that it may be considered as not less radically and permanently inherent in, than it is fatal to the object of, the present System.

2. Encroachments by the States on the federal authority.

☞

[39]2. Examples of this are numerous and repetitions may be foreseen in almost every case where any favorite object of a State shall present a temptation. Among these examples are the wars and Treaties of Georgia with the Indians – The unlicensed compacts between Virginia and Maryland, and between Pena. & N. Jersey – the troops raised and to be kept up by Massts.

3. Violations of the law of nations and of treaties.

☞

3. From the number of Legislatures, the sphere of life from which most of their members are taken, and the circumstances under which their legislative business is carried on, irregularities of this kind must frequently happen. Accordingly not a year has passed without instances of them in some one or other of the States. The Treaty of peace – the treaty with France – the treaty with Holland have each been violated. [See the complaints to Congress on these subjects]. The causes of these irregularities must necessarily produce frequent violations of the law of nations in other respects.

---

[37] James Madison, "Vices of the Political System of the U. States," May 7, 1787, Series 1, From July 5, 1783 to August 31, 1787, Image 1005, *The James Madison Papers*, LOC, http://hdl.loc.gov/loc.mss/mjm.02_1005_1013. *PJM*, 9:345–58. The editors of the *PJM* place this document under April 1787; it can be found on the Library of Congress' website under May 7, 1787.

[38] The editors of the *PJM* do not indicate the underlining in "Vices," noting that it was added at a later date. It is unknown who made these additions. *PJM*, 9:345.

[39] In general, the text of "Vices" is very generously spaced, indicating that perhaps Madison meant to insert addidional notes at a later date.

As yet foreign powers have not been rigorous in animadverting on us. This moderation however cannot be mistaken for a permanent partiality to our faults, or a permanent security agst. those disputes with other nations, which being among the greatest of public calamities, it ought to be least in the power of any part of the Community to bring on the whole.

4. Trespasses of the States on the rights of each other.

4. These are alarming symptoms, and may be daily apprehended as we are admonished by daily experience. See the law of Virginia restricting foreign vessels to certain ports – of Maryland in favor of vessels belonging to her own citizens – of N. York in favor of the same.

Paper money, instalments of debts, occlusion of Courts, making property a legal tender, may likewise be deemed aggressions on the rights of other States. As the Citizens of every State aggregately taken stand more or less in the relation of Creditors or debtors, to the Citizens of every other States, Acts of the debtor State in favor of debtors, affect the Creditor State, in the same manner, as they do its own citizens who are relatively creditors towards other citizens. This remark may be extended to foreign nations. If the exclusive regulation of the value and alloy of coin was properly delegated to the federal authority, the policy of it equally requires a controul on the States in the cases above mentioned. It must have been meant 1. to preserve uniformity in the circulating medium throughout the nation. 2. to prevent those frauds on the citizens of other States, and the subjects of foreign powers, which might disturb the tranquility at home, or involve the Union in foreign contests.

The practice of many States in restricting the commercial intercourse with other States, and putting their productions and manufactures on the same footing with those of foreign nations, though not contrary to the federal articles, is certainly adverse to the spirit of the Union, and tends to beget retaliating regulations, not less expensive & vexatious in themselves, than they are destructive of the general harmony.

5. want of concert in matters where common interest requires it.

5. This defect is strongly illustrated in the state of our commercial affairs. How much has the national dignity, interest, and revenue suffered from this cause? Instances of inferior moment are the want of uniformity in the laws concerning naturalization &

literary property; of provision for national seminaries, for grants of incorporation for national purposes, for canals and other works of general utility, wch. may at present be defeated by the perverseness of particular States whose concurrence is necessary.

6. want of Guaranty to the States of their Constitutions & laws against internal violence.

☞

6. The confederation is silent on this point and therefore by the second article the hands of the federal authority are tied. According to Republican Theory, Right and power being both vested in the majority, are held to be synonimous. According to fact and experience a minority may in an appeal to force, be an overmatch for the majority. 1. If the minority happen to include all such as possess the skill and habits of military life, & such as possess the great pecuniary resources, one third only may conquer the remaining two thirds. 2. One third of those who participate in the choice of the rulers, may be rendered a majority by the accession of those whose poverty excludes them from a right of suffrage, and who for obvious reasons will be more likely to join the standard of sedition than that of the established Government. 3. Where slavery exists the republican Theory becomes still more fallacious.

7. want of sanction to the laws, and of coercion in the Government of the Confederacy.

☞

7. A sanction is essential to the idea of law, as coercion is to that of Government. The federal system being destitute of both, wants the great vital principles of a Political Cons[ti]tution. Under the form of such a Constitution, it is in fact nothing more than a treaty of amity of commerce and of alliance, between[40] independent and Sovereign States. From what cause could so fatal an omission have happened in the articles of Confederation? from a mistaken confidence that the justice, the good faith, the honor, the sound policy, of the several legislative assemblies would render superfluous any appeal to the ordinary motives by which the laws secure the obedience of individuals: a confidence which does honor to the enthusiastic virtue of the compilers, as much as the inexperience of the crisis apologizes for their errors. The time which has since elapsed has had the double effect, of increasing the light and tempering the warmth, with which the arduous work may be revised. It is no longer doubted that a unanimous and punctual obedience of 13

[40] Madison wrote "so many" here but crossed it out.

independent bodies, to the acts of the federal Government, ought not be calculated on. Even during the war, when external danger supplied in some degree the defect of legal & coercive sanctions, how imperfectly did the States fulfil their obligations to the Union? In time of peace, we see already what is to be expected. How indeed could it be otherwise? In the first place, Every general act of the Union must necessarily bear unequally hard on some particular member or members of it. Secondly the partiality of the members to their own interests and rights, a partiality

a partiality which will be fostered by the Courtiers of popularity, will naturally exaggerate the inequality where it exists, and even suspect it where it has no existence. Thirdly a distrust of the voluntary compliance of each other may prevent the compliance of any, although it should be the latent disposition of all. Here are causes & pretexts which will never fail to render federal measures abortive. If the laws of the States, were merely recommendatory to their citizens, or if they were to be rejudged by County authorities, what security, what probability would exist, that they would be carried into execution? Is the security or probability greater in favor of the acts of Congs. which depending for their execution on the will of the state legislatures, wch. are tho' nominally authoritative, in fact recommendatory only.

8. Want of ratification by the people of the articles of Confederation. ☞

8. In some of the States the Confederation is recognized by, and forms a part of the constitution. In others however it has received no other sanction than that of the Legislative authority. From this defect two evils result: 1. Whenever a law of a State happens to be repugnant to an act of Congress, particularly when the latter[41] is of posterior date to the former, it will be at least questionable whether the latter must not prevail; and as the question must be decided by the Tribunals of the State, they will be most likely to lean on the side of the State.

2. As far as the Union of the States is to be regarded as a league of sovereign powers, and not as a political Constitution by virtue of which they are[42]

[41] Throughout this sentence, someone has crossed out "latter" and substituted "former" and crossed out "former" and substituted "latter."

[42] In the bottom-right corner is written "593 –" lightly. Such notes do not seem to be in Madison's hand and are omitted by the editors of the *PJM*.

are become one sovereign power, so far it seems to follow from the doctrine of compacts, that a breach of any of the articles of the confederation by any of the parties to it, absolves the other parties from their respective obligations, and gives them a right if they chuse to exert it, of dissolving the Union altogether.

9. Multiplicity of laws in the several States.

9. In developing the evils which viciate the political system of the U. S. it is proper to include those which are found within the States individually, as well as those which directly affect the States collectively, since the former class have an indirect influence on the general malady and must not be overlooked in forming a compleat remedy. Among the evils then of our situation may well be ranked the multiplicity of laws from which no State is exempt. As far as laws are necessary, to mark with precision the duties of those who are to obey them, and to take from those who are to administer them a discretion, which might be abused, their number is the

the price of liberty. As far as the laws exceed this limit, they are a nusance: a nusance of the most pestilent kind. Try the Codes of the several States by this test, and what a luxuriancy of legislation do they present. The short period of independency has filled as many pages as the century which preceded it. Every year, almost every session, adds a new volume. This may be the effect in part, but it can only be in part, of the situation in which the revolution has placed us. A review of the several codes will shew that every necessary and useful part of the least voluminous of them might be compressed into one tenth of the compass, and at the same time be rendered tenfold as perspicuous.

10. mutability of the laws of the States.

10. This evil is intimately connected with the former yet deserves a distinct notice as it emphatically denotes a vicious legislation. We daily see laws repealed or superseded, before any trial can have been made of their merits; and even before a knowledge of them can have reached the remoter districts within which they were to operate. In the regulations of trade this instability becomes a snare not only to our citizens but to foreigners also.[43]

[43] In the bottom-right corner is written "595" lightly.

11. Injustice of the laws of States.

11. If the multiplicity and mutability of laws prove a want of wisdom, their injustice betrays a defect still more alarming: more alarming not merely because it is a greater evil in itself, but because it brings more into question the fundamental principle of republican Government, that the majority who rule in such Governments, are the safest Guardians both of public Good and of private rights. To what causes is this evil to be ascribed?

These causes lie 1. in the Representative bodies.
2. in the people themselves.

1. Representative appointments are sought from 3 motives. 1. ambition 2. personal interest. 3. public good. Unhappily the two first are proved by experience to be most prevalent. Hence the candidates who feel them, particularly, the second, are most industrious, and most successful in pursuing their object: and forming often a majority in the legislative Councils, with interested views, contrary to the interest, and views, of their Constituents, join in a perfidious sacrifice of the latter to the former.
A succeeding election it might be supposed, would displace the offenders, and repair the mischief.
But how easily are base and selfish measures, masked by pretexts of public good and apparent expediency?

How frequently will a repetition of the same arts and industry which succeeded in the first instance, again prevail on the unwary to misplace their confidence?

How frequently too will the honest but unenligh[t]ened representative be the dupe of a favorite leader, veiling his selfish views under the professions of public good, and varnishing his sophistical arguments with the glowing colours of popular eloquence?

2. A still more fatal if not more frequent cause lies among the people themselves. All civilized societies are divided into different interests and factions, as they happen to be creditors or debtors – Rich or poor – husbandmen, merchants or manufacturers – members of different religious sects – followers of different political leaders – inhabitants of different districts – owners of different kinds of property &c &c. In republican Government the majority however composed, ultimately give the law. Whenever

therefore an apparent interest or common passion unites a majority what is to restrain them from unjust violations of the rights and interests of the minority, or of individuals? Three motives only 1. a prudent regard to their own good as involved in the general and permanent good of the Community. This consideration although of decisive weight in itself, is found by experience to be too often unheeded. It is too often forgotten, by nations as well as by individuals that honesty[44]

honesty is the best policy. 2dly. respect for character. However strong this motive may be in individuals, it is considered as very insufficient to restrain them from injustice. In a multitude its efficacy is diminished in proportion to the number which is to share the praise or the blame. Besides, as it has reference to public opinion, which within a particular Society, is the opinion of the majority, the standard is fixed by those whose conduct is to be measured by it. The public opinion without the Society, will be little respected by the people at large of any Country. Individuals of extended views, and of national pride, may bring the public proceedings to this standard, but the example will never be followed by the multitude. Is it to be imagined that an ordinary citizen or even an assembly-man of R. Island in estimating the policy of paper money, ever considered or cared in what light the measure would be viewed in France or Holland; or even in Masssts or Connect.? It was a sufficient temptation to both that it was for their interest: it was a sufficient sanction to the latter that it was popular in the State; to the former that it was so in the neighbourhood. 3dly. will Religion the only remaining motive be a sufficient restraint? It is not pretended to be such on men individually considered. Will its effect be greater on them considered in an aggregate view? quite the reverse. The conduct of every popular assembly acting on oath, the strongest of religious Ties, proves that individuals join without remorse in acts, against which their consciences would revolt if proposed to them under the like sanction, separately in their closets. When indeed Religion is kindled into enthusiasm, its force like that of other passions, is increased by the sympathy of a multitude.

[44] In the bottom-right corner is written "595" lightly.

But enthusiasm is only a temporary state of religion, and while it lasts will hardly be seen with pleasure at the helm of Government. Besides as religion in its coolest state, is not infallible, it may become a motive to oppression as well as a restraint from injustice.

Place three individuals in a situation wherein the interest of each depends on the voice of the others, and give to two of them an interest opposed to the rights of the third? Will the latter be secure? The prudence of every man would shun the danger. The rules & forms of justice suppose & guard against it. Will two thousand in a like situation be less likely to encroach on the rights of one thousand? The contrary is witnessed by the notorious factions & oppressions which take place in corporate towns limited as the opportunities are, and in little republics when uncontrouled by apprehensions of external danger. If an enlargement of the sphere is found to lessen the insecurity of private rights, it is not because the impulse of a common interest or passion is less predominant in this case with the majority; but because a common interest or passion is less apt to be felt and the requisite combinations less easy to be formed by a great than by a small number. The Society becomes broken into a greater variety of interests, of pursuits, of passions, which check each other, whilst those who may feel a common sentiment have less opportunity of communication and concert. It may be inferred that the inconveniences of popular States contrary to the prevailing Theory, are in proportion not to the extent, but to the narrowness of their limits.

The great desideratum in Government is such a modification of the Sovereignty[45] as will render it sufficiently neutral between the different interests and factions, to controul one part of the Society from invading the rights of another, and at the same time sufficiently controuled itself, from setting up an interest adverse to that of the whole Society.
In absolute Monarchies, the prince is sufficiently, neutral towards his subjects, but frequently sacrifices their happiness to his ambition or his avarice. In small Republics, the sovereign will is

[45] Someone has written "[governing power]" above "as will render it" and inserted a caret (^) after "sovereignty."

sufficiently controuled from such a Sacrifice of the entire Society, but is not sufficiently neutral towards the parts composing it.[46]

As a limited Monarchy tempers the evils of an absolute one; so an extensive Republic meliorates the administration of a small Republic.

An auxiliary desideratum for the melioration of the Republican form is such a process of elections as will most certainly extract from the mass of the Society the purest and noblest characters which it contains; such as will at once feel most strongly the proper motives to pursue the end of their appointment, and be most capable to devise the proper means of attaining it.

12. Impotence of the laws of the States[47]

[46] In the bottom-right corner is written "599" lightly.

[47] There is a note written lightly lengthways on the side of the page: "Vices of the Political System of the United States April 1787." Over top of this note is written "Cop."

C. Memorandums for the Convention of Virginia in 1788 on the federal Constitution

MEMORANDUMS FOR THE CONVENTION OF VIRGINIA[48] IN 1788 ON THE FEDERAL CONSTITUTION –

I[49]

[50] It appears that it was the design of Clodius to extend the suffrage to all the freedmen in the several tribes of the City, that the Tribunes might by corruption the more easily foment seditions. Cicero's Milo with the note[51]

Above 30,000. voters in some Counties of Engd. 3,000. only in all Scotland – Dalrymple F.P.[52]

—

Writ of Error lies from B.R. in Ireld. to B.R.[53] in Engd – Blackst.[54]

do. do. from Wales to B.R. Jenkins' Cent: & 1 W & M. c. 27.

as to Scotland into Parliament – see 6. Ann. c. 26. sect. 12.

———

difficulty of drawing line between laws apparent in Act of Union between Engd. & Scotland – 1. Art: 18. The laws concerning regulation of trade, Customs &c. see Abridgt. by Cay. Vol. 2. 384. under "Scotland"[55]. – For line between Courts – see art: 19.

48 James Madison, June 27, 1788, Series 1, From September 4, 1787 to June 5, 1790, Image 542, *The James Madison Papers*, LOC, http://hdl.loc.gov/loc.mss/mjm.03_0542_0563. The editors of the *PJM* believe Madison wrote these notes in November 1787; they can be found on the Library of Congress' website under June 27, 1788.

49 There is an "I" at the top of the page. The editors of the *PJM* believe Rives added this and the subsequent letters and page numbers.

50 This portion is prior to the rest, and the editors of the *PJM* note that it is written on the first half-size leaf. They put it at the end of the document.

51 Cicero, *Epistles to Atticus*. Madison listed this text in his "Memorandum of Books," *PJM*, 13:286.

52 John Dalrymple, *An Essay Towards a General History of Feudal Property in Great Britain*. According to Sowerby, *Catalogue of the Library of Thomas Jefferson*, II:317–18, Jefferson owned this text.

53 This is a reference to "Bancus Regis" – "the king's bench," which was the "supreme tribunal of the king after parliament."

54 William Blackstone, *Commentaries on the Laws of England*. Madison listed this text in his "Report on Books for Congress," *PJM*, 6:91.

55 Although it is not on his book list, Madison is probably referring to John Cay, *An Abridgement of the Publick Statutes in Force and of General Use From Magna Charta* …

Roman Empire more than 2000 M. from N. to. S. more than 3000 from W. to. E. Gibbon[56] population of do. abt. 120 Million including slaves who abt. ½. this more than in Europe. Id.

Spain	700 by 500 Miles	Engd. 360 by 300
France	600 by 500	Scotd. 300 by –150
Italy	– – 600 by 500	
Germany	600 by 500	Denmark 240 by 180
Poland	700 by 680	Norway 1000 by 900.
Sweeden	800 by 500[57]	

[1]

Examples shewing defect of[58] mere confederacies

Amphyctionic League. See
Lycian do.
Achæan do.
German do. – note Germany has more than 150 sovereignties
Swiss do.
Belgic do.
United Colonies – see
Albany project – see Albany papers.[59]
Articles of Confederation
Hanseatic do.
Union of Calmar. See p. 4.

Engd. & Scotland – formed in 1706. by 32 Commssrs. appd. for each Kgdom: they sat from April 18th. to middle of July – they were appd. by crwn by acts of two Parlts – restrained from treating of Religion

[56] Edward Gibbon, *The History of the Decline and Fall of the Roman Empire* ... Madison listed this as "Gibbon's on the decline of the Rom: Empire" in his "Report on Books for Congress," *PJM*, 6:77. He also refers to Gibbon in the "Notes on Government." See *MJM*, 128n18.

[57] This page is divided into three sections by using curly brackets on the left side. The first includes "It appears ... the note" and is labeled "I." The second includes "Above ... art: 19" and is labeled "B." The final section is labeled "I." The editors of the *PJM* believe Rives added these notes; they are in pencil.

[58] There is an "A" above "of." There is also a note: "Copd." above and to the left of the title, which seems to be in Rives' handwriting.

[59] Benjamin Franklin's Albany Plan of Union of 1754.

The Scotch had got the[60] notion of a fœderal Union like Holld. & Switzd. Engd. opposed decidedly amg. other reasons, because if differt. Parlts. eithr. cd. break it when pleased.

—

Many had despaired of Union as Burnet himself.[61]
In Scotland opposed violently, particularly by those who were for a new revolution, as Union fatal bar to it – carried in Parliamt. by inconsidble. majority – The presbyterians bro't into opposition by persuasion that religious rights wd. be in danger – this argt. used most by those known to be most adverse to that Religion – especially Dutchess of Hamilton & son, who as next in succession hoped for Crown if separate Kingdom.
Genl. argts. vs Union in Scotd.
1. antiquity & dignity of Kingdom to be given up & sold.
2. departing from Independt. State & to be swallowd by Engd.
3. wd. be outvoted in all questions by Engds: superiority in Parlt.
4. Scotland no more be regded. by foregin [*sic*] Nations.
5. danger to the Kirk.

Finally, Scotch parlt. prevailed on to annex conditions which advisers tho't wd. never be agd. to & thus the plan be defeated.

—

Opposers of Union findg. majority vs them – endeavd. to raise storm out of doors – petitions, addresses & Remonstrances came up from all quarters, instigated by Minority – Even riots excited abt Parlt. House.

—

In Engld. alarm also for Religion, & act passed to secure it – H. of Commons unan[im]ous – Lords 50 & 20.[62]

[2][63]

Sweeden

2 remarkable circumstances – 1. Citizens – elect by votes the multiples of their property – some rich merchts. have several hundred votes. 2. Country gentlemen between nobles & peasants – have no votes in electing the latter order – are not represented nor eligible at all. Constitn. Prior to 1772. alternately monarchical & aristocratic. Foreign powers had chief agency in producing the

[60] Madison sometimes abbreviated such words as these – that, the, etc. – with symbols commonly used during this time period. See Ronald A. Hill, "Interpreting the Symbols and Abbreviations in Seventeenth Century English and American Documents," *Genealogical Journal* 21 (1993), http://bcgcertification.org/blog/wp-content/uploads/2013/05/Hill-W141.pdf.

[61] Gilbert Burnet, *Bishop Burnet's History of His Own Time* ... Madison listed this text in his "Report on Books for Congress," *PJM*, 6:74.

[62] In the bottom-right corner is written "4289 R" lightly.

[63] This page has been labeled "D."

Revolution of 1772. King had at the time only 2 Companies of Guards. – [Power of King reduced to its lowest ebb at time of Revolution – Sheridan[64]] [the power of peasants predominant originally – hence alternate anarchy & tyranny. Id] – on death of Ch: XII. all prerogatives of Ex. abolished – hence, legisl: soon exercised Ex. & Judicl. power both – any 3 out of 4. houses competent to legislation.

[65] The Revol: of 72. owing to unpopularity of Diet owing to Abuse of power from union of Ex & Judl. with Legisl: – factions venality & foreign influence – The people favored the enterprize of the King.

Denmark.

The change in 1660. produced by the aversion to the Nobility – who as feudal lords had almost all power, the peasants being slaves to them – the two other orders being the Clergy – and Commons or represent[ative]s of Tuns. The Clergy were the great agents in the revolution & the King rather passive – Ld. Molesworth saith, Denmark differed little from an aristocracy when it became an absolute monarchy.

France –

The 3d. estate was composed accordg. to Robertson[66] of Reps. of Cities &c within King's demesne only – and the tillers of the earth the greatest body in all countries nothing or represented by the Nobles.

Spain –

Peasants never represented in Cortes – quere –

Poland

153 Senators – about 200 Nuncios –

[3][67]

Examples of hostile consequences of rival communities
not united by one Government.
All the antient & modern Confederacies.

Saxon Heptarchy (a) – England and Scotland (b) G.B. & Ireland Engd: & Wales –

Antient Republics of Italy – before Roman Empire
do – – – after dissolution of do.
[anno 827][68]

---

[64] Charles Francis Sheridan, *A History of the Late Revolution in Sweden* ... Madison listed this as "Sheridan's Revolutions of Sweeden" in his "Report on Books for Congress," *PJM*, 6:83.

[65] This note is written on the side of the page.

[66] William Robertson, *The History of the Reign of the Emperor Charles V*. Madison listed this as "Robinson's History of Charles V" in his "Report on Books for Congress," *PJM*, 6:78.

[67] This page is labeled "B."

[68] This portion appears above the text. In most cases, when Madison makes such a note, he writes a caret (ˆ) to show where the passage should be inserted. In this case, he did not.

(a) "Thus were united all the Kingdoms of the Heptarchy in on Great State near four hundd. years after 1st arrival of Saxons in Britain [& 250 after establisht.][69]; and the fortunate arms &c. of Egbert [King of Wessex] at last effectd. what had been so often attempted in vain by so many princes" Hume Vol. 1. p. 59.[70]

"Kent, Northumberland and Mercia had successively aspired to general dominion" Id. p. 60.

(b) question in 1713 in H. of Lords for dissolving Union as not answering & ruinous to Scotland, carried in negative by 4 voices only. Deb. Peers II. 313 – Burg. 3. 360.[71]

—

Harrington (pol. aphorisms 49. 50. 51 – page 517. pronounced the Union destructive to both Engd. & Scotland.[72]

—

Heptarchy reduced to two, after some ages – Mercia & W. Saxons – & then one (Egbert)
See Kennet. vol. 1. p. 37.[73] for an apt & short quotation as to Heptarchy
England & Wales prior to union under Edwd. 1 – & more fully under H. VIII[74]

4[75]

Union at Calmar in 1397 of Sweeden – Denmark – & Norway – formed by Margaret Queen of the 2 last & elected Queen also of the former. She convoked the deputies of the 3. Stas. Genl. at Calmar – 40 from each attended & formed the Union or Treaty – main argumt used by Queen – the contentions & wars when disunited. –

Union consisted of 3 principal articles:

1. that the 3 Kgdoms which were each elective – sd. have same King to be elected by turns out of each, with an exception however in favor of offspring whom the 3 Ks might elect.
2. The King to divide his residence by turns amg. each, & to spend in each the revenues of each Crown
3. The most important that each sd. keep its particular Senate – Customs – privileges. Govrs. Magistrs – Genls. Bishops & even troops & garrisons to be

[69] This bracketed note appears above the text and again there is no caret (^) to indicate where the passage should be inserted.

[70] David Hume, *The History of England* ... Madison listed this text in his "Report on Books for Congress," *PJM*, 6:80.

[71] James Burgh, *Political Disquisitions; or, An Enquiry Into Public Errors, Defects, and Abuses* ... Madison listed this as "Burgh's political disquisitions" in his "Report on Books for Congress," *PJM*, 6:88.

[72] James Harrington, *The Oceana and Other Works of James Harrington* ... Madison listed this as "Harrington's Works" in his "Report on Books for Congress," *PJM*, 6:85.

[73] White Kennett, *A Complete History of England* ... Madison listed this as "Kennett's English History" in his "Report on Books for Congress," *PJM*, 6:80.

[74] In the bottom-right corner is written "4291 R" lightly.

[75] This page is labeled "C."

taken from respective Kigdoms. so that King sd. never be allowed to employ subjects of one in another; being mutually regarded as strangers.

This Union, thus imperfect, increased the mutual enmity & laid foundation for fresh & more bitter animosities & miseries.

[5][76]

Danger, if disunited, – 1 of foreign Invasion by sea – 2. of Eastern invasion, on S. Sts.

Examples of invasions of defenseless Coasts x Such more formidable than by land, because more sudden & easily supported by supplies.

(a) Romans invade England
Saxons invade England
Danes – do
Normans do
(b) Danes do France
English Ireland
Europeans America
do. East Indies
do. Africa

Egyptians & Phonicians invade Greece
Greece do. Italy
Carthaginians do. Italy & Spain
Visigoths from Spain – Barbary

(a) See Hume Hist: Vol. 1.
(b) do. Vol. 1. p 69–70.

– Countries without navy conquerable in proportion to extent of Coast – England more frequently & thoroughly conquered than France or Spain.[77]

Sparta.[78]

2 Kings –
28 Senators } the two jointly forming a Council with power of life & death.

Senate – 1 for life
2 vacancies filled by popular election, out of Candidates 60 years old
3 had right of convoking & proposing to Assemblies – as had Kings X
4 decrees of no force till ratified by people –

Kings – were for life – in other respects like 2 Consuls
Generals during war – presided in assemblies & public sacrifices in peace – cd. propose to Assemblies – dissolve them when convoked by Kings – but cd do nothing with consent of nation – the 2 Kings alway's jealous & on ill terms with each other were watched by field deputies in war.

---

[76] This page is not numbered.

[77] In the bottom-right corner is written "4293 R" lightly.

[78] This page is not numbered. It is lettered "F."

People[79]
Assemblies general & particular – former of all Citizens – latter of Citizens of Sparta alone had power of peace & war – treaties – great affairs – & election of Magistrates.

Ephori – chosen annually by people, and concurred in their behalf with – Kings & Senate over both when they had authority –
X usurped this right
They had more authority than Tribunes – presided at elections of Magistrates demanded acct. of their administration – – could imprison Kings – had the adm[in]istration of Money – superintended Religion – in fine directed every thing.
lands divided in 39,000 shares –

Carthage –[80]
500 years, says Ari[s]totle without any considerable sedition – or tyrant-
3 different authorities – Suffetes – Senate – people[81]

Suffetes – like Consuls – and annual[82]
does not appear by whom chosen – assembled Senate presiding – proposing & collecting the votes – presided also in Judgmts. of most important affairs – sometimes commanded armies – at going out were made Pretors

Senate – composed of persons qualified by age – experience – birth – riches – were the Council of State – & the Soul of all public deliberation no. not known – must have been great since the 100 drawn out of it. – Senate treated of great affrs – read letters of generals – recd. plaints of provinces – gave auds: to ambassrs – and decided peace and War X When Senate unanimous decided finally – in case of division people decided – Whilst Senate retained its authority says Polybius[83] – wisdom & success marked every thing.

People – at first gave way to Senate – at length intoxicated by wealth & conquests, they assumed all power – then cabals & factions prevailed & were one of the principal causes of the ruin of the State.

Tribunal of 100 – composed of 104. persons –

79 "People" is above "general &." It could be a title or a word Madison meant to insert, although there is no obvious place for it to be inserted.
80 This page is also not numbered, although it is lettered "G."
81 Aristotle, *A Treatise on Government*... Madison listed this as "Aristotle's Republic," which the *Politics* was sometimes called, in his "Report on Books for Congress," *PJM*, 6:85.
82 The editors of the *PJM* format and align this portion differently. This line is centered and the paragraph does not continue here; perhaps Madison meant it to be a title.
83 Polybius, *The General History of Polybius*. Polybius: *Historiarum* is in Sowerby's *Catalogue of the Library of Thomas Jefferson*, I:25.

– were in place of Ephori at Sparta, according to Aristotle – & instituted to balance the Great & the Senate – with this differe[n]ce that here the Council was perpetual – Generals accounted to them –

Tribunal of 5 – taken out of 100 above – duration of office unknown – like the Council of 10 at Venice – filled vacancies – even in Senate – had great power – but no salaries – became tyranical.[84]

Rome[85]

power of Senate (exclusive of people). 1. care of Religion. 2. to regulate the provinces. 3. X[86] over public treasury and expences of Govt. with appt. of stipends to Generals – no. of troops, & provisions & cloathing for armies –[87]4 appd with such instructions & recd. ambassrs – & gave such answrs as they thought fit. 5 decreed thanksgivings – & conferred honor of triumphs 6 inquire into crimes & treasons at Rome & in Italy – & decide disputes among dependent cities 7 interpreting dispensing with, & even abrogating laws – 8 arm Consuls with absolute power – darent operam &c – 9. prorogue & postpone assemblies of people – pardon & reward – declared any one enemy – Middleton on R. Sen.[88]

power of Senate – to propose to people who cd. not originate laws – this taken away by the Tribunes – & Senate not only obliged to allow assemblies at all times to be called, but to agree before hand to whatever acts of the people Idem.

power of Senate unlimited almost at first – except legisl: power – choice of Magtres. and peace & war – all power in Senate – & a second Senatus consultum necessary – to ratify, act of people in consequence of proposition from Senate – Cod. d'Hum.

Senate consisted originally of 100 – usually abt. 300 – finally by Jul. Cæsar 1000 – not agreed how appd. (whether by Consuls & Censors – or people &) – on extraordy. occasions by Dictator – censors – on ordinary (Middleton) – by people out of annual magistrates till these became a regular supply [course?] – Middleton

Censors could expel – but other Censors reinstate – & Senators had an appeal from them to people – Id.

Vertot[89] thinks people had nothing to do in appointg Senators – power being first in Kings – then Consuls – then Censors – & on extra. occasions in

84 In the bottom-right corner is written "4294 R" lightly.

85 This page is not numbered. It is lettered "H."

86 The "X" refers to a note on the side of the page: "Gracchiis transferred their criml. jurisdiction to equestrian order."

87 There is a dot with a circle around it, referring to the note on the side of the page: "ambassors. taken from their own body – Code d Humanitè."

88 Conyers Middleton, *A Treatise on the Roman Senate* . . .

89 Although it is not on his book list, Madison is probably referring to René Aubert de Vertot, *The History of the Revolutions That Happened in the Government of the Roman Republic.*

Dictator – age required but not ascertained by antiquaries – so estate between £6 & 7000 Stng. Senate assembled by Kings – Consuls – Dicta[t]ors – Tribunes –

90

power of Consuls 1. Heads of Repub. 2. command of armies – levy troops in consequence of author[it]y from Commitia – 3. authy over Italy & provs – who cd. appeal to their tribunal – and could cite subjects to Rome & punish with death 4. convene Senate propose business – count votes – & draw up decrees – nor cd. any resol. pass if <u>one</u> of the Consuls <u>opposed</u> – 5 addressed letters to Kings &c – Gave audience to Ambasrs. introdd: them to Senate – & carried into execution decrees touchg all these matters – 6 convoked Commitia – presided therein 7. applied money. – Had all the power of the Kings – Must be 42 years

Tribunes – uncertain whether at first – 2 – 3 – or 5. estabd. in 260. increased to 10. in 297. confind to City & one mile. At first had no power but <u>to defend</u> people, their persons being sacred for that purpose – but soon arrogated right to call Senate & assembly of people – & propose to them –

They were – (1). protectors of people – under wch. title they interfered in all affairs – released malefactors – & imprisoned principal magistrates of Repub: as Consuls & after a time exerted their authority over dictators & censors – (2) had the <u>veto</u>, to stop the functions of all other Magistrs. & to negative all laws & decrees of Senate – to dissolve Comitia so that Repub: often in anarchy & once 5 years without other Magistrs: than Tribunes – by this veto particularly as opposed to levies of men by order of Senate, they extorted every thing they wanted. (3). sacredness of persons of wch. they availed themselves much – pretending that it was violated in the persons of their officers – (4) to convoke Senate – & people – at first sat at door of Senate waiting to be informed of result of its deliberations X and had no right to assemble people – but Junius Brutus caught at incautious acknowledgt. of consul – got comit: tribut. estabd. in place of Centuries where votes unequal – & of curiata where as in Centuries, auspices necessary – & in both concurrence of Senate to the calling them & coming to Resolns X to these They soon brought trial of principal Citizens by appeal – & all sorts of affairs – got plebiscite made laws by Coma. trib: which they ma[na] ged & directed as they pleased X – (5) disposed of Govts. & command of armies – finances – & lands of the public – Sylla as dictator humbled the Tribunes but they were restored & Jul: Cæsar caused himself to be perpetual Tribune. The shadow continued down to Constantine the Great.[91]

X[92]

[90] This page is not numbered. It is lettered "I."

[91] In the bottom-right corner is written "4301 R." lightly.

[92] There is a large "X" on the back of the page.

D. Letter to Mr. Jefferson on a Federal Negative on State Laws

Dear Sir[93] New York Octr. 24. 1787.

My two last, though written for the two last Packets, have unluckily been delayed till this conveyance. The first of them was sent from Philada. to Commodore Jones in consequence of information that he was certainly to go by the Packet then about to sail. Being detained here by his business with Congress, and being unwilling to put the letter into the mail without my approbation which could not be obtained in time, he detained the letter also. The second was sent from Philada. to Col. Carrington, with a view that it might go by the last packet at all events in case Commodore Jones should meet with further detention here. By ill luck he was out of Town, and did not return till it was too late to make use of the opportunity. Neither of the letters were indeed of much consequence at the time, and are still less so now. I let them go forward nevertheless as they may mention some circumstances not at present in my recollection, and as they will prevent a chasm in my part of [illegible] correspondence which I have so many motives to cherish by an exact punctuality.

Your favor of June 20. has been already acknowledged. The last Packet from France brought me that of August 2d. I have recd. also by the Mary Capt. Howland the three Boxes for W.H. B.F.[94] and myself. The two first have been duly forwarded. The contents of the last are a valuable addition to former literary remittances and lay me under additional obligations, which I shall always feel more strongly than I express. The articles included for Congress have been delivered & those for the two Universities and for General Washington have been forwarded, as have been the various letters for your friends in Virginia and elsewhere. The parcel of rice referred to in your letter to the Delegates of S. Carolina has met with[95]

with some accident. No account whatever can be gathered concerning it. It probably was not shipped from France. Ubbo's book[96] I find was not omitted as you seem to have apprehended. The charge for it however is, which I must beg you to supply. The duplicate vol. of the Encyclopedie,[97] I left in Virginia,

[93] James Madison to Thomas Jefferson, October 24, 1787, Series 1, From September 8, 1787 to February 16, 1788, Image 346, *The Thomas Jefferson Papers*, LOC, http://hdl.loc.gov/loc.mss/mtj.mtjbib003069. *PJM*, 10:205–20.

[94] The "Mary" is a ship (see Jefferson to Madison, August 2, 1787, *PJM*, 10:124). In this letter, Jefferson wrote that he sent "three boxes of books one marked I.M. for yourself, one marked B.F. for Doctr. Franklin, & one marked W.H. for William Hay in Richmond."

[95] This is the beginning of page 2, and there is a note at the bottom of the page. It appears to say "H 2. Vol. 34" but is not in Madison's handwriting. A page break occurs here.

[96] Ubbo Emmius, *Graecorum Respublicae*. Madison listed this text in his "Memorandum for Books," *PJM*, 13:288.

[97] Charles Joseph Panckoucke, *Encyclopédie Méthodique*. Madison listed this multi-volume set in his "Report on Books for Congress," *PJM*, 6:65.

and it is uncertain when I shall have an opportunity of returning it. Your Spanish duplicates will I fear be hardly vendible. I shall make a trial wherever a chance presents itself. A few days ago I recd. your favor of the 15 of Augst. via L'Orient & Boston. The letters inclosed along with it were immediately sent on to Virga.

You will herewith receive the result of the Convention, which continued its Session till the 17th. of September. I take the liberty of making some observations on the subject which will help to make up a letter, if they should answer no other purpose.[98]

It appeared to be the sincere and unanimous wish of the Convention to cherish and preserve the Union of the States. No proposition was made, no suggestion was thrown out, in favor of a partition of the Empire into two or more Confederacies.

It was generally agreed that the objects of the Union could not be secured by any system founded on the principle of a confederation of sovereign States. A voluntary observance of the federal law by all the members, could never be hoped for. A compulsive one could evidently never be reduced to practice, and if it could, involved equal calamities to the innocent & the guilty, the necessity of a military force both obnoxious & dangerous, and in general, a scene resembling much more a civil war, than the administration of a regular Government.

Hence was embraced the alternative of a Government which instead of operating, on the States, should operate without their intervention on the individuals composing them: and hence the change in the principle and proportion of representation.

This ground-work being laid, the great objects which presented themselves were 1. to unite a proper energy in the Executive and a proper stability in the Legislative departments, with the essential characters of Republican Government. 2. to draw a line of demarkation[99]

(3

demarkation which would give to the General Government every power requisite for general purposes, and leave to the States every power which might be most beneficially administered by them. 3. to provide for the different interests of different parts of the Union. 4. to adjust the clashing pretensions of the large and small States. Each of these objects was pregnant with difficulties. The whole of them together formed a task more difficult than can be well concieved by those who were not concerned in the execution of it. Adding to these considerations the natural diversity of human opinions on all new and complicated subjects, it is impossible to consider the degree of concord which ultimately prevailed as less than a miracle.

[98] There is a light "X" on the left side of the paper next to this paragraph.

[99] There is a note in the bottom-left corner – "V.34" – but it is not in Madison's handwriting.

The first of these objects as it respects the Executive, was peculiarly embarrassing. On the question whether it should consist of a single person, or a plurality of co-ordinate members, on the mode of appointment, on the duration in office, on the degree of power, on the re-eligibility, tedious and reiterated discussions took place. The plurality of co-ordinate members had finally but few advocates. Governour Randolph was at the head of them. The modes of appointment proposed were various, as by the people at large – by electors chosen by the people – by the Executives of the States – by the Congress, some preferring a joint ballot of the two Houses – some a separate concurrent ballot allowing to each a negative on the other house – some a nomination of several canditates [*sic*] by one House, out of whom a choice should be made by the other. Several other modifications were started. The expedient at length adopted seemed to give pretty general satisfaction to the members. As to the duration in office, a few would have preferred a tenure during good behaviour – a considerable number would have done so, in case an easy & effectual removal by impeachment could be settled. It was much agitated whether a long term, seven years for example, with a subsequent & perpetual ineligibility, or a short term with a capacity to be re-elected, should be fixed. In favor of the first opinion were urged the danger of a gradual degeneracy of re-elections from time to time, into first a life and then a heriditary tenure, and the favorable effect of an incapacity to be reappointed, on the independent exercise of the Executive authority. On the other side it was contended that the prospect of necessary degradation, would discourage the

4)

most dignified characters from aspiring to the office, would take away the principal motive to [illegible] faithful discharge of its duties – the hope of being rewarded with a reappointment, would stimulate ambition to violent efforts for holding over the constitutional term – and instead of producing an independent administration, and a firmer defence of the constitutional rights of the department, would render the officer more indifferent to the importance of a place which he would soon be obliged to quit for ever, and more ready to yield to the incroachmts. of the Legislature of which he might again be a member. The questions concerning the degree of power turned chiefly on the appointment to offices, and the controul on the Legislature. An absolute appointment to all offices – to some offices – to no offices, formed the scale of opinions on the first point. On the second, some contended for an absolute negative, as the only possible mean of reducing to practice, the theory of a free Government which forbids a mixture of the Legislative & Executive powers. Others would be content with a revisionary power to be overruled by three fourths of both Houses. It was warmly urged that the judiciary department should be associated in the revision. The idea of some was that a separate revision should be given to the two departments – that if either objected two thirds; if both three fourths, should be necessary to overrule.

In forming the Senate, the great anchor of the Government, the questions as they came within the first object turned mostly on the mode of appointment, and the duration of it. The different modes proposed were, 1. by the House of Representatives 2. by the Executive, 3. by electors chosen by the people for the purpose. 4. by the State Legislatures. On the point of duration, the propositions descended from good-behavior to four years, through the intermediate terms of nine, seven, six, & five years. The election of the other branch was first determined to be triennial, and afterwards reduced to biennial.

The second object, the due partition of power, between the General & local Governments, was perhaps of all, the most nice and difficult. A few contended for an entire abolition of the States; some for indefinite power of Legislation in the Congress, with a negative on the laws of the States: some for such a power without a negative: some for a limited power of legislation, with such a negative: the majority finally for a limited power without the negative. The question with regard to the Negative underwent

(5

underwent repeated discussions, and was finally rejected by a bare majority. [[100]As I formerly intimated to you my opinion in favor of this ingredient, I will take this occasion of explaining myself on the subject. Such a check on the States appears to me necessary 1. to prevent encroachments on the General authority. 2. to prevent instability and injustice in the legislation of the States.

1. Without such a check in the whole over the parts, our system involves the evil of imperia in imperio. If a compleat supremacy some where is not necessary in every Society, a controuling power at least is so, by which the general authority may be defended against encroachments of the subordinate authorities, and by which the latter may be restrained from encroachments on each other. If the supremacy of the British Parliament is not necessary as has been contended, for the harmony of that Empire; it is evident I think that without the royal negative or some equivalent controul, the unity of the system would be destroyed. The want of some such provision seems to have been mortal to the antient Confederacies, and to be the disease of the modern. Of the Lycian Confederacy little is known. That of the Amphyctions is well known to have been rendered of little use whilst it lasted, and in the end to have been destroyed by the predominance of the local over the federal authority. The same observation may be made, on the authority of Polybius, with regard to the Achæan League. The Helvetic System scarcely amounts to a Confederacy, and is distinguished by too many peculiarities, to be a ground of comparison. The case of

[100] The end bracket appears on p. 10.

the United Netherlands is in point. The authority of a Statholder, the influence of a Standing army, the common interest in the conquered possessions, the pressure of surrounding danger, the guarantee of foreign powers, are not sufficient to secure the authority and interests of the generality, agst. the antifederal tendency of the provincial sovereignties. The German Empire is another example. A Hereditary chief with vast independent resources of wealth and power, a federal Diet, with ample parchment authority, a regular Judiciary establishment, the influence of the neighbourhood of great & formidable Nations, have been found unable either to maintain the subordination

6)

-nation of the members, or to prevent their mutual contests & encroachments. Still more to the purpose is our own experience both during the war and since the peace. Encroachments of the States on the general authority, sacrifices of national to local interests, interferences of the measures of different States, form a great part of the history of our political system. It may be said that the new Constitution is founded on different principles, and will have a different operation. I admit the difference to be material. It presents the aspect rather of a feudal system of republics, if such a phrase may be used, than of a Confederacy of independent States. And what has been the progress and event of the feudal Constitutions? In all of them a continual struggle between the head and the inferior members, until a final victory has been gained in some instances by one, in others, by the other of them. In one respect indeed there is a remarkable variance between the two cases.[101] In the feudal system the sovereign, though limited, was independent; and having no particular sympathy of interests with the great Barons, his ambition had as full play as theirs in the mutual projects of usurpation. In the American Constitution The general authority will be derived entirely from the subordinate authorities. The Senate will represent the States in their political capacity; the other House will represent the people of the States in their individual capac[it]y. The former will be accountable to their constituents at moderate, the latter at short periods. The President also derives his appointment from the States, and is periodically accountable to them. This dependence of the General, on the local authorities, seems effectually to guard the latter against any dangerous encroachments of the former: Whilst the latter, within their respective limits, will be continually sensible of the abridgment of their power, and be stimulated by ambition to resume the surrendered portion of it. We find the representatives of Counties and corporations in the Legislatures of the States, much more disposed to sacrifice the aggregate interest, and even authority, to the local views of their

[101] There is an "X" written here lightly.

Constituents, than the latter to the former. I mean not by these remarks to insinuate that an esprit de corps will not exist in the national Government or that opportunities may not occur, of extending its jurisdiction in some points. I mean only that the danger of encroachments is much greater from the other side, and that the impossibility of dividing powers of legislation, in such a manner, as to be free from different constructions by different interests, or even from ambiguity in the judgment of the impartial, requires some such expedient as I contend for. Many illustrations might be given of this impossibility. How long has it taken to fix, and how imperfectly is yet fixed the legislative power of corporations, though that power is subordinate in the most compleat manner? The line of distinction between the power of regulating trade and that

(7

that of drawing revenue from it, which was once considered as the barrier of our liberties, was found on fair discussion, to be absolutely undefinable. No distinction seems to be more obvious than that between spiritual and temporal matters. Yet wherever they have been made objects of Legislation, they have clashed and contended with each other, till one or the other has gained the supremacy. Even the boundaries between the Executive, Legislative & Judiciary powers, though in general so strongly marked in themselves, consist in many instances of mere shades of difference.[102] It may be said that the Judicial authority under our new system will keep the States within their proper limits, and supply the place of a negative on their laws. The answer is, that it is more convenient to prevent the passage of a law, than to declare it void after it is passed; that this will be particularly the case, where the law aggrieves individuals, who may be unable to support an appeal agst. a State to the supreme Judiciary; that a State which would violate the Legislative rights of the Union, would not be very ready to obey a Judicial decree in support of them, and that a recurrence to force, which in the event of disobedience would be necessary, is an evil which the new Constitution meant to exclude as far as possible.

2. A constitutional negative on the laws of the States seems equally necessary to secure individuals agst. encroachments on their rights. The mutability of the laws of the States is found to be a serious evil. The injustice of them has been so frequent and so flagrant as to alarm the most stedfast friends of Republicanism. I am persuaded I do not err in saying that the evils issuing from these sources contributed more to that uneasiness which produced the Convention, and prepared the public mind for a general reform, than those which accrued to our national character and interest from the inadequacy of

[102] There is an "X" written here lightly.

the Confederation to its immediate objects. A reform therefore which does not make provision for private rights, must be materially defective. The restraints agst. paper emissions, and violations of contracts are not sufficient. Supposing them to be effectual as far as they go, they are short of the mark. Injustice may be effected by such an infinitude of legislative expedients, that where the disposition exists it can only be controuled by some provision which reaches all cases whatsoever

8)[103]
whatsoever. The partial provision made, supposes the disposition which will evade it. It may be asked how private rights will be more secure under the Guardianship of the General Government than under the State Governments, since they are both founded on the republican principle which refers the ultimate decision to the will of the majority, and are distinguished rather by the extent within which they will operate, than by any material difference in their structure. A full discussion of this question would, if I mistake not, unfold the true principles of Republican Government, and prove in contradiction to the concurrent opinions of theoretical writers, that this form of Goverment [*sic*], in order to effect its purposes, must operate not within a small but an extensive sphere. I will state some of the ideas which have occurred to me on this subject.[104] Those who contend for a simple Democracy, or a pure republic, actuated by the sense of the majority, and operating within narrow limits, assume or suppose a case which is altogether fictitious. They found their reasoning on the idea, that the people composing the Society, enjoy not only an equality of political rights; but that they have all precisely the same interests, and the same feelings in every respect. Were this in reality the case, their reasoning would be conclusive. The interest of the majority would be that of the minority also; the decisions could only turn on mere opinion concerning the good of the whole, of which the major voice would be the safest criterion; and within a small sphere, this voice could be most easily collected, and the public affairs most accurately managed. We know however that no Society ever did or can consist of so homogeneous a mass of Citizens. In the savage State indeed, an approach is made towards it; but in that State little or no Government is necessary. In all civilized Societies, distinctions are various and unavoidable. A distinction of property results from that very protection which a free Government gives to unequal faculties of acquiring it. There will be rich and poor; creditors and debtors; a landed interest, a monied interest, a mercantile interest, a manufacturing interest. These classes may again be subdivided according to the different productions of different situations & soils, & according to different

[103] There is an "X" written lightly at the top of the page.
[104] There is an "X" written here lightly.

branches of commerce, and of manufactures. In addition to these natural distinctions, artificial ones will be founded, on accidental differences in political, religious or other opinions, or an attachment to the persons of leading individuals. However erroneous or ridiculous these grounds of dissention and faction, may appear to the enlightened Statesman

(9

Statesman, or the benevolent philosopher, the bulk of mankind who are neither Statesmen nor Philosophers, will continue to view them in a different light. It remains then to be enquired whether a majority having any common interest, or feeling any common passion, will find sufficient motives to restrain them from oppressing the minority. An individual is never allowed to be a judge or even a witness in his own cause. If two individuals are under the biass of interest or enmity agst. a third, the rights of the latter could never be safely referred to the majority of the three. Will two thousand individuals be less apt to oppress one thousand, or two hundred thousand, one hundred thousand? Three motives only can restrain in such cases. 1. a prudent regard to private or partial good, as essentially involved in in[105] the general and permanent good of the whole. This ought no doubt to be sufficient of itself. Experience however shews that it has little effect on individuals, and perhaps still less on a collection of individuals, and least of all on a majority with the public authority in their hands. If the former are ready to forget that honesty is the best policy; the last do more. They often proceed on the converse of the maxim: that whatever is politic is honest. 2. respect for character. This motive is not found sufficient to restrain individuals from injustice, and loses its efficacy in proportion to the number which is to divide the praise or the blame. Besides as it has reference to public opinion, which is that of the majority, the Standard is fixed by those whose conduct is to be measured by it. 3. Religion. The inefficacy of this restraint on individuals is well known, the conduct of every popular Assembly, acting on oath, the strongest of religious ties, shews that individuals join without remorse in acts agst. which their consciences would revolt, if proposed to them separately in their closets. When Indeed Religion is kindled into enthusiasm, its force like that of other passions is increased by the sympathy of a multitude. But enthusiasm is only a temporary state of Religion, and whilst it lasts will hardly be seen with pleasure at the helm. Even in its coolest state, it has been much oftener a motive to oppression than a restraint from it. If then there must be different interests and parties in Society; and a majority when united by a common interest or passion can not be restrained from oppressing the minority, what remedy can be found in a republican Government

10)

Government, where the majority must ultimately decide, but that of giving such an extent to its sphere, that no common interest or passion will be likely to

[105] Madison has written "in" twice.

unite a majority of the whole number in an unjust pursuit. In a large Society, the people are broken into so many interests and parties, that a common sentiment is less likely to be felt, and the requisite concert less likely to be formed, by a majority of the whole. The same security seems requisite for the civil as for the religious rights of individuals. If the same sect form a majority and have the power, other sects will be sure to be depressed. Divide et impera, the reprobated axiom of tyranny, is under certain qualifications, the only policy, by which a republic can be administered on just principles. It must be observed however that this doctrine can only hold within a sphere of a mean extent. As in too small a sphere oppressive combinations may be too easily formed agst. the weaker party; so in too extensive a one, a defensive concert may be rendered too difficult against the oppression of those entrusted with the administration. The great desideratum in Government is, so to modify the[106] sovereignty as that it may be sufficiently neutral between different, parts of the Society to controul one part from invading the rights of another, and at the same time sufficiently controuled itself, from setting up an interest adverse to that of the entire Society. In absolute monarchies, the Prince may be tolerably neutral towards different classes of his subjects, but may sacrifice the happiness of all to his personal ambition or avarice. In small republics, the sovereign will is controuled from such a sacrifice of the entire Society, but is not sufficiently neutral towards the parts composing it. In the extended Republic of the United States, The General Government would hold a pretty even balance between the parties of particular States, and be at the same time sufficiently restrained by its dependence on the community, from betraying its general interests.]

Begging pardon for this immoderate digression I return to the third object abovementioned, the adjustment of the different interests of different parts of the Continent. Some contended for an unlimited power over trade including exports as well as imports, and over slaves as well as other imports; some for such a power, provided the concurrence of two thirds of both House were required; Some for such a qualification of the power, with an exemption of exports and slaves, others for an exemption of exports only. The result is seen in the Constitution.

(11

Constitution. S. Carolina & Georgia were inflexible on the point of the slaves.

[106] The editors of the *PJM* insert "the" before "sovereignty." There is a space before "sovereignty," but whatever word Madison may have written has faded. However, based on the spacing and context, the editors seem to be correct about their insertion.

The remaining object created more embarrassment, and a greater alarm for the issue of the Convention than all the rest put together. The little States insisted on retaining their equality in both branches, unless a compleat abolition of the State Governments should take place; and made an equality in the Senate a sine qua non. The large States on the other hand urged that as the new Government was to be drawn principally from the people immediately and was to operate directly on them, not on the States; and consequently as the States wd. lose that importance which is now proportioned to the importance of their voluntary compliances with the requisitions of Congress, it was necessary that the representation in both Houses should be in proportion to their size. It ended in the compromise which you will see, but very much to the dissatisfaction of several members from the large States.

It will not escape you that three names only from Virginia are subscribed to the Act. Mr. Wythe did not return after the death of his lady. Docr. MClurg left the Convention some time before the adjournment. The Governour and Col. Mason refused to be parties to it. Mr. Gerry was the only other member who refused. The objections of the Govr. turn principally on the latitude of the general powers, and on the connection established between the President and the Senate. He wished that the plan should be proposed to the States with liberty to them to suggest alterations which should all be referred to another general Convention, to be incorporated into the plan as far as might be judged expedient. He was not inveterate in his opposition, and grounded his refusal to subscribe pretty much on his unwillingness to commit himself, so as not to be at liberty to be governed by further lights on the subject. Col. Mason left Philada. in an exceeding ill humour indeed. A number of little circumstances arising in part from the impatience which prevailed towards the close of the business, conspired to whet his acrimony. He returned to Virginia with a fixed disposition to prevent the adoption of the plan if possible

12)

possible. He considers the want of a Bill of Rights as a fatal objection. His other objections are to the substitution of the Senate in place of an Executive Council & to the powers vested in that body – to the powers of the Judiciary – to the vice President being made President of the Senate – to the smallness of the number of Representatives – to the restriction on the States with regard to ex post facto laws – and most of all probably to the power of regulating trade, by a majority only of each House. He has some other lesser objections. Being now under the necessity of justifying his refusal to sign, he will of course muster every possible one. His conduct has given great umbrage to the County of Fairfax, and particularly to the Town of Alexandria. He is already instructed to promote in the Assembly the calling a Convention, and will probably be either not deputed to the Convention, or be tied up by express instructions. He did not object in general to the powers vested in the National Government, so much as to the modification. In some respects he admitted that some further powers would have improved the system. He acknowledged in particular that a negative on the State laws, and the appointment of the State Executives ought to be ingredients; but supposed that the public mind would not now bear them, and that experience would hereafter produce these amendments.

The final reception which will be given by the people at large to the proposed System can not yet be decided. The Legislature of N. Hampshire was sitting when it reached that State and was well pleased with it. As far as the sense of the people there has been expressed, it is equally favorable. Boston is warm and almost unanimous in embracing it. The impression on the Country is not yet known. No symptoms of disapprobation have appeared. The Legislature of that State is now sitting, through which the sense of the people at large will soon be promulged with tolerable certainty. The paper money faction in Rh. Island is hostile. The other party zealously attached to it. Its passage through Connecticut is likely to be very smooth and easy. There seems to be less agitation in this x[107] State than any where. The discussion of the subject seems

(13

Seems confined to the newspapers. The principal characters are known to be friendly. The Governour's party which has hitherto been the popular & most numerous one, is supposed to be on the opposite side; but considerable reserve is practised, of which he sets the example. N. Jersey takes the affirmative side of course. Meetings of the people are declaring their approbation, and instructing their representatives. Penna. will be divided. The City of Philada., the Republican party, the Quakers, and most of the Germans espouse the Constitution. Some of the Constitutional leaders, backed by the western Country will oppose. An unlucky ferment on the subject in their Assembly just before its late adjournment has irritated both sides, particularly the opposition, and by redoubling the exertions of that party may render the event doubtful. The voice of Maryland I understand from pretty good authority, is, as far as it has been declared, strongly in favor of the Constitution. Mr. Chase is an enemy, but the Town of Baltimore which he now represents, is warmly attached to it, and will shackle him as far as they can. Mr. Paca will probably be, as usual, in the politics of Chase.[108] My information from Virginia is as yet extremely imperfect. I have a letter from Genl. Washington which speaks favorably of the impression within a circle of some extent; and another from Chancellor Pendleton which

[107] This "x" refers to the note at the bottom of Madison's page 12: "N. York."

[108] There is an "X" written here lightly.

expresses his full acceptance of the plan, and the popularity of it in his district.[109] I am told also that Innis and Marshall are patrons of it. In the opposite scale are Mr. James Mercer, Mr. R. H. Lee, Docr. Lee and their connections of course, Mr. M. Page according to Report, and most of the Judges & Bar of the general Court. The part which Mr. Henry will take is unknown here. Much will depend on it. I had taken it for granted from a variety of circumstances that he wd. be in the opposition, and still think that will be the case. There are reports however which favor a contrary supposition. From the States South of Virginia nothing has been heard

14)
As the deputation from S. Carolina consisted of some of its weightiest characters, who have returned unanimously zealous in favor of the Constitution, it is probable that State will readily embrace it. It is not less probable, that N. Carolina will follow the example unless that of Virginia should counterbalance it. Upon the whole, although, the public mind will not be fully known, nor finally settled for a considerable time, appearances at present augur a more prompt, and general adoption of the Plan than could have been well expected.

[110][When the plan[111] came before Congs. for their sanction, a very serious effort was made by R. H. Lee & Mr. Dane from Masts. to embarrass it. It was first contended that Congress could not properly give any positive countenance to a measure which had for its object the subversion of the Constitution under which they acted. This ground of attack failing, the former gentleman urged the expediency of sending out the plan with amendments, & proposed a number of them corresponding with the objections of Col. Mason. This experiment had still less effect. In order however to obtain unanimity it was necessary to couch the resolution in very moderate terms.

Mr. Adams has recd. permission to return, with thanks for his Services. No provision is made for supplying his place, or keeping up any represen[ta]tion there. Your reappointment for three years will be notified from the Office of F. Affrs. It was *made without a negative eight states* being *present. Connecticut however put in a blank ticket* the *sense of* that *state having been declared against embassies. Massachusets betrayed some scruple* on *like ground.* Every *personal consideration* was *avowed* & *I believe with sincerity* to have *militated against these scruples.*[112] It seems to be understood that letters to & from the

[109] There is an "X" written here lightly.

[110] There is a faded mark here, along with the note: "Mr. Jefferson Oct 24. 1787."

[111] There is a caret (ˆ) with the note: "of Constitution proposed by the Convention."

[112] The words in italics are written in code and decoded above the numbers. The editors of the *PJM* note that Jefferson decoded "notwithstanding" incorrectly, as Madison wrote the code for "however."

foreign Ministers of the U.S. are not free of Postage: but that the charge is to be allowed in their accounts.

The exchange of our French for Dutch Creditors has not been countenanced

(15

tenanced either by Congress or the Treasury Board. The paragraph in your last letter to Mr. Jay, on the subject of applying a loan in Holland to the discharge of the pay due to the foreign Officers has been referred to the Board since my arrival here. No report has yet been made. But I have little idea that the proposition will be adopted. Such is the state & prospect of our fiscal department that any new loan however small, that should now be made, would probably subject us to the reproach of premeditated deception. The balance of Mr. Adams' last loan will be wanted for the interest due in Holland, and with all the income here, will, it is feared, not save our credit in Europe from further wounds. It may well be doubted whether the present Govt. can be kept alive thro' the ensuing year, or untill the new one may take its place.

Upwards of 100,000 Acres of the surveyed lands of the U.S. have been disposed of in open market. Five million of unsurveyed have been sold by private contract to a N. England Company, at $^2/_3$ of a dollar per acre, payment to be made in the principal of the public securities. A negociation is nearly closed with a N. Jersey Company for two million more on like terms, and another commenced with a Company of this City for four million.] Col. Carrington writes more fully on this subject.

You will receive herewith the desired information from Alderman Broome in the case of Mr. Burke. Also the Virga. Bill on crimes & punishments. Sundry alterations having been made in conformity to the sense of the House in its latter stages, it is less accurate & methodical than it ought to have been. To these papers I add a Speech of Mr. C. P. on the Missippi. business. It is printed under precautions of secrecy, but surely could not have been properly exposed to so much risk of publication. You will find also among the[113]

16)[114]

Pamplets & papers I send by Commodore Jones, another printed speech of the same Gentleman. The Musæum, Magazine, & Philada. Gazettes, will give you a tolerable idea of the objects of present attention.

The summer crops in the Eastern & Middle States have been extremely plentiful. Southward of Virga. They differ in different places. On the whole I do not know that they are bad in that region. In Virginia the drought has been unprecedented, particularly between the falls of the Rivers & the Mountains. The Crops of Corn are in general alarmingly

[113] There are two notes in the bottom-left corner – "&34" and "2."

[114] In the top-left corner is written "October 24. 1787. Mr. Jefferson. Cop."

short. In Orange I find there will be scarcely subsistence for the inhabitants. I have not heard from Albemarle. The crops of Tobo. are every where said to be pretty good in point of quantity; & the quality unusually fine. The crops of wheat were also in general excellent in quality & tolerable in quantity.

Novr. 1. Commodore*[115] Jones having preferred another vessel to the packet, has remained here till this time. The interval has produced little necessary to be added to the above. The Legislature of Massts. has it seems taken up the Act of the Convention, and have appointed or probably will appoint an early day for its State Convention. There are letters also from Georgia which denote a favorable disposition. I am informed from Richmond that the New Election – law from the Revised Code produced a pretty full House of Delegates, as well as a Senate, on the first day. It had previously had equal effect in producing full meetings of the freeholders for the County elections. A very decided majority of the Assembly is said to be zealous in favor of the New Constitution. The same is said of the Country at large. It appears however that individuals of great weight both within & without the Legislature are opposed to it. A letter I just have from Mr. A. Stuart, names Mr. Henry, Genl. Nelson, W. Nelson, the family of Cabels, St. George Tucker, John Taylor and

(17

and the Judges of the Genl. Court except P. Carrington. The other opponents he describes as of too little note to be mentioned, which gives a negative information of the Characters on the other side. All are agreed that the plan must be submitted to a Convention.

We hear from Georgia that that State is threatened with a dangerous war with the Creek Indians. The alarm is of so serious a nature, that law-martial has been proclaimed, and they are proceeding to fortify even the Town of Savannah. The idea there, is that the Indians derive their motives as well as their means from their Spanish neighbours. Individuals complain also that their fugitive slaves are encouraged by East Florida. The policy of this is explained by supposing that it is considered as a discouragement to the Georgians to form settlements near the Spanish boundaries.

There are but few States on the spot here which will survive the expiration of the federal year; and it is extremely uncertain when a Congress will again be formed. We have not yet heard who are to be in the appointment of Virginia for the next year.

With the most affectionate attachment I remain Dear Sr.
Your Obed friend & servant
Js. Madison Jr.[116]

[115] The * refers to a note on the left side of the page: "*Paul." Madison is referring to Revolutionary captain John Paul Jones.

[116] In the bottom-left corner is written: "Monsr. Monsr. Jefferson."

9

Party Press Essays

Population and Emigration
Consolidation
Dependent Territories
Money (Parts I and II)
Public Opinion
Government
Charters
Parties
British Government
Universal Peace
Government of the United States
Spirit of Governments
Republican Distribution of Citizens
Fashion
Property
The Union. Who Are Its Real Friends?
A Candid State of Parties
Who Are the Best Keepers of the People's Liberties?

For the NATIONAL GAZETTE.
POPULATION *and* EMIGRATION.[1]

BOTH in the vegetable and animal kingdoms, every species derives from nature, a reproductive faculty beyond the demand for merely keeping up its stock: the seed of a single plant is sufficient to multiply it one hundred or a thousand fold. The animal offspring is never limited to the number of its parents.[2,3]

This ordinance of nature is calculated, in both instances, for a double purpose. In both, it ensures the life of the species, which, if the generative principle had not a multiplying energy, would be reduced in number by every premature destruction of individuals, and by degrees would be extinguished altogether. In the vegetable species, the surplus answers, moreover, the essential purpose of sustaining the herbivorous tribes of animals; as in the animal, the surplus serves the like purpose of sustenance to the carnivorous tribes. A crop of wheat may be reproduced by one tenth of itself. The remaining nine tenths can be spared for the animals which feed on it. A flock of sheep may be continued by a certain proportion of its annual increase. The residue is the bounty of nature to the animals which prey on that species.

Man who preys both on the vegetable and animal species, is himself a prey to neither. He too possesses the reproductive principle far beyond the degree requisite for the bare continuance of his species. – What becomes of the surplus of human life to which this principle is competent?

It is either, 1st. destroyed by infanticide, as among the Chinese and Lacedemonians; or 2d. it is stifled or starved, as among other nations whose population is commensurate to its food; or 3d. it is consumed by wars and endemic diseases; or 4th. it overflows, by emigration, to places where a surplus of food is attainable.

What may be the greatest ratio of increase of which the human species is susceptible, is a problem difficult to be solved; as well because precise experiments have never been made, as because the result would vary with the

[1] James Madison, "Population and Emigration," *National Gazette* (Philadelphia, PA), November 21, 1791, http://docs.newsbank.com/openurl?ctx_ver=z39.88-2004&rft_id=info:sid/iw.newsbank.com:EANX&rft_val_format=info:ofi/fmt:kev:mtx:ctx&rft_dat=10EF6028E2FDE6A8&svc_dat=HistArchive:ahnpdoc&req_dat=0E8515E56BD9D19F. Also published in the *Daily Advertiser* in two parts on November 29, 1791, and November 30, 1791. *PJM*, 14:117–22. Compare this published article with Madison's notes on "Emigration," *PJM*, 14:113–16.

[2] This is Madison's footnote: "*The multiplying power in some instances, animal as well as vegetable, is astonishing. An annual plant of two seeds produces in 20 years, 1,048,576; and there are plants which bear more than 40,000 seeds. The roe of a Codfish is said to contain a million of eggs; mites will multiply to a thousand in a day; and there are viviparous flies which produce 2000 at once. See Stillingfleet and Bradley's philosophical account of nature.*"

[3] Stillingfleet, *Miscellaneous Tracts*, 58–63; Bradley, *A Philosophical Account of the Works of Nature*, 123–62.

circumstances distinguishing different situations. It has been computed that under the most favorable circumstances possible, a given number would double itself in ten years. What has actually happened in this country is a proof, that nature would require for the purpose, a less period than twenty years. We shall be safe in averaging the surplus at five per cent.[4]

According to this computation, Great Britain and Ireland, which contain about ten millions of people, are capable of producing annually for emigration, no less than five hundred thousand; France, whose population amounts to twenty five millions, no less than one million two hundred and fifty thousand; and all Europe, stating its numbers at one hundred and fifty millions, no less than seven and a half millions.

It is not meant that such a surplus could, under any revolution of circumstances, suddenly take place: yet no reason occurs why an annual supply of human, as well as other animal life, to any amount not exceeding the multiplying faculty, would not be produced in one country, by a regular and commensurate demand of another. Nor is it meant that if such a redundancy of population were to happen in any particular country, an influx of it beyond a certain degree ought to be desired by any other, though within that degree, it ought to be invited by a country greatly deficient in its population.[5] The calculation may serve, nevertheless, by placing an important principle in a striking view, to prepare the way for the following positions and remarks.

First. Every country, whose population is full, may annually spare a portion of its inhabitants, like a hive of bees its swarm, without any diminution of its number: nay, a certain portion must, necessarily, be either spared, or destroyed, or kept out of existence.[6,7]

---

[4] This is Madison's footnote: "*Emigrants from Europe*, enjoying freedom *in a climate similar to their own, increase at the rate of five per cent a year. Among Africans* suffering or *(in the language of some)* enjoying slavery *in a climate similar to their own, human life has been* consumed *in an equal ratio. Under all the mitigations latterly applied in the British West-Indies, it is admitted that an annual* decrease *of one per cent. has taken place. – What a comment on the African trade!*"

[5] The problem of population "surplus" and "redundancy" concerned Madison throughout his life. See, for example, Madison to Jefferson, June 19, 1786, *PJM*, 9:659–60. His proffered solution for the misery that attended the landless, urban poor of Europe was to emigrate to the vacant lands of America rather than work in dependent positions, such as household servants, the manufacturing of superfluous goods, etc. Cf. the Party Press Essay "Fashion." Cf. Drew R. McCoy, *The Elusive Republic* (Chapel Hill: University of North Carolina Press, 1980), 120–32.

[6] This is Madison's footnote: "*The most remarkable instances of the swarms of people that have been spared without diminishing the parent stock, are the colonies and colonies of colonies among the antient Greeks. Miletum, which was itself a colony, is reported by Pliny, to have established no less than* eighty *colonies, on the Hellespont, the Propontis, and the Euxine. Other facts of a like kind are to be found in the Greek historians.*"

[7] See Pliny, *Natural History*, trans. H. Rackham (Cambridge, MA: Harvard University Press), II:305. Madison likely copied this reference to Pliny from Barthélemy, *Voyage*, 6:190–91.

Secondly. It follows, moreover, from this multiplying faculty of human nature, that in a nation, sparing or losing more than its proper surplus, the level must soon be restored by the internal resources of life.

Thirdly. Emigrations may even augment the population of the country permitting them. The commercial nations of Europe, parting with emigrants, to America, are examples. The articles of consumption demanded from the former, have created employment for an additional number of manufacturers. The produce remitted from the latter, in the form of raw materials, has had the same effect – whilst the imports and exports of every kind, have multiplied European merchants and mariners. Where the settlers have doubled every twenty or twenty-five years, as in the United States, the encrease of products and consumption in the new country, and consequently of employment and people in the old, has had a corresponding rapidity.

Of the people of the United States, nearly three millions are of British descent.[8] The British population has notwithstanding increased within the period of our establishment. It was the opinion of the famous Sir Josiah Child,[9] that every man in the British colonies found employment, and of course, subsistence, for four persons at home. According to this estimate, as more than half a million of the adult males in the United States equally contribute employment at this time to British subjects, there must at this time be more than two millions of British subjects subsisting on the fruits of British emigrations. This result, however, seems to be beyond the real proportion. Let us attempt a less vague calculation.

The value of British imports into the United States including British freight, may be stated at about fifteen millions of dollars, Deduct two millions for foreign articles coming through British hands; there remain thirteen millions. About half our exports, valued at ten millions of dollars, are remitted to that nation. From the nature of the articles, the freight cannot be less than three millions of dollars; of which about one fifth[10,11] being the share of the United States, there is to be added

8 This is Madison's footnote: "*Irish is meant to be included.*"

9 Sir Josiah Child, *A New Discourse of Trade*, 2nd edn. (London, 1694). Child was a merchant, an economist, a member of Parliament, and a governor of the East India Company. He was an early proponent of the free trade doctrine, although he also advocated a commercial policy that favored Britain over her colonial holdings.

10 This is Madison's footnote: "*This is stated as the fact is, not as it ought to be. The United States are reasonably entitled to half the freight, if, under regulations* perfectly reciprocal in every channel of navigation, *they could acquire that share. According to Lord Sheffield, indeed, the United States are well off, compared with other nations; the tonnage employed in the trade with the whole of them, previous to the American Revolution, having belonged to British subjects, in the proportion of more than eleven twelfths. In the year* 1660, *other nations owned about* 1/4; *in* 1700 *less than* 1/6; *in* 1725 1/19; *in* 1750 1/12; *in* 1774, *less than that proportion. What the proportion is now, is not known. If such has been the operation of the British navigation law on other nations, it is our duty, with enquiring into their acquiescence in its monopolizing tendency, to defend ourselves against it, by all the fair and prudent means in our power.*"

11 John Baker Holroyd, Sheffield, *Observations on the Commerce of the American States* (1784), 137.

to the former remainder; two millions four hundred thousand. The profit accruing from the articles as materials or auxiliaries for manufactures, is probably at least fifty per cent, or five millions of dollars.[12] The three sums make twenty millions four hundred thousand dollars; call them in round numbers twenty millions. – The expence of supporting a labouring family in Great-Britain, as computed by Sir John Sinclair, on six families containing thirty-four persons, averages £ 4: 12:10 1/2 sterling, or about twenty dollars a head.[13] As his families were of the poorer class, and the subsistence a bare competency, let twenty-five per cent. be added, making the expence about twenty five dollars a head, dividing twenty millions by this sum, we have eight hundred thousand for the number of British persons whose subsistence may be traced to emigration for its source: or allowing eight shillings sterling a week, for the support of a working man, we have two hundred sixteen thousand three hundred forty-five of that class, for the number derived from the same source.

This lesson of fact, which merits the notice, of every commercial nation, may be enforced by a more general view of the subject.

The present imports of the United States, adding to the first cost, &c. one half the freight as the reasonable share of foreign nations, may be stated at twenty-five millions of dollars. Deducting five millions on account of East-India articles, there remain in favour of Europe, twenty millions of dollars. The foreign labour incorporated with such part of our exports as are subjects or ingredients for manufactures, together with half the export freight, is probably not of less value than fifteen millions of dollars. The two sums together make thirty-five millions of dollars, capable of supporting two hundred thirty-three thousand three hundred thirty-three families of six persons in each: or three hundred seventy-eight thousand six hundred and five men, living on eight shillings sterling a week.

The share of this benefit, which each nation is to enjoy, will be determined by many circumstances. One that must have a certain and material influence, will be, the taste excited here for their respective products and fabrics. This influence has been felt in all its force by the commerce of Great-Britain, as the advantage originated in the emigrations from that country to this; among the means of retaining it, will not be numbered a restraint on emigrations. Other nations, who have to acquire their share in our commerce, are still more interested in aiding their other efforts, by permitting, and even

[12] This is Madison's footnote: "*This is admitted to be a very vague estimate. The proportion of our exports which are either necessaries of life, or have some profitable connection with manufactures, might be pretty easily computed. The actual profit drawn from that proportion is a more difficult task; but if tolerably ascertained and compared with the proportion of such of our imports as are not for mere consumption, would present one very interesting view of the commerce of the United States.*"

[13] Sir John Sinclair, *Queries Drawn Up for the Purpose of Elucidating the Natural History and Political State of Scotland* (London, 1790), 3.

promoting emigrations to this country, as fast as it may be disposed to welcome them. The space left by every ten or twenty thousand emigrants will be speedily filled by a surplus of life that would otherwise be lost. The twenty thousand in their new country, calling for the manufactures and productions required by their habits, will employ and sustain ten thousand persons in their former country, as a clear addition to its stock. In twenty or twenty-five years, the number, so employed and added, will be twenty thousand. And in the mean time, example and information will be diffusing the same taste among other inhabitants here, and proportionally extending employment and population there.

Fourthly. Freedom of emigration is due to the general interests of humanity. The course of emigrations being always, from places where living is more difficult, to places where it is less difficult, the happiness of the emigrant is promoted by the change: and as a more numerous progeny is another effect of the same cause, human life is at once made a greater blessing, and more individuals are created to partake of it.

The annual expence of supporting the poor in England amounts to more than one million and a half sterling.[14,15] The number of persons, subsisting themselves not more than six months in the year, is computed at one million two hundred sixty eight thousand, and the number of beggars at forty eight thousand. In France, it has been computed that seven millions of men women and children live one with another, on twenty five livres, which is less than five dollars a year. Every benevolent reader will make his own reflections.

Fifthly. It may not be superfluous to add, that freedom of emigration is favorable to morals. A great proportion of the vices which distinguish crouded from thin settlements, are known to have their rise in the facility of illicit intercourse between the sexes, on one hand, and the difficulty of maintaining a family, on the other. Provide an outlet for the surplus of population, and marriages will be increased in proportion. Every four or five emigrants will be the fruit of a legitimate union which would not otherwise have taken place.

Sixthly. The remarks which have been made, though in many respects little applicable to the internal situation of the United States, may be of use as far

[14] This is Madison's footnote: "*From Easter 1775 to Easter 1776, was expended the sum of £ 4,556,804 : 6–3 sterling. See Anderson vol. 5. p. 275.* This well informed writer conjectures the annual expence to be near £.2,000,000 *sterling. It is to be regretted that the number and expence of the poor in the United States cannot be contrasted with such statements. The subject well merits research, and would produce the truest eulogium on our country.*"

[15] Anderson, *An Historical and Chronological Deduction of the Origin of Commerce*, 5:275. Specifically, Anderson estimates England's expenses on the poor to be £1,523,163 compared to £1,679,585 raised. For a comparison of Anderson's and Hume's very different ways of conceiving of the history of commerce, see Daniele Francesconi, "The Language of Historical Causation in David Hume's *History of England*," *Cromohs* 6 (2001), 1–11, www.cromohs.unifi.it/6_2001/francesconi.html.

as they tend to prevent mistaken and narrow ideas on an important subject. Our country being populated in different degrees in different parts of it, removals from the more compact to the more spare or vacant districts are continually going forward – The object of these removals is evidently to exchange a less easy for a more easy subsistence. The effect of them must therefore be to quicken the aggregate Population of our country. Considering the progress made in some situations towards their natural complement of inhabitants, and the fertility of others, which have made little or no progress, the probable difference in their respective rates of increase is not less than as three in the former to five in the latter. Instead of lamenting then a loss of *three* human beings to Connecticut, Rhode-Island, or New-Jersey, the *Philanthropist*, will rejoice that *five* will be gained to New-York, Vermont or Kentucky; and the *patriot* will be not less pleased that *two* will be added to *the citizens of the United States*.

Philadelphia, Nov. 19, 1791.

For the National Gazette. *CONSOLIDATION.*[16]

MUCH has been said, and not without reason, against a consolidation of the States into one government. Omitting lesser objections, two consequences would probably flow from such a change in our political system, which justify the cautions used against it. *First*, it would be impossible to avoid the dilemma, of either relinquishing the present energy and responsibility of *a single* executive magistrate, for some *plural* substitute, which by dividing so great a trust might lessen the danger of it; or suffering so great an accumulation of powers in the hands of that officer, as might by degrees transform him into a monarch. The incompetency of one Legislature to regulate all the various objects belonging to the local governments, would evidently force a transfer of many of them to the executive department; whilst the encreasing splendour and number of its prerogatives supplied by this source, might prove excitements to ambition too powerful for a sober execution of the elective plan, and consequently strengthen the pretexts for an hereditary designation of the magistrate. *Second*, were the state governments abolished, the same space of country that would produce an undue growth of the executive power, would prevent that controul on the Legislative body, which is essential to a faithful discharge of its trust, neither the voice nor the sense of ten or twenty millions of people, spread through so many latitudes as are comprehended within the United States, could ever be combined or called into effect, if deprived of those local organs, through which both can now be conveyed. In such a state of things, the impossibility of acting together, might be succeeded by the inefficacy of partial expressions of the public mind, and this at length, by a universal silence and insensibility, leaving the whole government to that *self directed course*, which, it must be owned, is the natural propensity of every government.

But if a consolidation of the states into one government be an event so justly to be avoided, it is not less to be desired, on the other hand, that a consolidation should prevail in their interests and affections; and this too, as it fortunately happens, for the very reasons, among others, which lie against a governmental consolidation. For, in the first place, in proportion as uniformity is found to prevail in the interests and sentiments of the several states, will be the practicability of accommodating *Legislative* regulations to them, and thereby of withholding new and dangerous prerogatives from the executive. Again, the greater the mutual confidence and affection of all parts of the Union, the

[16] James Madison, "Consolidation," *National Gazette* (Philadelphia, PA), December 5, 1791, http://docs.newsbank.com/openurl?ctx_ver=z39.88-2004&rft_id=info:sid/iw.newsbank.com:EANX&rft_val_format=info:ofi/fmt:kev:mtx:ctx&rft_dat=10EF5F184516893 8&svc_dat=HistArchive:ahnpdoc&req_dat=0E8515E56BD9D19F. *PJM*, 14:137–39. Also published in the *New-York Daily Gazette* on December 10, 1791.

more likely they will be to concur amicably, or to differ with moderation, in the elective designation of the chief magistrate; and by such examples, to guard and adorn the vital principle of our republican constitution. Lastly, the less the supposed difference of interests, and the greater the concord and confidence throughout the great body of the people, the more readily must they sympathize with each other, the more seasonably can they interpose a common manifestation of their sentiments, the more certainly will they take the alarm at usurpation or oppression, and the more effectually will they *consolidate* their defence of the public liberty.

Here then is a proper object presented, both to those who are most jealously attached to the separate authority reserved to the states, and to those who may be more inclined to contemplate the people of America in the light of one nation. Let the former continue to watch against every encroachment, which might lead to a gradual consolidation of the states into one government. Let the latter employ their utmost zeal, by eradicating local prejudices and mistaken rivalships, to consolidate the affairs of the states into one harmonious interest; and let it be the patriotic study of all, to maintain the various authorities established by our complicated system, each in its respective constitutional sphere; and to erect over the whole, one paramount Empire of reason, benevolence and brotherly affection.

Philadelphia, Dec 3.

For the NATIONAL GAZETTE. DEPENDENT TERRITORIES[17]

ARE of two kinds. *First* – Such as yield to the superior state at once a monopoly of their useful productions, and a market for its superfluities. These, by exciting and employing industry, might be a source of beneficial riches, if an unfavorable balance were not created by the charge of keeping such possessions. – The *West Indies* are an example. *Second* – those, which, though yielding also a monopoly and a market, are principally lucrative, by means of the wealth which they heap on individuals, who transport and dissipate it within the superior state. This wealth is not only like the former, overbalanced by the cost of maintaining its sources, but resembles that drawn, not from industry, but from mines, and is productive of similar effects. – The *East Indies* are an example.

All dependent countries are to the superior state, not in the relation of children and parent, according to the common phrase, but in that of slave and master, and have a like influence on character. By rendering the labour of the one, the property of the other, they cherish pride, luxury, and vanity on one side; on the other, vice and servility, or hatred and revolt.

---

[17] James Madison, "Dependent Territories," *National Gazette* (Philadelphia, PA), December 12, 1791, http://docs.newsbank.com/openurl?ctx_ver=z39.88-2004&rft_id=info:sid/iw.newsbank.com:EANX&rft_val_format=info:ofi/fmt:kev:mtx:ctx&rft_dat=10EF5F3B256EE2C0&svc_dat=HistArchive:ahnpdoc&req_dat=0E8515E56BD9D19F. *PJM*, 17:559–60. Also published in *Dunlap's American Daily Advertiser* on January 4, 1792, and the *General Advertiser* on August 14, 1792.

For the NATIONAL GAZETTE.
MONEY.[18]

[OBSERVATIONS written *posterior to the circular* Address of Congress *in Sept.* 1779, *and prior to their Act of March*, 1780.][19]

IT has been taken for an axiom in all our reasonings on the subject of finance, that supposing the quantity and demand of things vendible in a country to remain the same, their price will vary according to the variation in the quantity of the circulating medium; in other words, that the value of money will be regulated by its quantity. I shall submit to the judgment of the public some considerations which determine mine to reject the proposition as founded in error. Should they be deemed not absolutely conclusive, they seem at least to shew that it is liable to too many exceptions and restrictions to be taken for granted as a fundamental truth.

If the circulating medium be of universal value as specie, a local increase or decrease of its quantity, will not, whilst a communication subsists with other countries, produce a correspondent rise or fall in its value. The reason is obvious. When a redundancy of universal money prevails in any one country, the holders of it know their interest too well to waste it in extravagant prices, when it would be worth so much more to them elsewhere. When a deficiency happens, those who hold commodities, rather than part with them at an undervalue in one country, would carry them to another. The variation of prices in these cases, cannot therefore exceed the expence and insurance of transportation.

Suppose a country totally unconnected with Europe, or with any other country, to possess specie in the same proportion to circulating property that Europe does; prices there would correspond with those in Europe. Suppose that so much specie were thrown into circulation as to make the quantity exceed the proportion of Europe tenfold, without any change in commodities, or in the demand for them: as soon as such an augmentation had produced its effect, prices would rise tenfold; or which is the same thing, money would be depreciated tenfold. In this state of things, suppose again, that a free and ready communication were

[18] James Madison, "Money," *National Gazette* (Philadelphia, PA), December 19, 1791, http://docs.newsbank.com/openurl?ctx_ver=z39.88-2004&rft_id=info:sid/iw.newsbank.com:EANX&rft_val_format=info:ofi/fmt:kev:mtx:ctx&rft_dat=10EF5F5CE60B6528&svc_dat=HistArchive:ahnpdoc&req_dat=0E8515E56BD9D19F. *PJM*, 1:302–5.

[19] Madison refers here to the Continental Congress' 1779 entreaty (penned by John Jay) to the states to support the American War for Independence with men, money, and materials. See William Jay, *The Life of John Jay: With Selections From His Correspondence and Miscellaneous Papers* (New York: J. J. Harper, 1833), I:476–90. Madison's reference to the Act of 1780 likely concerns the March 18 establishment by Congress of an exchange rate governing gold, silver, and bills (relating the last to the Spanish milled dollar). In Walter S. Franklin, *Resolutions, Laws, and Ordinances, Relating to the Pay, Half Pay, Commutation of Half Pay, Bounty Lands, and Other Promises Made by Congress to the Officers and Soldiers of the Revolution* (Washington, DC: T. Allen, 1838), 39.

opened between this country and Europe, and that the inhabitants of the former, were made sensible of the value of their money in the latter; would not its value among themselves immediately cease to be regulated by its quantity, and assimilate itself to the foreign value?

Mr. Hume in his discourse on the balance of trade supposes, "that if four fifths of all the money in Britain were annihilated in one night, and the nation reduced to the same condition, in this particular, as in the reigns of the Harrys and Edwards, that the price of all labour and commodities would sink in proportion, and every thing be sold as cheap as in those ages: That, again, if all the money in Britain were multiplied fivefold in one night, a contrary effect would follow." This very ingenious writer seems not to have considered that in the reigns of the Harrys and Edwards, the state of prices in the circumjacent nations corresponded with that of Britain; whereas in both of his suppositions, it would be no less than four fifths different. Imagine that such a difference really existed, and remark the consequence. Trade is at present carried on between Britain and the rest of Europe, at a profit of 15 or 20 per cent. Were that profit raised to 400 per cent. would not their home market, in case of such a fall of prices, be so exhausted by exportation – and in case of such a rise of prices, be so overstocked with foreign commodities, as immediately to restore the general equilibrium? Now, to borrow the language of the same author, "the same causes which would redress the inequality were it to happen, must forever prevent it, without some violent external operation."[20]

The situation of a country connected by commercial intercourse with other countries, may be compared to a single town or province whose intercourse with other towns and provinces results from political connection. Will it be pretended that if the national currency were to be accumulated in a single town or province, so as to exceed its due proportion five or tenfold, a correspondent depreciation would ensue, and every thing be sold five or ten times as dear as in a neighboring town or province?

If the circulating medium be a municipal one, as paper currency, still its value does not depend on its quantity. It depends on the credit of the state issuing it, and on the time of its redemption; and is no otherwise affected by the quantity, than as the quantity may be supposed to *endanger* or *postpone* the redemption.

That it depends in part on the credit of the issuer, no one will deny. If the credit of the issuer, therefore be perfectly unsuspected, the time of redemption alone will regulate its value.

To support what is here advanced, it is sufficient to appeal to the nature of paper money. It consists of bills or notes of obligation payable in specie to the bearer, either on demand or at a future day. Of the first kind is the paper currency of Britain, and hence its equivalence to specie. Of the latter kind is the paper currency of the United States, and hence its inferiority to specie. But if

[20] See David Hume, "Of the Balance of Trade," in *David Hume: Essays, Moral, Political, and Literary*, ed. Eugene F. Miller (Indianapolis: Liberty Classics, 1985), 312. Hume's actual wording is: "... the same cause, which redresses the inequality when it happens, must for ever prevent it, without some violent external operation."

its being redeemable not on demand but at a future day, be the cause of its inferiority, the distance of that day, and not its quantity, ought to be the measure of that inferiority.

It has been shewn that the value of specie does not fluctuate according to local fluctuations in its quantity. Great Britain, in which there is such an immensity of circulating paper, shews that the value of paper depends as little on its quantity as that of specie, when the paper represents specie payable on demand. Let us suppose that the circulating notes of Great Britain, instead of being payable on demand, were to be redeemed at a future day, at the end of one year for example, and that no interest was due on them. If the same assurance prevailed that at the end of the year they would be equivalent to specie, as now prevails that they are every moment equivalent, would any other effect result from such a change, except that the notes would suffer a depreciation equal to one year's interest? They would in that case represent, not the nominal sum expressed on the face of them, but the sum remaining after a deduction of one year's interest. But if when they represent the full nominal sum of specie, their circulation contributes no more to depreciate them, than the circulation of the specie itself would do; does it not follow, that if they represented a sum of specie less than the nominal inscription, their circulation ought to depreciate them no more than so much specie, if substituted, would depreciate itself? We may extend the time from one, to five, or to twenty years; but we shall find no other rule of depreciation than the loss of the intermediate interest.

What has been here supposed with respect to Great Britain has actually taken place in the United States. Being engaged in a necessary war without specie to defray the expence, or to support paper emissions for that purpose redeemable on demand, and being at the same time unable to borrow, no resource was left, but to emit bills of credit to be redeemed in future. The inferiority of these bills to specie was therefore incident to the very nature of them. If they had been exchangeable on demand for specie, they would have been equivalent to it; as they were not exchangeable on demand, they were inferior to it. The degree of their inferiority must consequently be estimated by the time of their becoming exchangeable for specie, that is the time of their redemption.

To make it still more palpable that the value of our currency does not depend on its quantity, let us put the case, that Congress had, during the first year of the war, emitted five millions of dollars to be redeemed at the end of ten years; that, during the second year of the war, they had emitted ten millions more, but with due security that the whole fifteen millions should be redeemed in five years; that, during the two succeeding years, they had augmented the emissions to one hundred millions, but from the discovery of some extraordinary sources of wealth, had been able to engage for the redemption of the whole sum in one year: it is asked, whether the depreciation, under these circumstances, would have increased as the quantity of money increased – or whether on the contrary, the money would not have risen in value, at every accession to its quantity?

[To be continued.]

For the NATIONAL GAZETTE.
MONEY.[21]

[OBSERVATIONS *written posterior to the circular* Address of Congress *in Sept.* 1779, *and prior to their Act of March*, 1780.]

[Concluded.]

IT has indeed happened, that a progressive depreciation of our currency has accompanied its growing quantity; and to this is probably owing in a great measure the prevalence of the doctrine here opposed. When the fact however is explained, it will be found to coincide perfectly with what has been said. Every one must have taken notice that, in the emissions of Congress, no precise time has been stipulated for their redemption, nor any specific provision made for that purpose. A general promise entitling the bearer to so many dollars of metal as the paper bills express, has been the only basis of their credit. Every one therefore has been left to his own conjectures as to the time the redemption would be fulfilled; and as every addition made to the quantity in circulation, would naturally be supposed to remove to a proportionally greater distance the redemption of the whole mass, it could not happen otherwise than that every additional emission would be followed by a further depreciation.

In like manner has the effect of a distrust of public credit, the other source of depreciation, been erroneously imputed to the quantity of money. The circumstances under which our early emissions were made, could not but strongly concur, with the futurity of their redemption, to debase their value. The situation of the United States resembled that of an individual engaged in an expensive undertaking, carried on, for want of cash, with bonds and notes secured on an estate to which his title was disputed; and who had besides, a combination of enemies employing every artifice to disparage that security. A train of sinister events during the early stages of the war likewise contributed to increase the distrust of the *public ability* to fulfil their engagements. Before the depreciation arising from this cause was removed by the success of our arms, and our alliance with France, it had drawn so large a quantity into circulation, that the quantity itself soon after begat a distrust of the *public disposition* to fulfil their engagements; as well as new doubts, in timid minds, concerning the issue of the contest. From that period, this cause of depreciation has been incessantly operating. It has first conduced to swell the amount of necessary emissions, and from that very amount has derived new force and

[21] James Madison, "Money," *National Gazette* (Philadelphia, PA), December 22, 1791, http://infoweb.newsbank.com/iw-search/we/HistArchive/?p_product=EANX&p_theme=ahnp&p_nbid=Q4CD53FHMTQxNTE0MzYxMS40OTEzNDE6MToxNDoxNTMuMTA0LjE1OS41MA&p_action=doc&s_lastnonissuequeryname=2&d_viewref=search&p_queryname=2&p_docnum=1&p_docref=v2:10E6125A1E3BBB18@EANX-10EF5F6CE6566078@2375565-10EF5F6D1E2CA7B8@1-10EF5F6DECFE6308@For%20the%20National%20Gazette.%20Money. *PJM*, 1:305–9.

efficacy to itself. Thus, a further discredit of our money has necessarily followed the augmentation of its quantity; but every one must perceive, that it has not been the effect of the quantity, considered in itself, but considered as an omen of public bankruptcy.[22,23]

Whether the money of a country, then, be gold and silver, or paper currency, it appears that its value is not regulated by its quantity. If it be the former, its

---

[22] This is Madison's footnote:

As the depreciation of our money has been ascribed to a wrong cause, so, it may be remarked, have effects been ascribed to the depreciation, which result from other causes. Money is the instrument by which men's wants are supplied, and many who possess it will part with it for that purpose, who would not gratify themselves at the expence of their visible property. Many also may acquire it, who have no visible property. By increasing the quantity of money therefore, you both increase the means of spending, and stimulate the desire to spend; and if the objects desired do not increase in proportion, their price must rise from the influence of the greater demand for them. Should the objects in demand happen, at the same juncture, as in the United States, to become scarcer, their prices must rise in a double proportion.

It is by this influence of an augmentation of money on demand, that we ought to account for that proportional level of money, in all countries, which Mr. Hume attributes to its direct influence on prices. When an augmentation of the national coin takes place, it may be supposed either, 1. not to augment demand at all; or, 2. to augment it so gradually that a proportional increase of industry will supply the objects of it; or, 3. to augment it so rapidly that the domestic market may prove inadequate, whilst the taste for distinction natural to wealth, inspires, at the same time, a preference for foreign luxuries. The first case can seldom happen. Were it to happen, no change in prices, nor any efflux of money, would ensue; unless indeed, it should be employed or loaned abroad. The superfluous portion would be either hoarded or turned into plate. The second case can occur only where the augmentation of money advances with a very slow and equable pace; and would be attended neither with a rise of prices, nor with a superfluity of money. The third is the only case, in which the plenty of money would occasion it to overflow into other countries. The insufficiency of the home market to satisfy the demand would be supplied from such countries as might afford the articles in demand; and the money would thus be drained off, till that and the demand excited by it, should fall to a proper level, and a balance be thereby restored between exports and imports.

The principle on which Mr. Hume's theory, and that of Montesquieu's before him, is founded, is manifestly erroneous. He considers the money in every country as the representative of the whole circulating property and industry in the country; and thence concludes, that every variation in its quantity must increase or lessen the portion which represents the same portion of property and labor. The error lies in supposing, that because money serves to measure the value of all things, it represents and is equal in value to all things. The circulating property in every country, according to its market rate, far exceeds the amount of its money. At Athens oxen, at Rome sheep, were once used as a measure of the value of other things. It will hardly be supposed, they were therefore equal in value to all other things.

[23] See Hume, "Of Money," 281–94. For an analysis of Hume's monetary theory, see *David Hume: Writings on Economics*, ed. Eugene Rotwein (London: Thomas Nelson, 1955), liv–lxvii; cf. Robert W. McGee and Barry University, "The Economic Thought of David Hume: A Pioneer in the Field of Law & Economics," *Hume Studies* 15, no. 1 (1989): 184–204. See also Montesquieu, *SOL*, 22:2, *passim*, especially Chapter 2, in which Montesquieu argued: "Metal is taken for this sign, as being durable, because it consumes but little by use; and because, without being destroyed, it is capable of many divisions ... The Athenians, not having the use of metals, made use of oxen, and the Romans of sheep; but one ox is not the same as another ox in the manner that one piece of metal may be the same as another."

value depends on the general proportion of gold and silver, to circulating property throughout all countries having free inter communication. If the latter, it depend[s] on the credit of the state issuing it, and the time at which it is to become equal to gold and silver.

Every circumstance which has been found to accelerate the depreciation of our currency naturally resolves itself into these general principles. The spirit of monopoly hath affected it in no other way than by creating an artificial scarcity of commodities wanted for public use, the consequence of which has been an increase of their price, and of the necessary emissions. Now it is this increase of emissions which has been shewn to lengthen the supposed period of their redemption, and to foster suspicions of public credit. Monopolies destroy the natural relation between money and commodities; but it is by raising the value of the latter, not by debasing that of the former. Had our money been gold or silver, the same prevalence of monopoly would have had the same effect on prices and expenditures; but these would not have had the same effect on the value of money.

The depreciation of our money has been charged on misconduct in the purchasing departments: but this misconduct must have operated in the same manner as the spirit of monopoly. By unnecessarily raising the price of articles required for public use, it has swelled the amount of necessary emissions, on which has depended the general opinion concerning the time and the probability of their redemption.

The same remark may be applied to the deficiency of imported commodities. The deficiency of these commodities has raised the price of them; the rise of their price has increased the emissions for purchasing them; and with the increase of emissions, have increased suspicions concerning their redemption.

Those who consider the quantity of money as the criterion of its value, compute the intrinsic depreciation of our currency by dividing the whole mass by the supposed necessary medium of circulation. Thus supposing the medium necessary for the United States to be 30,000,000 dollars, and the circulating emissions to be 200,000,000 the intrinsic difference between paper and specie will be nearly as 7 for 1. If its value depends on the time of its redemption, as hath been above maintained, the real difference will be found to be considerably less. Suppose the period necessary for its redemption to be 18 years, as seems to be understood by Congress; 100 dollars of paper 18 years hence will be equal in value to 100 dollars of specie; for at the end of that term, 100 dollars of specie may be demanded for them. They must consequently at this time be equal to as much specie as, with compound interest, will amount, in that number of years, to 100 dollars. If the interest of money be rated at 5 per cent. this present sum of specie will be about 41 1-2 dollars. Admit, however the use of money to be worth 6 per cent. about 35 dollars will then amount in 18 years to 100. 35 dollars of specie therefore is at this time equal to 100 of paper; that is, the man who would exchange his specie for paper at this discount, and lock it in his desk for 18 years, would get 6 per cent. for his money. The proportion of 100 to 35 is less than 3 to 1. The intrinsic depreciation of our money therefore, according to this rule of computation, is less than 3 to 1; instead of 7 to 1, according to the rule espoused in the circular address, or 30 or 40 to 1, according to its currency in the market.

I shall conclude with observing, that if the preceding principles and reasoning be just, the plan on which our domestic loans have been obtained, must have operated in a manner directly contrary to what was intended. A loan-office certificate differs in nothing from a common bill of credit, except in its higher denomination, and in the interest allowed on it; and the interest is allowed, merely as a compensation to the lender, for exchanging a number of small bills, which being easily transferable, are most convenient, for a single one so large as not to be transferable in ordinary transactions. As the certificates, however, do circulate in many of the more considerable transactions, it may justly be questioned, even on the supposition that the value of money depended on its quantity, whether the advantage to the public from the exchange, would justify the terms of it. But dismissing this consideration, I ask whether such loans do in any shape, lessen the public debt, and thereby render the discharge of it less suspected or less remote? Do they give any new assurance that a paper dollar will be one day equal to a silver dollar, or do they shorten the distance of that day? Far from it: The certificates constitute a part of the public debt no less than the bills of credit exchanged for them, and have an equal claim to redemption within the general period; nay, are to be paid off long before the expiration of that period, with bills of credit, which will thus return into the general mass, to be redeemed along with it. Were these bills, therefore, not to be taken out of circulation at all, by means of the certificates, not only the expence of offices for exchanging, reexchanging, and annually paying the interest, would be avoided; but the whole sum of interest would be saved, which must make a formidable addition to the public emissions, protract the period of their redemption, and proportionally increase their depreciation. No expedient could perhaps have been devised more preposterous and unlucky. In order to relieve public credit sinking under the weight of an enormous debt, we invent new expenditures. In order to raise the value of our money, which depends on the time of its redemption, we have recourse to a measure which removes its redemption to a more distant day. Instead of paying off the capital to the public creditors, we give them an enormous interest to change the name of the bit of paper which expresses the sum due to them; and think it a piece of dexterity in finance, *by emitting loan-office certificates*, to elude the necessity of *emitting bills of credit*.

PUBLIC OPINION.[24]

PUBLIC opinion sets bounds to every government, and is the real sovereign in every free one.

As there are cases where the public opinion must be obeyed by the government; so there are cases, where not being fixed, it may be influenced by the government. This distinction, if kept in view, would prevent or decide many debates on the respect due from the government to the sentiments of the people.

In proportion as government is influenced by opinion, it must be so, by whatever influences opinion. This decides the question concerning *a Constitutional Declaration of Rights*, which requires an influence on government, by becoming a part of the public opinion.

The larger a country, the less easy for its real opinion to be ascertained, and the less difficult to be counterfeited; when ascertained or presumed, the more respectable it is in the eyes of individuals. – This is favorable to the authority of government. For the same reason, the more extensive a country, the more insignificant is each individual in his own eyes. – This may be unfavorable to liberty.

Whatever facilitates a general intercourse of sentiments, as good roads, domestic commerce, a free press, and particularly *a circulation of newspapers through the entire body of the people*, and *Representatives going from, and returning among every part of them*, is equivalent to a contraction of territorial limits, and is favorable to liberty, where these may be too extensive.

[24] James Madison, "Public Opinion," *National Gazette* (Philadelphia, PA), December 19, 1791, http://docs.newsbank.com/openurl?ctx_ver=z39.88-2004&rft_id=info:sid/iw.newsbank.com:EANX&rft_val_format=info:ofi/fmt:kev:mtx:ctx&rft_dat=10EF5F5D041C5A58&svc_dat=HistArchive:ahnpdoc&req_dat=0E8515E56BD9D19F. *PJM*, 14:170. Also published in the *New-York Daily Gazette* on December 22, 1791.

GOVERNMENT.[25]

IN monarchies there is a two fold danger – 1st, That the eyes of a good prince cannot see all that he ought to know – 2d, That the hands of a bad one will not be tied by the fear of combinations against him. Both these evils increase with the extent of dominion; and prove, contrary to the received opinion, that monarchy is even more unfit for a great state, than for a small one, notwithstanding the greater tendency in the former to that species of government.

Aristocracies, on the other hand, are generally seen in small states: where a concentration of the public will is required by external danger, and that degree of concentration is found sufficient. The *many*, in such cases, cannot govern on account of emergencies which require the pr[omp]titude and precautions of a *few*; whilst the few themselves, resist the usurpations of a *single* tyrant. In Thessaly, a country intersected by mountainous barriers into a number of small cantons, the governments, according to Thucydides, were in most instances, oligarchical. Switzerland furnishes similar examples. – The smaller the state, the less intolerable is this form of government, its rigors being tempered by the facility and the fear of combinations among the people.

A republic involves the idea of popular rights. A representative republic *chuses* the wisdom, of which hereditary aristocracy has the *chance*; whilst it excludes the oppression of that form. And a confederated republic attains the force of monarchy, whilst it equally avoids the ignorance of a good prince, and the oppression of a bad one. To secure all the advantages of such a system, every good citizen will be at once a centinel over the rights of the people; over the authorities of the confederal government; and over both the rights and the authorities of the intermediate governments. Dec. 31.

[25] James Madison, "Government," *National Gazette* (Philadelphia, PA), January 2, 1792, http://docs.newsbank.com/openurl?ctx_ver=z39.88-2004&rft_id=info:sid/iw.newsbank.com:EANX&rft_val_format=info:ofi/fmt:kev:mtx:ctx&rft_dat=10EF5FAB606FF1B8&svc_dat=HistArchive:ahnpdoc&req_dat=0E8515E56BD9D19F. *PJM*, 14:178–79. Also published in *Dunlap's American Daly Advertiser* on January 4, 1792.

CHARTERS.[26]

IN Europe, charters of liberty have been granted by power. America has set the example and France has followed it, of charters of power granted by liberty. This revolution in the practice of the world, may, with an honest praise, be pronounced the most triumphant epoch of its history, and the most consoling presage of its happiness. We look back, already, with astonishment, at the daring outrages committed by despotism, on the reason and the rights of man; We look forward with joy, to the period, when it shall be despoiled of all its usurpations, and bound for ever in the chains, with which it had loaded its miserable victims.

In proportion to the value of this revolution; in proportion to the importance of instruments, every word of which decides a question between power and liberty; in proportion to the solemnity of acts, proclaiming the will, and authenticated by the seal of the people, the only earthly source of authority, ought to be the vigilance with which they are guarded by every citizen in private life, and the circumspection with which they are executed by every citizen in public trust.

As compacts, charters of government are superior in obligation to all others, because they give effect to all others. As trusts, none can be more sacred, because they are bound on the conscience by the religious sanctions of an oath. As metes and bounds of government, they transcend all other land-marks, because every public usurpation is an encroachment on the private right, not of one, but of all.

The citizens of the United States have peculiar motives to support the energy of their constitutional charters.

Having originated the experiment, their merit will be estimated by its success.

The complicated form of their political system, arising from the partition of government between the states and the union, and from the separations and subdivisions of the several departments in each, requires a more than common reverence for the authority which is to preserve order thro' the whole.

Being republicans, they must be anxious to establish the efficacy of popular charters, in defending liberty against power, and power against licentiousness: and in keeping every portion of power within its proper limits; by this means discomfiting the partizans of anti-republican contrivances for the purpose.

All power has been traced up to opinion. The stability of all governments and security of all rights may be traced to the same source. The most arbitrary

[26] James Madison, "Charters," *National Gazette* (Philadelphia, PA), January 19, 1792, http://docs.newsbank.com/openurl?ctx_ver=z39.88-2004&rft_id=info:sid/iw.newsbank.com:EANX&rft_-val_format=info:ofi/fmt:kev:mtx:ctx&rft_dat=10EF5FD4A1451A28&svc_dat=HistArchive:ahnpdoc&req_dat=0E8515E56BD9D19F. *PJM*, 14:191–92.

government is controuled where the public opinion is fixed. The despot of Constantinople dares not lay a new tax, because every slave thinks he ought not. The most systematic governments are turned by the slightest impulse from their regular path, when the public opinion no longer holds them in it. We see at this moment the *executive* magistrate of Great-Britain, exercising under the authority of the representatives of the *people*, a *legislative* power over the West-India commerce.

How devoutly is it to be wished, then, that the public opinion of the United States should be enlightened; that it should attach itself to their governments as delineated in the *great charters*, derived not from the usurped power of kings, but from the legitimate authority of the people; and that it should guarantee, with a holy zeal, these political scriptures from every attempt to add to or diminish from them. Liberty and order will never be *perfectly* safe, until a trespass on the constitutional provisions for either, shall be felt with the same keenness that resents an invasion of the dearest rights; until every citizen shall be an ARGUS to espy, and an ÆGEON to avenge, the unhallowed deed?[27]

Jan. 18.

[27] In Greek mythology, Argus (the "all seeing") was a many-eyed (perhaps one-hundred-eyed) monster used by the gods as a guard; Aegaeon (or Briareus), one of the Hekatoncheires, was a hundred-armed, fifty-headed sea monster, whom Thetis employed to protect Zeus from an attempt by the Olympian gods to put him in chains.

PARTIES.[28]

IN every political society, parties are unavoidable. A difference of interests, real or supposed, is the most natural and fruitful source of them. The great object should be to combat the evil: 1. By establishing a political equality among all. 2. By withholding *unnecessary* opportunities from a few, to increase the inequality of property, by an immoderate, and especially an unmerited, accumulation of riches. 3. By the silent operation of laws, which, without violating the rights of property, reduce extreme wealth towards a state of mediocrity, and raise extreme indigence towards a state of comfort. 4. By abstaining from measures which operate differently on different interests, and particularly such as favor one interest at the expence of another. 5. By making one party a check on the other, so far as the existence of parties cannot be prevented, nor their views accommodated. – If this is not the language of reason, it is that of republicanism.

In all political societies, different interests and parties arise out of the nature of things, and the great art of politicians lies in making them checks and balances to each other. Let us then increase these *natural distinctions* by favoring an inequality of property; and let us add to them *artificial distinctions*, by establishing *kings*, and *nobles*, and *plebeians*. We shall then have the more checks to oppose to each other: we shall then have the more scales and the more weights to perfect and maintain the equilibrium. This is as little the voice of reason, as it is that of republicanism.

From the expediency, in politics, of making natural parties, mutual checks on each other, to infer the propriety of creating artificial parties, in order to form them into mutual checks, is not less absurd than it would be in ethics, to say, that new vices ought to be promoted, where they would counteract each other, because this use may be made of existing vices.

[28] James Madison, "Parties," *National Gazette* (Philadelphia, PA), January 23, 1792, http://docs.newsbank.com/openurl?ctx_ver=z39.88-2004&rft_id=info:sid/iw.newsbank.com:EANX&rft_val_format=info:ofi/fmt:kev:mtx:ctx&rft_dat=10EF5FD68B0303E0&svc_dat=HistArchive:ahnpdoc&req_dat=0E8515E56BD9D19F. *PJM*, 14:197–98.

BRITISH GOVERNMENT.[29]

THE boasted equilibrium of this government, (so far as it is a reality) is maintained less by the distribution of its powers, than by the force of public opinion. If the nation were in favour of absolute monarchy, the public liberty would soon be surrendered by their representatives. If a republican form of government were preferred, how could the monarch resist the national will? Were the public opinion neutral only, and the public voice silent, ambition in the House of commons could wrest from him his prerogatives, or the avarice of its members, might sell to him its privileges.

The provision required for the civil list, at every accession of a king, shews at once his dependence on the representative branch, and its dependence on the public opinion. Were this establishment to be made from year to year, instead of being made for life (a change within the legislative power) the monarchy, unless maintained by corruption, would dwindle into a name. In the present temper of the nation, however, they would obstruct such a change, by taking side with their king, against their representatives.

Those who ascribe the preservation of the British government to the form in which its powers are distributed and balanced, forget the revolutions which it has undergone. – Compare its primitive with its present form.

A king at the head of 7 or 800 barons, sitting together in their own right, or (admitting another hypothesis) some in their own right, others as representatives of a few lesser barons, but still sitting together as a single House; and the judges holding their offices during the pleasure of the king; such was the British government at one period.

At present a king is seen at the head of a legislature, consisting of two Houses, each jealous of the other, one sitting in their own right, the other representing the people; and the judges forming a distinct and independent department.

In the first case the judiciary is annexed to the executive, and the legislature not even formed into separate branches: In the second, the legislative, executive and judiciary are distinct; and the legislative subdivided into rival branches.

What a contrast in these forms? If the latter be self balanced, the former could have no balance at all. Yet the former subsisted as well as the latter, and lasted longer than the latter, dating it from 1688, has been tried.

The former was supported by the opinion and circumstances of the times, like many of the intermediate variations, through which the government has passed; and as will be supported, the future forms through which it probably remains to be conducted, by the progress of reason, and change of circumstances. Jan.18.

[29] James Madison, "British Government," *National Gazette* (Philadelphia, PA), January 30, 1792, http://docs.newsbank.com/openurl?ctx_ver=z39.88-2004&rft_id=info:sid/iw.newsbank.com:EANX&rft_val_format=info:ofi/fmt:kev:mtx:ctx&rft_dat=10EF5FD9DCED8A80&svc_dat=HistArchive:ahnpdoc&req_dat=0E8515E56BD9D19F. *PJM*, 14:201–02. Also published in the *General Advertiser* on January 31, 1792.

For the NATIONAL GAZETTE
UNIVERSAL PEACE.[30]

AMONG the various reforms which have been offered to the world, the projects for universal peace have done the greatest honor to the hearts, though they seem to have done very little to the heads of their authors. Rousseau, the most distinguished of these philanthropists, has recommended a confederation of sovereigns, under a council of deputies, for the double purpose of arbitrating external controversies among nations, and of guaranteeing their respective governments against internal revolutions.[31] He was aware, neither of the impossibility of executing his pacific plan among governments which feel so many allurements to war, nor, what is more extraordinary, of the tendency of his plan to perpetuate arbitrary power wherever it existed; and, by extinguishing the hope of one day seeing an end of oppression, to cut off the only source of consolation remaining to the oppressed.

A universal and perpetual peace, it is to be feared, is in the catalogue of events, which will never exist but in the imaginations of visionary philosophers, or in the breasts of benevolent enthusiasts. It is still however true, that war contains so much folly, as well as wickedness, that much is to be hoped from the progress of reason; and if any thing is to be hoped, every thing ought to be tried.

Wars may be divided into two classes; one flowing from the mere will of the government, the other according with the will of the society itself.

Those of the first class can no otherwise be prevented than by such a reformation of the government, as may identify its will with the will of the society. The project of Rousseau was, consequently, as preposterous as it was impotent. Instead of beginning with an external application, and even precluding internal remedies, he ought to have commenced with, and chiefly relied on the latter prescription.

He should have said, whilst war is to depend on those whose ambition, whose revenge, whose avidity, or whose caprice may contradict the sentiment of the community, and yet be uncontrouled by it; whilst war is to be declared by

[30] James Madison, "Universal Peace," *National Gazette* (Philadelphia, PA), February 2, 1792, http://docs.newsbank.com/openurl?ctx_ver=z39.88-2004&rft_id=info:sid/iw.newsbank.com:EANX&rft_val_format=info:ofi/fmt:kev:mtx:ctx&rft_dat=10EF5FDB2E787B40&svc_-dat=HistArchive:ahnpdoc&req_dat=0E8515E56BD9D19F. *PJM*, 14:206–09. Also published in the *General Advertiser* on February 3, 1792, the *Federal Gazette/Philadelphia Evening Post* on February 4, 1792, the *Argus* on February 14, 1792, the *Norwich Packet* on February 16, 1792, and the *Diary/Loudon's Register* on April 10, 1792.

[31] Jean-Jacques Rousseau, *Extrait du Projet de Paix Perpétuelle de M. l'Abbé de Saint-Pierre* (Amsterdam, 1761). Rousseau's *Extrait* was a terse rewrite and revision of Charles Irénée Castel de Saint-Pierre's *Projet pour Rendre la Paix Perpétuelle en Europe* (1713).

those who are to spend the public money, not by those who are to pay it; by those who are to direct the public forces, not by those who are to support them; by those whose power is to be raised, not by those whose chains may be riveted the disease must continue to be *hereditary* like the government of which it is the offspring. A(s) the first step towards a cure, the government itself must be regenerated. Its will must be made subordinate to, or rather the same with, the will of the community.

Had Rousseau lived to see the constitutions of the United States and of France, his judgment might have escaped the censure to which his project has exposed it.

The other class of wars, corresponding with the public will, are less susceptible of remedy. There are antidotes, nevertheless, which may not be without their efficacy. As wars of the first class were to be prevented by subjecting the will of the government to the will of the society, those of the second, can only be controuled by subjecting the will of the society to the reason of the society; by establishing permanent and constitutional maxims of conduct, which may prevail over occasional impressions, and inconsiderate pursuits.

Here our republican philosopher might have proposed as a model to lawgivers, that war should not only be declared by the authority of the people, whose toils and treasures are to support its burdens, instead of the government which is to reap its fruits: but that each generation should be made to bear the burden of its own wars, instead of carrying them on, at the expence of other generations. And to give the fullest energy to his plan, he might have added, that each generation should not only bear its own burdens, but that the taxes composing them, should include a due proportion of such as by their direct operation keep the people awake, along with those, which being wrapped up in other payments, may leave them asleep, to misapplications of their money.

To the objection, if started, that where the benefits of war descend to succeeding generations, the burdens ought also to descend,[32] he might have answered: that the exceptions could not be easily made; that, if attempted, they must be made by one only of the parties interested; that in the alternative of sacrificing exceptions to general rules, or of converting exceptions into general rules, the former is the lesser evil; that the expense of *necessary* wars, will never exceed the resources of an *entire* generation; that, in fine, the objection vanishes before the *fact*, that in every nation which has drawn on posterity for the support of its wars, *the accumulated interest* of its perpetual debts, has soon become more than *a sufficient principal*, for all its exigencies.

---

[32] See Madison to Jefferson, February 4, 1790, *PJM*, 13:23. Cf. Jefferson to Madison, September 6, 1789, *PJM*, 12:382–88, 469. Cf. *Federalist* 49 and 50. See Adrienne Koch's analysis of the exchange between Jefferson and Madison on the theory of generational sovereignty in Koch, *Jefferson & Madison: The Great Collaboration* (New York: Oxford University Press, 1964), 62–96; cf. my treatment of the issue in *James Madison and the Spirit of Republican Self-Government*, 124–55.

Were a nation to impose such restraints on itself, avarice would be sure to calculate the expences of ambition; in the equipoise of these passions, reason would be free to decide for the public good; and an ample reward would accrue to the state, first, from the avoidance of all its wars of folly, secondly, from the vigor of its unwasted resources for wars of necessity and defence. Were all nations to follow the example, the reward would be doubled to each; and the temple of Janus[33] might be shut, never to be opened more.

Had Rousseau lived to see the rapid progress of reason and reformation, which the present day exhibits, the philanthropy which dictated his project would find a rich enjoyment in the scene before him: And after tracing the past frequency of wars to a will in the government independent of the will of the people; to the practice by each generation of taxing the principal of its debts on future generations; and to the facility with which each generation is seduced into assumptions of the interest, by the deceptive species of taxes which pay it; he would contemplate, in a reform of every government subjecting its will to that of the people, in a subjection of each generation to the payment of its own debts, and in a substitution of a more palpable, in place of an imperceptible mode of paying them, the only hope of UNIVERSAL AND PERPETUAL PEACE.

Philadelphia, January 31, 1792.

[33] The temple of Janus was part of the Roman forum, representing the god of beginnings and endings, after whom the month of January is named. The temple was equipped with double gates – one set at each end; the gates were kept open in times of war and closed in times of peace.

GOVERNMENT OF THE UNITED STATES.[34]

POWER being found by universal experience liable to abuses, a distribution of it into separate departments, has become a first principle of free governments. By this contrivance, the portion entrusted to the same hands being less, there is less room to abuse what is granted; and the different hands being interested, each in maintaining its own, there is less opportunity to usurp what is not granted. Hence the merited praise of governments modelled on a partition of their powers into legislative, executive, and judiciary, and a repartition of the legislative into different houses.

The political system of the United States claims still higher praise. The power delegated by the people is first divided between the general government and the state governments; each of which is then subdivided into legislative, executive, and judiciary departments. And as in a single government these departments are to be kept separate and safe, by a defensive armour for each; so, it is to be hoped, do the two governments possess each the means of preventing or correcting unconstitutional encroachments of the other.

Should this improvement on the theory of free government not be marred in the execution, it may prove the best legacy ever left by lawgivers to their country, and the best lesson ever given to the world by its benefactors. If a security against power lies in the division of it into parts mutually controuling each other, the security must increase with the increase of the parts into which the whole can be conveniently formed.

It must not be denied that the *task* of forming and maintaining a division of power between different governments, is greater than among different departments of the same government; because it may be more easy (though sufficiently difficult) to separate, by proper definitions, the legislative, executive, and judiciary powers, which are more distinct in their nature, than to discriminate, by precise enumerations, one class of legislative powers from another class, one class of executive from another class, and one class of judiciary from another class; where the powers being of a more kindred nature, their boundaries are more obscure and run more into each other.

If the task be difficult, however, it must by no means be abandoned. Those who would pronounce it impossible, offer no alternative to their country but schism, or consolidation; both of them bad, but the latter the worst, since it

[34] James Madison, "Government of the United States," *National Gazette* (Philadelphia, PA), February 6, 1792, http://docs.newsbank.com/openurl?ctx_ver=z39.88-2004&rft_id=info:sid/iw.newsbank.com:EANX&rft_val_format=info:ofi/fmt:kev:mtx:ctx&rft_dat=10EF5FDD7A888AF8&svc_dat=HistArchive:ahnpdoc&req_dat=0E8515E56BD9D19F. *PJM*, 14:217–19. Also published in *Dunlap's American Daily Advertiser* on February 7, 1792, the *General Advertiser* on February 7, 1792, and the *Diary/Loudon's Register* on May 23, 1792.

is the high road to monarchy, than which nothing worse, in the eye of republicans, could result from the anarchy implied in the former.

Those who love their country, its repose, and its republicanism, will therefore study to avoid the alternative, by elucidating and guarding the limits which define the two governments; by inculcating moderation in the exercise of the powers of both, and particularly a mutual abstinence from such as might nurse present jealousies, or engender greater.

In bestowing the eulogies due to the partitions and internal checks of power, it ought not the less to be remembered, that they are neither the sole nor the chief palladium of constitutional liberty. The people who are the authors of this blessing, must also be its guardians. Their eyes must be ever ready to mark, their voice to pronounce, and their arm to repel or repair aggressions on the authority of their constitutions; the highest authority next to their own, because the immediate work of their own, and the most sacred part of their property, as recognising and recording the title to every other. Feb. 4.

For the NATIONAL GAZETTE.
SPIRIT OF GOVERNMENTS.[35]

NO Government is perhaps reducible to a sole principle of operation. Where the theory approaches nearest to this character, different and often heterogeneous principles mingle their influence in the administration. It is useful nevertheless to analyse the several kinds of government, and to characterize them by the spirit which predominates in each.

Montesquieu has resolved the great operative principles of government into fear, honor, and virtue, applying the first to pure despotisms, the second to regular monarchies, and the third to republics.[36] The portion of truth blended with the ingenuity of this system, sufficiently justifies the admiration bestowed on its author. Its accuracy however can never be defended against the criticisms which it has encountered. Montesquieu was in politics not a Newton or a Locke, who established immortal systems, the one in matter, the other in mind. He was in his particular science what Bacon was in universal science: He lifted the veil from the venerable errors which enslaved opinion, and pointed the way to those luminous truths of which he had but a glimpse himself.

May not governments be properly divided, according to their predominant spirit and principles into three species of which the following are examples?

First. A government operating by a permanent military force, which at once maintains the government, and is maintained by it; which is at once the cause of burdens on the people, and of submission in the people to their burdens. Such have been the governments under which human nature has groaned through every age. Such are the governments which still oppress it in almost every country of Europe, the quarter of the globe which calls itself the pattern of civilization, and the pride of humanity.

Secondly. A government operating by corrupt influence; substituting the motive of private interest in place of public duty; converting its pecuniary dispensations into bounties to favorites, or bribes to opponents; accommodating its measures to the avidity of a part of the nation instead of the benefit of the whole: in a word, enlisting an army of interested partizans, whose tongues, whose pens, whose intrigues, and whose active combinations, by supplying the terror of the sword, may support a real domination of the few, under an apparent liberty of the many. Such a government, wherever to be found, is an

[35] James Madison, "Spirit of Governments," *National Gazette* (Philadelphia, PA), February 20, 1792, http://docs.newsbank.com/openurl?ctx_ver=z39.88-2004&rft_id=info:sid/iw.newsbank.com:EANX&rft_val_format=info:ofi/fmt:kev:mtx:ctx&rft_dat=10EF5FE58113 5EF8&svc_dat=HistArchive:ahnpdoc&req_dat=0E8515E56BD9D19F. *PJM*, 14:233–34. Also published in the *General Advertiser* on February 21, 1792, and the *Daily Advertiser* on February 23, 1792.

[36] Montesquieu, *SOL*, 3:3–9, 20–27.

imposter. It is happy for the new world that it is not on the west side of the Atlantic. It will be both happy and honorable for the United States, if they never descend to mimic the costly pageantry of its form, nor betray themselves into the venal spirit of its administration.

Thirdly. A government, deriving its energy from the will of the society, and operating by the reason of its measures, on the understanding and interest of the society. Such is the government for which philosophy has been searching, and humanity been sighing, from the most remote ages. Such are the republican governments which it is the glory of America to have invented, and her unrivalled happiness to possess. May her glory be compleated by every improvement on the theory which experience may teach; and her happiness be perpetuated by a system of administration corresponding with the purity of the theory.

February 18, 1792.

For the NATIONAL GAZETTE.
Republican distribution of Citizens.[37]

A PERFECT theory on this subject would be useful, not because it could be reduced to practice by any plan of legislation, or ought to be attempted by violence on the will or property of individuals: but because it would be a monition against empirical experiments by power, and a model to which the free choice of occupations by the people, might gradually approximate the order of society.

The best distribution is that which would most favor *health, virtue, intelligence* and *competency* in the *greatest number* of citizens. It is needless to add to these objects, *liberty* and *safety*. The first is presupposed by them. The last must result from them.

The life of the husbandman is pre-eminently suited to the comfort and happiness of the individual. *Health*, the first of blessings, is an appurtenance of his property and his employment. *Virtue*, the health of the soul, is another part of his patrimony, and no less favored by his situation. *Intelligence* may be cultivated in this as well as in any other walk of life. If the mind be less susceptible of polish in retirement than in a croud, it is more capable of profound and comprehensive efforts. Is it more ignorant of some things? It has a compensation in its ignorance of others. *Competency is* more universally the lot of those who dwell in the country, when liberty is at the same time their lot. The extremes both of want and of waste have other abodes. 'Tis not the country that peoples either the Bridewells or the Bedlams.[38] These mansions of wretchedness are tenanted from the distresses and vices of overgrown cities.[39]

The condition, to which the blessings of life are most denied is that of the sailor. His health is continually assailed and his span shortened by the stormy element to which he belongs. His virtue, at no time aided, is occasionally exposed to every scene that can poison it. His mind, like his body, is imprisoned within the bark that transports him. Though traversing and circumnavigating

---

37 James Madison, "Republican Distribution of Citizens," *National Gazette* (Philadelphia, PA), March 5, 1792, http://docs.newsbank.com/openurl?ctx_ver=z39.88-2004&rft_id=info:sid/iw.newsbank.com:EANX&rft_val_format=info:ofi/fmt:kev:mtx:ctx&rft_dat=10EF5FEC78877A78&svc_dat=HistArchive:ahnpdoc&req_dat=0E8515E56BD9D19F. *PJM*, 14:244–46. Also published in the *General Advertiser* on March 6, 1792, the *Freeman's Journal/North-American Intelligencer* on March 7, 1792, the *Diary/Loudon's Register* on March 16, 1792, the *National Aegis* on January 16, 1811, and the *Vermont Gazette* on April 6, 1792.

38 Bridewell was a prison and poorhouse and Bedlam was a notorious insane asylum in England.

39 Thomas Jefferson gave perhaps the best classic expression of the virtues of farming and the cherished place an agrarian lifestyle should hold in the political economy: "Those who labour the earth are the chosen people of God. The mobs of great cities add just so much support to the government, as sores do to the strength of the body" (*Jefferson Writings: Autobiography, Notes on the State of Virginia Public and Private Papers, Addresses, Letters*, ed. Merrill D. Peterson [New York: Library of America, 1984], 290–91).

the globe, he sees nothing but the same vague objects of nature, the same monotonous occurrences in ports and docks; and at home in his vessel, what new ideas can shoot from the unvaried use of the ropes and the rudder, or from the society of comrades as ignorant as himself. In the supply of his wants he often feels a scarcity, seldom more than a bare sustenance; and if his ultimate prospects do not embitter the present moment, it is because he never looks beyond it. How unfortunate, that in the intercourse, by which nations are enlightened and refined, and their means of safety extended, the immediate agents should be distinguished by the hardest condition of humanity.

The great interval between the two extremes, is, with a few exceptions, filled by those who work the materials furnished by the earth in its natural or cultivated state.

It is fortunate in general, and particularly for this country, that so much of the ordinary and most essential consumption, takes place in fabrics which can be prepared in every family, and which constitute in deed the natural ally of agriculture. The former is the work within doors, as the latter is without; and each being done by hands or at times, that can be spared from the other, the most is made of every thing.

The class of citizens who provide at once their own food and their own raiment, may be viewed as the most truly independent and happy. They are more: they are the best basis of public liberty, and the strongest bulwark of public safety. It follows, that the greater the proportion of this class to the whole society, the more free, the more independent, and the more happy must be the society itself.

In appreciating the regular branches of manufacturing and mechanical industry, their tendency must be compared with the principles laid down, and their merits graduated accordingly. Whatever is least favorable to vigor of body, to the faculties of the mind, or to the virtues or the utilities of life, instead of being forced or fostered by public authority, ought to be seen with regret as long as occupations more friendly to human happiness, lie vacant.

The several professions of more elevated pretensions, the merchant, the lawyer, the physician, the philosopher, the divine, form a certain proportion of every civilized society, and readily adjust their numbers to its demands, and its circumstances.

March 3.

For the NATIONAL GAZETTE.
FASHION.[40]

AN humble address has been lately presented to the Prince of Wales by the BUCKLE MANUFACTURERS of Birmingham, Wassal, Wolverhampton, and their environs, stating that the BUCKLE TRADE gives employment to more than TWENTY THOUSAND persons, numbers of whom, in consequence of the prevailing fashion of SHOESTRINGS & SLIPPERS, are at present without employ, almost destitute of bread, and exposed to the horrors of want at the most inclement season; that to the manufactures of BUCKLES and BUTTONS, Birmingham owes its important figure on the map of England; that it is to no purpose to address FASHION herself, she being void of feeling and deaf to argument, but fortunately accustomed to listen to his voice, and to obey his commands: and finally, IMPLORING his Royal Highness to consider the deplorable condition of their trade, which is in danger of being ruined by the *mutability of fashion*, and to give that direction to the *public taste*, which will insure the lasting gratitude of the petitioners.[41]

Several important reflections are suggested by this address.

I. The most precarious of all occupations which give bread to the industrious, are those depending on mere fashion, which generally changes so suddenly, and often so considerably, as to throw whole bodies of people out of employment.

II. Of all occupations those are the least desirable in a free state, which produce the most servile dependence of one class of citizens on another class. This dependence must increase as the *mutuality* of wants is diminished. Where the wants on one side are the absolute necessaries; and on the other are neither absolute necessaries, nor result from the habitual œconomy of life, but are the mere caprices of fancy, the evil is in its extreme; or if not,

III. The extremity of the evil must be in the case before us, where the absolute necessaries depend on the caprices of fancy, and the caprice of a single fancy directs the fashion of the community. Here the dependence sinks to the lowest

[40] James Madison, "Fashion," *National Gazette* (Philadelphia, PA), March 22, 1792, http://docs.newsbank.com/openurl?ctx_ver=z39.88-2004&rft_id=info:sid/iw.newsbank.com:EANX&rft_val_format=info:ofi/fmt:kev:mtx:ctx&rft_dat=10EF5FF5F82E1480&svc_dat=HistArchive:ahnpdoc&req_dat=0E8515E56BD9D19F. *PJM*, 14:257–59. Also published in the *Essex Journal* on April 11, 1792, and the *Columbian Centinel* on April 25, 1792.

[41] By the late eighteenth century, shoestrings rather than buckles had become the prevalent fashion in England. In 1791, distressed buckle manufacturers petitioned the Prince of Wales (later George IV) to do what he could to revive their trade. The Prince himself resumed wearing buckles on his shoes and decreed that no shoe should be tied by strings in his household. Despite his efforts, his attempt to set a new fashion among the English failed and the buckle industry did not recover.

point of servility. We see a proof of it in the *spirit* of the address. *Twenty thousand* persons are to get or go without their bread, as a wanton youth, may fancy to wear his shoes with or without straps, or to fasten his straps with strings or with buckles. Can any despotism be more cruel than a situation, in which the existence of thousands depends on one will, and that will on the most slight and fickle of all motives, a mere whim of the imagination.

IV. What a contrast is here to the independent situation and manly sentiments of American citizens, who live on their own soil, or whose labour is necessary to its cultivation, or who were occupied in supplying wants, which being founded in solid utility, in comfortable accommodation, or in settled habits, produce a reciprocity of dependence, at once ensuring subsistence, and inspiring a dignified sense of social rights.

V. The condition of those who receive employment and bread from the precarious source of fashion and superfluity, is a lesson to nations, as well as to individuals. In proportion as a nation consists of that description of citizens, and depends on external commerce, it is dependent on the consumption and caprice of other nations. If the laws of propriety did not forbid, the manufacturers of Birmingham, Wassal, and Wolverhampton, had as real an interest in supplicating the arbiters of fashion in America, as the patron they have addressed. The dependence in the case of nations is even greater than among individuals of the same nation: for besides the *mutability of fashion* which is the same in both, the *mutability of policy* is another source of danger in the former. March 20.

For the NATIONAL GAZETTE.
PROPERTY.[42]

THIS term in its particular application means "that dominion which one man claims and exercises over the external things of the world, in exclusion of every other individual."[43]

In its larger and juster meaning, it embraces every thing to which a man may attach a value and have a right; and *which leaves to every one else the like advantage*,

In the former sense, a man's land, or merchandize, or money is called his property.

In the latter sense, a man has a property in his opinions and the free communication of them.

He has a property of peculiar value in his religious opinions, and in the profession and practice dictated by them.

He has a property very dear to him in the safety and liberty of his person.

He has an equal property in the free use of his faculties and free choice of the objects on which to employ them.

In a word, as a man is said to have a right to his property, he may be equally said to have a property in his rights.

Where an excess of power prevails, property of no sort is duly respected. No man is safe in his opinions, his person, his faculties, or his possessions.

Where there is an excess of liberty, the effect is the same, tho' from an opposite cause.

Government is instituted to protect property of every sort; as well that which lies in the various rights of individuals, as that which the term particularly expresses. This being the end of government, that alone is a *just* government, which *impartially* secures to every man, whatever is his *own*.

According to this standard of merit, the praise of affording a just security to property, should be sparingly bestowed on a government 'which, however scrupulously guarding the possessions of individuals, does not protect them in

[42] James Madison, "Property," *National Gazette* (Philadelphia, PA), March 29, 1792, http://docs.newsbank.com/openurl?ctx_ver=z39.88-2004&rft_id=info:sid/iw.newsbank.com:EANX&rft_val_format=info:ofi/fmt:kev:mtx:ctx&rft_dat=10EF5FF9A5A66716&svc_dat=HistArchive:ahnpdoc&req_dat=0E8515E56BD9D19F. *PJM*, 14:266–68.

[43] Sir William Blackstone, *Commentaries on the Laws of England in Four Books. Notes Selected From the Editions of Archibold, Christian, Coleridge, Chitty, Stewart, Kerr, and Others, Barron Field's Analysis, and Additional Notes, and a Life of the Author by George Sharswood. In Two Volumes* (Philadelphia: J. B. Lippincott, 1893), http://oll.libertyfund.org/titles/2141. Blackstone wrote that the right of property is the "sole and despotic dominion which one man claims and exercises over the external things of the world, in total exclusion of the right of any other individual in the universe."

the enjoyment and communication of their opinions, in which they have an equal, and in the estimation of some, a more valuable property.

More sparingly should this praise be allowed to a government, where a man's religious rights are violated by penalties, or fettered by tests, or taxed by a hierarchy. Conscience is the most sacred of all property; other property depending in part on positive law, the exercise of that, being a natural and unalienable right. To guard a man's house as his castle, to pay public and enforce private debts with the most exact faith, can give no title to invade a man's conscience which is more sacred than his castle, or to withhold from it that debt of protection, for which the public faith is pledged, by the very nature and original conditions of the social pact.

That is not a just government, nor is property secure under it, where the property which a man has in his personal safety and personal liberty, is violated by arbitrary seizures of one class of citizens for the service of the rest. A magistrate issuing his warrants to a press gang, would be in his proper functions in Turkey or Indostan, under appellations proverbial of the most compleat despotism.

That is not a just government, nor is property secure under it, where arbitrary restrictions, exemptions, and monopolies deny to part of its citizens that free use of their faculties, and free choice of their occupations, which not only constitute their property in the general sense of the word; but are the means of acquiring property strictly so called. What must be the spirit of legislation where a manufacturer of linen cloth is forbidden to bury his own child in a linen shroud, in order to favour his neighbour who manufactures woolen cloth; where the manufacturer and wearer of woolen cloth are again forbidden the æconomical use of buttons of that material, in favor of the manufacturer of buttons of other materials!

A just security to property is not afforded by that government, under which unequal taxes oppress one species of property and reward another species: where arbitrary taxes invade the domestic sanctuaries of the rich, and excessive taxes grind the faces of the poor; where the keenness and competitions of want are deemed an insufficient spur to labor, and taxes are again applied, by an unfeeling policy, as another spur; in violation of that sacred property, which Heaven, in decreeing man to earn his bread by the sweat of his brow, kindly reserved to him, in the small repose that could be spared from the supply of his necessities.

If there be a government then which prides itself in maintaining the inviolability of property; which provides that none shall be taken *directly* even for public use without indemnification to the owner, and *yet directly* violates the property which individuals have in their opinions, their religion, their persons, and their faculties; nay more, which *indirectly* violates their property, in their actual possessions, in the labor that acquires their daily subsistence, and in the hallowed remnant of time which ought to relieve their fatigues and soothe their cares, the influence will have been anticipated, that such a government is not a pattern for the United States.

If the United States mean to obtain or deserve the full praise due to wise and just governments, they will equally respect the rights of property, and the property in rights: they will rival the government that most sacredly guards the former; and by repelling its example in violating the latter, will make themselves a pattern to that and all other governments.

March 27.

For the NATIONAL GAZETTE.

THE UNION.

Who are its real friends?[44]

NOT those who charge others with not being its friends, whilst their own conduct is wantonly multiplying its enemies.

Not those who favor measures, which by pampering the spirit of speculation within and without the government, disgust the best friends of the Union.

Not those who promote unnecessary accumulations of the debt of the Union, instead of the best means of discharging it as fast as possible; thereby encreasing the causes of corruption in the government, and the pretexts for new taxes under its authority, the former undermining the confidence, the latter alienating the affection of the people.

Not those who study, by arbitrary interpretations and insidious precedents, to pervert the limited government of the Union, into a government of unlimited discretion, contrary to the will and subversive of the authority of the people.

Not those who avow or betray principles of monarchy and aristocracy, in opposition to the republican principles of the Union, and the republican spirit of the people; or who espouse a system of measures more accommodated to the depraved examples of those hereditary forms, than to the true genius of our own.

Not those, in a word, who would force on the people the melancholy duty of chusing between the loss of the Union, and the loss of what the union was meant to secure.

The real FRIENDS *to the Union are those,*

Who are friends to the authority of the people, the sole foundation on which the Union rests.

Who are friends to liberty, the great end, for which the Union was formed.

Who are friends to the limited and republican system of government, the means provided by that authority, for the attainment of that end.

Who are enemies to every public measure that might smooth the way to hereditary government; for resisting the tyrannies of which the Union was first planned, and for more effectually excluding which, it was put into its present form.

Who considering a public debt as injurious to the interests of the people, and baneful to the virtue of the government, are enemies to every contrivance for

[44] James Madison, "The Union. Who Are Its Real Friends?" *National Gazette* (Philadelphia, PA), April 2, 1792, http://docs.newsbank.com/openurl?ctx_ver=z39.88-2004&rft_id=info:sid/iw.newsbank.com:EANX&rft_val_format=info:ofi/fmt:kev:mtx:ctx&rft_dat=10EF5FFBD922DC38&svc_dat=HistArchive:ahnpdoc&req_dat=0E8515E56BD9D19F. *PJM*, 14:274–75. Also published in the *Argus* on April 27, 1792, and the *Diary/Loudon's Register* on April 10, 1792.

unnecessarily increasing its amount, or protracting its duration, or extending its influence.

In a word, those are the real friends to the Union, who are friends to that republican policy throughout, which is the only *cement* for the Union of a republican people; in opposition to a spirit of usurpation and monarchy, which is the *menstruum* most capable of dissolving it. March 31.

For the NATIONAL GAZETTE.
A *candid State of* PARTIES.[45]

AS it is the business of the contemplative statesman to trace the history of parties in a free country, so it is the duty of the citizen at all times to understand the actual state of them. Whenever this duty is omitted, an opportunity is given to designing men, by the use of artificial or nominal distinctions, to oppose and balance against each other those who never differed as to the end to be pursued, and may no longer differ as to the means of attaining it. The most interesting state of parties in the United States may be referred to three periods: Those who espoused the cause of independence and those who adhered to the British claims, formed the parties of the first period; if, indeed, the disaffected class were considerable enough to deserve the name of a party. This state of things was superseded by the treaty of peace in 1783. From 1783 to 1787 there were parties in abundance, but being rather local than general, they are not within the present review.

The Federal Constitution, proposed in the latter year, gave birth to a second and most interesting division of the people. Every one remembers it, because every one was involved in it.

Among those who embraced the constitution, the great body were unquestionably friends to republican liberty; tho' there were, no doubt, some who were openly or secretly attached to monarchy and aristocracy; and hoped to make the constitution a cradle for these hereditary establishments.

Among those who opposed the constitution, the great body were certainly well affected to the union and to good government, tho' there might be a few who had a leaning unfavourable to both. This state of parties was terminated by the regular and effectual establishment of the federal government in 1788; out of the administration of which, however, has arisen a third division, which being natural to most political societies, is likely to be of some duration in ours.

One of the divisions consists of those, who from particular interest, from natural temper, or from the habits of life, are more partial to the opulent than to the other classes of society; and having debauched themselves into a persuasion that mankind are incapable of governing themselves, it follows with them, of course, that government can be carried on only by the pageantry of rank, the influence of money and emoluments, and the terror of military force. Men of those sentiments must naturally wish to point the measures of government less to the interest of the many than of a few, and less to the reason of the many than to their weaknesses; hoping perhaps in proportion to the

45 James Madison, "A Candid State of Parties," *National Gazette* (Philadelphia, PA), September 26, 1792, http://docs.newsbank.com/openurl?ctx_ver=z39.88-2004&rft_id=info:sid/iw.newsbank.com:EANX&rft_val_format=info:ofi/fmt:kev:mtx:ctx&rft_dat=10EF605ED29E3088&svc_dat=HistArchive:ahnpdoc&req_dat=0E8515E56BD9D19F. *PJM*, 14:370–72.

ardor of their zeal, that by giving such a turn to the administration, the government itself may by degrees be narrowed into fewer hands, and approximated to an hereditary form.

The other division consists of those who believing in the doctrine that mankind are capable of governing themselves, and hating hereditary power as an insult to the reason and an outrage to the rights of man, are naturally offended at every public measure that does not appeal to the understanding and to the general interest of the community, or that is not strictly conformable to the principles, and conducive to the preservation of republican government.

This being the real state of parties among us, an experienced and dispassionate observer will be at no loss to decide on the probable conduct of each.

The antirepublican party, as it may be called, being the weaker in point of numbers, will be induced by the most obvious motives to strengthen themselves with the men of influence, particularly of moneyed, which is the most active and insinuating influence. It will be equal their true policy to weaken their opponents by reviving exploded parties, and taking advantage of all prejudices, local, political, and occupational, that may prevent or disturb a general coalition of sentiments.

The Republican party, as it may be termed, conscious that the mass of people in every part of the union, in every state, and of every occupation must at bottom be with them, both in interest and sentiment, will naturally find their account in burying all antecedent questions, in banishing every other distinction than that between enemies and friends to republican government, and in promoting a general harmony among the latter, wherever residing, or however employed.

Whether the republican or the rival party will ultimately establish its ascendance, is a problem which may be contemplated now; but which time alone can solve. On one hand experience shews that in politics as in war, stratagem is often an overmatch for numbers: and among more happy characteristics of our political situation, it is now well understood that there are peculiarities, some temporary, others more durable, which may favour that side in the contest. On the republican side, again, the superiority of numbers is so great, their sentiments are so decided, and the practice of making a common cause, where there is a common sentiment and common interest, in spight of circumstancial and artificial distinctions, is so well understood, that no temperate observer of human affairs will be surprised if the issue in the present instance should be reversed, and the government be administered in the spirit and form approved by the great body of the people.

Philadelphia, Sept. 22.

For the NATIONAL GAZETTE
WHO ARE THE BEST KEEPERS OF THE PEOPLE'S LIBERTIES?[46]

Republican. – *The* people themselves. – The sacred trust can be no where so safe as in the hands most interested in preserving it.

Anti-republican. – *The* people are stupid, suspicious, licentious. They cannot safely trust themselves. When they have established government they should think of nothing but obedience, leaving the care of their liberties to their wiser rulers.

Republican. – *Although* all men are born free, and all nations might be so, yet too true it is, that slavery has been the general lot of the human race. Ignorant – they have been cheated; asleep – they have been surprized; divided – the yoke has been forced upon them.[47] But what is the lesson? That because the people *may* betray themselves, they ought to give themselves up, blindfold, to those who have an interest in betraying them? Rather conclude that the people ought to be enlightened, to be awakened, to be united, that after establishing a government they should watch over it, as well as obey it.

Anti-republican. – *You* look at the surface only, where errors float, instead of fathoming the depths where truth lies hid. It is not the government that is disposed to fly off from the people; but the people that are ever ready to fly off from the government. Rather say then, enlighten the government, warn it to be vigilant, enrich it with influence, arm it with force, and to the people never pronounce but two words – *Submission* and *Confidence.*

Republican. – The centrifugal tendency then is in the people, not in the government, and the secret art lies in restraining the tendency, by augmenting the attractive principle of the government with all the weight that can be added to it. What a perversion of the natural order of things! to make *power* the primary and central object of the social system, and *Liberty* but its satellite.

[46] James Madison, "Who Are the Best Keepers of the People's Liberties?" *National Gazette* (Philadelphia, PA), December 22, 1792, http://docs.newsbank.com/openurl?ctx_ver=z39.88-2004&rft_id=info:sid/iw.newsbank.com:EANX&rft_val_format=info:ofi/fmt:kev:mtx:ctx&rft_dat=10EF5F2CC631E448&svc_dat=HistArchive:ahnpdoc&req_dat=0E8515E56BD9D19F. *PJM*, 14:426–27. Also published in the *Argus* on January 8, 1793.

[47] Madison is clearly invoking Rousseau's famous opening lines of the *Social Contract*: "Man is born free, and everywhere he is in chains. One who believes himself the master of others is nonetheless a greater slave than they." See Jean-Jacques Rousseau, "On the Social Contract," in *Social Contract, Discourse on the Virtue Most Necessary for a Hero, Political Fragments, and Geneva Manuscript*, trans. Judith R. Bush, Roger D. Masters, and Christopher Kelly, eds. Roger D. Masters and Christopher Kelly, vol. 4 of *The Collected Writings of Rousseau*, eds. Roger D. Masters and Christopher Kelly (Hanover: University Press of New England, 1994), 131; the allusion to Rousseau's phraseology is intended to prepare readers for a substantially different analysis than the Genevan offered.

Anti-republican. – *The* science of the stars can never instruct you in the mysteries of government. Wonderful as it may seem, the more you increase the attractive force of power, the more you enlarge the sphere of liberty; the more you make government independent and hostile towards the people, the better security you provide for their rights and interests. Hence the wisdom of the theory, which, after limiting the share of the people to a third of the government, and lessening the influence of that share by the mode and term of delegating it, establishes two grand hereditary orders, with feelings, habits, interests, and prerogatives all inveterately hostile to the rights and interests of the people, yet by *a mysterious* operation all combining to fortify the people in both.[48]

Republican. – Mysterious indeed! – But mysteries belong to religion, not to government; to the ways of the Almighty, not to the works of man. And in religion itself there is nothing mysterious to its author; the mystery lies in the dimness of the human sight. So in the institutions of man let there be no mystery, unless for those inferior beings endowed with a ray perhaps of the twilight vouchsafed to the first order of terrestrial creation.

Anti-republican. – You are destitute, I perceive, of every quality of a good citizen, or rather of a good *subject.* You have neither the light of faith nor the spirit of obedience. I denounce you to the government as an accomplice of atheism and anarchy.

Republican. – And I forbear to denounce you to the people, though a blasphemer of their rights and an idolater of tyranny. – Liberty disdains to persecute.

Dec. 20.

[48] The "Anti-republican" Madison ridicules for searching for "the mysteries of government" in the "science of the stars" (as well as by "fathoming the depths") bears no small resemblance to John Adams and his argument in the chapter on "Dr. Franklin" in the *Defence*. Adams defended bicameralism against Benjamin Franklin's advocacy of unicameralism via an appeal to James Harrington's cosmology. In response to Franklin's advocacy of unicameralism, Harrington may have remarked (as he did when he offered the example of two girls dividing a cake): "O! the depth of the wisdom of God, which, in the simple invention of a carter, has revealed to mankind the whole mystery of a commonwealth; which consists ... in dividing and equalizing forces. ..." For Adams, Franklin ignored the "centripetal and centrifugal forces by which the heavenly bodies are continued in their orbits, instead of rushing to the sun, or flying off in tangents among comets and fixed stars impelled or drawn by different forces in different directions, they are blessings to their own inhabitants and the neighboring systems; but if they were drawn only by one, they would introduce anarchy wherever they should go." There must be "more powers than one," Adams insisted. In Adams, *Defence*, vol. 1, *WJA*, 4:390–91.

Index

CPSIA information can be obtained
at www.ICGtesting.com
Printed in the USA
LVOW12s1754300517
536317LV00011B/178/P